Elementary School Curriculum

second edition

Elementary School Curriculum

Jeff Passe
University of North Carolina

Boston Burr Ridge, IL Dubuque, IA Madison, WI New York San Francisco St. Louis
Bangkok Bogotá Caracas Lisbon London Madrid
Mexico City Milan New Delhi Seoul Singapore Sydney Taipei Toronto

McGraw-Hill College

A Division of The **McGraw-Hill** *Companies*

ELEMENTARY SCHOOL CURRICULUM, SECOND EDITION

This book is printed on acid-free paper.

1 2 3 4 5 6 7 8 9 0 DOC/DOC 9 3 2 1 0 9 8

ISBN 0-697-29883-3

Editorial director: *Jane E. Vaicunas*
Sponsoring editor: *Beth Kaufman*
Developmental editor: *Cara Harvey*
Marketing manager: *Daniel M. Loch*
Project manager: *Mary Lee Harms*
Production supervisor: *Deborah Donner*
Freelance design coordinator: *Mary L. Christianson*
Senior photo research coordinator: *Lori Hancock*
Supplement Coordinator: *Rita Hingtgen*
Compositor: *Carlisle Communications Ltd.*
Typeface: *10/12 Palatino*
Printer: *R. R. Donnelley & Sons Company/Crawfordsville, IN*

Freelance cover designer: *Jamie O'Neal*

The credits section for this book begins on page 302 and is considered an extension of the copyright page.

Library of Congress Cataloging-in-Publication Data

Passe, Jeff.
Elementary school curriculum / Jeffrey Passe. —2nd ed.
p. cm.
Includes bibliographical references and index.
ISBN 0-697-29883-3
1. Elementary schools—Curricula. 2. Education, Elementary—
-United States—Curricula. 3. Teacher participation in curriculum
planning—United States. I. Title.
LB1570.P284 1999
372.19—dc21 98-30206
CIP

www.mhhe.com

Dedicated to All of My Students—Past, Present, and Future.

Contents

Part Two
CURRICULUM GOALS

Part Three
ELEMENTARY CURRICULUM ISSUES

Preface

The field of elementary school curriculum has become increasingly important over the past several years. Research on teacher development has brought out the crucial role teachers play in determining what is taught and learned. Concurrently, the new movement toward decentralization has given teachers even greater responsibility in making curricular decisions.

These changes demand that teacher preparation programs prepare their students to take on greater responsibility in curriculum development. Until now, the educational publishing community has been slow in responding to this need. Most curriculum textbooks are not designed for novices who are just entering the profession. Instead, they are geared to the graduate-level student. They tend to be abstract and wordy, and assume that the reader is already teaching.

This book has been written for the preservice education major. The writing style speaks directly to that student's needs, explaining how the curriculum is determined, what needs to be changed, and how to change it. The emphasis is on practical application, relating theory to practice. Rather than assume students will make those connections in their own minds, the text helps them see how various forces influence what is taught and learned, and how they, as teachers, can contribute to that process.

Most preservice teachers have had courses in the topics that are addressed in this book. They have studied child development, the history of education, and the various arts and sciences. Yet, they rarely gain the opportunity to tie all those strands together—to relate the abstract stages of cognitive development to the decisions about which concepts are taught in which grade levels, to make connections between their studies of the political process and the government's role in education, and to translate one's own educational philosophy into actual classroom goals. This book helps them answer that age-old vexing question, Why do we have to learn this stuff? The way that question is answered influences the quality of the curriculum that is presented.

After reading this book, students may look at each subject area with new eyes, as they reevaluate their own educational experiences. They will probably become committed to the process of educational change, for this book shows that there is much a teacher can do to improve the quality of the curriculum. It is hoped that readers of this book will become armed with the power of reason and be able to use the knowledge and skills presented herein to become educational leaders in their schools and communities. This goal has become increasingly crucial as the mania for testing has risen to new levels.

Some textbooks attempt to combine the teaching of instructional methods with the study of curriculum. That approach serves neither field well. Instructional issues are well addressed in the numerous textbooks devoted solely to that topic. But curriculum deserves its own text, reflecting the idea that curricular goals should be clear before planning instruction. The best methods in the world will be wasted if the content is of little worth.

Some popular curriculum textbooks cover K through 12, which may be helpful for superintendents but not future elementary school teachers. This text focuses on the elementary curriculum. After an introduction to the field of curriculum (Part 1), the chapters in Part 2 establish the foundations of societal, human, and developmental needs, with particular emphasis on young children. Students can use the content in these chapters to evaluate the history and philosophies of elementary school curriculum presented in Chapter 4. Professors who advocate student self-theorizing will find this chapter helpful.

Part 3 looks at the curriculum of each major subject area. These chapters promote application of the foundations developed earlier. Each chapter presents the goals of a subject area with an analysis of the forces that have prevented the translation of theory to practice. Upon concluding Part 3, students should be able to identify the specific curricular goals they wish to set for their own classrooms. This section is useful as an introduction for students entering the teacher education program or a synthesis for students who have completed their methods courses.

Parts 2 and 3 are designed to overcome the perception that curricular change is impractical. Special features in each chapter offer examples of successful application, thereby demonstrating the practicality of the curricular ideas that are presented. The Instructor's Manual also offers suggestions for helping novice teachers process the textbook content in a meaningful fashion. When professors themselves apply what is proposed in the text, students are better able to grasp both the value and practicality of a curriculum geared toward democratic, active, concrete learning. The discussion questions at the end of each chapter should prove particularly helpful in promoting depth of understanding.

Part 4, the final section, emphasizes application. Students will learn the basics of planning an integrated unit. This part may be introduced earlier in courses in which a student-prepared curricular unit is a course requirement. Then, after a section on the political process of curriculum development (a rarity in undergraduate curriculum texts!), a final section is devoted to the text's central theme—that teachers can make a difference in improving the curriculum.

There has been much talk about the empowerment of teachers. With the rise of school-based management, teachers now have greater power in shaping the curriculum. This text goes beyond mere talk. It presents strategies for offering a curriculum that will strengthen our society and the individuals that contribute to it. With a strong base of theory and research presented in language that students can understand and enjoy, this text may be the one that new teachers take with them to their first teaching assignment.

ACKNOWLEDGEMENTS

It would be impossible to acknowledge all of those who contributed to this book. Many contributions were subtle and, perhaps, unappreciated at the time they were made. The editors at McGraw-Hill, however, have earned my deepest gratitude: Beth Kaufman, Cara Harvey, and Terry Routley are consummate professionals who are dedicated to quality educational publishing. I am lucky to have worked with them! The excellent comments of the manuscript reviewers were quite helpful; these included:

Cheryl Stanley Westfield State

Audrey Wright Central Missouri State University

Lawrence Lyman Emporia State University

Wilma Longstreet University of New Orleans

I must also thank Laurence Demers for her research, and all my colleagues and students for critiquing my work and letting me pick their brains. My professors from the University of Florida should be able to recognize their contributions. The energy to write was a direct result of love from Mindy, Sarah, and Ryan Passe. Thank you all.

PART ONE

Introduction

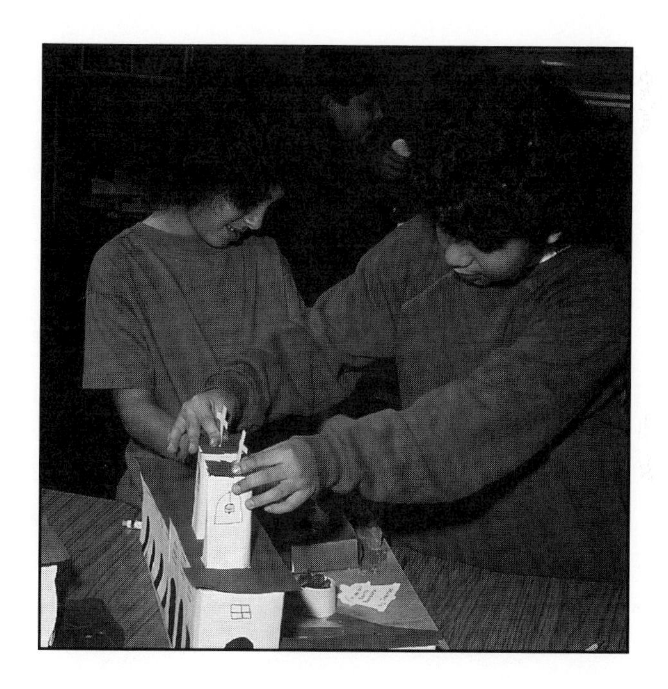

CHAPTER 1

Introduction

Consider your own educational experiences. Were you well prepared for today's world? Did you receive a quality education? Did your schooling help you understand yourself and your culture? Are your human relations skills strong? Are you politically savvy? Are you an effective consumer?

I always present these questions to students in my university classes. At first they usually insist that they came from strong school systems and received high-quality educations. When they focus on specific aims of the curriculum, however, many identify gaps. For instance, most of my students indicate serious deficits in their knowledge of government. Many claim that they lack a strong understanding of how the economic system works. Some cite a weakness in

Teachers can pool their knowledge to create a dynamic curriculum.

mathematics, especially problem solving. A few feel deficient in their abilities to speak before a group, read critically, or write effectively. The more they study the matter, the more dissatisfied they become with the quality of their educational experiences.

The sum of what is learned in school is often referred to as the curriculum. Throughout this book, we shall examine the elementary school curriculum. The knowledge you gain from this study will enable you to analyze the curriculum of your school or district so that you can engage in the ongoing process of improving it.

A DEFINITION OF CURRICULUM

It has been said that "one can find as many definitions of curriculum as one can find curriculum textbooks" (Gress & Purpel, 1978). In your hands is another curriculum textbook, but it will not present a new definition. The current ones are adequate for our purposes.

But which current ones? Can we just use any definition? No. The meanings behind language are important because they influence our thinking and behavior. For instance, the original use of the word curriculum comes from a Greek word meaning "race course." That interpretation defines the curriculum as a course of study, or a body of courses offered by an educational institution (Morris, 1981). This definition implies that the curriculum is a list that can be found in some document, like the teacher education courses listed in your college catalog.

Implications of the Race Course Definition

The race course definition is a popular interpretation of *curriculum.* However, if you think of the curriculum as a fixed list of courses, you face two major implications:

1. If the curriculum is fixed, then teachers are merely technicians who carry out what has been handed down from on high. That implication can lead to boring classrooms and irrelevant knowledge, unsuited to the needs of children and society. It can also lead to disaffected teaching professionals; bright, young people leave the field or never enter it because their professional judgment is not valued. Throughout this book, it will be argued that education is enhanced when teachers become an integral part of the curriculum development process.

   A fixed curriculum implies stability, but American education has witnessed a succession of curricular changes throughout the years. As you will see in Chapter 4, many changes did not last. At the present time, however, such curricular reforms as whole language, multiculturalism, and technology-oriented education are popular. While much of the traditional curriculum remains in place, there is no doubt that change is occurring. Teachers must take an active part in shepherding educational reform efforts if they are to succeed.

2. If a school's curriculum is only a set of courses, we must assume that that is what students learn there. Yet it is well recognized that the curriculum of a district or school accounts for only a portion of what students learn. A large amount of learning in schools is not found on any lists of objectives. This has been called the "hidden curriculum" (Jackson, 1968). There is also a body of knowledge that does not get taught, even though it is included in the official curriculum. Therefore, educators speak of the "delivered curriculum" as different from the "official curriculum." These differentiations, however, imply that students learn what is taught, and we all recognize the fallacy there. Thus, the "received curriculum" is different from the "delivered curriculum" (Jackson, 1992).

The Search for a Perfect Definition

In an effort to replace the race course definition, curriculum theorists have argued among themselves about a more accurate term. Their arguments have focused on whether the curriculum includes experiences as well as lessons; if so, whether those experiences are planned, whether they are directed or undirected, and whether they take place in school or in the community (Jackson, 1992). This discussion has seldom gone beyond the university walls.

As helpful as an all-encompassing definition might be, this book will not present one. Instead, curriculum will be examined in all its varieties: the official curriculum, the delivered curriculum, the received curriculum, the hidden curriculum, and also the "null curriculum," which is not written, taught, or received (Eisner, 1979). Our goal is to understand the process of curriculum development: what the curriculum looks like, how it got to be that way, how it might change, and how to achieve that change. By the conclusion of the text, you may be able to construct your own definition of the term.

WHY STUDY CURRICULUM?

In the past, curriculum was primarily a graduate school topic. Those seeking to become educational leaders would study it as preparation for determining their school or district's curriculum. That responsibility belonged to college professors, superintendents, principals, and other administrators.

In recent years, there has been a growing recognition of the need for teachers to study curriculum. Two major trends have led to this realization. One is the body of qualitative research focusing on the role of teachers in curriculum development. Studies have pinpointed the key influence of teachers on the success or failure of a curricular innovation. Curriculum researchers have also isolated various teacher characteristics that contribute to the decisions about what is taught in schools (Clark & Peterson, 1986). These findings contradict the notion that administrators and college professors make curricular decisions which are merely carried out by teachers. Teachers are actually making choices at their level of implementation. To make informed decisions, preservice teachers need to study curriculum.

Models of Curriculum

Different Kinds of Curriculum

HIDDEN CURRICULUM

Some of what we learn in school is not part of any plan. As a fourth grader, for instance, recess time included the ritual of having two captains select their teams by choosing one player at a time. Through this sometimes horrible experience, I learned that being friendly with those in power (i.e., the captains) can help in gaining favorable treatment. That valuable lesson was not my teacher's instructional goal (if she even had one!), and it certainly did not appear in the official curriculum documents, yet I learned it well from the "hidden" curriculum.

Sometimes the hidden curriculum contradicts the official curriculum. When my teachers were supposed to be emphasizing the joys of reading poetry, the poems they chose were so boring that I learned to dislike the subject for many years. For a more extensive discussion of the hidden curriculum, see Chapter 10.

OFFICIAL CURRICULUM

Every school district has a document outlining its curriculum. This document identifies a plan set forth by an official body, usually a Board of Education at the state or district level. As you will read in Chapter 13, the process by which the official curriculum is decided can be rather complex.

DELIVERED CURRICULUM

How many times do you recall finishing a history textbook? Even though the official curriculum specifies content from the twentieth century, it is a rare class that gets that far. I never learned about World War I until college! The same is true in every subject area. A lot of curricular content is never delivered.

Part of the problem is that parts of the delivered curriculum are not official. I once had a teacher who loved to discuss movies. I learned a lot about the history of film from that teacher, but I am sure that content was not included in the district's curriculum guide. Most of the hidden curriculum falls also into the category of delivered curriculum.

RECEIVED CURRICULUM

Every teacher bemoans the fact that students do not learn what has been taught. Whether because of inappropriate content, poor instructional techniques, or distracted students, there is often a large gap between the delivered curriculum and the received curriculum. Consider the poetry lesson that was delivered to promote poetry, but did the opposite. What was delivered was definitely not received.

NULL CURRICULUM

Some topics are not included in the official curriculum, nor are they delivered or received in schools. You may not have been taught the study of differences between various religious sects (e.g., Lutherans, Baptists, Episcopalians.) Perhaps it was homosexuality or birth control that was left out. These are all topics that are perceived to be controversial and are, thus, avoided both on paper and in lessons.

Many times, a topic is in the null curriculum due to rapid cultural change. Knowledge of the Internet, for example, may be part of the null curriculum in school districts that lack the necessary technology.

All in all, with so many aspects of curriculum to consider, the race course definition of a set of courses is a misleading interpretation of the term.

The second trend, which will be discussed in Chapter 13, is the decentralization of educational administration. A variety of factors, including the knowledge of teacher behavior cited above, have been moving the locus of decision making from the state and superintendent's offices to individual schools.

A casual observer may expect decentralized decisions to be concerned with such bureaucratic matters as personnel and budget, but with a curriculum that is constantly changing, the scope of decision making is broadened. This new movement has teachers officially deciding, within limits, what should be taught to their students. Such a major process change demands teachers who understand curricular issues. Preservice teacher education programs will need to include a significant curriculum component.

In a year or two, you may be a novice teacher attending a school curriculum meeting. You may have the opportunity to contribute to your school's official curriculum. At the very least, you will be the curriculum master of your classroom. Are you ready for that responsibility? This book may move you in that direction.

CURRICULUM VS. INSTRUCTION

For the purposes of this text, curriculum is viewed as separate from instruction. In other words, what we teach is different from how we teach it. Without this simple differentiation, a curriculum textbook would have to include both topics and would be very long, complicated, and expensive. Methods of instruction are addressed in other teacher education courses and textbooks.

The separation of curriculum from instruction in this book, however, is only a convenience. In actuality, the two topics can hardly be separated, since the ends influence the means (Dewey, 1933). For instance, a curriculum goal that stresses knowledge of the state capitals (the end) will encourage instructional techniques stressing memorization (the means).

The means influence the ends too. Consider a mathematics lesson designed to promote skills in problem solving. On paper, this meets the curriculum goal of students applying their knowledge of mathematics. But if the lesson is taught with an emphasis on copying what the teacher does, the curriculum has been altered. How the lesson is taught does affect what is learned. Teachers must therefore ensure that their instructional techniques do not conflict with their curriculum goals. This text shall frequently address the means-ends continuum, but, for the reasons cited, will not attempt to prescribe methods of instruction.

AIMS OF THE CURRICULUM

Over the years, there has been considerable debate concerning the purpose of schooling. Most theorists identify four main categories of aims, although different weight is given to each. These aims, issued by the Educational Policies Commission of the National Education Association (1938), appear to have stood the test of time: (1) self-realization, (2) human relations, (3) economic efficiency, and (4) civic responsibility.

Self-Realization

Self-realization refers to the process of socialization, which is one of the original purposes of education, in or out of school. When individuals become self-realized, they have developed the tools for thinking, which include the basic skills of communication and mathematics. Self-realization also involves the ability to care for oneself in terms of health and recreation as well as developing an appreciation of the arts. Graduates of schools that are successful in this area are expected to become autonomous members of the society.

Human Relations

Human relations deals with the affective and humanistic aims of the curriculum. The purpose of this set of aims is to develop people of good character who are respectful, friendly, cooperative, and courteous. A successful curriculum in this area anticipates producing graduates who are able to get along with one another.

Economic Efficiency

Economic efficiency reflects the societal need to make the economic system work properly. Schools are expected to contribute to the development of careers and skills in consumer economics. When they are successful in this area of the curriculum, graduates are supposed to be productive workers and wise consumers.

Civic Responsibility

Civic responsibility refers to the requirements of democratic citizenship. American citizens play a role in determining their country's leaders and policies. Education has always been viewed as a key component of the democratic process. Thomas Jefferson's famous quote summarizes this viewpoint:

> I know of no safe depository of the ultimate powers of the society but the people themselves; and if we think them not enlightened enough to exercise their control with a wholesome discretion, the remedy is not to take it from them, but to inform their discretion by education. (Boyer, 1990, p. 5)

Civic responsibility goes beyond the right to vote. It also includes obeying the law, social action, tolerance, and protection of the democratic system. If this set of curriculum aims is reached, the society should operate in a just manner.

THE DYNAMIC CURRICULUM

Each group of aims appears to be very important, but our society has continually shifted in the priority it has placed on each. Shifting aims could be regarded as a sign of instability but is more accurately viewed as a response to changing needs. Schools are created by society. When societal needs of individuals within the society change, the schools try to adjust. The curriculum is, therefore, regarded as dynamic.

The concept of a dynamic curriculum is sometimes surprising to beginning teachers. They expect to be told what the curriculum is and then teach it. If that were the case, this would be a very short book. With an ever-changing curriculum, the role of educators is different. They must be sensitive to the needs of the society and the needs of individuals so that the proper adjustments can be made.

A word of caution is in order, however. Use of the terms "societal needs" and "individual needs" implies that a consensus has been reached. Yet all of us are painfully aware of deep divisions concerning the best way to address societal problems. In many instances, groups have resorted to violence to achieve their own version of the best solution. Although educational circles have not experienced violent disputes, there is certainly no wide-ranging agreement as to what society or the individual needs.

Teachers can and should engage in debates about societal and individual needs. After all, if one purpose of education is to address those needs, it makes sense to include educators in the deliberations. Teachers are the ones who implement the curriculum. Their role is crucial to its success, but that success will only be reached when teachers are committed to the goals of the curriculum (Fullan, 1991). This book is designed to prepare teachers to participate in the development of a dynamic curriculum from the earliest stages and to maximize the effectiveness of whatever plan is produced.

THE OUTLINE OF THIS BOOK

To help you in your quest to contribute to a dynamic curriculum, the next two chapters focus on needs. Chapter 2 addresses the changing needs of individuals in our society, particularly the young ones who attend our elementary schools. Societal needs are also analyzed. People put much faith in the ability of schools to solve social problems. If the curriculum is to respond accordingly, teachers must contemplate the nature of those problems. This chapter, indeed the entire book, reflects the belief that the curriculum should be designed to meet children's needs during childhood, not just those necessary for adult success. Chapter 3 focuses on the developmental needs of young children. Because children rapidly change throughout the elementary school years, their developmental needs are a crucial consideration in curriculum development.

Once you have a sense of those needs the curriculum should address, you can place them in historical perspective in Chapter 4. Besides tracing how the curriculum has changed, this chapter orients you to the major curricular philosophies. These two topics are frequently separated, but that strategy often leads to excessive abstraction. I have combined the two topics because I believe that matters of philosophy can be made more concrete by being placed in historical context. Chapter 4 may help you decide on a particular set of beliefs or recognize aspects of your own educational philosophy. Knowledge of your own philosophical leanings is helpful in developing curriculum.

Chapters 5 through 11 examine the traditional subject areas: social studies, science and health, language arts and reading, mathematics, the arts, and physical education. Each subject area has its own set of goals and problems but you will also see a number of similarities. Each chapter includes an in-depth analysis of an issue that cuts across all subjects. Besides learning about the curriculum, you will also gain insight into the nature of those subjects. The ones that you dislike may become more attractive when you look at them from a different perspective. Chapter 11 focuses on school and classroom organization, a topic whose relationship to the curriculum is surprisingly strong.

After this thorough study of the elementary curriculum and its problems, Chapters 12 and 13 suggest how to improve it. Chapter 12 considers methods of developing a meaningful curriculum that will address the concerns described in the previous chapters. The ideas in this chapter may broaden the way you think about teaching. Chapter 13 explains how the official curriculum is determined, and methods of influencing its development, including what the individual teacher can do.

A FINAL COMMENT

Much of what you read in this book may influence your views about education. That is one of my goals. If an idea strikes you as particularly extreme or impractical, do not be quick to reject it. Instead, try to place it in the context of ends and means. Discuss the matter with educators who can add their professional perspective. Major educational reform may require substantial changes from the status quo. Being responsive to the range of possibilities is an essential ingredient for success.

If, after thinking about whether an idea is valid, you choose to reject it, so be it. I ask only that you be reflective in your dealings with the curriculum. The quality of our educational system is at stake!

Questions

1. Many teacher education students assume that the teacher's role is to work from a curriculum that has been decided beforehand. What were your original conceptions concerning curriculum?
2. How comfortable do you feel about teachers playing an active role in curriculum development? Would you prefer to have these decisions made by others?
3. Of the various aims of education, which ones do you see as most important? Why?
4. What experiences have you had with the hidden curriculum?

References

BOYER, E. L. (1990). Civil education for responsible citizens. *Educational Leadership, 48,* 4–7.

CLARK, C., & PETERSON, P. (1986). Teachers' thought processes. In M. Wittrock (Ed.), *Handbook of research on teaching* (3rd ed.), (pp. 255–296). New York: Macmillan.

DEWEY, J. (1933). *How we think.* Lexington, MA: Heath.

EDUCATIONAL POLICIES COMMISSION OF THE NATIONAL EDUCATION ASSOCIATION. (1938). *Purpose of education in American democracy.* Washington, DC: National Education Association.

EISNER, E. (1979). *The educational imagination.* New York: Macmillan.

FULLAN, M. G. (1991). *The new meaning of educational change.* (2nd ed.). New York: Teachers College Press.

GRESS, J. R., & PURPEL, D. E. (1978). *Curriculum: An introduction to the field.* Berkeley, CA: McCutchan.

JACKSON, P. (1968). *Life in classrooms.* New York: Holt, Rinehart & Winston.

JACKSON, P. (1992). Conceptions of curriculum and curriculum specialists. In P. W. Jackson (Ed.), *Handbook of research on curriculum* (pp. 1–40). New York: Macmillan.

MORRIS, W. (Ed.). (1981). *The American heritage dictionary of the English language.* Boston: Houghton Mifflin.

PART TWO

Curriculum Goals

CHAPTER 2

Meeting the Changing Needs of Individuals in Our Society

If you're like most prospective teachers, you probably have fantasies about your future classes. You may imagine a collection of students similar to what you were like as a child, in a classroom similar to yours, in a neighborhood similar to yours. Don't be too disappointed if it doesn't happen like that. Most new teachers find students who are quite different from what they were like as children.

Children are different today because our society is no longer the same. Every aspect of our lives has been altered in some way by massive social, economic, political, and technological changes that have taken place in recent decades. By analyzing some of the more significant societal changes, you can better prepare your curriculum for the individual students in your future classrooms.

I can recall an incident during my first year of teaching when I was teaching my fourth graders about similes. To develop the concept of "chilling," I referred to the sound of a dentist's drill. Expecting to see children groaning and gritting their teeth, I was surprised to see many blank looks. I found that many of my students, who lived in poverty, had never been to the dentist's office. A closer scrutiny of their mouths supported that finding.

I was shocked. I had always assumed that my students' backgrounds would be similar to my middle-class upbringing. Now I had to reframe all of my assumptions. As the school year went on I found many more differences between myself and my students.

As a college professor, I frequently share that experience with my undergraduates to accentuate the need to question one's assumptions as a teacher. One time, my own seven-year-old daughter was present during the class. After I finished the story, Sarah's hand shot into the air. "Daddy," she asked, "what is a dentist's drill?" Once again my assumption was shattered. With my own child yet! Sarah didn't know what a dentist's drill was because she had never had a cavity. Going to the dentist, for her, was a strictly pleasurable activity. The message is, even as a veteran teacher, you must never stop thinking about your students' backgrounds.

SOCIETAL CHANGES

To begin thinking about backgrounds, we must consider several influential factors. The following list of factors is not meant to be conclusive. Change will constantly occur. It is the one thing we can count on.

Poverty

The first major change we must examine is in the economic realm. A distressing trend is that, since 1970, students are more likely to live under conditions of poverty (see Figure 2.1). In 1970, 14.9 percent of children age 0–17 lived in poverty. That percentage rose to 17.9 in 1980, then to 19.9 in 1990. It has leveled off around 20.0 percent in the 1990s (U.S. Bureau of the Census, 1997). Of particular interest to elementary educators are the children under age five who live in poverty. In 1986, that number was at its highest point in the previous thirty years (Hodgkinson, 1986).

Children who live in poverty have different needs than more well-to-do children. They must adapt to a middle-class culture in which their language, behavior patterns, and values are regarded as deficiencies (Comer, 1988). Their

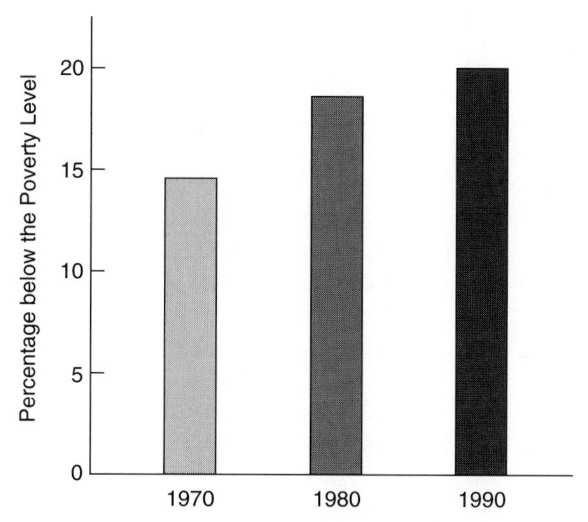

FIGURE 2.1. Children under age 17 living below the poverty level in the United States.
Source: Statistical Abstract of the United States, 1992.

parents are less likely to have had a successful formal education (Holman, 1997). They are also less likely to use academic skills outside the classroom and thus need help in seeing the purposes behind educational activities (Knapp & Shields, 1990). The resulting sense of alienation and lack of motivation can seriously harm any chances for school success. Consider Minnesota's 94 percent graduation rate, which is attributed to the low incidence of poverty there. By contrast, many states in the South, which has the highest poverty rate in the nation, have dropout rates of over 30 percent (Duckett, 1988). Indeed, a study of standardized tests discovered that students' scores increased with every additional $10,000 of the family's annual income (FairTest, 1989).

Rather than blame the victim, schools can do more to meet the needs of poor children. A curriculum that respects the backgrounds of poor children and allows more opportunity for application and integration can break the connection between poverty and school failure.

Poor children are also more likely to suffer from malnutrition and other health problems than other children (Horday, 1986). These factors are associated with learning disabilities and poor school achievement (Duckett, 1988). Thus, if we intend to teach poor children, we may need to include education in nutrition and personal health.

Another problem for poor children is the lack of adult supervision (Horday, 1986). One reason for this is the fact that a large percentage of poor families are headed by single parents, usually mothers. A single parent is likely to be very busy trying to run a family, especially with small children at home. For poor, single parents with jobs, the time for high-quality interaction with youngsters is negligible. Their children may arrive at school with little appreciation for learning, only limited experience with books, and an absence of consistent behavior guidelines.

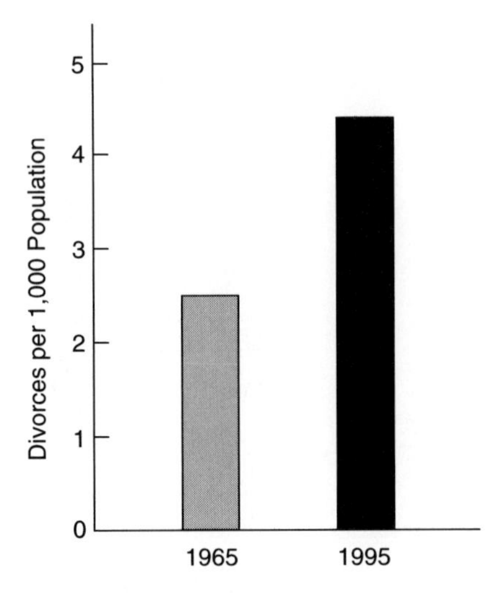

FIGURE 2.2. Divorce rate in the United States.
Source: Information Please Almanac, 1990, New York: Houghton Mifflin.

How can the elementary school help them? It can provide a program that develops feelings of self-sufficiency and self-worth (Duckett, 1988). A sense of self-sufficiency is important because, in the absence of parental guidance, the children may have to function by themselves. Self-worth must be developed because it is usually through adult love and support that a child feels validated. Your own elementary school may not have had goals of self-sufficiency and self-worth. The one in which you teach may need to have them.

One must be careful not to overgeneralize concerning children from poor families. Various levels of poverty exist, with differing characteristics (Levitan, 1990). For instance, the size of the family, the number of breadwinners, the length of time the family has experienced a low income, the extent to which the family relies on social services, and other factors all contribute to variations of poverty. Some circumstances, such as a strong family support system and parental involvement, increase the chances for school success. After all, there are numerous examples of people who have experienced extraordinary success despite their impoverished backgrounds. Teachers must be careful not to lower their expectations based on the appearance or fact of poverty. But the curriculum can be designed to better meet poor children's needs.

Single-Parent Families

The United States has undergone several major social changes in recent years, many of which get overlooked until we stop to notice them. For instance, single parenting is more and more common. Divorce is one explanation for this trend (see Figure 2.2). Since 1967, the American divorce rate has practically doubled

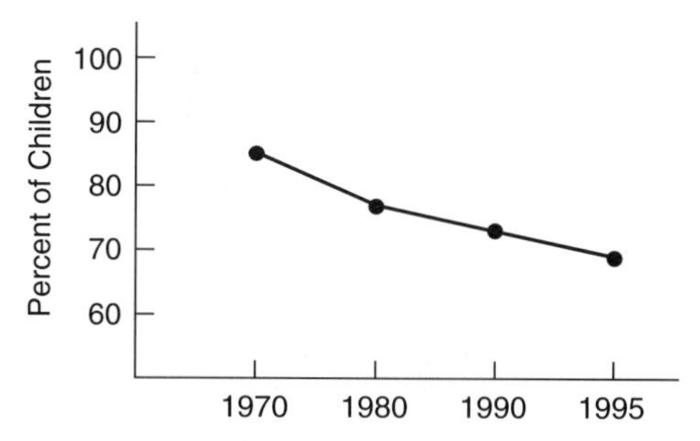

FIGURE 2.3. Percent of children under age 18 living with both parents.
Source: Statistical Abstract of the United States, 1992.

(U.S. Bureau of the Census, 1997). The number of children living with both parents has declined from 85 percent in 1970 to 69 percent in 1995 (U.S. Bureau of the Census, 1997) (see Figure 2.3).

Divorce alone, however, does not account for this change; many single parents have never been married. In 1993, 31 percent of all births were to unmarried women (U.S. Bureau of the Census, 1997.) That number was only 3.3 percent in 1950 and only 7.7 percent in 1965. Today, half of all American five-year-olds have experienced living with only one parent (Duckett, 1988).

Children of single parents grow up with a perspective on family life that is different from that of children in "traditional" families. They experience much more independence. Children are expected to take care of themselves and other members of the family. They are likely to have major household chores. As a result, they tend to grow up faster (Elkind, 1988).

The price paid for this accelerated maturity is a loss of childhood. The trend is a general, societal one but particularly applies to children of single parents. If the children are unable to handle the pressure of being a grown-up with a child's mind and body, they are likely to suffer from stress, low self-esteem, and anxiety. Unfortunately, they may receive little help from their parents (Elkind, 1988). Single parents are often so busy with the tasks of running a household that they cannot attend to emotional needs, their own or those of their children (Louv, 1991).

Researchers have recently identified delayed effects of divorce. They cite the findings that, ten years after a divorce, 41 percent of children whose parents divorced were "doing poorly" in an emotional sense. They were likely to have trouble forming loving relationships and difficulty achieving their desired goals. They were characterized as worried, underachieving, and often angry (Louv, 1991).

Although many children of divorced or single parents do not seem to be suffering, schools must help children of single parents overcome whatever problems they may have so that learning can take place. Many of these children appear to need lessons in making decisions, in avoiding stress, and in communicating intimate feelings (Whitfield & Freeland, 1981). Such topics are traditionally part of the guidance curriculum. It may be helpful if that curriculum is expanded and integrated into the regular course of study.

Latchkey Kids

A profound change in American life has been the movement of women into the workplace. The number of working mothers has increased from 27 percent in 1960 to 70 percent in 1995 (U.S. Bureau of the Census, 1997). The resulting phenomenon is the "latchkey child." The term comes from the key that children may carry to let themselves into their homes after school. In 1987, 41 percent of children were left on their own between the end of school and 5:30 P.M. at least once a week. For 25 percent, this was a daily occurrence (Tyler-Wilkins, 1988). Today, those numbers are probably even higher.

Like children of single parents, latchkey kids have a lot of responsibility thrust upon them. They are often instructed to stay in the house at all times, especially in high-crime areas. Many times they have household chores to do. Older children may also have to supervise their younger siblings. As a result, latchkey kids tend to suffer from the same maladies as other children who grow up fast (Elkind, 1988).

What do latchkey kids do with their time? If they are not doing chores or homework, it is likely that they are watching television. One has to wonder about the effects of so much television watching on young minds. That topic will be explored later in the chapter.

Another concern is the effect of so much solitude on children. Over half of all teachers in a recent poll said that being alone after school was the primary cause of student classroom problems. Indeed, research indicates that latchkey kids are more likely than other children to abuse alcohol, tobacco, and marijuana (Louv, 1991).

Latchkey kids do not have much opportunity for physical play. Being confined to the house prevents them from getting fresh air. It also deprives them of the opportunity to play with neighborhood friends. All of these factors may lead to more serious problems.

Schools can help latchkey kids by providing more opportunity for physical activity. Expanded recess and physical education can provide the outlet that children need. Schools can also teach how to productively pursue recreational activities that can be done alone, besides television. Exposure to a range of hobbies and educational activities would be beneficial. Schools can teach more about home safety and security too.

To deal with some of the changes in American lifestyles, some schools are adapting to meet families' needs. For instance, growing numbers of year-round schools, after-school programs, recreation centers for neighborhood youth, and other similar services are available. These adaptations, which would have been unthinkable generations ago, are testimony to the idea that institutional change can take place if there is enough demand.

The Increasingly Mobile Society

Noneducators may be surprised to learn that 23 percent of all primary grade children have moved at some time in their lives (Lash & Kirkpatrick, 1990). However, elementary school teachers are well aware of that recent increase in American mobility because they have had to adjust their classrooms for the constant arrival and departure of children.

Many of us can painfully recall the difficulties inherent in changing schools. The experience of being the new kid is not a pleasant one. Being unfamiliar with the curriculum is just one part of it. There is also the embarrassment of not knowing where the bathroom is or how to go through the lunch line. Even worse is the feeling of being an outsider, especially if you lack self-confidence. If a child has changed schools because of divorce, there are additional adjustment problems. When a move is to a new region of the country or even another country, the stress is further multiplied.

Can we provide a curriculum to help children who have moved? At the very least, we can teach children how to make friends. We can teach about accepting others who appear to be different. We can also develop self-confidence so transitions will not be so painful.

When one usually thinks about the curriculum, the thought of mathematics or language arts comes to mind, not the affective goals that are suggested above. It may have been sufficient, at one time, to merely teach the three R's, but the United States has changed so much that a different curriculum is needed. As educators, we must lead the way in adjusting the curriculum to meet individual needs by alerting the public to the shifting demands of children and proposing alterations in what we teach.

The Changing Cultural Mix

Another major trend is the change in the racial and cultural character of the United States. In the past few decades, an enormous increase in the number of Americans from Asian and from Hispanic nations has taken place (see Figure 2.4). At the same time, the number of African-American children has steadily risen. The result is that the American mosaic is developing more tones of color. The U.S. Census Bureau predicts that American schools will be 47 percent nonwhite by the year 2050 (Riche, 1996). Already, minorities are actually the majority in most large urban school systems.

What is the significance of these changes? Does heritage and skin color affect student needs? Apparently, they do. One challenge is having to learn content in a language different from the one spoken at home. That dilemma (and poverty) helps to explain why the dropout rate for Hispanics is 45 percent compared to 5 percent for non-Hispanic whites. Better bilingual education programs may be necessary to help meet this challenge.

Minorities also require more content related to their heritage (Estrada, 1988). Learning about the contributions of one's ethnic group promotes a sense

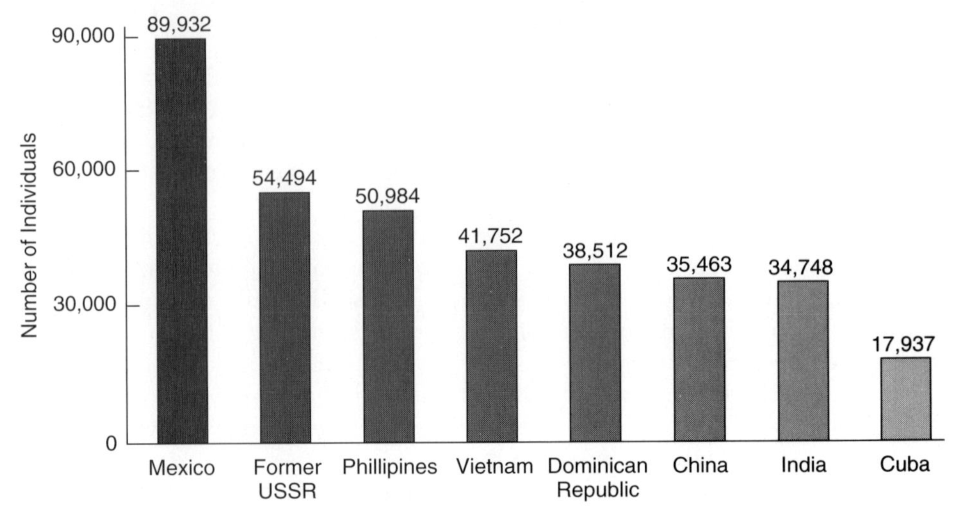

FIGURE 2.4. Immigrants admitted 1995.
Source: Statistical Abstract of the United States, 1992.

of self-worth (Gollnick & Chinn, 1990). It also makes the study of history and anthropology more relevant.

An additional consideration is the need for all children to learn about other cultures. It is easy to react negatively to unfamiliar cultures, especially if you're an egocentric seven-year-old. For instance, knowing that many Asian-Americans are not Christian and do not celebrate Christmas may help to reduce negative judgments during the winter holiday season. In order to live peacefully, it helps to know each other's cultural characteristics. Rather than be upset by odd-sounding languages, unfamiliar foods and clothing, or different attitudes, children can study these attributes to better understand one another. Awareness of differences can also help in understanding one's own culture.

Technological Change

A mere glance around your home will provide numerous examples of machines that have transformed American life. What may be surprising is how recent many of them are. For instance, it is only in the past twenty years that Walkman stereos, compact disc players, personal computers, microwave ovens, telephone answering machines, portable telephones, remote control television, videocassette recorders, Nintendo games, and electronic toys have become popular.

Sociologists are still trying to measure all the changes that technological improvements have brought to American life, but a few distressing trends are clearly discernible. First is the increasing solitude of American children. So much of the new technology is geared to individuals rather than groups. One sits under stereo headphones separated from the rest of the world. Personal computers and electronic games also promote solitary recreation.

Other items, like remote-control televisions and VCRs, can be used by groups, but are often controlled by a single individual. Witness the "channel surfer" who flips through channels at a rapid pace, oblivious to others' needs or interests. VCRs are frequently used to entertain youngsters at various times during the day, apart from their parents.

Convenient as they are, these machines are depriving children of a basic need: interaction. In combination with the latchkey phenomenon and single-parent families, there is less interpersonal communication than ever before. Children are more likely than ever to stay in the house and play with their marvelous new machines than go outside and play with neighbors. Within families, we find children staring at portable televisions in their own rooms, apart from the family. Instead of helping parents prepare the meal, children are relegated to the VCR. The car was one place where families could talk, insulated from the distractions of the home. Now we need only glance into the window of the car in the next lane to see the adult talking on the car phone while the teenager listens to her Walkman and the younger child plays an electronic game.

Of course, the technology itself is not at fault. It is how we choose to use it. In the meantime, children arrive at school desperate for interaction. The last thing they need is to sit still for a teacher lecture or be handed a pile of worksheets and told to work on them quietly. Schools must provide outlets for children to speak, listen, and play. Otherwise, serious behavior problems will result. On one extreme is the child "acting out" for attention; at the other is the child who lacks the necessary interpersonal skills to form a friendship.

Another major change brought on by technology is "information overload." The amount of data that is now available through technology is far more than any child can manage. Compounding the challenge is the disturbing nature of some of the information, whether it be terrorist activities, natural disasters, or disease. Young children need adults to help them interpret what they see and hear (Passe, 1994).

One of the benefits of recent technological change has been the ease of access. Through the Internet, public access television, and fax machines, even obscure groups can now communicate their ideas to the public. Children can easily get a distorted picture of society unless adults assist them in assessing validity, reliability, and bias of information sources (Passe, 1994).

Changes in the Workplace

Why do we rely on so many technological aids? It may be because adults are busier than ever. In 1973 the average American had 26.2 hours per week for recreation (see Figure 2.5). That decreased to 16.6 in 1987, a drop of 37 percent (Louv, 1991).

The cause of that drop can be attributed to job demands. A Harris Poll revealed that the work week is not the 40 hours for which labor unions had historically been fighting. The average is 46.8 hours per week, increasing to 52.2 for professionals and 57.3 for small business owners (Louv, 1991).

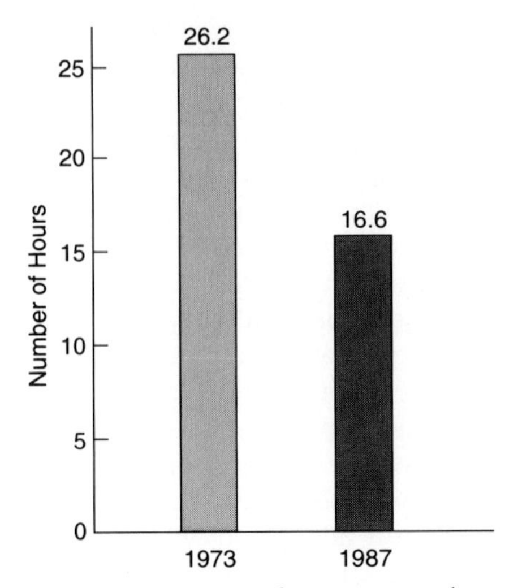

FIGURE 2.5. Average hours per week of recreation in the United States.
Source: Data from Childhood's Future by R. Louv, 1991, Boston: Houghton Mifflin.

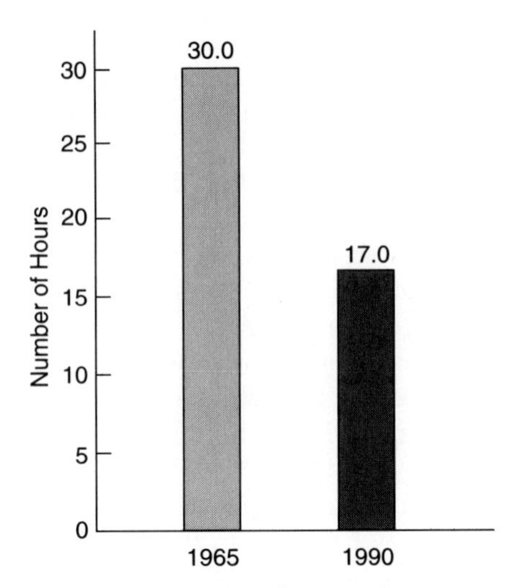

FIGURE 2.6. Hours of contact between parents and children.
Source: Data from Childhood's Future by R. Louv, 1991, Boston: Houghton Mifflin.

The cost of economic success is great. It requires time and dedication. Unfortunately, it is the children who feel the brunt of these workplace changes. In 1965 the average parent had 30 weekly hours of contact with children (see Figure 2.6). In 1990 that number was 17 (Louv, 1991).

In the early years of industrialization, grandparents filled the gap when parents were working. They often lived in the same home. In today's mobile society, the extended family is less likely to congregate, much less live together. Indeed, the size of the average American household today is 2.65 persons (see Figure 2.7). In 1930 it was 4.11 persons (Johnson, 1996).

Teachers can no longer expect the kind of adult support and involvement that used to help children develop positive values, attitudes, and knowledge. More and more that role is being filled by the child's peers, the media, and an assortment of child-care workers.

Is it a coincidence that between 1984 and 1994 the arrest rate for violent crime among juveniles more than doubled in rural and suburban areas, and more than tripled in urban areas? (*U.S. News & World Report*, 1996). It may not have been necessary to teach about values in the old days. It seems essential now!

Television

As one of the major changes of the twentieth century, television, and its effect on children, deserves a careful analysis. It can be examined on a general level, but also can be studied for the changes it has brought over the past few years.

Television can be a positive force. Quality programs bring the world into the child's home. They can orient the viewer to artistic achievements in acting,

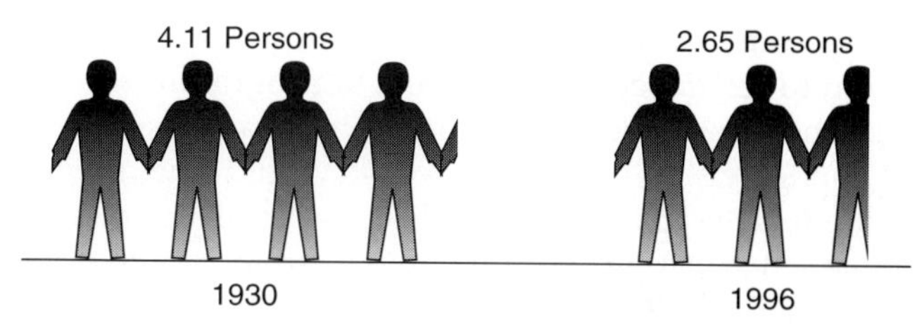

FIGURE 2.7. Average size of American household.
Source: Data from Information Please Almanac, 1990, New York: Houghton Mifflin.

writing, directing, and other technical aspects of video production. Television provides exposure to the arts, nature, other cultures, and current events in a way that no other medium can approach. Young adults will tell you that they learned much of what they know through television.

Television watching has significant drawbacks, however, many of which are of great concern to educators. For instance, research reveals that children who watch a lot of television tend to be less creative than other children. This finding can be explained by the passive nature of television watching which allows the senses to be stimulated without much thinking taking place (Postman, 1982).

At one time, television was a relatively tame medium. Programs with violent or sexual content were rare. When they were shown at all, it was during the 10:00 P.M. time slot when most children would be expected to be in bed. Times have changed! Today, sitcoms and dramas that frequently focus on such matters as loss of virginity and sexually transmitted diseases are shown in earlier time slots when elementary children are watching. Reruns of violent movies are shown throughout the day on cable channels.

Talk shows and soap operas are staples of daytime television. Many of these programs' themes revolve around sordid sexual misconduct, deviancy, and other sensitive issues. Yet they are shown during midmorning when preschoolers are likely to be present or during late afternoon when elementary-aged children are flicking through the channels. Some of these programs are beneficial. The problem is that young children are being exposed to topics that may confuse or disturb them, especially when an adult may not be present or able to help them understand.

This challenge is multiplied with cable channels and videocassettes. Just a generation ago, one had to pay to enter a theater to see movies that were made strictly for adults. In fact, a movie rating system was designed to insure that children not be present during the showing of these movies. Now, in many families, children merely have to push the right buttons to observe language, sexual activity, and violence that most adults would never recommend for children.

As a result, children in today's schools are likely to have a far greater awareness of adult matters than ever before. They are also likely to have large amounts of misinformation because their "teacher" (i.e., the television) has not explained the content in a positive manner that is suited to children's developmental needs.

Many educators are concerned about the effects of television on children. Proposals abound to restrict children's access to programming of a sexual or violent nature. In the meantime, the students in your class are likely to have watched scenes on television that many people would find offensive. What can we do to help them? Is it appropriate to discuss the nature of sex and violence in the elementary school? A generation ago educators would not endorse such a radical proposal. It doesn't seem so radical anymore.

Mental Illness

Psychologists have noted a rise in reports of mental illness in recent years. Of particular concern is the increase among children. It is estimated that between 12 percent and 22 percent of children suffer from some emotional or mental disorder, such as depression, hyperactivity, drug abuse, and anorexia. Yet only one-third receive psychological treatment (Louv, 1991). Many of these children are victims of child abuse. Three million cases were reported in 1994 (U.S. Bureau of the Census, 1997), nearly three times that of 1976 (see Figure 2.8).

The sad consequence of this trend is that the suicide rate for children age 10–14 rose 128 percent from 1980 to 1994 (U.S. Bureau of the Census, 1997). A related issue is the rise in adolescent childbearing. Perhaps the choice of keeping the child reflects the perception by many teenagers that a baby can provide unconditional love, love that can overcome feelings of inadequacy (Beane & Lipka, 1984).

Teachers are not psychologists. They cannot provide therapy in a professional sense. They can, however, provide the kind of curriculum that allows

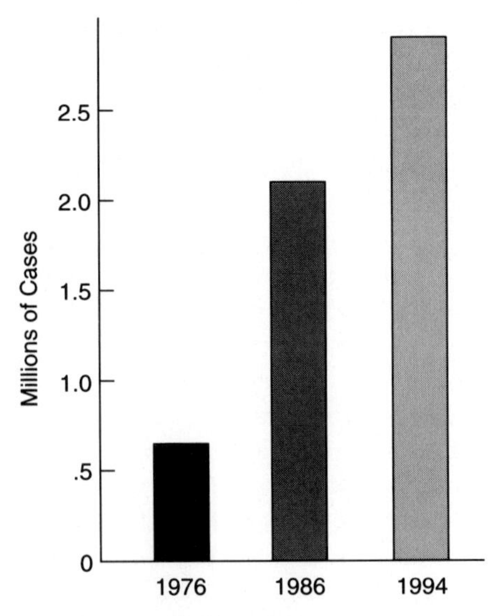

FIGURE 2.8. Child maltreatment cases. *Source: Statistical Abstract of the United States, 1997.*

children to learn how to deal with problems. They can provide an atmosphere that encourages self-expression and individuality. These may not have been the original goals of those who developed the first schools. They certainly seem appropriate now.

Do all these developments depress you? If they didn't, you wouldn't be human. But we educators can look at these changes from a positive standpoint. If we can influence the curriculum so that it begins to meet the needs of children, we will provide a major societal service. Rather than shrink from the teaching profession because the challenges we face rob it of glamour, instead we can seek to make the profession even more valuable. Professionals who are aware of what needs to be done are essential. You can make a difference!

SOLVING SOCIETAL PROBLEMS

While it is true that elementary schools could better meet the needs of children with a more effective curriculum, schools are expected to meet other goals too. From the earliest days of schooling, in America and elsewhere, people have assumed that society will solve its problems through education (Reitman, 1992). This can occur directly or indirectly. Take the challenges of teenage pregnancy and

Elementary school students are usually quite interested in environmental issues.

the spread of sexually transmitted diseases as an example. A direct solution would be the development of a sex education curriculum to combat teenage pregnancy and the spread of sexually transmitted diseases. An indirect solution would be the creation of a curriculum that promotes literacy. Through expanded literacy, the society would then have access to ideas that may be used to solve particular problems. For instance, after reading what the experts have to say about teenage pregnancy, people can choose their own best solution to the problem.

Though most people agree that education is the key to solving problems, there is substantial debate concerning what content should be included in the curriculum to meet that goal. As you will see in later chapters, there are a number of influences on the curriculum, especially when addressing societal challenges. Because teachers are gaining a greater voice in the curriculum debate, they need to study the issues to become informed participants in the discussions.This section of the chapter analyzes some of our societal needs in an effort to help teachers with curriculum decisions. Because of the changing nature of our society, the topics that are discussed in this chapter cannot be completely inclusive or up-to-date. Between the time this book is written and the time you read it, there will be new issues and (we hope) solutions that make old issues irrelevant. Yet the themes will probably remain similar.

Violent Conflict

At any one time, there are dozens of armed conflicts around the globe. We know the names of those that involve our country's armed forces, and those that may lead to American involvement, but a number of regional conflicts and civil wars go unnoticed by most Americans.

The key question for us has usually been, Should we get involved? This question is of great importance because of the threat to people's lives and the enormous expenditures required. Because only Congress has the power to officially declare war, the American people have a say in matters of war and peace through their elected representatives. (There have been numerous examples of American military action without congressional authorization, but that too is an issue for the people to address.)

To exercise the judgment that is granted to citizens in a democracy, the people must know the issues. We must be familiar with the relevant region(s) of the world, the causes of the conflicts, the political, social, and economic factors, and the projected outcomes of various courses of action.

Of course, we cannot spend valuable school hours learning the characteristics of every nation in the world, preparing for the possibility of a war anywhere. We could not retain all this material. We can, however, study certain trouble spots where conflicts are most likely. For instance, there have been wars in the Middle East since time immemorial and there probably will continue to be, as long as the volatile combination of crude oil and ethnic conflict is present. Political instability in South America, Eastern Europe, and equatorial Africa is also likely to persist. Studying these regions will help prepare Americans to make decisions about the role of the United States in world affairs.

Theory to Practice

The Clark Family

Every school has a family like the Clarks. On my first day as a fifth grade teacher, a colleague pulled me over to confide, "Oh, you have Patricia Clark in your class. Those Clarks are nothing but trouble. They're always late. They never have their homework done." Then, she whispered, "They smell!"

Patricia Clark did smell. Her hair was often uncombed and her clothes did not fit. The other children teased her. But Patricia was bright. She worked hard and was sufficiently successful to move on to middle school.

The following year I had her brother Paul in my class. After an evening performance of that year's class play, I noticed Paul walking home alone. No one had come to watch his acting. I offered to drive him home on that chilly night. He seemed uncomfortable, but climbed in nonetheless.

Paul directed me across a busy highway and told me to let him off near its intersection with a dirt road. "This is where the bus drops me. I'll walk from here," but I insisted on door to door service. The road was a mile long, and it was the worst one I had ever traveled. We navigated across huge potholes that were still holding water from the previous day's rain. It was no wonder that the bus driver stopped where he did.

Finally, we arrived at Paul's house, which was really only a tiny shack. He was embarrassed to have me see his home. I was embarrassed too, for a society that would force people to live under those conditions.

The next day, I learned all about the Clarks. There were five kids, all in elementary or middle school. The father was a distant memory. A few years earlier, the mother went out and never came back. The children were nominally cared for by an alcoholic grandmother who slept on the couch. In reality, it was Paul and Patricia who served as caregivers. A relative or neighbor would stop by from time to time to drop off charitable donations.

That incident transformed me as a teacher. Imagine being angry because Paul was late to school. It was a miracle he arrived at all! Sometimes I have trouble getting my own children cleaned, dressed, and fed in the morning. Try doing it when you're ten years old, when there's no heat, no washing machine, and no support.

Why did the Clarks even bother? Why come to a school where the teachers sneer at you, your classmates tease you, and you have trouble learning? It's because school is a haven for these kids. It's a place where they have their own desks, their own books. It's a place where they no longer have to be adults. They can regain their childhood innocence for a brief period of time.

My knowledge of the Clarks tempted me to take it easy on Paul, to hold him to a lower standard. But I realized that was the worst thing for him. He needed to learn, to succeed, to gain the skills that will enable him to provide for his brothers and sisters. I chose to encourage him, push him a little, and stimulate him with the joys of learning. I also worked with my principal to be sure that the community was helping the Clarks. (Say what you want about welfare dependence. This family needed it!)

Later that school year, one of the Clark kids was a little slow and all the kids missed the bus. They ran across the busy highway to get to school on time, but only three of them made it. Paul's little sister was killed by a speeding truck. Paul took the responsibility on himself. He may still be punishing himself.

Today, twenty years later, I wonder what happened to Paul Clark and his family. As a naive, beginning teacher, I did the best I could but I suspect it wasn't enough. He needed more than reading, writing, and arithmetic. He needed counseling, problem-solving skills, and all the other so-called frills. Our schools are too bureaucratic and our classes too large for any teacher to personally rescue Paul from a lifetime of failure.

An end-of-course test will not solve Paul's problems. Neither will extra homework, school uniforms, or suspensions for misbehavior. They may help a little. What we need to address is the curriculum. Are we giving our students an education to meet their individual needs. Could we? Will we? In education,

Conflict Resolution

A more general issue regarding war and peace is the process of conflict resolution. Many times the crucial decision is whether to go to war. Long before that decision is made, however, diplomats struggle to prevent matters from escalating to that point. Some educators believe that the study of peace may help the cause of preventing war (Hicks, 1988).

The need for conflict resolution is not limited to international affairs. Our national political process has recently been stymied by legislative gridlock. Various interest groups have crossed swords over such matters as abortion rights, the environment, and the mistreatment of animals. Family violence is at an all-time high.

Elementary schools, of course, are not immune from the presence of violence. Teachers are more concerned than ever about students' physical conflict. They also worry about verbal abuse by students. Fortunately, the threat of students possessing weapons is still relatively small (Shen, 1997). Even counting the tragic 1998 shootings at a Jonesboro, Arkansas middle school, the number of school-related murders is not rising (Males, 1998). Such violence receives attention, not because it is common, but because it is rare.

Still, developing skills in conflict resolution could help overcome these problems. Fortunately, some highly regarded curriculum plans are available for this purpose (Johnson, Johnson, Stevahn & Hodne, 1997; Kriedler, 1984; Berman, 1983).

The Environment

Environmental problems are less of an immediate threat to human life than war, but their consequences can be just as dangerous. The safety of the air, land, and water is a matter of growing concern. Scientists believe that recent increases in cancer and other diseases are linked to the pollution our industrial society has created, but the precise cause-effect relationships have yet to be clarified (Pitot, 1990).

In the meantime, we nonscientists must make decisions concerning our own individual behavior as well as the actions of the overall society. How do we prevent the destruction of our natural resources? How do we clean up the messes we have made?

To answer these questions, we need scientific knowledge. We must understand the ecological system of which we are a part. For instance, a seemingly inconsequential action like dumping a pan of used motor oil into a sewer may lead to a poisoned water supply that can adversely affect the lives of animals, plants, and humans. A governmental farm policy that encourages the use of pesticides can also have serious consequences that may not be immediately apparent. Conversely, individual decisions to compost natural waste or governmental policies that require trees to be planted along roadsides may contribute to solutions.

Many environmental issues have financial considerations. The decision to halt the destruction of ancient forests, for instance, may save endangered species, but it carries with it economic costs in terms of jobs and community growth. Citizens need to be comfortable with the mathematical thinking required to make logical decisions.

Environmental appreciation involves more than dollars and cents, however; feelings are involved. You cannot calculate the aesthetic value of a waterfall, a redwood tree, or clean mountain air. Schools can help children become aware of these feelings. Environmental awareness can be accomplished through the arts, including photography, film, poetry, and prose. It may seem odd, but a basic strategy in attacking environmental problems may be through such nonscientific means as reading Thoreau or examining the photos of Ansel Adams.

Ethnic Discord

In recent years there has been a series of disturbances in major American cities. The most prominent, in Los Angeles, Miami, and New York, have involved clashes between ethnic groups. We have also seen "hate crimes," which include beatings, vandalism of religious property, and other acts that promote intolerance. Sociologists indicate that mistrust between ethnic groups exists, with economic and political causes at its root (Gollnick & Chinn, 1990).

In this land that has often been regarded as a "melting pot," it is remarkable how little we know about each other. We may be able to identify people's origins by their facial features or by the food, clothing, and music that is associated with certain ethnic groups, but we often know little beyond that.

Some popular stereotypes associate particular groups with such negative connotations as mob activity, drunkenness, shady business practices, and shiftlessness. There are also positive connotations regarding intelligence, work ethic, athletic skill, and thriftiness. These stereotypes persist because we lack the firsthand knowledge and communication skills that would allow us to replace them with deep and accurate understanding.

Schools can play a role in correcting the ignorance that leads to ethnic divisions. Many schools already have a broad ethnic mix that allows students intercultural interaction. Getting to know people who are different helps us understand ourselves as well as others.

Unfortunately, goals related to intercultural understanding have seldom been emphasized in the elementary curriculum. There may be an occasional holiday celebration or story about another cultural group, but intercultural learning is usually incidental to some other goal. Students are seldom encouraged to discuss their cultural similarities and differences with each other, perhaps for fear of conflict. But that conflict is inevitable, and is not necessarily harmful. It is better to have a serious or lively discussion under a teacher's guidance than to have a riot in the streets.

Poverty

Like ethnic discord, poverty is a subject that makes teachers and students uncomfortable. In the interest of sensitivity, we are hesitant to point out economic differences between children or neighborhoods. There is no question that many children are aware of these differences and often have strong feelings about them. Nevertheless, we avoid addressing the topic directly (Moore, Lare, & Wagner, 1985).

The reasons for this reluctance (as with most curriculum issues) are varied. One factor is the topic's strong ethical component. The school curriculum has seldom addressed matters of societal right and wrong. Much time is spent in elementary schools on such individual moral behaviors as manners, cleanliness, and respect, but societal norms are rarely addressed, and certainly not criticized. Controversy is shunned.

Criticism of our society has considerable historical baggage attached to it. In the past, the idea of examining the weaknesses of the capitalist economic system has been considered by some to be unpatriotic or even subversive. But blind endorsement of the status quo without considering how to improve it is also problematic. The gap between the haves and have-nots in America has steadily widened (U.S. Bureau of the Census, 1997). Research suggests that delaying children's exposure to political conflict may be detrimental to the democratic process (Moore, Lare, & Wagner, 1985). Addressing this challenge requires a deep understanding of how the system works. By necessity, this includes looking at weaknesses and alternatives. A shift in the curriculum may be worth the criticism that would be generated.

Criminal Justice

Some experts believe that eradicating poverty would substantially eliminate crime (Hagan, 1993). Until that happens, the study of justice and the law can promote understanding of crime, its causes, and its consequences.

Unlike some of the previously mentioned topics, justice and law are already part of the elementary school curriculum. Students are presented with rules and consequences from the moment they enter the classroom, and every school day provides varied experiences in the operation of the justice system. Much of this education is unplanned and often undiscussed, leading to a less effective curriculum. Allowing students to participate in the development of rules and the procedures for enforcing them can provide a deeper understanding of justice and the law (Passe, 1991). Classroom justice issues can also be related to other aspects of the curriculum. The problem of how to share access to the classroom's lone computer, for instance, can be related to the issue of scarcity of natural resources (Passe, 1988a).

Elementary students can also examine justice issues that occur beyond the classroom. The newspapers are filled with reports of crime, arrests, trials, and punishments in local communities and around the world. Children's interest in these matters can be used to focus attention on the students' own behavior. A series of car thefts in the community, for example, can call attention to the consequences of stolen property in the classroom (Passe, 1991). Moving the curriculum in this direction is not difficult if teachers see the need for this type of learning.

Immoral Behavior

One approach to improving the nature of society is promoting a sense of caring and responsibility. These characteristics along with respect, empathy, values, and action help define the morally educated person (Wilson, 1973). If people are educated to behave morally, it is reasoned, they will make individual decisions that do not harm society (e.g., to not steal, to not litter) and make group or societal decisions based on moral principles (e.g., to protect children).

This approach is not new. One of the earliest goals of American schools was to develop individuals of high moral character (Ornstein & Levine, 1989). To meet this need in the past, the curriculum included a strong religious component. Religious training has since been eliminated from the public school curriculum in line with the constitutional separation of church and state.

The prohibition against the advancement of religion by state action does not, however, rule out moral education. Schools have always been active in developing moral behavior (Sockett, 1993). We see it in fairy tales and fables, classroom rules, and the emphasis on patriotism. There are several proposals for a more comprehensive approach to character education (e.g., Raths, Harmin, & Simon, 1978; Kohlberg, 1985; Lickona, 1987; Bennett, 1980), but they tend to be controversial. Ironically, even though the topic seems highly traditional, one objection to character education is that it deviates from the traditional elementary school emphasis on basic skills. If educators wish to promote character education as part of the curriculum, these objections must be addressed.

Political Participation

Citizen interest in the political process has been steadily dropping (see Figure 2.9). This trend is best exemplified by the low voter turnouts in local, state, and national elections. It would be easy to blame the quality of politicians or the role of television news anchors for citizen disinterest, but the situation is more complex. Other variables, such as the political environment, the age distribution of

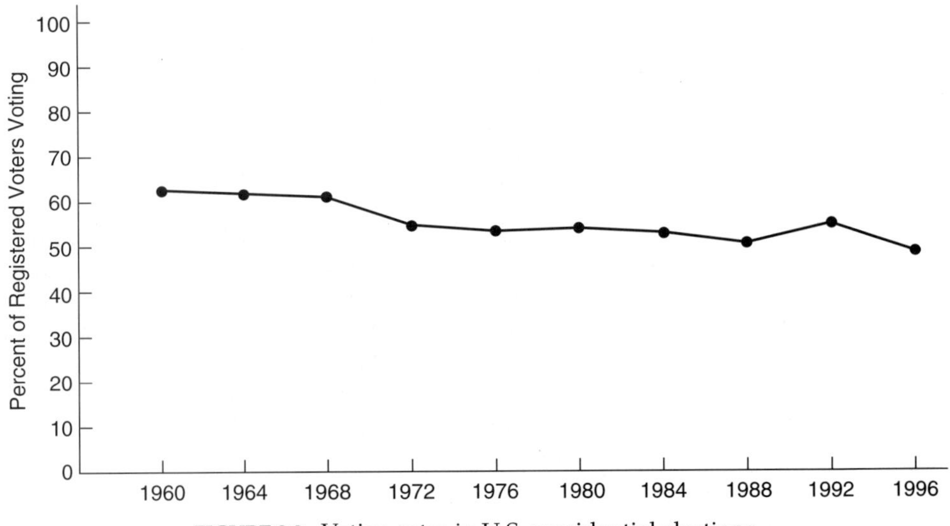

FIGURE 2.9. Voting rates in U.S. presidential elections.
Source: Statistical Abstract of the United States, 1996.

the electorate, and changes in societal value orientations, also play a role (Conway, 1991).

Research on political participation has identified two key areas in which schools can play a part. One is newspaper reading, which is linked to political interest and activity (Teixeira, 1987). Students can be exposed to the pleasures and responsibilities of newspaper reading at an early age. Development of this habit can promote depth of understanding concerning political issues. It can also lead to discussions of current events in the classroom, which provides the foundation for political analysis (Passe, 1988b). Of course, this approach requires that teachers regularly follow the news, which is not always the case in elementary schools (Passe, 1988c).

The second area in which schools can foster political involvement is participation in decision making. A series of studies suggests that when children have engaged in the discussion and choice of alternatives, they will be more likely to participate in the political system as adults (Conway, 1991). This idea has been instituted in a number of classrooms and schools (Wood, 1990; Goodman, 1992; Passe, 1996). The topic will be further explored in Chapter 11.

Communication Skills

Many societal problems are caused or exacerbated by poor communication between individuals and between groups. Members of different ethnic groups, religions, and social classes sometimes have difficulty getting along because of their limited interaction. If schools can develop communication skills, our society may benefit in several ways.

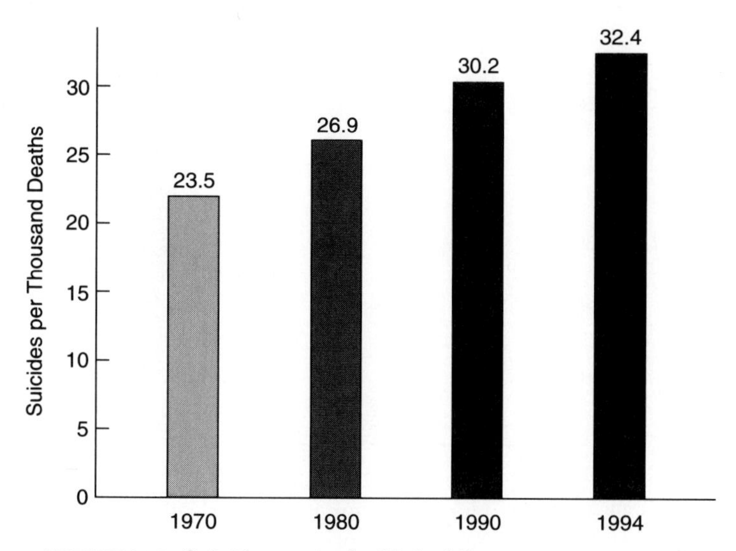

FIGURE 2.10. Suicide rate in the United States.
Source: Statistical Abstract of the United States, 1992.

Political Communication

An essential element of successful political participation is "thoughtful discourse" (Boyer, 1990). Some of the ideas presented earlier can promote the necessary thought, but measures must be taken to promote the quality of the discourse. That means "teaching students to think critically, listen with discernment, and communicate with power and precision. If students learn to listen and speak more carefully, as well as read and write, they will not only be critically empowered; they will also know how to distinguish between the authentic and the fraudulent in human discourse. Indeed, the destiny of this nation may be threatened not so much by weapons systems but by the inclination of public officials to send messages that obscure truth". (Boyer, 1990, pp. 5–6)

Interpersonal Communication

As important as thoughtful discourse is to the political process, it is also crucial in interpersonal relationships. Our society is suffering from a breakdown in communication. We see it in the divorce rate, the level of street violence, the number of lawsuits, and the rise in mental illness and suicide (see Figures 2.10 and 2.11). If individuals can be taught to effectively communicate their thoughts and feelings, their capacity to handle problems improves (Goldstein & Michaels, 1985). Advances in this area may reverse many of these trends.

The elementary school has always been responsible for teaching communication skills, but usually in a formal sense. Correct use of punctuation, clear oral expression, and knowing how to structure a term paper each has value, but such skills are insufficient to address interpersonal communication problems. The

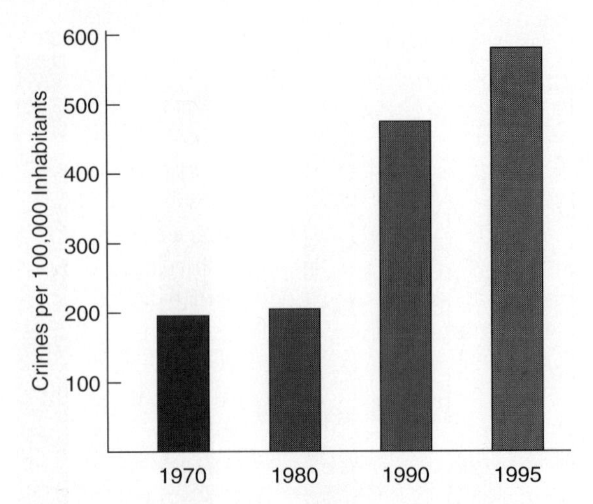

FIGURE 2.11. Number of inmates in local jails, state prisons, and federal prisons.
Source: Bronfenbrenner, McClelland, Wethington, Moen, and Ceci. (1996). The State of Americans, New York: The Free Press.

focus must shift to quality of expression and to skills in decoding what others are trying to communicate.

Economic Communication

Another aspect of communication skill is related to economic efficiency. Business and industry leaders have decried the weaknesses of high school graduates. A series of reports on education called nearly unanimously for improvement in student communication competencies (Ornstein & Levine, 1989).

The consumer side of economic efficiency is also weak. The inability to effectively analyze product warranties, life insurance policies, or television advertisements can lead to calamitous financial mistakes. Wasted money, whether it is spent on unnecessary purchases or contributed to corrupt fund-raising organizations, is also a drain on the economy. Students should be taught how to become wise consumers.

Political, interpersonal, and economic communication has not been adequately addressed by the traditional curriculum. Educators must make adjustments in order to meet those societal needs.

Health Care

Health care is an individual matter. We each make dozens of daily choices concerning our bodies, ranging from matters of nutrition and skin care to drug use and sexual activity. The decisions we make can have major personal consequences, such as the development of an incapacitating disease. But each personal choice has societal implications too, for the economic system suffers when a productive worker stops contributing and starts to draw benefits from the government. Therefore, it is in society's interest to promote healthy living.

Proper health care is of particular concern to educators because of the strong relationship between health and learning. For instance, a baby with a low birth weight (under 5.5 pounds) is likely to require special education services. Between 15 and 20 percent of such babies will have significant disabilities. This problem is correctable, however, because the major cause of low birth weight is unsatisfactory prenatal care. When pregnant mothers delay their visits to a physician, they do not learn about proper health habits. Thus, they are more likely to eat poorly and use drugs and tobacco during pregnancy, all of which are linked to low birthweight babies (Merenstein, 1992).

Over the years, the schools have responded strongly to this need. Many health topics such as dental care and nutrition are addressed in the science curriculum, sometimes in conjunction with the school nurse. For major societal concerns, special programs such as sex education and drug abuse prevention have been added to the curriculum. Some teachers have been critical of this approach because of the difficulty in squeezing new topics into an already cramped schedule. The total curriculum has suffered as a result (Wise, 1988). This concern will be addressed in later chapters.

Over the past several years, there has been considerable public debate over the future of our country's health care system. No matter what changes are proposed and implemented, the discussion will continue. Programs will be constantly evaluated and revised until some level of individual and societal satisfaction is achieved.

In-depth discussion of this topic requires much background knowledge. We must be acquainted with the range of services, the relative costs, and the consequences of various choices. Comparisons with health care in Canada and other countries demand knowledge of those nations and the cultural characteristics that make their situations similar to or different from that in the United States.

Mathematics plays a key role in the study of health care. To financially assess a new program, we must compare it to the current system. Many Americans do not know how much they pay for health insurance, even when payroll deductions are printed on their paychecks. The public may also be unfamiliar with the costs of various health care options or the salaries of health care practitioners. This mathematical ignorance, called "innumeracy" by one commentator (Paulos, 1990) must be addressed by the curriculum if students are to make optimum health care choices.

Sexual Activity

Sexual activity among teenagers has increased from 10 percent to more than 50 percent since the 1960s (Elkind, 1988). A survey in a typical urban area found that 65 percent of tenth-grade students were sexually active (Mecklenburg Council on Adolescent Pregnancy, 1989). Students need to understand that the consequences of early sexual behavior are profound. Pregnancy can seriously

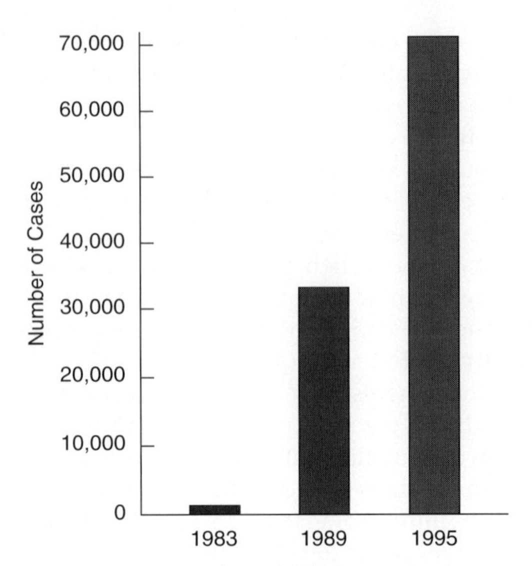

FIGURE 2.12. Number of AIDS cases in the United States.
Source: The World Almanac and Book of Facts, New York: Pharos Books.

harm teenagers' lives—physically, financially, socially, and academically. The community is affected because 72 percent of teen parents are on welfare for at least one year (Mecklenburg Council on Adolescent Pregnancy, 1988). The alternative of abortion has physical and emotional consequences, not to mention the societal furor attached to it. The threat of sexually transmitted diseases, which annually affect 2.5 million U.S. teens (Centers for Disease Control, 1989), must also be considered. AIDS (see Figure 2.12) is also a threat to this group. The teenagers' children are more likely to suffer from physical and emotional disabilities, leading to an additional annual societal cost of $19 billion to provide special education (Wattleton, 1992). Finally, the threat of overpopulation must be discussed. Rapid population growth creates numerous environmental, health, and employment problems that are difficult to remedy.

What are the implications for the elementary school curriculum? Sex education must begin early. If almost two-thirds of students are sexually active by tenth grade, we cannot wait until high school for detailed discussion to take place. The issue of when to begin, however, is a matter of controversy.

Despite its promise, sex education is not a cure-all. There are other factors to address. Children must learn to analyze the barrage of sexual messages from the media, especially television. True love as it is often portrayed in the media can be unrealistic (e.g., passionate love at first sight, living happily ever after following a one-night stand) and irresponsible (e.g., failing to use contraceptives, going off with a stranger). Discussion of media portrayals may help reduce inappropriate sexual activity and, in general, prevent youngsters from being manipulated (Wattleton, 1992).

Another approach to this problem that is not limited to sexual matters is decision making. We can all benefit from a more cautious consideration of consequences, consultation with accurate information sources, and a reasoned approach to weighing the pros and cons. Helping youngsters learn to make decisions could be the best thing elementary school teachers can do for their students.

EVALUATING YOUR OWN EDUCATION

The second half of this chapter has suggested a number of competencies that may be instrumental in meeting societal needs. At this point, it should be interesting to assess your own educational experience. Did your schooling leave you well prepared in these areas?

- international relations
- methods of conflict resolution
- ecological science
- mathematical problem solving
- aesthetic awareness and appreciation
- the lifestyles and belief systems of other ethnic groups
- the strengths and weaknesses of the economic system
- issues of justice
- your character development
- the political process
- your ability to express your feelings
- effective communication skills
- critical thinking
- consumer awareness
- societal health issues
- personal health care
- sexual matters
- media analysis
- decision making

You will probably identify a few areas in which you were well prepared. Most of my students cite less than five. It is at this point that they recognize the importance of curricular decisions.

If you compare totals with your classmates, you may discover quite a variation, especially in particular areas. Some school districts have strong programs to promote multicultural understanding, for instance, while others make no reference to the topic at all. Many times it is a particular teacher who provides the necessary experiences. Reasons for these variations will be discussed throughout this book.

The Need for Teacher Knowledge

The paramount concern for many prospective teachers is their lack of knowledge as they enter the field. Teachers who are not well prepared in, say, international relations can hardly be expected to teach the topic effectively. They often end up ignoring the topic, teaching it shallowly, or spreading misinformation. Each outcome leaves students inadequately prepared to confront the problems of the world.

How can you be a well-prepared teacher? I suggest a positive approach to overcoming your weaknesses. Here are a few helpful strategies.

Start following the news. This can be done in a variety of ways. The daily newspaper is a good start, if the articles provide some depth. Otherwise, weekly news magazines provide significant background information on many topics. Public radio news programming is often quite entertaining while it informs, and can be listened to while you commute. Television news is also good, but usually only at the national level. Local news tends to focus on sensational crime and human interest stories at the expense of more significant issues. However, you do need to be aware of events in your own community. Whatever choice you make, the key is to develop a news habit. You may be surprised how knowledgeable you become in a short time.

Make a conscious effort to correct deficiencies. Your local librarian can recommend general interest books about most of the topics mentioned earlier in this chapter. Take a college course; it may even be applied toward a degree. Community centers and churches sometimes offer evening classes on a variety of topics. Perhaps you know someone who likes to talk about current issues. Many experts enjoy sharing their knowledge with novices, especially when they know you plan to use it in your teaching.

Acquire teacher's guides and other educational materials. Most curriculum publishers prepare background materials to help round out teacher presentations. After all, many teachers attended school long before certain issues, such as ecological awareness, were appreciated.

Don't let a sense of embarrassment prevent you from seeking remediation. Any deficiencies are not necessarily your fault! You cannot be blamed for the failure of your school system, if it is to blame. Once you recognize an area of weakness, you can take responsibility for correcting it. That responsibility begins today, so use your time well. Your students will benefit from your new knowledge!

Questions

1. In view of the concerns identified in the chapter, what goals should schools emphasize?
2. Are you familiar with anyone who has experienced some of the problems identified in the chapter (including yourself)? Are these concerns justified?
3. What should be the role of the school in addressing these problems? Is it possible for schools to make a difference?
4. Why do you think some of the challenges identified in the chapter have not been addressed by the school curriculum?

References

BEANE, J., & LIPKA, R. (1984). *Self-concept, self-esteem, and the curriculum.* Boston: Allyn & Bacon.

BENNETT, W. J. (1980). The teacher, the curriculum and values education development. *New Directions for Higher Education, 31,* 27–34.
BERMAN, S. (Ed.). (1983). *Perspectives: A teaching guide to concepts of peace.* Cambridge, MA: Educators for Social Responsibility.
BOYER, E. (1990). Civic education for responsible citizens. *Educational Leadership, 48,* 5.
CENTERS FOR DISEASE CONTROL. (1989). *Annual report.* Atlanta: Author.
COMER, J. P. (1988). Educating poor minority children. *Scientific American, 88,* 42–48.
CONWAY, M. M. (1991). *Political participation in the United States.* (2nd ed.). Washington, DC: Congressional Quarterly Press.
DUCKETT, W. (1988). Using demographic data for long-range planning. *Phi Delta Kappan, 70,* 166–171.
ELKIND, D. (1988). *The hurried child.* Boston: Allyn & Bacon.
ESTRADA, L. (1988). Anticipating the demographic future. *Change, 20,* 14–17.
FAIRTEST. (1989). *Annual SAT and ACT scores share continued flaws.* Cambridge, MA: National Center for Fair and Open Testing.
GOLDSTEIN, A., & MICHAELS, G. (1985). *Empathy: Development, training, and consequences.* Hillsdale, NJ: Erlbaum.
GOLLNICK, D. M., & CHINN, P. C. (1990). *Multicultural education in a pluralistic society.* New York: Macmillan.
GOLLNICK, D. M., & CHINN, P. C. (1990). *Multicultural education in a pluralistic society.* Columbus, OH: Macmillan.
GOODMAN, J. (1992). *Elementary schooling for critical democracy.* Albany, NY: State University of New York Press.
HAGAN, J. (1993). Structural and cultural disinvestment and the new ethnographics. *Contemporary Sociology, 22,* 327–333.
HICKS, D. (1988). *Education for peace.* London: Routledge.
HODGKINSON, H. (1986). *The schools we need for the kids we've got.* Paper presented at the annual meeting of the American Association of Colleges for Teacher Education, Washington, DC.
HOLMAN, L. J. (1997). Meeting the needs of Hispanic immigrants. *Educational leadership, 54*(7), 37–38.
HORDAY, J. (1986). Poverty kills children. *In World Health* (pp. 12–16).
JOHNSON, D. W., JOHNSON, R. T., STEVAHN, L., & HODNE, P. (1997). The three Cs of safe schools, *Educational Leadership, 55*(2), 8–13.
JOHNSON, O. (Ed.). (1990). *Information please almanac.* New York: Houghton Mifflin.
KNAPP, M. S., & SHIELDS, P. M. (1990). Reconceiving academic instruction for the children of poverty. *Phi Delta Kappan, 71,* 753–758.
KOHLBERG, L. (1985). The just community approach to moral education. In M. W. Berkowitz and F. Oser (Eds.), *Moral education: Theory and application* (pp. 27–87). London: Erlbaum.
KRIEDLER, W. (1984). *Creative conflict resolution.* Glenview, IL: Scott, Foresman.
LASH, A., & KIRKPATRICK, S. (1990). A classroom perspective on student mobility. *The Elementary School Journal, 91,* 176–185.
LEVITAN, S. A. (1990). Poverty. *Academic International Encyclopedia.* New York: Academic International.
LICKONA, T. (1987). Character development in the elementary school classroom. In K. Ryan and G. F. Maclean (Eds.), *Character development in schools and beyond* (pp. 177–206). Westport, CN: Praeger.
LOUV, R. (1991). *Childhood's future.* Boston: Houghton Mifflin.

MALES, M. A. (1998). Five Myths and Why Adults Believe They are True. *New York Times,* April 29, 1998, p. 9.
MECKLENBURG COUNCIL ON ADOLESCENT PREGNANCY (1989, April 29). *1988 statistical report on adolescent pregnancy: Mecklenburg County.* [News release, Charlotte, NC].
MERENSTEIN, G. B. (1992). At risk at birth. *NEA Today, 10*(7), 29.
MOORE, S. W., LARE, J., & WAGNER, K. A. (1985). *The child's political world: A longitudinal perspective.* New York: Praeger.
ORNSTEIN, A. C., & LEVINE, D. U. (1989). *An introduction to the foundations of education* (4th ed.). Boston: Houghton Mifflin.
PASSE, J. (1988a). Citizenship behavior: Its role in improving classroom behavior. *Social Studies and the Young Learner, 1,* 19–21.
PASSE, J. (1988b). Developing current events awareness in children. *Social Education, 52,* 531–533.
PASSE, J. (1988c). The role of internal factors in the teaching of current events. *Theory and Research in Social Education, 16,* 83–89.
PASSE, J. (1991). Citizenship knowledge in young learners. *Social Studies and the Young Learner, 3,* 15–17.
PASSE, J. (1994). Media literacy in a global age. *Social Studies and the Young Learner,* 6(4), 7–9.
PASSE, J. (1996). *When students choose content.* Thousand Oaks, CA: Corwin Press.
PAULOS, J. A. (1990). *Innumeracy: Mathematical illiteracy and its consequences.* New York: Vintage.
PITOT, H. C. (1990). Cancer. In A. K. Ranson (Ed.), *Academic international encyclopedia* (pp. 101–106). Academic International.
POSTMAN, N. (1982). *The disappearance of childhood.* New York: Delacorte.
RATHS, L., HARMIN, M., & SIMON, S. B. (1978). *Values and teaching: Working with values in the classroom* (2nd ed.). Columbus, OH: Merrill.
REITMAN, S. (1992). *The educational messiah complex: American faith in the culturally redemptive power of schooling.* Sacramento: Caddo Press.
RICHE, M. F. (1996). A profile of America's diversity—The view from the Census Bureau, 1996. *The world almanac and book of facts.* Mahwah, NJ: World Almanac Books.
SHEN, J. (1997). The evolution of violence in schools. *Educational Leadership, 55*(2), 18–21.
SOCKETT, H. (1993). The moral aspects of the curriculum. In P. W. Jackson (Ed.), *Handbook of research on curriculum.* New York: Macmillan, 543–568.
TEIXEIRA, R. (1987). *Why Americans don't vote: Turnout decline in the United States, 1960–1984.* Westport, CT: Greenwood Press.
TYLER-WILKINS, A. (1988). *Latchkey children.* Washington, DC: U.S. Government Printing Office.
U.S. BUREAU OF THE CENSUS. (1988). *Statistical abstract of the United States, 1988* (108th ed.). Washington, DC: U.S. Government Printing Office.
U.S. BUREAU OF THE CENSUS. (1997). *Statistical abstract of the United States.* Washington, DC: Author.
WATTLETON, F. (1992). Teenage pregnancy: The case for national action. In F. Schultz (Ed.), *Education 92/93* (pp. 182–184). Guilford, CT: Dushkin.
WHITFIELD, E., & FREELAND, K. (1981). Divorce and children: What teachers can do. *Childhood Education, 58,* 88–89.
WILSON, J. (1973). *A teacher's guide to moral education.* London: Chapman.
WISE, A. E. (1988). Legislated learning revisited. *Phi Delta Kappan, 69,* 328–333.
WOOD, G. H. (1990). Teaching for democracy. *Educational Leadership, 48,* 32–37.

CHAPTER 3

How Can the Curriculum Meet the Developmental Needs of Elementary Children?

In my university classes, when I begin to teach about developmental needs of elementary school children, my students groan. They insist that they have studied the topic ad nauseum in other classes. I respond by offering them the chance to explain its importance. Are there topics that should be introduced in later grades because of developmental considerations? Should some skills be taught earlier? Which ones? On what basis should these decisions be made? How can development inform our decisions concerning classroom organization? Usually, few can answer these questions.

The problem is that students cannot remember what was taught. Because they had few opportunities to apply the knowledge, it becomes another interesting but useless set of facts that is quickly forgotten after the exam. Knowledge is of little benefit unless it can be applied. The significance of developmental needs only becomes apparent when we analyze how well the elementary school curriculum meets them. It would not be an exaggeration to say that meeting developmental needs is the most crucial issue in the elementary school curriculum.

To explain how this is so, this chapter will identify important developmental changes and discuss how the curriculum is set up to meet children's needs or, as is too often the case, how it is harmful to them. This chapter will focus only on the developmental needs of elementary school children. No attempt will be made to provide in-depth analysis of human development from birth to old age; if you have an interest in or need for more information in this area, references are provided in the bibliography.

TYPES OF DEVELOPMENT

Humans are complex beings. As we age, we change physically, cognitively, and socially. Although each type of development has its own timetable, developments influence each other. For instance, when infants develop the physical ability to grasp an object, they are likely to learn (cognitively) about objects, which promotes social maturity.

Loss of a tooth is a developmental milestone for young children.

Each type of development is important in the elementary curriculum because young children change so rapidly during their early years. To teach physical skills such as throwing a ball, holding a pencil, or playing a musical instrument, a teacher must be aware of what children can and can't do.

The same is true of cognitive skills such as alphabetizing a list of words, developing an outline, or interpreting a poem. The best teacher in the world cannot instruct a child in one of those skills if the child's thinking ability is not sufficiently mature to learn it.

Social development is also a factor. Teachers often tell kindergartners not to worry or ask them to share their toys, but the children may not be able to do what the teacher wants. Teachers who know the levels of their students' social development will be more likely to give appropriate directions, such as telling the worrier what will happen next or instructing the toy hoarder to let another child use a specific toy for a certain amount of time.

In the sections that follow, each type of development will be analyzed to highlight the major needs that exist during elementary school. Then those needs will be related to the curriculum as it exists. You will discover that schools do a good job, in most cases, of matching the curriculum to the child's needs. But you will also be confronted with practices that cry out to be changed.

Physical Development

Elementary school-age children experience a number of physical changes including changes in height, weight, and body proportion. Appearance changes so dramatically that it is difficult not to exclaim, "You've gotten so big!" even when you know it is a cliche. Major physical changes influence a child's self-esteem. A child who is unusually tall, short, thin, or fat must deal with a lot of teasing, both good-natured and otherwise.

Elementary school children are particularly proud of changes inside their mouths. The loss of "baby" teeth is a notable achievement for every youngster. Yet teachers must also be aware of the effects of new and missing teeth on speech, eating habits, and dental health.

During the later elementary years, many children begin to undergo changes associated with adolescence. The development of breasts, body odor, facial hair, and a deepening voice become noticeable. Other aspects of puberty, such as growth spurts, changes in sex organs, growth of body hair, and menstruation are also occurring. Changes in size often bring on adult-like expectations and pressures.

At one time, these changes would not be discussed in a book about elementary school children, but the onset of puberty is occurring earlier and earlier among Americans. For example, one recent study indicates that nearly half of black girls and 15 percent of white girls had begun developing breasts, pubic hair, or both by age 8 (Herman-Giddens, Slora, Wasserman, Bourdony, Bhapkar, Koch and Hasemeier, 1998). Improvements in nutrition and health are believed to account for the general trend toward early puberty (Elkind, 1988), while the cause of the racial differences are unclear (Herman-Giddens, Slora, Wasserman, Bourdony, Bhapkar, Koch & Hasemeier, 1998). Regardless of the cause, if more and more second graders are reaching puberty, the elementary curriculum must be adapted to meet their changing needs. Youngsters seek to understand what is happening to them; how their relationships with family, friends, and the other sex may be influenced; how to deal with early or late adolescent development; and how to deal with sexual urges and expectations.

Motor development is also rapid during the elementary school years. Consider kindergartners who are just mastering such basic skills as tying their shoes, hopping, and manipulating a crayon. By the end of elementary school, most children can competently engage in complex motor activities that range from building intricate models to playing piano to performing gymnastics.

Because physical development is cephalocaudal (progressing from the head to the extremities), gross motor skills develop before fine motor skills. Just as the infant could sit up before it could walk, elementary children are also slower in learning to perform skills that involve small muscles in the fingers than they are in, say, running and jumping. It is not unusual for first graders to have difficulty writing their letters on the lines of their paper or cutting along a straight line with scissors.

Although children's physical changes during elementary school are noticeable, they are often overlooked when the curriculum is planned. This oversight can create problems, which will be discussed later in the chapter.

Cognitive Development

The aspect of education that is least understood by noneducators is cognitive development. Many educational commentators appear to regard learning as simply a matter of gaining more information. They imply that children differ from adults only by having less knowledge. Therefore, they conclude, we only need to start teaching sooner and everyone will be successful. As a result, in recent years, our society has seen three-year-olds thrown into formal classroom situations, flash cards developed for quizzing infants, and even cassette recordings played for those who are still in the womb!

Most elementary educators look at the work of Jean Piaget as their guide to cognitive development. His research and that of hundreds of replicative studies conclude that children think *differently* than adults do. Three-year-olds are not able to do the mental manipulations that eight-year-olds can. Nor can eight-year-olds think like fourteen-year-olds. Piaget's developmental theory is regarded as a stage theory because there are qualitative differences between children at each stage.

The first stage is the sensorimotor stage, which runs from birth to about age two. Sensorimotor children are not capable of thinking before they act. (Many adults also do not think before they act, but are capable of doing so!) Infants in the sensorimotor stage are busy learning that causes have effects and that an object that is hidden still exists. You will not find children at this stage in a regular elementary classroom, so we will move on to the more relevant preoperational stage.

Contrasts between Preoperational and Concrete-Operational Thought

When children show evidence of thinking before acting, we call them preoperational. Preoperational children do not think logically but rely on their perceptions instead. In contrast are concrete-operational children, who can reason logically to solve a problem. Several classic experiments illustrate preoperational and concrete-operational thinking.

The most famous one involves two beakers with identical amounts of water (see Figure 3.1). One beaker is tall and thin, the other short and wide. When you ask a preoperational child if one has more water or they both have the same amount, the child will insist that the tall, thin beaker has more. The child relies on the perception that the tall one has more because the water is higher. Children who are not able to measure changes like this are said to lack the ability to conserve.

This conservation experiment illustrates preoperational characteristics. First, the child can only focus on one variable; in this case, height. Second, the child is thinking perceptually, relying on how things look. A concrete-operational child, who is able to think logically, can think through the situation to conclude that the beakers hold equal amounts of water. Concrete-operational children can focus on more than one variable at a time. In their minds' eye, they can mentally pour the water from one beaker into another and measure the change. This mental manipulation is called an operation. Children who cannot perform this operation are, thus, preoperational.

Piaget reminds us that the difference in the two types of thinking is not simply a matter of getting the answer correct. We can easily train a child to give the right

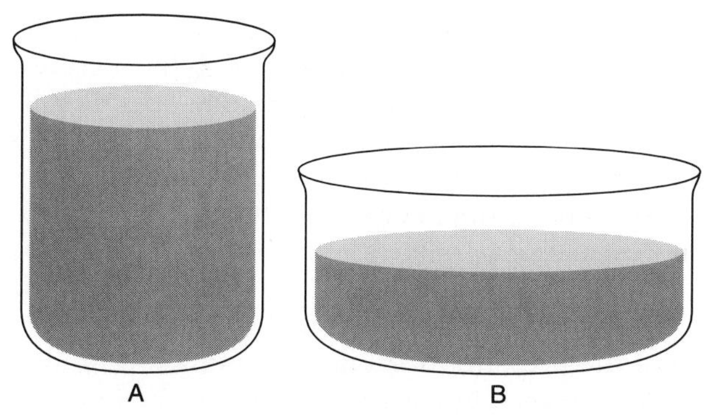

FIGURE 3.1. Piagetian beaker experiment.

answer, but the child will not understand. It is like a three-year-old repeating a mathematical equation, such as $8 \times 9 = 72$, without understanding the process.

Classification

Their inability to focus on more than one variable at a time prevents preoperational children from successfully classifying data. They can divide items by color or by shape, but not both at once. However, concrete-operational children delight in classifying anything and everything. They will sort out baseball cards, seashells, and doll clothing according to well-defined criteria. Like anyone else who learns a new skill, these children enjoy practicing it. It is to be expected that concrete-operational children would actively seek to measure themselves against their classmates in terms of such characteristics as strength, reading ability, and handwriting skill.

The ability to classify enables children to manipulate symbols. Thus, children can now grasp the hierarchical system of numbers. When my neighbor, Chris, was five, he was trying to meet the prerequisites for entering kindergarten in his school district. Among the requirements was understanding the number system. When I asked him how he was doing, he replied, "I know 4 and 7, but I'm still working on 6." Chris's reply demonstrated that he had no idea what he was talking about! Knowing one's numbers isn't being able to recite them in order, but to understand that 4 is larger than 3 and smaller than 5 (thus being able to handle two variables, one larger and one smaller, simultaneously). Once the hierarchical nature of the system is grasped, children can use numerals to solve problems.

Concrete operations also permit children to use rules to decode words. To try and teach reading before this ability develops can be harmful to the child's academic development, as we shall see. Rules are also used in writing proper sentences and playing complex games (Elkind, 1988).

Animism

Another important distinction between preoperational and concrete-operational thought is the presence of animism in younger children. They give human characteristics to inanimate objects. For instance, if you ask some youngsters whether a car is alive, they will tell you that it is. Why? Because it moves. The same is true of clouds, waves, and the sun. Concrete-operational children, however, understand the concept of an organism, and are thus able to correctly differentiate between living and nonliving things. Surprisingly, however, some elements of animism continue until age twelve (Good, 1977).

If one gives human characteristics to inanimate objects, it becomes easy to explain confusing events. For instance, we can conclude that the sun has appeared through the clouds because it wanted to be nice to all the cold people. Or we can explain the presence of a big rock along a trail by saying that the rock chose to be where people will sit, so it won't be lonely. Preoperational children excel in such illogical thought, but it makes them a lot of fun to be around.

Many adults, who initially express disbelief when they hear such descriptions of younger children, eventually conclude that preoperational children are indeed animistic. Why are they so surprised? In many cases, it is because adults do not ask children questions about why things happen. The adult assumes that the difference between living and nonliving things is understood. This kind of mistake is often made by noneducators who make proposals to improve the curriculum. Even some educators make such mistakes because they spend too much time talking to children instead of listening to their ideas. Another explanation is that some adults form conclusions based on the comments of brighter children without considering that most of their age-mates have not yet reached higher stages of cognitive development.

Egocentrism

An important developmental concept is egocentrism. Young children have a lot of it. Egocentrism is the inability to consider viewpoints other than your own. When young children give some of the unusual explanations we often hear, it never occurs to them that they may be wrong. They don't think about their own thought. In fact, they assume that others see and feel things the exact same way. So, a child may say, "My tooth hurts. Can't you feel it?" A good example of egocentrism appeared in the comic strip "Family Circus" when five-year-old Billy gave directions to a matronly woman: "You go down here to the climbin' tree, over Mrs. Cobb's fence, left at Max's house, through Boyd's back yard, under the hedge. . . ." As if this woman knows Max or Mrs. Cobb, or would crawl under hedges or climb over fences!

As children get older they gradually lose their egocentrism. Through maturity and interaction with others, they develop. In concrete operations they begin to logically challenge their ideas. Many will chuckle when they realize how silly some of their conclusions were.

How Children Develop

While the research on cognitive stages is fairly conclusive, the actual process of development remains unclear. It is generally accepted, however, that children

"It's OK if they hafta pull your tooth, Grandma. Your second one will grow in in no time!"

Reprinted with special permission of King Features Syndicate.

develop through a combination of maturity and experience. The key to this idea is that both factors have to be present.

Think about those rare cases of unfortunate children who have been isolated from society, locked in a closet or basement. Even though their brains may have developed enough to allow concrete-operational thought, their lack of experience prevents them from reaching that stage. Maturity by itself is inadequate for cognitive growth.

Neither is experience. Just as a boy cannot walk until his muscles are adequately developed, he cannot think concretely until his brain is sufficiently mature. When both brain growth and appropriate environmental conditions are present, developmental growth will occur.

Formal Operations

Formal operations follow concrete operations for many people. Researchers report that less than half of all Americans reach formal operations (Dulit, 1975). In elementary schools, therefore, aspects of formal thought are most likely to occur among a small number of children in the upper grades, if at all.

Formal thinkers are able to deal with abstract concepts, ideas that exist only in one's head. Concrete thinkers, on the other hand, can only deal with events they have experienced. For instance, formal thinkers can understand nuclear physics; concrete-operational children cannot because the process is not observable. Metaphors represent words, not concrete ideas, so they can be appreciated only by those who have reached the stage of formal operations. In contrast to concrete thinkers, formal thinkers enjoy intellectual discussions concerning such matters as belief systems and values.

Some abstract ideas can be made concrete. For instance, a formal operational thinker can read a definition of an inflationary spiral, "a continuous rise in prices that is sustained by the tendency of wage increases and cost increases to react with each other," and understand the process. Concrete thinkers need a real (concrete) experience in order to understand. A savvy teacher could set up a class store that uses play money. The teacher would keep raising prices so the student workers would demand more money. Raises would be granted by providing even more play money. When the children realized that the value of the money decreased, they would be able to recognize the inflationary spiral, even if they couldn't recite the definition.

Much of the university curriculum is at the formal operational level. Even introductory courses such as economics, sociology, and mathematics emphasize theoretical models of understanding the world. Students are often uncomfortable with these courses' high level of abstraction because their previous school experience did not prepare them for that kind of content. Discomfort, however, is not an indication that one continues to think on a concrete-operational level. Everyone, including college professors, prefers concrete examples. Students with even a modest degree of success at the college level can safely assume themselves to be capable of formal operational thought.

Cognitive development is a difficult topic to teach and learn. It is so complex (and so abstract!) that many educators gloss over it. Yet, as we will see, we must take it into account when planning the curriculum.

Social Development

Children's social development has so many characteristics that it would be impossible to describe them all in this chapter. More detailed examination of the many fascinating aspects of social change is essential for anyone working closely with children. In this section, the focus will be on those changes that most directly concern the curriculum.

Peers

One of the major changes that parents notice is the rise in the importance of the peer group. Until about the age of five or six, parents are the primary socializing force. Gradually, peers become more important until they eventually surpass parents in influence (LeFrancois, 1984). Accordingly, the intimacy of friendships will also increase during this period (Bigelow & LaGaipa, 1975).

An aid in developing friendship is the ability to understand emotions. Whereas younger children can identify with the emotions of people similar to themselves, school-age children can empathize with those who are dissimilar.

Furthermore, they are better able to analyze the causes of people's emotions (Flapan, 1968).

Role Taking

Selman (1976) developed a model of children's role-taking abilities. According to his research, it is not until ages nine and ten that a child can take another's role, but the child then still cannot take his or her own role simultaneously. At age ten through twelve, mutual role taking can occur. Later, the adolescent regards different viewpoints as part of a social system.

Using Selman's model, we can analyze a playground fistfight. Children who hurt others on the playground may realize the pain their victims are suffering, but they cannot do so while they're thinking of their own anger. Thinking of only one role at a time prevents proper consideration of the circumstances. As children develop, they can handle simultaneous role taking and thus are more likely to exercise restraint. After that stage, they can grasp the complex factors that contribute to playground altercations.

These changes in role-taking ability enable children to get along better. They can understand other people's intentions, instead of merely focusing on their behaviors (Schickidanz, Schickidanz & Forsyth, 1982). As a result, the study of literature or other cultures and even general playground activity become fertile learning opportunities for older children.

Selman's work (1976) exemplifies the overlap between social and cognitive development. Children's ability to think about more than one variable is linked to the ability to think about two roles at once. Thus, as children grow cognitively, they also grow socially.

Another example of the link between cognitive and social development involves sharing. Young children regard possessions as part of themselves. Therefore, the idea of sharing toys or even sharing a parent is objectionable (Elkind, 1988).

Psychosocial Development

Erik Erikson (1963) has theorized about the major psychosocial tasks that people face as they develop. According to his theory, kindergartners have the task of developing initiative. In their innocence, they are eager learners, excited about using their new skills to solve problems. If successful, they will develop a sense of purpose and a willingness to take chances.

Sometimes, however, the sense of initiative is thwarted, resulting in guilty feelings. Children who are prevented from exercising a reasonable amount of initiative because of adult restrictions may avoid future opportunities to do so. In this way, they can escape their anticipated guilty feelings. Guilt may also arise from unbridled exercise of initiative. When children are too aggressive in their physical or verbal play, others can be hurt. The self-condemnation that results often prevents subsequent expressions of initiative. Children, thus, seek a balance between initiative and guilt.

Teachers can help children achieve psychosocial development by structuring the curriculum appropriately. Sufficient time and materials must be provided to let young children engage in acts of exploration and discovery.

Not coincidentally, preoperational thinkers have the same need. But in many primary grade classrooms the curriculum limits student initiative by emphasizing worksheets, memorization, and passive listening.

Erikson's theory (1982) posits industry as the primary task of the next psychosocial stage. Children work enthusiastically on projects, eager to demonstrate their prowess. If successful, they feel competent and proud.

If children do not achieve a sense of industry, inferiority is the result. Children who do not have the opportunity to apply themselves to meaningful work or whose work is belittled will feel incompetent. Like guilt, a sense of inferiority can disrupt normal development. A curriculum that is filled with trivial tasks can, thus, be harmful. So can the expectation to perform tasks that are beyond the child's capabilities.

Erikson's theory emphasizes that a healthy balance is needed at both psychosocial stages. Schools can teach children to be cautious when they take initiative. They can also insure that a child experiences occasional failure to help them see their strengths and weaknesses.

Multiple Intelligences

Piagetian cognitive-developmental theory emphasizes logical-mathematical reasoning. Because our society reveres logic, we often form conclusions about intelligence from student performance in this area. For instance, children who can solve equations well before their peers are considered geniuses.

In a similar fashion, linguistic intelligence is also highly regarded. Children with advanced vocabularies and strong reading skills are usually the stars of their classrooms. These children are more likely to go on to prestigious colleges and successful careers than their classmates. It is, therefore, easy to understand how IQ or intelligence tests came to be based on linguistic and mathematical performance.

Recently, Howard Gardner (1993) has proposed an alternative conception of intelligence he calls "multiple intelligences." In addition to the two types we have identified, Gardner adds spatial intelligence, musical intelligence, bodily-kinesthetic intelligence, interpersonal intelligence, intrapersonal, and naturalist intelligence. Table 3.1 provides descriptions and examples.

Though there is debate over Gardner's categories (e.g., Kohlberg & DeVries, 1987), many educators are beginning to reassess their curriculum and methods with an eye toward the needs of children with different types of intelligence. For instance, how well is the school curriculum developing engineers or artists or therapists? These issues will be addressed throughout this text.

Emotional Intelligence

Gardner's (1995) conception of intrapersonal intelligence inspired the concept of emotional intelligence: "abilities such as being able to motivate oneself and persist in the face of frustrations; to control impulse and delay gratification; to regulate one's moods and keep distress from swamping the ability to think; to empathize and to hope" (Goleman, 1995, p. 34). While cognitive intelligence is certainly important in academics, it does not always translate into successful

TABLE 3.1. Multiple Intelligences

Intelligence	Manifested in These Abilities	Demonstrated by These Individuals
Logical-mathematical	Math, science, logic	Newton, Einstein, Grace Hopper
Linguistic	Writing, poetry, public speaking	Shakespeare, Churchill, Anne Tyler
Interpersonal	Diplomacy, compromise, manipulation	Gandhi, Madeleine Albright, Martin Luther King, Jr.
Spatial	Visualizing, transforming, creating images	Michaelangelo, daVinci, Annie Liebowitz
Musical	Composing, orchestrating, performing	Bach, Sarah Caldwell, Stevie Wonder
Kinesthetic	Athletics, dance, choreography	Michael Jordan, Martha Graham, Marcel Marceau
Intrapersonal	Self-understanding, personal problem solving	Virginia Woolf, Freud
Naturalist	Solving nature-related problems	Charles Darwin, Carl Sagan, Jacques Cousteau

Adapted from *Multiple Intelligences: The Theory in Practice* by H. Gardner, 1993, New York: HarperCollins.

careers and relationships or general happiness (Goleman, 1995). It may account for as little as 4 to 20 percent of career performance. Emotional intelligence, on the other hand, has been correlated with about 80 percent of a person's success in life (Pool, 1997).

Salovey (1990) proposes five domains of emotional intelligence:

- *Knowing one's emotions.* People with self-awareness make better personal decisions.
- *Managing emotions.* Children are better able to avoid violence, drug abuse, and teen pregnancy by learning to handle their emotions responsibly.
- *Motivating oneself.* Emotional self-control and being able to get into the "flow" promotes productivity and effectiveness.
- *Recognizing emotions in others.* Children can learn how to be empathetic, thus promoting their ability to respond to others' needs.
- *Handling relationships.* Learning social skills enables people to get along better.

The curriculum can promote social development. It does not have to be an extra. Dozens of social and emotional learning programs are in operation, many as a response to the work of Gardner (1993) and Goleman (1995). Research on these programs indicates that integrating social and emotional learning goals into the curriculum strengthens the academic work of children (Goleman, 1995; Elias, Breune-Butler, Blum & Schuyler, 1997).

DEVELOPMENT AND THE CURRICULUM

A teacher's task in planning the curriculum is to choose subject matter that is developmentally appropriate. If the content is beyond the child's capabilities, the result will be failure.

Consider the topic of subtraction with regrouping. In exchanging one of the tens for ten ones, we are performing an operation. This task is no problem for a concrete-operational child who can handle the multiple variables of subtracting from the tens column to add to the ones column. If the initial experience with regrouping is done concretely, say with beads and sticks to represent ones and tens, the concrete thinker will be successful.

Preoperational children cannot understand this procedure. Being unable to handle the two variables, they may be forced to memorize the process. They will mindlessly cross out the numeral in the tens column, replace it with the next lower number, and put a one in front of the numeral in the ones column. In that case, they may answer correctly, but they will not have learned any mathematics! When confronted with a more complex process, such as subtracting 13 from 10,000, their memorized system is unlikely to work. Their lack of true understanding becomes apparent when we see the numbers added, subtracted without any regrouping, or skipped over.

For many preoperational students, matters become worse. The teacher often tells them to do the assignment over, to try harder, or perhaps teaches the process again, only in a louder voice. Students blame themselves, assuming that they had not been paying attention or that they are dumb. Such a process will probably lead to a series of failures.

Curriculum Disabilities

When children are confronted with an inappropriate curriculum, it leads to what Elkind (1976) calls a "curriculum disability." Unlike other disabilities, such as hearing deficits, emotional disturbance, or muscular problems, which children bring to school, curricular disabilities are caused by the school itself. The inappropriate curriculum guarantees failure in that children are incapable of successfully learning the content. The failure may take the form of low grades or it may take the form of memorizing words and procedures with little comprehension (Smith, 1975). Either type of failure easily leads to feelings of guilt and inferiority, a dislike of the subject, a dislike of the teacher, and a dislike of school (Wadsworth, 1978). Learning by rote is boring and failure is worse. Students who continually experience these feelings are unlikely to enjoy school.

This unfortunate sequence is very common in elementary schools. We see it when concrete-operational children are taught such abstract shortcuts as inverting a fraction in order to divide by it. A fraction such as 3/5 is changed to 5/3 and then multiplied, but few of us can explain why. We get by with a memorized formula, but really haven't learned any mathematics.

Consider other examples of developmentally inappropriate curriculum. The reading class has some kindergartners who are baffled when confronted with a system of arbitrary symbols called letters that combine to form words. First-grade children, barely able to properly grip a pencil, are chastised for sloppy handwriting. The third-grade social studies class is expected to deal with the abstract relationships between city, county, and state. In physical education some children feel humiliated when they cannot throw a ball according to the teacher's standards. In music, we see children who cannot seem to grasp the abstract concept of a quarter note. Some sixth graders are helpless when it comes to interpreting the metaphors in a piece of poetry.

A comical example of children dealing with content beyond their capability is the pledge of allegiance. They recite it proudly, but are unable to tell you what it means. What is allegiance? What is a republic? And who on earth is Richard Stans (in the phrase "and to the republic for Richard Stans")? Because so much of the pledge is abstract (though it can be explained concretely), it is no wonder that children do not attempt to derive meaning from its words.

Appropriate Curriculum

Despite these problems, much of the elementary curriculum is developmentally appropriate. The tradition of learning to read at about age six is probably not an accident. The movement to concrete operations at about that age enables the child to apply class-inclusion principles to the irregularities of language. One example of classification in reading is described by Wadsworth (1978): "The letter 'a' has a class of regular pronunciations (*able*) and a class of not regular pronunciations (*father, any, senate*). In addition, the 'long-a' sound (as in *able*) is written by letter patterns other than 'a' (as in *vein, they,* and *break*)" (pp. 135–136).

Another appropriately placed skill is mathematical regrouping in second grade when many children are capable of handling multiple variables. In social studies, the emphasis on abstract notions of government and ancient history is part of most states' curricula for fifth and sixth grades, when the movement to formal operations has begun.

Curriculum Discrepancies

Unfortunately, there are discrepancies too. One analysis of elementary science textbooks concludes that most of the content is developmentally inappropriate (Good, 1977). No wonder the teaching and learning of science is so unpopular among elementary school students and teachers! When one considers the remarkably strong interest of preschoolers in scientific topics, it is reasonable to conclude that curriculum disabilities are at work, with memorization replacing curiosity.

In many states, the elementary language arts curriculum emphasizes learning the parts of speech, but concrete-operational students are unable to engage in abstract discussions of adverbs and conjunctions. Instead, they memorize the examples of those parts of speech (e.g., words that end in *-ly* are adverbs). It is to be expected that teachers complain that their students still have not learned to diagram sentences. It is beyond most children's capabilities!

Brain Research

Recent advances in medicine and computer technology have allowed researchers to study changes in the brain. These have led to new perspectives on the ways the brain processes information. Much of the recent research on the brain is directly relevant to the elementary school curriculum.

One key finding is that multiple complex experiences are essential for meaningful learning and teaching. The brain can make connections from a variety of perspectives at one time. Immersion in a topic is, therefore, an effective way to learn (Caine & Caine, 1991). Achievement may be lower when the curriculum is designed to "cover" a variety of topics in a shallow fashion, while depth of study allows the brain to truly grasp content. This finding can help guide teachers in making curricular decisions.

A finding that supports other principles of cognitive development is that multiple *concrete* experiences are also essential for meaningful learning and teaching. If content is related to some aspect of students' lives, brain activation is at its height (Caine & Caine, 1991).

Brain research concludes that the brain's basic function is to search for novelty and challenge. Curriculum developers must, therefore, insure that school content is, indeed, challenging and interesting. Review, drill, and practice, which compose a substantial portion of the traditional elementary school classroom, is insufficient to engage the students' brains. In contrast, when the curriculum includes new, complex stimuli, the brain will seek to organize the information by creating some sort of pattern. That new pattern makes it easier for the brain to grasp and retrieve information (Caine & Caine, 1991). That finding may help to explain why so much school content is quickly forgotten.

THE PROBLEM OF VARIATIONS IN DEVELOPMENT

Some may conclude that the curriculum is generally appropriate, except for some glaring errors that can be corrected. However, that would only be true if all children acquired the required cognitive abilities at the same time. Unfortunately, variations in maturation and environment negate that premise. While some children come to kindergarten already able to read (less than 3 percent), the overwhelming majority do not (Elkind, 1988). In the upper elementary grades, when some children are moving into formal operations, there may still be students who are preoperational.

One of the earliest curriculum disabilities occurs when children are first taught handwriting. Those with well-developed fine motor skills excel at forming letters and staying on the line. Others, who are barely able to control the pencil, unsuccessfully struggle to copy their teacher's and classmate's models. Immediately, a message is sent: neatness counts! Because so much of the day in primary classrooms is spent on handwriting, the slower-developing students learn to dread school. They hate concentrating so hard to create something that can never be as neat as the model. Some give up, some seek diversion by chatting or looking out the window, and some get angry at the teacher and misbehave.

Gender Differences

Who are these slower-developed students? For the most part, they are boys. At age six, boys, on the average, lag a full year behind girls in physical development! One would never expect kindergartners to do what first graders can, but in essence, that is what many schools do. As a result of situations like this (there are other issues too), boys tend to dislike school more than girls do in the elementary grades. The general assumption that girls are neater than boys may evolve from these initial developmental differences, rather than from innate long-term personality characteristics.

Socioeconomic Differences

Another group that tends to be less developed upon entering school is the poor. Children from environments of poverty often lack the parental interaction, exposure to books, travel experiences, and other environmental influences that promote maturity. Due to this factor, and others (as discussed in Chapter 2), the students most likely to have difficulty in school are those who especially need a strong initiation into the educational world.

The fact that children have vastly different levels of maturity is what makes teaching so challenging. Some of your students may be quite skillful with scissors while others cannot seem to close the blades with enough force to cut the paper. A few will be able to solve complex math problems while others are just learning the number system. There will be those who are adept at relating to their peers and some who may lash out physically at every perceived slight. How, then, does one plan for such a varied group?

Curriculum Differentiation

Variations in development require variations in the curriculum. The conventional view of an elementary school classroom is of a group of children working on a common task under a teacher's direction. This view may no longer be realistic, if it ever was. Today, more and more teachers are offering a differentiated curriculum, with different work for different students, depending on their needs.

To make curriculum differentiation easier, some educators use ability grouping and tracking. Despite their immediate appeal, these two methods of organizing students for learning have substantial drawbacks. Fortunately, there are other, less harmful methods of differentiating curriculum. They will be discussed in Chapter 11.

The idea of a differentiated curriculum means that all students are not treated the same. Is this wrong? Think about physicians. Do they walk into the waiting room and prescribe the same medicine for each patient, even though one suffers from a cold, another from cancer, and another from a broken arm? Of course not! Differing needs require different prescriptions. The trick, in education as in medicine, is diagnosing the situation to be sure each student's needs are met.

Identifying Developmental Capabilities

Identifying a student's developmental capabilities is not as difficult as it may seem at first. Teachers can basically rely on their powers of observation to make a rough estimate. By watching how the student reasons through a mathematics problem or by asking questions to determine the child's sense of animism, differences in children may readily appear. More formal diagnosis is possible using the tests that Piaget used, including the famous beaker experiment. Wadsworth (1978) offers a series of developmental assessments in his excellent volume relating Piagetian theory to practice.

Sometimes a teacher acts very much like a detective. The mystery is the child who is not learning. Is it a lack of effort on the child's part? Is it poor instructional techniques on the teacher's part? Is there some sort of physical or emotional problem hindering learning? Or is the curriculum developmentally inappropriate?

For the sake of the child, each of these possibilities, plus others, must be considered. To engage in this kind of detective work (which is tremendously rewarding when successful), teachers must be comfortable with the concepts of development. Those who are will find themselves effectively using developmental principles throughout the school day. Those who never quite grasp the topic are like detectives who ignore evidence. If you find this chapter to be an insufficient review, consult some development textbooks. The knowledge you gain will make you a better curriculum planner.

To meet the developmental needs of elementary school children, the curriculum must be appropriate. It must provide sufficient challenge to stimulate development but also be within the child's capabilities. As you will study later in the text, curricular decisions are often made by noneducators who have little knowledge of development. It is up to the classroom teacher to become involved in curriculum matters to prevent the kinds of problems discussed in this chapter.

Questions

1. Do you think you have a curricular disability? How did you acquire it?
2. Which type of intelligence is strongest for you? How has it helped you? Were you encouraged to use it in your schooling?
3. Which type of development is stressed most in schools? Why do you think that is?
4. Some people believe that we can reduce developmental differences by addressing some of the challenges identified in Chapter 2. Do you agree? Why or why not?

References

BIGELOW, B. J., & LAGAIPA, J. J. (1975). Children's written descriptions of friendship: A multidimensional analysis. *Developmental Psychology, 11*, 857–858.

CAINE, R., & CAINE, G. (1991). *Making connections: Teaching and the human brain.* Alexandria, VA: Association for Supervision and Curriculum Development.

DULIT, E. (1975). Adolescent thinking a la Piaget: The formal stage. In R. Grinter (Ed.), *Studies in adolescence* (pp. 535–556). New York: Macmillan.

ELIAS, M. J., BREUNE-BUTLER, L., BLUM, L., & SCHUYLER, T. (1997). How to launch a social and emotional learning program. *Educational Leadership, 54*(8), 15–19.

ELKIND, D. (1976). *Child development and education.* New York: Oxford University Press.

ELKIND, D. (1988). *The hurried child.* Reading, MA: Addison-Wesley.

ERIKSON, E. (1963). *Childhood and society* (2nd ed.). New York: Norton.

FLAPAN, D. (1968). *Children's understanding of social interaction.* New York: Teachers College Press.

GARDNER, H. (1993). *Multiple intelligences: The theory in practice.* New York: Basic Books.

GOLEMAN, D. (1995). *Emotional intelligence.* New York: Bantam Books.

GOOD, R. G. (1977). *How children learn science.* New York: Macmillan.

HERMAN-GIDDINGS, M. E., SLORA, E. J., WASSERMAN, R. C., BOURDONY, C. J., BHAPKAR, M. V., KOCH, G. G., & HASEMEIER, C. M. (1998). Secondary sexual characteristics and menses in young girls seen in office practice: A study from the pediatric research in office settings systems, *Pediatrics, 99*(4), 505–512.

KOHLBERG, L., & DEVRIES, R. (1987). Psychometric and Piagetian measures of intelligence: Their nature and educational uses. In L. Kohlberg (Ed.), *Child psychology and childhood education* (pp. 110–111). White Plains, NY: Longman.

LEFRANCOIS, G. R. (1984). *Of children: An introduction to child development* (4th ed.). Belmont, CA: Wadsworth.

POOL, C. R. (1997). Up with emotional health. *Educational Leadership, 54*(8), 12–14.

SCHICKIDANZ, J., SCHICKIDANZ, D., & FORSYTH, P. (1982). *Toward understanding children.* Boston: Little, Brown.

SELMAN, R. (1976). Social-cognitive understanding: A guide to educational and clinical practice. In T. Lickona (Ed.), *Moral development and behavior: Theory, research, and social issues* (pp. 219–240). New York: Holt, Rinehart & Winston.

SMITH, F. (1975). *Comprehension and learning.* New York: Henry Holt.

WADSWORTH, B. (1978). *Piaget and the classroom teacher.* New York: Longman.

CHAPTER 4

The Impact of History and Philosophy on the Elementary Curriculum

Why should we study the history of the elementary school curriculum? To answer that question, consider why we study history at all. The main benefit of historical study is that it enables us to better understand the present and prepare for the future. In the field of education, nothing could be more crucial. In fact, many argue that in the field of curriculum, too many of us are *ahistorical;* we know little about what has happened in the past (Kliebard, 1986).

Many mistakes that educational reformers have made over the years could have been prevented by consideration of the history of reform. Only recently

While the physical aspects of classrooms may have changed substantially, the curriculum has been slower to adapt to societal needs.

has there been careful historical analysis of the process of educational change, with recommendations on how to avoid the pitfalls (Fullan & Miles, 1992). For instance, one generally accepted lesson from educational history is that when educational change is mandated by school officials it is rarely effective. This is known as top-down change. For a reform to be successful, there must also be support from those who will implement the change (Fullan & Miles, 1992).

A classic example of unsuccessful top-down change is the "new math" curriculum of the 1950s and 1960s. It was considered a great idea by elected officials and university professors, but somehow teachers and parents were neglected in the process. The new math required different ways of thinking from the traditional math curriculum. When it came time to implement the program, the instructors were uncertain about its goals, unsure of the best instructional methods, and unprepared to effectively teach it. Matters were not helped when the bewildered students sought homework assistance from their parents, who were equally baffled by the new concepts and approaches. Subsequent complaints to teachers multiplied the confusion. As you might expect, the program ultimately failed, although there are still remnants of it in today's math curriculum.

It would be reassuring to state that we have learned from such mistakes and will never repeat them. Unfortunately, top-down curriculum reform proposals are still with us. Educators and members of the public who want to shape the curriculum may not have adequately studied the past to avoid repeating mistakes.

Although this chapter cannot provide a thorough analysis of the history of the elementary curriculum, it offers basic observations that will be useful in understanding the present and preparing for the future. These observations are presented in the form of generalizations that are applicable to many times and places; thus, they will be more useful than a mere presentation of the facts of one particular circumstance.

Throughout the chapter, in addition to historical generalizations, you will find discussion of major educational philosophies. Those philosophies influenced the curriculum at various times throughout history and remain powerful today. Your understanding of educational philosophy will help you clarify your own beliefs about schooling, and thus help you develop as a teacher.

THE ELEMENTARY CURRICULUM IN COLONIAL TIMES

> *Generalization: One cannot assume that one's own experiences are similar to those of other times and places*

In the period before the American Revolution, the fledgling colonial governments were not primarily involved with education. Matters of economic viability, political process, and other basic issues were the major governmental concerns. As a result, education was provided by various sources, including the home, church, and workplace. The school itself may have been only a minor educational influence. Therefore, it would be misleading to speak of a school curriculum for that time period (Bidwell & Dreeben, 1992).

Generalization: Cultural traditions have a strong influence

Because most colonial Americans came from Europe, they copied that continent's curriculum when they established schools. As a result, the Latin grammar school was offered to the sons of the upper classes (Morison, 1956). (Exclusion of women and other social classes was another European practice that was carried over.)

The Latin grammar school was preparation for college. Children entered around age eight, studying Latin and the classics for eight years. Before beginning Latin grammar school, the child would have been privately tutored in English.

The Latin grammar school reflects the educational philosophy of intellectual traditionalism, the dominant mode of thought at that time (Goodlad & Su, 1992). To understand the intellectual traditionalists, it is necessary to closely examine their philosophy of education, generally known as perennialism.

Generalization: The issue regarding a particular curriculum is not whether it works; if implemented properly, the major curriculums tend to achieve their goals; a more important issue is whether the goals they achieve are the best ones for the society

Perennialism was successful in teaching the sons of the upper classes in colonial America. The students of that curriculum were the leaders of our new nation: Washington, Jefferson, Adams, Madison. Judging by their work—our constitutional system, a political masterpiece that has guided our nation for over 200 years—their educational preparation must have been exceptional.

Models of Curriculum

Perennialism

Perennialists believe that the goal of education is development of intelligence. With proper training, the mind will develop, much as a muscle develops under the right regimen. To achieve that goal, the curriculum must emphasize intellectual skills, especially reasoning, rhetoric, and writing. A perennialist classroom would include a great deal of argument and debate, both written and oral. The intended result is a society of citizens who think carefully and critically.

The content of the perennialist curriculum is the classic works of literature and art. Perennialists tend to be idealists, who believe that truth is universal and unchanging. In other words, the great ideas have already been articulated. Therefore, through careful, reasoned study of the classics, students can learn those ideas as they develop their minds (Eisner, 1992; Ornstein & Levine, 1989). The term perennial refers to endurance. Just as perennial flowers continually reappear in the garden (unlike annuals), so the perennial ideas will endure.

True to its title, the perennialist philosophy has always been present, primarily in exclusive preparatory schools and highly competitive universities. It has been successful in developing national leaders in government, industry, and academia.

Yet perennialism has been criticized for being elitist. Some say that the development of the mind is a worthy goal for those who will move into positions of wealth and power, usually the children of wealthy parents like the aforementioned Founding Fathers. These critics claim that most children are not so fortunate; they need an education that addresses the basic needs of citizenship and vocational preparation. Thus, they say, perennialism is not for all children.

A related criticism is that the study of philosophy and the reading of difficult literature insures that only the intellectually gifted will succeed under a perennialist curriculum, thus widening the gap between the social classes (Johnson et al., 1988). As you will see, this issue of whether perennialism best meets society's needs will resurface in the twentieth century.

Generalization: The curriculum reflects the views of the community's leaders

In colonial New England, the Puritan church was powerful. One of the tenets of that church's Calvinist philosophy was that those who were educated in God's word would be most likely to resist worldly temptations. Thus, it was the Puritans who established the earliest community schools (Ornstein & Levine, 1989).

The Puritans regarded the child as naturally depraved. To root out sin, their curriculum was heavy in religious dogma. When the children learned to read, they read the Ten Commandments, the Lord's Prayer, and other religious matter (Ornstein & Levine, 1989). Discipline was harsh, reflecting the Puritan emphasis on hard work and subservience to authority.

The mid-Atlantic colonies were more culturally diverse than New England, so their schools differed considerably. The heavy emphasis on mercantile trading in those colonies inspired some colonial leaders to create academies. The academy was a private school whose curriculum focused on such skills as navigation, surveying, bookkeeping, Spanish, French, and geography (Ornstein & Levine, 1989). In essence, the mercantile leaders developed academies as training grounds for future workers. We shall see this theme repeated in the nineteenth and twentieth centuries, with public schools.

THE ELEMENTARY CURRICULUM IN THE 1800s

Generalization: Changes in philosophic thought encourage radical reforms in the school curriculum but, ultimately, those reforms tend to have only minor effects

The work of Pestalozzi and Froebel in Europe inspired the development of the "infant school" in America for children under eight. Their humanistic approach viewed the child as innately good, quite a change from the Puritans. According to this belief, the use of song, dance, stories, and pictures would develop the child's interest in learning and serve as an introduction to schooling. The only essential would be reading, but even that would be taught in a low-key manner, emphasizing the enjoyment of that skill (Tanner & Tanner, 1980). In practice, however, infant schools evolved into miniature grammar schools. Recitation, memorization, and fear pervaded the curriculum. The long-term impact of the infant schools was not the change in curriculum but the precedent of providing education for younger children.

> *Generalization: The curriculum often changes in an attempt to solve other societal problems*

Upon independence, the new nation's leaders were troubled by the overwhelming cultural influence of Britain, its former mother country. They identified the need to develop an American cultural identity and unity. One leader, Noah Webster, tried to change the curriculum by writing textbooks in spelling and grammar. Those textbooks and his famous dictionary were influential in creating an American language, with rules that differed from classic English. Because his textbooks were so popular, Webster also helped to develop "a common past" in that all school-going Americans read his books as part of their childhoods (Tanner & Tanner, 1980). Another successful textbook author, William Holmes McGuffey, wrote a popular series of readings that emphasized patriotic material, such as speeches by Patrick Henry and George Washington (Ornstein & Levine, 1989).

In the nineteenth century, the Industrial Revolution altered American lifestyles. Factories began to replace farms as the primary American workplace. Many rural families gave up agriculture to move to the cities for factory jobs. This created a problem of idle urban youth. In an agricultural society, children worked on the farm alongside their parents or were cared for by relatives as part of an extended family. When families moved to the city, limited housing forced households to become smaller.

At first, children also worked in the factories. But the dangerous conditions led to a series of child labor laws that discouraged the practice. As a result, many children were left on their own while their parents worked (usually for twelve hours a day).

At the same time, European immigration increased substantially. Most of the immigrants also settled in cities. So, not only were there idle youth on the streets, but many of them were perceived as non-American, with different languages, clothing, and customs. As expected, quite a few of these idle children got into mischief, which alarmed community leaders. The answer: put the children in school.

Most of the factory workers' children were too poor to afford private school tuition, and public schools did not exist. However, there were parochial schools, run by churches, that subsidized the costs of education for its church members.

This situation created a particularly acute problem in Boston. That city, controlled by English Protestants since early colonial times, had become inundated by Irish Catholic immigrants. The Irish and English had been feuding for centuries, often violently. The city leaders wanted the immigrant children in school, but not in parochial schools. They were afraid that more religious training would shift the balance of power in favor of the Irish Catholics. The so-called true Americans would become political and social minorities.

The alternative was the development of common schools. Common schools were public schools, provided for by taxpayer money. Students were required to attend them by the Massachusetts Compulsory Schooling Act of 1852. By requiring attendance at common schools, Massachusetts leaders could address several issues at once: they could get idle youth off the streets, provide a non-Catholic education, and retain power.

In addition, the common schools were seen as an instrument for developing an informed American citizenry capable of participating in the political process. The new republic, after all, was built on the principles of democracy, in which literate voters were important.

Generalization: Social class and expectations influence the school's curriculum

Because the Irish and other immigrants lived in poverty, they were believed to have a lower intelligence than the rest of the community. The educational leaders of the day did not expect them to succeed at the challenging perennialist curriculum. Accordingly, a different type of curriculum was developed, a simpler one, more suited to lower expectations of educational success.

Models of Curriculum

Essentialism

Essentialists are most concerned about basic skills. They believe that emphasizing the "essentials" of reading, writing, and arithmetic will ensure that students will be able to function in society. In addition, the development of such attitudes as effort and self-discipline are also deemed essential (Hessong & Weeks, 1987).

Whereas the perennialists are concerned with the development of the mind, essentialists focus on the "adjustment of the individual to the physical and social environment" (Kneller, 1971, p. 61). Essentialism reflects the philosophy of realism in which the emphasis is on the unchanging, universal truths of the physical world. Other than the three R's, basic subject matter knowledge in history, foreign language, and science is taught. These subjects would enable citizens to solve personal, social, and civic problems (Ornstein & Levine, 1989).

The essentialist classroom includes a great deal of lecture, memorization, repetition, and examination as tools to enable students to acquire the essential knowledge that its name evokes. As with perennialism, the teacher's role is to pass on the knowledge that the children need.

The curriculum was different for another important reason—its goals differed. Whereas the perennialist curriculum sought to develop leaders of the society, the common schools were established, in part, to develop workers for the trades and factories. Leadership and a powerful mind were not needed to run a machine. Obedience, honesty, and conformity were (Tanner & Tanner, 1980). Factory owners were quite concerned about the quality of their immigrant workers. They wanted workers whom they could depend upon to work hard and provide an honest day's labor. They viewed the school as a means to that end. Thus, the common school was guided by what is now known as the philosophy of essentialism. (See box)

THE ELEMENTARY CURRICULUM IN THE 1900s

Generalization: The school does not exist in a vacuum; political, social, economic, and philosophic forces come to bear upon what we teach and how we teach it

The beginning of the twentieth century was a time of upheaval and reform in American life. Political corruption was attacked by a series of reform candidates who attempted to clean up government. Concern about the growing power of business interests led to attempts to curb monopolies and trusts. At the same time, reformers called attention to the poor living conditions of immigrants and other urban residents.

In this wave of reform, the educational system was also critically scrutinized. Many educators at this time became excited about the theories of G. Stanley Hall. Hall and his followers objected to the lack of activity in classrooms. They claimed that scientific "child study" had proven that the curriculum should be built around students' needs and interests. Believing that children relive the history of mankind in their activities, Hall advocated an elementary school based on play. This curriculum would presumably allow students to interact with nature, ancient myths and fables, and other aspects of life from centuries before. Intellectual training would come later (Kliebard, 1986).

Hall's reputation as a scientist and his claims of scientific child study helped confer legitimacy on his ideas. Indeed, a number of leading educators endorsed the child study philosophy (Kliebard, 1986). Yet further analysis reveals that Hall's child study approach was based more on the romanticist philosophies of Rousseau than on any scientific data. Nonetheless, it caught the attention of the reformers who began looking critically at the essentialist and perennialist curriculum philosophies. It was in this atmosphere that progressivism evolved.

Generalization: Labels can be misleading

Progressivism had numerous versions. The version considered most representative of the progressive curriculum was established in the early 1900s by John Dewey, director of the University of Chicago Laboratory School. Dewey felt that mastery of subject matter would follow from students' interest in social occupations, such as cooking, carpentry, and growing food.

Dewey pointed out that each occupation integrates subject matter for the child to discover. For instance, cooking involves the chemistry and physics of heat, the mathematics of weights, measurement, and fractions, and the historical and cultural aspects of food. Reading was the core study that facilitated learning in the other areas. Students at the Dewey School moved cooperatively from one problem to the next based on interest. Teachers constantly experimented (Kliebard, 1986).

Dewey took pains to emphasize that there must be purpose to the activities. The teacher cannot let the children choose "acts that are immediately and sensationally appealing, but which lead to nothing in particular" (Dewey, 1936, p. 469). Instead, he wanted the teacher to help children choose problems and activities that would lead to the learning of generalizations about subject matter as well as the development of intellectual skills (Kliebard, 1986).

W. H. Kilpatrick, one of Dewey's students, popularized the "project method," a curriculum that violated Dewey's standards. Kilpatrick's curriculum encouraged teachers to let the students choose a purposeful activity, regardless of its value for intellectual growth, subject matter learning, or societal improvement. As long as the children had problems they wished to solve, Kilpatrick saw their experience as valuable (Tanner & Tanner, 1980).

Models of Curriculum

Progressivism

Progressives emphasize the concept of experience. Experience, in their view, is the interaction between the organism and the environment. Because people and their environment are constantly changing, their experiences are constantly changing. These experiences create knowledge. Thus, knowledge is constantly changing. This way of thinking is considerably different from the perennialist and essentialist view of knowledge as universal, unchanging truth (Ornstein & Levine, 1989).

The content of the progressive curriculum combines problem solving and the study of society. Progressives believe that by using the scientific method to solve problems that interest children, preferably in group situations, students will form generalizations about their physical and social worlds. The teacher is to serve as a facilitator, not as one who merely imparts knowledge.

Progressives emphasize community study as a laboratory for problem solving. Using a broad definition of community (which may include the classroom community, the local town, or the international community), the intent is that students will be able to apply what they have learned to make their community a better place. Therefore, as progressives are fond of saying, school is not preparation for life, it is life.

The progressive curriculum was very appealing to reformers. It reflected Hall's child-centered approach but also emphasized using schools as a means of improving the quality of life in America. Yet, as with the infant school movement, the anticipated final product was often transformed through implementation.

Because Kilpatrick was Dewey's student, and because of his leadership in the Progressive Education Association, the project method is often associated with the progressive curriculum. Both types of curriculum are child-centered, but their differences are significant. Yet in the public's mind and among many educators the project method was sometimes viewed as the practical implementation of Dewey's ideas (Lucas, 1984).

Another strand of the progressive curriculum evolved among educators who felt Dewey's ideas did not sufficiently address the problems of society. This new curriculum, reconstructionism, is now regarded as a major curriculum theory, separate from progressivism.

Generalization: For every action there is a reaction

Although attempts by progressives and reconstructionists to redesign the curriculum had only limited success, there was substantial opposition to their ideas. The critics' reactions reflected a strong belief in conservatism, both in an educational sense and a political sense.

Models of Curriculum
Reconstructionism

Reconstructionists believe the progressive curriculum should be beyond the development of intellectual skills and learning of subject matter. To them, schools should create a new society in which people work to solve the serious problems facing the world.

To achieve this goal, the reconstructionist curriculum focuses student attention on social problems such as war, injustice, poverty, and environmental concerns. Rather than maintain a neutral posture, teachers assist students in challenging the status quo. In response to charges of imposing certain values on students, leaders of this movement, led by George Counts, argued that values are already being imposed—the values of the ruling class. Neutrality, they believed, is impossible (Tanner & Tanner, 1980).

Reconstructionism began in the 1930s. Conditions at that time were frightening. The Great Depression had caused massive unemployment and poverty. At the same time in Europe, Hitler and the Nazis were threatening the freedom of millions of people. Calls for change in the social order were being made. Reconstructionists believed that the schools could provide leadership in that movement.

The Reconstructionists were not successful in influencing the curriculum. What they proposed was deemed impractical, even by those who supported its goals (Lucas, 1984). Yet, because its leaders evolved from the progressive camp, and because the approach has numerous similarities to progressivism, reconstructionism was often regarded as a form of progressive thought. When critics spoke of the progressive curriculum, at times they referred to Kilpatrick's project method, at times to Counts's reconstructionism, and occasionally to Dewey's ideas. This mislabeling would cause problems in the future.

In terms of education, the critics argued that the purpose of schools is to pass on the cultural inheritance of the nation. They cited numerous examples in which students did not receive an adequate education in basic skills and knowledge because of the overemphasis on peripheral social concerns and frills. Most of the weaknesses were deemed the result of Deweyan progressivism. The society cannot be maintained, they implored, if the schools do not serve as an agency to conserve it. Higher standards must be maintained to insure that students master the bodies of knowledge found in the basic subject areas (Lucas, 1984). This form of educational conservatism, the careful reader will note, is essentialism.

Surprisingly, there was little response from leading educators to the serious charges of the essentialists. To understand why, consider the political situation. The essentialist position was established in 1938, but the debate was interrupted by World War II. When it resumed after the war, the specter of communism was casting its shadow on America. Talk of restructuring society, especially in terms of economic injustice, was viewed with suspicion. Senator Joseph McCarthy and his followers were seeking to rid the country of those whom they viewed as anti-American. A number of innocent people were accused of being communist sympathizers because of their political statements. The atmosphere was not conducive to an open discussion concerning the role of the schools (Tanner & Tanner, 1980).

In addition to squelching discussion, the country's political conservatives strengthened the hand of the essentialists in another way. Rather than seek change in our major institutions, there were now calls for promoting patriotism, discipline, and obedience (Lucas, 1984). The essentialist curriculum was put forth as the best vehicle to achieve those goals. Once again, the need to solve America's problems resulted in curricular change. This time, however, the change was a return to a traditional mode of schooling. It would not be long before another societal need triggered another curricular change, followed by yet another reaction.

Generalization: Schools tend to receive the blame for societal weaknesses

A major crisis in American schooling occurred when the Soviet Union launched a communications satellite, *Sputnik I,* in 1957. Americans were stunned to see their archenemy surpass them in technology. Surely, they reasoned, there must be something wrong with the schools.

Immediately, there ensued a series of blue-ribbon panels and commissions to propose solutions to America's perceived educational failure. Predictably, the essentialists resumed their campaign against Dewey as they called for an educational system similar to the Soviet Union's, one that emphasized rigorous, no-nonsense study of the traditional subjects (Kliebard, 1986). Perennialists, led by Admiral Hyman Rickover (1959), argued that "the school's concern is with the intellect alone" (p. 154). Progressives emphasized the need for children to solve problems rather than have subject knowledge merely handed down (Lucas, 1984).

TABLE 4.1.

	Perennialism	Essentialism	Progressivism	Reconstructionism
View of Knowledge	Unchanging truths	Proven knowledge	Ever-changing and individually constructed	Ever-changing and individually constructed
Role of Teacher	Use Socratic method to help students learn the unchanging truths	Present proven knowledge to students	Prepare and facilitate problem-solving opportunities	Prepare and facilitate problem-solving opportunities
Role of Students	Read and debate	Learn knowledge	Solve problems	Solve societal problems
Content	Classic works of literature and art	Essential knowledge	Children's interests	Societal problems
Goals	Intelligent leaders	Competent citizens	Problem solvers	Citizens who will transform society

The curricular approach that evolved from the national discussion on the crisis in education did not fit neatly into any one curricular philosophy. The new plan, supported by a massive federal infusion of funds, encouraged the development of thinkers. In each subject area, students would learn to think like academics. Thus, in math, rather than memorize step-by-step procedures, students would learn to reason like a mathematician. The scientific method would be applied in the sciences and social sciences with each subject area emphasizing the characteristics that are unique to its study. For instance, chemistry class would have students solving problems by hypothesizing and then testing their hypotheses in a laboratory.

Perhaps because it was developed by a committee, the new math, new science, and new social studies had something for everybody. The essentialists were pleased with the emphasis on subject area learning as well as the move toward rigor and high standards. Perennialists applauded the renewal of learning to think as a major educational goal. Progressives were delighted to see the traditional lecture and recitation approach rejected in favor of student problem solving.

Unfortunately, the new curriculum was poorly implemented. Yet, as with other radical reforms, there were unintended effects that lasted. One was the major federal role in education. Previously, matters of schooling belonged to the states under constitutional mandate. Now, although the federal government could not mandate curricular reform, it began to use its financial power to persuade states to comply. Subsequent efforts to promote civil rights and education for the handicapped evolved from this precedent (Kliebard, 1986).

A second influence of the new curriculum was a change in orientation. The new curriculum was aimed at the academically gifted. Previous efforts at educational reform had been geared to all students. Excellence replaced equal opportunity as the major goal. International competition was the driving force, rather than internal strength and unity. This change would also influence the tone of later curricular discussions.

Generalization: Successful curricular change must be guided by a theoretical perspective

In the mid-1960s, the United States again experienced a period of self-analysis. In a reaction against the conformity of the 1950s, every aspect of American life was challenged. Protests against poverty, the Vietnam War, racial discrimination, sexism, and environmental damage occupied much of the political stage. In the social realm, people were experimenting in dress, language, music, marriage, drug use, religion, and most other aspects of day-to-day life.

In this era of rebellion, the essentialist nature of schooling was found wanting. Critics complained about irrelevant content that stifled initiative, creativity, and attention to social problems.

In response, educational reformers popularized new approaches, such as the addition of topics of concern to students (e.g., pollution, rock-and-roll music), emphasis on interpersonal relationships (e.g., nonverbal communication, expression of feelings), and alternatives to traditional classroom activities (e.g., more small-group work, less memorization, more projects). Of course, these ideas were not new at all; they are all variations on the progressive curriculum. Yet, in the ahistorical atmosphere of the schools, people were excited about what they believed to be revolutionary changes (Tanner & Tanner, 1980).

As educators enthusiastically implemented these various reforms, which generally lacked a theoretical framework, problems appeared. For instance, in response to the impersonal nature of essentialist schools, a popular reform was to develop student self-esteem. A portion of the curriculum was devoted to developing students' sense of personal and cultural identity. Unfortunately, in their zeal to make a difference, some teachers lost sight of the purpose of the reform. Instead of helping students to feel good about themselves through their educational achievements, teachers encouraged them merely to feel good. Development of cognitive skills was deemphasized in favor of affective activities. Many students did come to feel good about themselves, but ultimately returned to a lower self-concept when they were unsuccessful in reading and other academic areas (Tanner & Tanner, 1980). Some teachers even avoided giving low grades because they were afraid of hurting the students' self-concepts.

Failure to work from a theoretical framework has led to other problems. Parents, teachers, and other citizens have become justifiably wary of new ideas. Indeed, new curricular approaches, even those with strong philosophical bases,

Theory to Practice

Combining Philosophies

Each curricular philosophy has aspects that are appealing. Most readers will endorse, for example, the perennialists' emphasis on critical thinking. They will, likewise, be drawn to the essentialists' stress on basic skills as a foundation for learning. The goal of developing problem solvers, associated with the progressive and reconstructionist philosophies, is also very attractive. Therefore, some students may seek to combine the philosophies, thus creating a hybrid philosophy that combines their strengths but avoids their weaknesses.

If only it were that simple! While the field of philosophy is always open to new ideas, hybrid philosophies tend to suffer from irreconcilable conflicts. Essentialists believe, for example, that teachers should present proven knowledge to students. That role cannot be combined with the progressive emphasis on students learning through problem solving. Once the teacher takes on the role of knowledge giver, students will no longer be constructing their own knowledge, which is the foundation of progressivism.

The philosophies have remained different primarily because they reflect different views of knowledge. If you believe that knowledge is a set of unchanging truths, your job as a teacher is to bring out those truths using the Socratic method. That involves students debating with you until they form your predetermined conclusion. That is very different from the views of knowledge and the roles of teacher and student in the other philosophies. In progressivism and reconstructionism, students are thinking for themselves, while in essentialism students are receiving knowledge.

Being distinctly different, however, does not rule out overlapping concerns. Learning the basics, for instance, is not limited to the essentialists. All of the philosophies have students learning basic skills and knowledge. The difference is that essentialists view basic skills and knowledge as their primary content goal. The other philosophies seek to go beyond that content. The perennialist emphasis on the classics is another example. The fact that perennialists build their curriculum around classic works of art and literature does not preclude their use under other curricular philosophies.

As indicated earlier, each philosophy has been shown to be somewhat successful in achieving its goals. Teachers (and citizens) need to decide what those goals should be. That decision will probably reflect a particular view of knowledge. If you wish to combine philosophies, you must reconcile any potential conflicts.

are often referred to as fads. Another concern is the problem of mixed messages. If teachers and schools seek to be eclectic, combining theories, students are apt to become confused. On one hand, they may be encouraged to develop their thinking skills and creativity with instruction designed under the progressive approach; on the other, they may be confronted with essentialist-type exams that require memorization and penalize creativity. Numerous other conflicts of this sort will be addressed throughout this book.

Generalization: When schools are viewed as inferior, the government's role in education increases

As noted earlier, the 1960s were a time of significant cultural change. Many of the changes that appeared during that period tended to be harmful to the educational process. The major alterations to family life, the immense popularity of television, and increases in drug and alcohol abuse all negatively influenced educational achievement. When those changes were combined with poorly planned educational reform, the results were alarming. Newspaper headlines blurted out the bad news: crime was up, teenage pregnancy was increasing, violence was becoming rampant, and to prove the point, test scores were dropping (Lucas, 1984).

A backlash against the social changes of the sixties took place. Conservatives were elected at the local, state, and national level who promised to crack down on the permissive institutions of society.

Schools bore the brunt of the blame. Citizens lamented the other social causes of student failure, but claimed they were impotent to change it. Schools were different; they were part of the government's responsibility. Taxpayers were reminded that they weren't getting their money's worth. They demanded a change, so the government stepped in.

The call went out for a return to the old ways—"Back to basics." Throw out the fads and return the teacher to the front of the room. Assign more homework and maintain discipline. Increase testing (Lucas, 1984). By now, this cycle of reaction should be familiar.

To enforce their essentialist demands, each state developed a series of competency tests. Students should not graduate, it was argued, unless they prove they have acquired basic skills in reading, writing, and arithmetic. Some states instituted competency tests at other grade levels and for other subject areas, but the overall message was clear: the schools would have to emphasize the basics.

Governmental action did not stop with testing. State legislators and education officials became involved in the review of textbooks, the setting of course requirements, the evaluation of teachers, and other aspects of management that were heretofore left to the local school districts.

Generalization: Financial support is a powerful weapon

Most school systems jumped into the back-to-basics movement with both feet. They had to. The public was now carefully scrutinizing test scores. At stake was a variety of supports to education. At the local level, there would be community support for bond issues only if the school system was viewed as worthy. Bond issues are multimillion-dollar, multiyear loans to a community to pay for capital improvements, such as new buildings, buses, and athletic facilities, that are too expensive to be supported by the regular budget. Many school systems were disappointed during the tax-conscious 1980s when their public financial support vanished (Ornstein & Levine, 1989).

At the state level, legislatures and governors were also hesitant to support education without evidence of more successful performance. Such high budget items as teacher pay and funds for the purchase of books and supplies were often reduced from previous years' expenditures by state governmental leaders (Ornstein & Levine, 1989).

Local school systems responded by emphasizing topics that are measured by standardized tests. Creative writing, oral expression, art, and music were viewed as frills (Ornstein & Levine, 1989). Minimal competency replaced consumer education and citizenship development as goals (Tanner & Tanner, 1980). Instruction became even more teacher-centered, with constant drill, daily homework, and frequent testing (Lucas, 1984).

Because the back-to-basics reforms were top-down, the movement was not totally successful. Pockets of progressivism remained in each state and school district. Another impediment to reform was the differing definitions of what back-to-basics meant. Yet there is little doubt that the accountability movement of recent years cemented the essentialist nature of American schools. Only recently have cracks begun to appear in that foundation.

Generalization: Leaders control the agenda

During the economic recession of the 1980s, the curricular emphasis refocused on meeting occupational needs. This has been described by Labaree (1997) as the goal of "social efficiency." "Social efficiency . . . is the perspective of the taxpayer and the employer, from which education is seen as a public good designed to prepare workers to fill structurally necessary market roles" (Labaree, 1997, p. 42).

The social efficiency movement reached a crescendo with the 1983 publication of *A Nation at Risk* (National Commission on Excellence in Education, 1983). That document, written in the midst of America's seeming failure in competition with Japanese industry, essentially blamed the schools for the country's economic woes. The recommendations of the National Commission on Excellence in Education dealt largely with changes within the sphere of educational policy, such as better teacher training and more challenging content, but politicians and corporate leaders cited the report to promote the idea that schools exist to strengthen the economy (Ray & Mickelson, 1990).

Politicians, seeking to appease voters and avoid blame for the country's economic slide, could now demonstrate their ability to solve the problem by reforming the educational system (Apple, 1996). Ronald Reagan, who was president at the time, sought to highlight the federal role in education when he cited the *A Nation at Risk* report in calling for an essentialist curricular approach to guarantee that graduates are capable of basic skills.

The public responded positively to the shift in educational goals. Taxpayers, concerned about the ever-rising cost of public education, especially during a recession, wanted to see direct economic benefits of their tax expenditures, such as greater American productivity. Business leaders, fearful of the cost of inadequately trained workers, wanted to be sure that the schools did actually meet their needs. Students and their parents, concerned about job prospects in a tide of rising unemployment, wanted to be sure that schools prepared them for work, so they too joined the bandwagon (Labaree, 1997).

Eight years later, President George Bush endorsed the essentialist shift with his support of *America 2000* (U.S. Department of Education, 1991), which was described by its authors as a plan for a "revolutionary" transformation of schools. The document identified six educational goals to be met by the year 2000, three of which (Goals 3, 4, and 5) are directly relevant to the elementary school curriculum:

> *Goal 3:* U.S. students will leave grades four, eight, and twelve and have demonstrated competency in the five core subjects of English, mathematics, science, history, and geography; and all students will learn to use their minds well, so they may be prepared for further learning and productive employment in the modern economy;
>
> *Goal 4:* U.S. students will be first in the world in science and mathematics achievement;
>
> *Goal 5:* Every adult will be literate and possess the knowledge and skills necessary to compete in a global economy and exercise the rights and responsibilities of citizenship.

Upon his election to succeed President Bush, Bill Clinton issued his own education plan, called Goals 2000, which was similar to the Bush plan in its position on the curriculum. The two plans, which were obviously committed to social efficiency goals, unequivocally established the position of national leaders concerning education.

In response, most of the associations representing school subject areas created academic standards for their disciplines. The associations, overwhelmingly comprised of classroom teachers, tried to influence the debate over academic standards by identifying specific objectives within the broad goals. Teachers of mathematics, for example, stressed the need for problem-solving skills, and science teachers called for more attention to scientific methods. The teaching profession had clearly been placed in a defensive position.

During this process, the public's attention would occasionally be drawn away from test scores when a controversial set of standards was proposed. (Chapters 5–10 discuss details of the various subject-area recommendations.) In one such incident, the proposed standards for history created a firestorm when some commentators objected to their seeming underemphasis on traditional heroes and symbols of American history. It turns out that the critics were not focusing on the history standards themselves, but on examples that were provided to clarify them (Elson, 1994). Nonetheless, in this rare instance of public debate over curricular issues, the teaching profession lost some respect from a public growing skeptical of teachers' ability to handle the challenges of educating today's youth.

Generalization: Conflicting movements may occur simultaneously

As federal and state governmental control of education has increased, due to the emphasis on accountability, a contradictory movement for local control has occurred. Many state governments have delegated some decision-making responsibilities to local school districts. In those cases, while all districts are expected to conform to state curricular guidelines, usually measured by a state-designed exam, the districts have been granted the freedom to decide how best to meet those guidelines. In other words, the states have maintained control of the official curriculum but some states are allowing instructional decisions to be made by local districts and schools.

Conflicting movements are likely to occur simultaneously under a democratic system that permits ideological pluralism. While some nations are controlled by a single political party or ideology, the system in the United States grants relatively greater freedom for the expression and application of minority views. Thus, individual schools or school districts may offer considerable diversity in their programs.

One way that school districts have diversified is by creating magnet schools. Magnet schools are schools that focus on one particular philosophy or concentration. North Carolina's Charlotte-Mecklenburg school district, for example, offers 42 magnet programs in open education, traditional education, classical studies, and Paideia (a type of perennialist approach), in addition to schools that specialize in science and technology, communication arts, performing arts, Montessori, and many others. Parents and students are able to choose the philosophy or emphasis that best matches their preferences. Teachers also benefit from the opportunity to apply for a position in a school that is closely aligned with their educational philosophies. For those parents, teachers, and students who are not interested in a magnet school, they can attend one of the vast majority of the district's schools that do not have a specialization.

Some states have sought to promote diversity by establishing charter schools. Charter schools are public schools, governed and paid for by the state, that were created to encourage alternative methods of administration, instruction, and curriculum. Since the nation's first charter school law in Minnesota, close to 800 charter schools now exist (Manno, Finn, Bierlein & Vanourek, 1998.) The rules concerning charter schools are different from state to state, so they tend to be quite varied. Because charter schools may be excused from some of the regulations that limit curricular experimentation in public schools, they are better able to align themselves with a particular curricular philosophy. A charter school, therefore, may be the best place to go to see an unfamiliar curriculum in action.

Charter schools and magnet schools were not born solely out of a desire by state officials to diversify their curricular offerings. Both movements can be linked to a variety of public and political pressures, including demands for desegregation, neighborhood schools, local control, vouchers, and anti-teachers' union sentiment. Yet, their presence on the educational menu may help to improve the quality of the elementary school curriculum in ways that are not yet foreseen.

USING THIS CHAPTER

This historical review was designed to emphasize key generalizations that can be learned by studying curricular trends and their causes and effects. The generalizations here are not meant to be comprehensive. Many other lessons can be learned from the rich history of curricular change, especially if one expands that study to include international trends. Nonetheless, the few generalizations presented here will be useful in subsequent chapters, when each curricular area is examined.

As a matter of review, consider each generalization that has been presented. Can you find other examples of that generalization in other periods of history? For instance, the idea that for every action there is a reaction has been evident in the various pendulum swings between essentialism and progressivism. Can you find others?

The four major curricular philosophies—perennialism, essentialism, progressivism, and reconstructionism—are incorporated in this review. Considerable reference to these belief systems will be made throughout the book. Reading more about curricular philosophies will help you understand the curriculum and be a better teacher. This is especially important if there is a philosophy that is attractive to you. The end-of-chapter references may be helpful in that regard.

Questions

1. If you could choose a single curricular philosophy, which one would it be? Why?
2. On what points would perennialists disagree with essentialists? On what points would progressives disagree with reconstructionists?
3. What are some conflicts that may result from an eclectic curriculum?
4. What period of curricular change is most similar to today's situation? Explain.

References

APPLE, M. (1996). *Cultural politics and education.* New York: Teachers College Press.

BIDWELL, C. E., & DREEBEN, R. (1992). School organization and curriculum. In P. A. Jackson (Ed.), *Handbook of research on curriculum* (pp. 345–362). New York: Macmillan.

DEWEY, J. (1936). The theory of the Chicago experiment. In H. M. Kliebard, (1986), *The struggle for the American curriculum 1893–1958* (p. 469). Boston: Routledge & Kegan Paul.

EISNER, E. (1992). Curriculum ideologies. In P. A. Jackson (Ed.), *Handbook of research on curriculum* (pp. 302–326). New York: Macmillan.

ELSON, J. (1994). History, the sequel: A controversial new set of recommendations generates a debate on what's important about America's past. *Time, 144*(19), 64.

FULLAN, M. G., & MILES, M. B. (1992). Getting reform right: What works and what doesn't. *Phi Delta Kappan, 73,* 744–752.

GOODLAD, J. I., & SU, Z. (1992). Organization of the curriculum. In P. A. Jackson (Ed.), *Handbook of research on curriculum* (pp. 327–344). New York: Macmillan.

HESSONG, R. F., & WEEKS, T. H. (1987). *Introduction to education.* New York: Macmillan.
JOHNSON, J. A., COLLINS, H. W., DUPUIS, V. L., & JOHANSEN, J. H. (1988). *Introduction to the foundations of American education.* Boston: Allyn & Bacon.
KLIEBARD, H. M. (1986). *The struggle for the American curriculum 1893–1958.* Boston: Routledge & Kegan Paul.
KNELLER, G. F. (1971). *Introduction to the philosophy of education.* New York: Wiley.
LABAREE, D. (1997). Public goods, private goods: The American struggle over educational goals, *American Educational Research Journal, 34,* 39–82.
LUCAS, C. J. (1984). *Foundations of education.* Englewood Cliffs, NJ: Prentice-Hall.
MANNO, B. V., FINN, C. E., BIERLEIN, L. A., & VANOUREK, G. (1998). How charter schools are different. *Phi Delta Kappan, 79,* 488–498.
MORISON, S. E. (1956). *The intellectual life of colonial New England.* New York: New York University Press.
NATIONAL COMMISSION ON EXCELLENCE IN EDUCATION. (1983). *A nation at risk: The imperative for educational reform.* Washington, DC: U.S. Department of Education.
RAY, C., & MICKELSON, R. (1990). Business leaders and the politics of school reform. In D. Mitchell & M. Goertz (Eds.), *Education politics for the new century.* London: Falmer Press, 119–136.
RICKOVER, H. (1959). *Education and freedom.* New York: E. P. Dutton.
TANNER, D., & TANNER, L. (1980). *Curriculum development: Theory into practice.* New York: Macmillan.
U.S. DEPARTMENT OF EDUCATION. (1991). *America 2000: An education strategy.* Washington, DC: U.S. Department of Education, p. 3.

PART THREE

Elementary Curriculum Issues

CHAPTER 5

Social Studies

You may either love or hate social studies, depending on your definition of the term. Many students hate it (Schug, Todd & Beery, 1984). To them, it means names and dates, the heights of mountains, the location of Civil War battles, and how a bill becomes a law—boring memorized trivia.

Many others love social studies. They see it as the explanation of their grandparents' way of life, the comparison between American and Japanese lifestyles, the course of action for fighting a tuition increase, and a discussion of the effects of computer games on teenagers.

Why is there such a difference in perspective? One major reason is teachers' beliefs about the social studies curriculum.

WHAT IS SOCIAL STUDIES

Social studies is an integration of social sciences and humanities. It is not just history, despite what your own classroom experience may tell you. According to the National Council for the Social Studies, "Social studies is the integrated study of the social sciences and humanities to promote civic competence. Within the school program, social studies provides coordinated, systematic study drawing upon such disciplines as anthropology, archeology, economics, geography, history, law, philosophy, political science, psychology, religion, and sociology, as well as appropriate content from the humanities, mathematics, and natural sciences" (NCSS, 1993).

The National Council for the Social Studies (1994) identified ten themes on which to build a social studies program. They are:

I. Culture
II. Time, Continuity, and Change
III. People, Places, and Environments
IV. Individual Development and Identity
V. Individuals, Groups, and Institutions
VI. Power, Authority, and Governance
VII. Production, Distribution, and Consumption
VIII. Science, Technology, and Society
IX. Global Connections and Independence
X. Civic Ideals and Practice

You may note, from reading this list, that the ten themes are integrated, in that they cut across social sciences, as well as across other subject areas in the elementary school curriculum. This is no accident. It reflects the very basic beliefs of most social educators.

By briefly examining the major social sciences (see Figure 5.1), you will see how each is an integral part of our understanding of human social behavior. You will also recognize how neglecting a social science may be like putting a puzzle together when there are missing pieces.

History

History is the study of the past. We study the past to understand the present and prepare for the future. For instance, by learning about the Great Depression of the 1930s, we begin to understand why some people—elderly people are so conservative in their spending: they developed their shopping habits when there was little money to spend. Their fear of economic hard times makes them want to save money, even now, when they may be fairly comfortable. Understanding the Great Depression is also helpful when we examine the recent failure of Asian

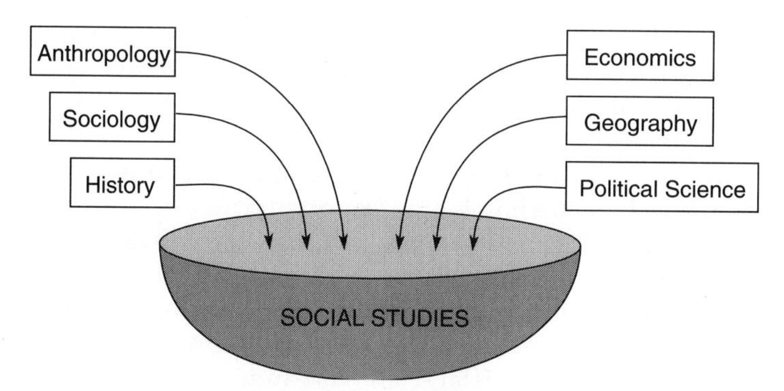

FIGURE 5.1. Components of social studies.

banks. When banks were closing in the 1930s, how did the government protect people's savings? What should be done today?

Geography

Some geographers organize their discipline by five basic themes: location, place, relationships within places, movement, and regions. Geography is most useful as the study of people's interaction with the environment. Though you may associate it with the location of rivers and the study of state capitals, it is much more than that. For instance, consider the fact: Mount Mitchell is the tallest mountain in the Appalachian Chain (6,684 ft.). It may be helpful to know this on a quiz show, but the information is not very useful unless you intend to climb the mountain. Of greater importance is the effect of the Appalachian Mountains on people. That they isolated the people who lived there, causing differences in speech, music, dance, and recreation is significant. Even more significant is that the mountains served as an obstacle to economic development, creating poverty conditions and limiting access to basic services such as electricity. One may also notice how the mountains affect weather to the east and west. To understand these effects, one needs to know the relative size of the mountains, not their precise heights.

We must also recognize the effects of people on mountains. On a trip to Mount Mitchell you might notice how roads have been blasted into mountainsides, how forests have been converted to ski resorts, how wildlife is disappearing, and how erosion has become a problem. Mount Mitchell's apex has been ravaged by acid rain. Environmental damage affects people no matter where they live. Geography helps us understand its effects, and gives us clues about how we can promote a healthy environment.

Political Science

Political science is the study of power. Like the other social sciences, it is regarded as a dry subject—we think of numerous charts concerning governmental processes—but political science can be remarkably relevant. There are all kinds of government. Think about the times when you were younger and needed permission to do something that was ordinarily against the rules. To whom did you go? Your mother? Your father? Another relative? The choice you made shows that, even back then, you were a political scientist, conscious of where power resided.

If you have ever been the victim of an unfair punishment or the buyer of damaged merchandise, you know how important it is to know the rules for appeal. On another level, if you were upset about something an authority or institution was overlooking, such as an unsafe playground or low teacher salaries, would you know how to change things? Could you be effective in developing a new school program and convincing the school board to approve it?

Those who know their political science are more effective as change agents. They are able to influence policies because they know how the system works. Those who do not may become pawns, the weakest pieces on the chessboard, who get pushed around by all the other pieces.

Anthropology

Anthropology is a subject that often gets little attention in elementary schools. It is the study of cultures, how they develop and how they change. If you have traveled to other states and nations you have probably noticed how people are very different. So many aspects of your life that you take for granted may be viewed as odd by those who do not live in your community. For instance, in Singapore indicating OK with your thumb and forefinger is considered obscene. In Venezuela the gift of a handkerchief is regarded as bad luck because it signifies tears (Schreiber, 1992).

Similarly, some of the behaviors we see in our travels may appear inappropriate or strange. Yet such behaviors as bowing as a way of greeting or the wearing of loincloths are regarded as perfectly normal by the cultures that practice them.

Anthropology is particularly important today. America has always been a nation of immigrants, but now many of the new arrivals to our communities come from cultures substantially different from those of European immigrants. For example, many Asian-Americans are Buddhists or Hindus, with beliefs quite different from those of Judeo-Christian heritage. Not only do they not celebrate Christmas, they may not necessarily believe in one god. In addition, their language system, in both its spoken and written forms, is quite different from Western languages.

Are you prepared to teach children from another culture? Can you help your students celebrate their commonalities and differences? Anthropology is a tool for doing so.

Economics

Economics is the study of the choices people make to meet their needs and wants. It can be horribly abstract, with references to monetary policy, gross national product, and the Keynesian model. On the other hand, economics concerns such concrete ideas as taxes, unemployment, and interest rates.

Many Americans prefer not to think about economic issues, but avoiding them will only make one's life harder. Too many people are suffering because of unwise investments, foolish spending, and failure to plan properly. For instance, some California residents who lost their homes to mudslides discovered too late that they had inadequate insurance. On the other hand, there are numerous success stories of those who waited for the right time to buy a home, sell a car, or make a deal. We can help students become happier and more successful when we prepare them for the real world, where economic awareness counts.

Recent advertising campaigns aimed at children show that businesses recognize their economic power. Indeed, it has been estimated that youngsters between the ages of four and twelve spend $2 billion of their own money annually. They also influence their parents' spending to the tune of $33 billion (Grayard, 1992). The spending power of children and teens makes economic education important.

Economic knowledge is also integral to citizenship. Political scientists tell us that voters tend to consider economic issues when choosing presidential candidates. If the electorate does not understand issues like foreign trade and fiscal policy, can they make knowledgeable decisions? When candidates vow not to raise taxes, will the public ask what services will be cut? Only if they develop a strong sense of economics.

Sociology

Sociology is the study of groups and human interaction within groups. It is the social science that predominates in primary grade social studies. It is also cited by critics as a weak social science because it is not as rigorous as history and geography.

Most of us are amateur sociologists. We may enjoy observing frazzled parents dealing with their children in the supermarket or studying the types of people waiting in line at the movie theater. Trends in clothing, music, hairstyles, and language all come under the purview of the sociologist.

On a more serious note, sociology is also the study of television's effects on our society, how we treat the elderly, the causes of drug addiction, and the symptoms of child abuse. Studying these topics can provide valuable insights to individuals who seek to make their lives happier and the world a better place to live. Sociology, as its name reminds us, deals with people. If we seek to get along with others, we need to understand them. Sociology is a tool for doing so.

HOW DO THE SOCIAL SCIENCES FIT TOGETHER?

Think of a recent world event, such as the El Niño phenomenon in 1998. Can you identify the perspective of each social science in the event?

Anthropologists would be interested in the name, El Niño. It literally means, "the Christ child," reflecting its occasional appearance near the Christmas season. Anthropologists would also study the influence of El Niño's weather patterns on the cultures of people who live on the Pacific coasts of North and South America, where the winds and rain hit hardest. They would also be interested in how various cultures explain the El Niño phenomenon.

Geographers would discuss how El Niño originates in the South Pacific Ocean during the summer months in that region. They would analyze causes of mudslides in California, effects of heavy rains on agricultural production, and preventive measures that can be taken to protect people and property.

Economists would address the financial costs of El Niño. They would discuss the effects of bad weather on food prices, housing, and insurance premiums. Economists would also study the expenses of federal, state, and local governments in providing emergency assistance to people who lost their farms, homes, or belongings due to the storms. The effect on taxes, budget deficits, and interest rates would be a major consideration.

Political scientists would also be interested in the role of governments in providing assistance. They would look at how decisions are made to deal with El Niño's effects, including emergency management, governmental policies to promote preparedness, and programs to safeguard the environment. They would also study the role of nonprofit organizations, such as the Red Cross and the Sierra Club, to determine their influence in the decision-making process.

Historians can tell us the story of El Niño. They can explain how Chileans fishing for anchovies gave a name to the unusual weather patterns that began in December. They can offer evidence of how people have dealt with El Niño's effects and the lessons we can learn from those experiences. They can also predict the ripple effects of El Niño on people's lives, based on historical trends.

Sociologists look at El Niño's influence on affected groups such as farmers or families. They may examine the divorce rate or crime rate in areas that were ravaged by weather disturbances. They would study how communities form bonds during emergencies, with neighbors, relatives, and even strangers helping each other deal with adversity. They would also analyze the way that mass media reports about El Niño, thus contributing to public reaction.

If you see overlap between various social sciences, do not be concerned. It is difficult to place some concepts, such as agriculture, under either geography or economics. The ways that severe weather affects community life is equally fascinating to the sociologist, historian, and anthropologist. (As for the difference between sociology and anthropology, remember that anthropology usually focuses on a particular culture, while sociology looks at groups, such as teachers, consumers, or vegetarians, that cut across many cultures.) Fortunately, there is no need to make a distinction, unless you crave a good intellectual argument. The many overlaps call attention to the need for *social studies,* a combining of the social sciences. It is only by looking at all the perspectives that we can get a complete picture of the event.

Can you imagine studying El Niño without mentioning economics or sociology? The result would be a distorted picture, one which could mislead the learner about the reality of the situation. That is how you may have received much of your social education—with a lot of history, a smattering of geographic facts, and no attempt to tie in the other social sciences, or focus on events as a whole.

Many elementary school teachers complain that they do not have much interest in or knowledge of social studies. If they learned social studies as a series of unconnected facts, their complaints are not surprising. Not being able to see the "big picture" keeps students from appreciating the depth and excitement of our complex world. Social studies, for them, is something to be memorized and forgotten. Not so for those who learned about the world from many perspectives. They are the ones who are most comfortable assuming the responsibilities of citizenship.

It is up to you, a future teacher, to develop a social studies program that will attract students to the topic. The challenge may be daunting if you know little about the field. But, fortunately, it is not that hard to catch up. If you can develop the habit of reading or watching the daily news, engaging in discussions with knowledgeable people, and becoming actively involved with community or local governmental groups, you will soon begin to feel a sense of citizenship. It is a good feeling, one of being able to make a difference!

WHAT ARE THE GOALS OF SOCIAL STUDIES?

Most citizens regard social studies as a body of knowledge that must be learned, usually through memorization. Such a narrow view of the topic is in conflict with the overall goal of social studies, which is to develop responsible citizens.

Conceptual Goals: Application of Knowledge

A responsible citizen has to make decisions, many of which are quite difficult: which candidate will provide the best leadership, how to address the problem of homelessness, what to do about the loss of the ozone layer. To make such decisions, we certainly need knowledge, a lot of it. We must be able to apply all that we know about the social sciences, as well as science, mathematics, and other subjects. The key word is *apply.* All of the knowledge in the world is of little value unless we are able to use it.

That is the problem with social studies as most of us know it: we never got to apply the content we were taught. You may have heard the saying, If you don't use it, you lose it. Though not normally used in reference to social studies, the saying is apropos. We have memorized so many facts for exams and then forgotten them. For instance, those of us who were taught the state capitals and the order of presidents would have difficulty performing those tasks today because they were not used in solving meaningful problems. Those facts that we do remember, such as the multiplication tables, the names of the most recent presidents, and our own state capital, are never forgotten because they are relevant to our daily lives.

Knowledge of facts is not the goal of a social studies program, but only the means to an end. This view, however, conflicts with the orientations of many noneducators, and certainly with the experiences of legions of school children.

Reprinted by permission: Tribune Media Services.

For most students, social studies is nothing but a collection of dreary, trivial facts to be memorized for the exam and quickly forgotten. This conception of social studies poisons the atmosphere in schools, stifles intellectual growth, and handicaps citizens in their exercise of democracy. These are serious consequences. Educators must carefully examine the liabilities of a social studies program that is dedicated to the teaching of facts:

Facts are Easily Forgotten. Almost all children are taught the state capitals, but only a few can remember more than a dozen. Some of us had to memorize the nation's presidents in sequential order, but would be unlikely to reproduce that feat today. You probably had to study the main products of particular states and countries, but no doubt that knowledge was lost within twenty-four hours of the exam. Teaching facts is a waste of time. It bores students. It also causes undue burdens on children who have difficulty memorizing. What is truly criminal is that emphasizing facts deprives us of the opportunity to achieve the depth of understanding that is needed for effective citizenship.

Facts Do Not Develop the Mind. Recall of facts is the lowest level of thinking. It does not require analytical skills, problem solving, synthesis, or application. In learning factual content, we do not develop skills that can be applied to other situations. If a teacher's goal is for me to learn that Jacques Chirac is France's president, I merely assimilate the knowledge. No further processing is necessary.

Facts Change. We could have our students learn the names of each of the world's leaders, but that information would become obsolete as soon as the next election, governmental overthrow, or death in office occurs. The actual nations of those world leaders may even change. After all, there is no U.S.S.R. anymore, nor is there an East Germany or Czechoslovakia. The nations of Rhodesia, Byelorussia, and Burma have become Zimbabwe, Belarus, and Myanmar, respectively. It is anyone's guess what other changes are in store. In the meantime, students are spending valuable class time memorizing information that may soon become inaccurate.

The globe is still round, but the names and boundary lines are constantly being altered.

Facts are Limited. Of what value is a fact? Merely knowing the name of my state's governor will be of little value when trying to influence events in the state capital. My knowledge that West Virginia is a mountainous state will not enable me to get along better with someone who comes from there. Being able to recite the fact that Hindu is the dominant religion in India will not make me a better person. We must go beyond the immediate facts to reach the goals of social studies education.

There are Too Many Facts. The primary complaint of most social studies teachers is the overwhelming amount of content to be covered. Teachers constantly feel rushed to include all the content in the textbook, with numerous quizzes and review sessions to be sure all the facts are crammed into students' heads. Unfortunately, even a superhuman effort will not achieve the goal of teaching all the facts that need to be learned. There are always ideas that will be excluded, usually those found at the end of the book. Plus, there are facts that the textbook authors had to leave out for space considerations, not to mention those they did not know or care about. In the meantime, new facts are being created at an ever increasing rate.

It may be clear, at this point, that an emphasis on teaching and learning facts is more than inefficient and boring; it is harmful to the development of thoughtful, knowledgeable citizenry. Fortunately, there is an alternative: emphasizing generalizations.

Facts vs. Generalization

To reduce the emphasis on facts, we must be clear what we mean by the term. A fact is a specific statement that is true for a particular time and place. Thus, the statement, "West Virginia is a mountainous state" is a fact because it is only true for one place—West Virginia. The statement, "Jacques Chirac has replaced Francois Mitterand as President of France" is only true for one brief period of time—the 1990s, and one place—France.

Facts are different from generalizations. A generalization is a general statement that is true for many times and places. Generalizations do not refer to specific times, people, or places; they are supposed to be general. Thus, the statement, "Geographical obstacles prevent interaction between cultures" is a generalization because it is true not just today, but was true long ago. The Atlantic Ocean, for instance, prevented interaction between Native Americans and Europeans for centuries. The statement is also true for a variety of places. The Appalachian Mountains have served as a barrier between West Virginians and coastal residents just as the Sahara Desert has done the same for various African peoples.

PEANUTS reprinted by permission of United Feature Syndicate, Inc.

The Benefits of Using Generalizations

The goal of learning generalizations is better suited to social studies education than the mere learning of facts. By providing relevance, depth, application, and efficiency, generalizations are more likely to be learned, understood, and used than factual content.

Relevance. Because generalizations are true for many times and places, they are likely to be relevant to individuals. Knowledge of West Virginia's separation from the coast is only relevant to those who are interested in that particular region, presumably those who live there. For everyone else, it is a fact of slight, if any, interest. In contrast, the generalization that geographic barriers prevent interaction between cultures can be applied to any region of interest. Students in Michigan can contemplate the differences between residents of the upper and lower peninsulas of that state, Northwesterners can study the differences between eastern and western Washington, and children in New Jersey can appreciate how the general *lack* of geographic barriers has promoted cultural interaction in their state.

Depth. Because generalizations are true for many times and places, students benefit from multiple examples. The West Virginia fact illustrates an interesting development, but adding the examples from Michigan and Washington, with the nonexample from New Jersey, gives us greater depth of understanding. Students may perceive the West Virginia fact to be about mountains or about an unusual situation; but the other examples make it clear that the idea is not a shallow one. As the students confront further examples of the generalization in later grades, it further reinforces their learning.

Application. When the learning of facts is a goal, students only use them in a testing situation. Generalizations, by contrast, are designed to be applied. In later grades, in the study of Australia, teachers will be pleased when their students apply their knowledge of geographic barriers to the Great Desert that divides the cultures of Eastern and Western Australia. When citizens read the newspaper about fighting between ethnic groups in Turkey, they will find themselves better able to understand the conflict by noticing how water and mountains have kept these groups separate for so many years. On an interpersonal level, you may have a better understanding of a new friend when you learn where he or she grew up. All of these applications—whether related to scholastics, citizenship, or interpersonal relations, make knowledge from generalizations much more useful than mere facts.

Efficiency. Many social studies teachers like generalizations because they make learning more efficient. Teachers do not have time to teach about every geographic barrier and its effects on cultural interaction, nor do students need all that information. Instead, with the generalization as a goal, students only have to learn the main idea. That frees classroom time for other important ideas and activities.

Understandings

Imagine Johnny, a second grader, coming home from school. When his parents ask what he learned that day, he says, "Geographic barriers prevent interaction between cultures." His parents would either faint from surprise or else enroll Johnny in a program for precocious children, because second graders do not speak like that!

Most second graders are not capable of understanding the wording of Johnny's generalization. As we have studied in Chapter 3, second graders tend to be concrete-operational. They cannot handle such abstractions as "geographic barriers" and "interaction between cultures." We want them to learn the principle, even if they don't use the abstract wording. When they do understand the language, they still need concrete examples to learn the idea.

Instead of being taught an abstract generalization, children work with "understandings," which are concrete, specific examples of the generalization. Thus, Johnny would be more likely to tell his parents that he learned about how the Appalachian Mountains have made it hard for West Virginians to trade with coastal residents. This content, which is an example of the generalization, is concrete, very specific, and in a second grader's language. It is, therefore, developmentally appropriate.

Elementary school teachers must teach understandings to help their students learn generalizations. Most students need at least a few examples before they grasp an idea. This is called *convergent thinking.* Convergent thinking is a good way for students to form generalizations. In a third grade study of communities, for instance, the teacher may point out how the city's police officers are paid by the local government using tax dollars. Students may then research the source of pay for other public servants, including firefighters, sanitation workers, and teachers. As they study the examples, they will eventually form the generalization, "Taxes are used to pay the salaries of public servants."

All of these examples, whether supplied by the teacher or the student, are understandings because they are concrete, specific examples of the generalization. Understandings are valuable in helping students learn generalizations. Without understandings, the generalization will remain inaccessible to the students. They may memorize the words, but must have concrete examples to truly learn it.

Students are more likely to remember understandings because they are tied to generalizations. Instead of memorizing which workers are paid by their city government, they can instead apply the generalization to specific jobs. Drivers for the city's bus service are public servants; their salaries are, therefore, paid by tax money. In this case, students are using the generalization as an organizer. Instead of metaphorically, tossing facts into their brains, they can organize their brains into compartments, one of which addresses the source of pay for public servants. Recall is easier when your brain is organized.

In later grades, students will have the opportunity to apply their generalizations to other situations. This is called *divergent thinking.* In fourth grade, after reviewing how the city's public servants are paid, students may then consider the pay source of the state's governor, park rangers, and highway patrol officers. This content is easier to learn because the new understandings relate to a familiar generalization. Thus, conceptual goals are more effectively reached by using understandings.

Understandings also help us learn the basic facts of social studies. As they learn the understanding about the Appalachian Mountains serving as an obstacle to West Virginians, students are also learning specific locations. But, in this case they are learning them as part of a key idea, rather than doing it for the purpose of memorization. Because the specific locations are essential to learning the understanding, students are far more likely to remember them. Thus, in a strong social studies program, children learn specific facts, but unlike traditional programs, the learning of facts is only an intermediate step on the way to learning valuable generalizations. It is a means to an end.

You may have noticed that the use of understandings makes teaching more efficient. The social studies class does not have to devote time to memorizing the locations of specific mountain ranges or states. Instead they learn those basic ideas as they learn the understandings. The boredom of low-level fact reviews is eliminated. Thus, along with saving time, the class is also likely to be more motivated to learn and less bored by the content. Social studies becomes a meaningful, enjoyable course of study.

All of these benefits result in a social studies program that meets its conceptual goals. Generalizations and understandings allow teachers and students to focus on the important ideas that children need to become effective citizens. At the same time, students engage in higher-level thinking activities that are necessary for lifelong learning. Finally, they grow to enjoy learning social studies and recognize its relevance and value. The contrast between that approach and the dreary, facts-based social studies of yesteryear is astounding!

The Role of Teachers in Determining Specific Conceptual Goals

An added benefit of using generalizations as a social studies learning goal is the additional power that is granted to teachers. For many years, teachers have not been heavily involved in the curriculum development process. They have been assigned to teach content that had already been decided by others. As discussed in the previous chapter, this situation limits teachers' effectiveness in meeting students' needs. It also results in the deskilling of teachers as their curriculum development abilities become rusty.

Under the traditional facts-based program, teachers are not expected to use their professional knowledge. When teachers are working with generalizations as their learning goal, they are actively involved in the curriculum development process. All facts are not equally important. Teachers must thoughtfully analyze the content to identify which important ideas the students need. They are expected to emphasize what is important and de-emphasize what may not be useful in reaching the goals of the program.

The additional power that comes with a generalization-based program can transform the professional lives of teachers. Teachers may find their jobs more rewarding when they are working toward important goals instead of presenting content that they know is not relevant, interesting, or useful to students in the long term. Teachers find it gratifying to see students interested in the content as a result of thoughtful curricular decisions. Developing a curriculum based on generalizations promotes the type of pride that keeps teachers motivated to do their best, stay in the profession, and improve the quality of schooling their students receive. Thus, the empowerment of teachers through their expanded role in curriculum development can be a major step in achieving excellence in our schools.

Process Skills

The goal of social studies is more than the development of knowledge; it is also the development of process skills. Process skills are tools for learning, such as research and critical thinking skills. We need process skills because, even if we learned all the knowledge there is to know, there will always be more. New knowledge is constantly being created. We must be prepared to learn, even after graduation.

Theory to Practice
Social Studies

As part of their study of the ancient world, some sixth graders in Martinsburg, West Virginia, are creating cultural artifacts (Passe & Passe, 1985). Cultural artifacts are objects that humans have created and used.

But the Martinsburg artifacts are not from the present day. They represent ancient civilizations. Each group of students has secretly chosen a civilization. One has ancient Rome, another ancient Egypt, while a third chose ancient Greece. There is even a group that devised an imaginary civilization.

Each group must research the civilization to decide what artifacts best represent the culture. Possibilities include money, jewelry, tools, weapons, and clothing. Obviously, ancient artifacts are not readily available, so part of the project is to create them.

The teacher has prepared a section of the playground where each group buries its artifacts. The next day, the class will perform an archaeological dig. They will tag each finding using standard archaeological techniques (which they developed by going through classroom trash baskets).

When all the artifacts have been discovered, the students will analyze the findings and make a guess as to the nature of the civilization. This requires careful consideration of the materials in use at that time, the cultural beliefs that guided each civilization, and any relevant historical events (e.g., volcanic eruptions, wars).

This activity is designed to capture the excitement and importance of anthropology and archaeology. It also develops a sense of history and the way historical knowledge is constructed. Working as a team to create the artifacts of a civilization promotes process goals. Affective goals are reached as students consider what things members of their civilization considered important. Through activities like this, the students construct their knowledge of ancient civilizations while taking delight in creating and solving a mystery.

Fortunately, social studies lends itself to simultaneous development of knowledge and process skills. For instance, suppose your third graders want to learn about the duties of the mayor. They can write to the mayor to request an interview, develop questions they want to have answered, and create a skit to present what they learned. Such a project helps them develop such valuable skills as letter writing, interviewing, notetaking, outlining, scriptwriting, and performing.

Do these activities sound like fun? You may be wondering why your third-grade class didn't do projects like this. It may be because of your teacher's view of the curriculum. A teacher who does not see the value of process goals is more likely to deliver a lecture on a topic, provide a textbook explanation, or skip the topic altogether. These methods are certainly quick, but they're not necessarily effective. Students are more likely to remember information that they discover themselves than information that was merely transmitted to them.

The use of process skills does more than make the learning enjoyable. Many would argue that learning how to take notes may be more useful than knowledge of a mayor's duties. An old saying sums it up: Give someone a fish and you've given food for one meal. Teach someone to fish and you've given food for a lifetime. If the teacher provides a list of mayoral duties, the students have been given some information (have been handed a fish). But if they are taught how to gather the information, they will be able to find out anything they need to know (have been taught how to fish). If the mayor's duties change or the children move to a different city, they will still be able to find the information they need.

Values, Feelings, and Appreciations

Another goal of social studies is in the affective realm—the development of values, feelings, and appreciations. This goal, too, is frequently underemphasized by social studies teachers (Scott, 1991).

Social studies is rich with human emotions and beliefs. Whatever the topic of study, be it war, homelessness, justice, or family, there is a cavalcade of affect. Why would a pioneer choose to leave a secure home for a dangerous life on the

DILBERT reprinted by permission of United Feature Syndicate, Inc.

frontier? What motivates farmers to maintain their family farms in the face of economic uncertainty? How do African-Americans feel about their heritage as slaves?

Each of these questions (and there are so many others!) considers the affective side of experience. Social studies is, after all, much more than a collection of facts; it is the study of the rationales for the decisions we make. It gives us insight into ourselves and into each other. By studying the values of pioneers, for instance, we consider whether we would be willing to take similar chances. Whatever the answer, we learn about our own preferences and, perhaps, those of our classmates. We gain an understanding of one another. What could be a more worthy educational goal than that?

Many teachers avoid lessons about values because they believe values are the responsibility of the church or the home. Critics respond by pointing out how few Americans attend church and how many parents are not capable or willing to teach about values (Fraenkel, 1977). Indeed, a vast majority of Americans believe that schools should teach values (Scott, 1991).

Other teachers argue that affective lessons are controversial and divisive, that they will lead to classroom conflict and parental objection (Fraenkel, 1977). On one hand, they're correct. A discussion of values may bring out differing viewpoints. But what better preparation for democratic citizenship can there be? Students must learn to respect the views of others, gain insight into the reasoning behind their choices, and be able to explain their own beliefs. A healthy exchange of views can facilitate these goals. As long as it's fairly conducted, classroom discussion of differing views can also be quite enjoyable.

Joyce (1970, p. 255) argues that, "The natural world of childhood is filled with conflict, aggression, independence, and warmth. To pretend that their world is bland is false." As discussed in earlier chapters, children no longer come to school as innocent lambs, if they ever did. Concerns about crime, injustice, and poverty, which may promote heated discussion, are already a daily topic of conversation outside of the classroom.

Another reason that elementary school teachers tend to avoid values lessons is the legitimate fear of indoctrination. That concern is based, however, on the essentialist model of teacher as the source of all knowledge. Progressives and reconstructionists, on the other hand, view the teacher's role as facilitator. Under those philosophies, teachers help students learn *about* values, to help them realize what they, themselves, consider important. They also help students learn about the values of others, including people from different cultures and time periods. Your views on the issue of values education may be helpful in clarifying your own curricular philosophy.

You may be wishing that you had experienced lessons in the affective realm. If so, your teachers, in their concern for the facts and their fear of criticism, probably didn't consider the human aspects of their lessons. As a result, student interest was not as high as it could have been. This avoidance of values helps to explain the wide dislike of social studies. The teacher's beliefs about the curriculum make a difference!

THE ROLE OF TEXTBOOKS

If a teacher's beliefs about the curriculum are so important, it is worthwhile to analyze how they are formed. Numerous influences shape a teacher's approach, including teacher education courses, school board policies, and state laws. One very significant factor is the classroom textbook.

Teachers tend to think of the textbook as the curriculum. As a result, texts are the dominant source of classroom content and activities, especially in social studies (McCutcheon, 1982).

On the surface, heavy reliance on textbooks makes a lot of sense, especially for beginning teachers. It is much easier to plan a lesson based on a textbook chapter than it is to plan an original lesson. Textbooks also provide content that may be unfamiliar to the teacher. A third benefit is the teacher's guide which supplies numerous suggestions concerning instructional techniques, questioning, and evaluation (Thornton, 1991).

Many teachers use the textbook because they are also concerned about reading skills. They argue that through a textbook-based approach students can improve their reading abilities and learn social studies content at the same time (Peters & Hayes, 1989).

The emphasis on reading is very appealing to elementary educators. Successful reading ability is generally regarded as the most crucial goal of elementary education (Stake & Easley, 1978). Accordingly, reading is the subject area that receives the most classroom time and the one that is tested most heavily. Public concern about reading test scores has been high for decades (Goodlad, 1984).

As a result of reading's dominance in the curriculum, many social studies lessons are taught in the same fashion as traditional reading lessons. Students are initially introduced to new vocabulary words. Then they read the textbook, answer comprehension questions, and complete skill sheets. This approach is a comfortable one for many elementary teachers since they usually follow that format in their reading lessons as well as in other areas of the curriculum. Most reading programs are built around the textbook. Thus, the social studies program has become similarly structured (Goodlad, 1984; Peters & Hayes, 1989).

What happens when the textbook becomes the curriculum? While there are numerous benefits, such as shorter lesson planning time, efficient classroom routines, and praise from the public for emphasizing reading skills, there are dangers too.

Bias

Singular Viewpoints

If the textbook is the sole source of knowledge, students are exposed to only one point of view (English, 1986). This may not be an area of concern if you believe that textbooks are totally objective. However, many critics of education characterize textbooks as quite ideological in nature, whether intentionally or not (Anyon, 1979; Ellington, 1986; Wald, 1989). Consider the following.

Some adults recall learning, in their early schooling, how North America was settled by the Puritans and other Europeans who were seeking religious freedom and a better life. This presentation, common in most social studies textbooks, portrayed early America as a white Christian nation, ignoring the contributions of Native Americans, enslaved Africans, and the masses of poor Catholics and Jews immigrating for reasons of economic hardship and religious injustice. It was not until college that these students learned that American culture was not as pure as their elementary school textbooks implied.

Other adults remember their textbooks stressing the multicultural nature of American society. They assumed that all children were presented with the same ideas.

Not everyone has received the same education. The viewpoints and biases of the textbook authors and publishers influence what is learned. Whether you believe that one textbook's approach is better than another is immaterial. The point is that using only one textbook is likely to promote only one viewpoint among many.

Contrast this approach with the use of multiple sources of information—textbooks, nonfiction, fiction, films, videotapes, magazine articles, guest speakers, newspapers, and so on. Working with different materials exposes children to many perspectives, especially if the teachers are determined to meet that goal.

The presentation of numerous viewpoints encourages critical thinking, as students must decide which arguments are most persuasive. It is also a realistic approach, for life is complex; causes and effects are seldom simple. This awareness is important, for students will be confronted throughout life with politicians, advertisers, and religious leaders who promote simplistic solutions. They may be less likely to be drawn to religious cults or demagogues like Hitler if they have the ability to question and reject easy explanations (Carlson, 1989).

Philosophical Bias

Another type of textbook bias deals with educational philosophy. If a teacher teaches by the book with a text that promotes content learning at the expense of thinking skills, the students are deprived of valuable learning experiences. The same is true for any other emphasis in content or philosophy. The publishers are not necessarily trying to promote their vision of society. They may only be emphasizing a particular goal because of their perceptions of what the public wants (Graham, 1986). But if their books become the curriculum, the textbook publishers become the ones who determine the school curriculum, rather than the educators and citizens of the community.

Interest Groups

Textbook content is not decided by a group of scholars in an ivory tower. State education officials and lawmakers conduct intense political negotiations among a variety of interest groups which produce additional textbook content, compromises between competing views, and occasional deletions. The interest groups that engage in these negotiations do so because of their awareness of the power of textbooks to mold people's beliefs (Apple, 1988).

When interest groups have set out to influence textbook content, changes have occurred. For instance, when a series of studies identified glaring distortions and trivialization concerning the role of women in history, publishers responded. However, most of their changes were minor, such as highlighting "the usual famous women," without presenting alternative female perspectives (AAUW, 1992). Similar compromises have been made in other subject areas. Thus, despite the protests and negotiations, many textbooks continue to promote versions of "the truth" that differ substantially from current thinking in educational and academic circles.

Effects on Students

A second problem with overemphasizing textbooks is the effect on students. For many years, textbooks have been criticized for dull, lifeless prose (Tyson-Bernstein & Woodward, 1986). The problem is understandable when one considers the pressures on textbook authors to include massive amounts of information in their chapters (Graham, 1986). Yet the problem is not necessarily the lack of high-quality writing. Even with improvements in textbook writing, the student is still merely a passive recipient of knowledge.

As you learned in Chapter 3, on developmental needs, elementary children require concrete experiences and active learning. One cannot expect textbooks to provide those activities; books are for reading, not doing. As important as reading is, it is not the only way, or even the best way, for young children to learn. Teachers who overuse the textbook often have to deal with uninterested students who fail to learn the content. Children also lose out on the opportunity to develop their process skills (Taxel, 1989).

Textbooks are written for national or international populations. Authors must generalize about the interests or needs of the youngsters who will use the book. Thus, textbook lessons may include content or skills that are not relevant to students or even needed by them (Tyson-Bernstein & Woodward, 1986). These lessons are taught, though, wasting classroom time that could be better spent. If teachers use the textbooks as one source among many, they will be more likely to take the opportunity to skip, adapt, or resequence lessons when appropriate.

Deskilling of Teachers

A third major problem with relying on textbooks is the deskilling of teachers. Many teachers rely on the book for lesson goals, instructional activities, and evaluation exercises. What is left for teachers to do? In effect, those teachers no longer exercise the principles and practices they were trained to implement. They become paper-pushers skilled in recording test scores and hushing unruly students, but unskilled in meeting individual student needs with meaningful activities and appropriate evaluation (Apple, 1986).

You may have had such teachers, whose total program consisted of having students read the text, answer the questions at the end, and then grade the responses according to the teacher's guide. Teachers like this give the field of education a bad name. They contribute to the belief that anyone can be a teacher. Indeed, one merely needs the ability to read in order to run such an instructional program. That approach is not teaching; it's following directions. True teachers make dozens of decisions each day as they consider student interests and needs, the demands of the curriculum, instructional methods, evaluation issues, and numerous other factors.

You do not have to fall into the trap of letting the textbook become your entire curriculum. Thousands of teachers use their brains and apply what they have learned in their educational careers. These teachers have fought to resist a textbook-based program. Teachers have a lot of power that they may not know they have. In Chapter 13 you will learn how to use your power effectively.

Questions

1. Of the various social sciences that make up social studies, which ones did not receive enough emphasis in your schooling? Has it harmed you?
2. How do you feel about the development of process and affective goals?
3. What can teachers do to prevent textbooks from having undue influence on the curriculum?
4. How would your education be different if the curriculum had been built around generalizations?

References

AMERICAN ASSOCIATION OF UNIVERSITY WOMEN. (1992). *How schools shortchange girls.* Washington, DC: American Association of University Women Educational Foundation.

ANYON, J. (1979). Ideology and United States history textbooks. *Harvard Educational Review, 49,* 361–368.

APPLE, M. (1986). *Teachers and texts: A political economy of class and gender relations in education.* London: Routledge & Kegan Paul.

APPLE, M. (1992). The text and cultural politics. *Educational Researcher, 21*(7), 4–11.

CARLSON, D. (1989). Legitimation and delegitimation. In S. de Castell, A. Luke, & C. Luke (Eds.), *Language, authority and criticism: Readings on the school textbook* (pp. 46–55). London: Falmer.

ELLINGTON, L. (1986). Blacks and Hispanics in high school economics texts. *Social Education, 50*(1), 64–67.

ENGLISH, R. (1986). Can social studies textbooks have scholarly integrity? *Social Education, 50*(1), 46–48.

FRAENKEL, J. (1977). *How to teach about values: An analytic approach.* Englewood Cliffs, NJ: Prentice-Hall.

GOODLAD, J. (1984). *A place called school.* New York: McGraw-Hill.

GRAHAM, A. (1986). Elementary social studies texts: An author-editor's viewpoint. *Social Education, 50*(1), 54–55.

GRAYARD, H. (1992, June 15). Financially, they're no babes in the woods. *Charlotte Observer,* p. D1.

JOYCE, B. (1970). Social action for the primary schools. *Childhood Education, 46,* 254–258.

McCUTCHEON, G. (1982). How do elementary school teachers plan? The nature of planning and influences on it. *Elementary School Journal, 82*(5).

NATIONAL COUNCIL FOR THE SOCIAL STUDIES. (1993). Definition approved. *The Social Studies Professional,* January/February, 3.

NATIONAL COUNCIL FOR THE SOCIAL STUDIES. (1994). *Curriculum standards for social studies.* Washington, DC: Author.

PASSE, J., AND PASSE M. (1985). Archaeology: A unit to promote thinking skills. *The Social Studies, 76,* 238–239.

PETERS, C., & HAYES, B. (1989). The role of reading instruction in the social studies classroom. In D. Lapp, J. Flood, & N. Farnam (Eds.), *Content area reading and learning.* Englewood Cliffs, NJ: Prentice-Hall.

SCHREIBER, P. (1992, August 2). Don't bare your sole in Singapore, and never point. *Charlotte Observer,* p. 7B.

SCHUG, M. C., TODD, R., & BEERY, R. (1984). Why kids don't like social studies. *Social Education, 48,* 382–387.

SCOTT, K. P. (1991). Achieving social studies affective aims: Values, empathy, and moral development. In J. P. Shaver (Ed.), *Handbook of research on social studies teaching and learning* (pp. 357–369). New York: Macmillan.

STAKE, R., & EASLEY, J. (1978). *Case studies in science education: Vol. 2. Design, overview, and general findings.* Urbana-Champaign: University of Illinois Center for Instructional Research and Curriculum Evaluation.

TAXEL, J. (1989). Children's literature: A research proposal. In S. de Castell, A. Luke, & C. Luke (Eds.), *Language, authority and criticism: Readings on the school textbook* (pp. 32–43). London: Falmer.

THORNTON, S. (1991). Teacher as curricular-instructional gatekeeper in social studies. In J. Shaver (Ed.), *Handbook of research on social studies teaching and learning.* New York: Macmillan.

TYSON-BERNSTEIN, H., AND WOODWARD, A. (1986). The great textbook machine and prospects for reform. *Social Education, 50*(1), 41–45.

WALD, A. (1989). Hegemony and literary tradition in the United States. In S. de Castell, A. Luke, & C. Luke (Eds.), *Language, authority and criticism: Readings on the school textbook* (pp. 3–16). London: Falmer.

CHAPTER 6

Science and Health

Children come to school with a strong interest in matters of science. They are fascinated by animal behavior, intent on observing plant growth, and puzzled by the behavior of the moon and stars. A simple shadow is a topic of intense study. Yet, by the end of the elementary school years, science is rated as the least liked subject in the curriculum (Goodlad, 1984).

When interest in a subject drops so precipitously, there must be something wrong with the curriculum. To understand that phenomenon, we must explore the nature of science.

WHAT IS SCIENCE?

If you think of science as a series of definitions, the periodic table of elements, and the Latin names of flora and fauna, your teachers may have missed the point. There are two main aspects of science, each influencing the other.

Science Knowledge

The most familiar aspect of science is the body of knowledge that has been learned about the physical universe. That body is voluminous and growing rapidly. There is considerably more scientific knowledge today than there was even a generation ago. In 1978, there were 41,000 science research journals. In 1993, there were 29,000 additional journals, representing a 70 percent growth rate over fifteen years (Fort, 1993). Not long ago, entire fields of scientific study such as genetic engineering did not exist. Now, there are genetic engineering professors, genetic engineering conferences, and numerous genetic engineering journals. It is reasonable to expect scientific discovery to maintain this rapid pace and maybe even intensify.

With so much scientific knowledge it is impossible, as in social studies, to learn all there is to know. Therefore, science educators have taught generalizations that will allow students to comprehend and organize scientific knowledge (Duschl & Hamilton, 1992). Generalizations are broad statements that apply to numerous circumstances.

An example of a scientific generalization (or principle or law) is, Objects may be classified according to common properties. The wording in this statement is somewhat abstract and therefore not suitable for presenting to most elementary students. However, young children can learn that the plant kingdom is divided into vascular plants, which have a system of tubes running through them, and nonvascular plants like mosses and fungi, which have no vascular system.

When children move on to the study of animals, they can observe another classification system for vertebrates and invertebrates. A unit on physical science can include the classification of simple and complex machines. Earth science introduces metamorphic, sedimentary, and igneous rock. The applications go on and on.

Generalizations like these are useful because they can be applied in many ways. Facts are useful too, but mostly for learning generalizations. As we saw with social studies, facts are most beneficial when they can be applied to a broader idea. As children apply the concept of classification in each field, their learning of the generalization is reinforced.

Another scientific generalization is, Air exerts pressure. By itself, that is a rather abstract statement that is of little value. However, the concept of air pressure can be related to the power of our lungs, the creation of weather conditions, the popping of the eardrums as we climb or fly, and the ability of balloons to soar above the earth. In essence, the statement is quite useful, but only if it is applied to the types of questions that interest children.

TABLE 6.1. Science Process Skills

Science process skills are divided into two categories: primary and integrated skills. Primary process skills are fairly simple, designed for grades K–3. Integrated process skills combine various primary skills and are emphasized in higher grades.

Primary Process Skills	Integrated Process Skills
Observing	Formulating hypotheses
Classifying	Naming variables
Measuring	Controlling variables
Communicating	Making operational definitions
Inferring	Experimenting
Predicting	Interpreting data
Recognizing space-time relations	Investigating
Recognizing number relations	

Source: Adapted from *Teaching Elementary Science* (6th ed.), by W. K. Esler, and M. K. Esler, 1993, Belmont, CA: Wadsworth.

Science Process

The second crucial aspect of science is process. As in social studies, it is not enough to know facts or even generalizations. If you absorbed all the scientific knowledge there is, would that make you a scientist? Of course not. A scientist, after all, is one who investigates science. Therefore, students must learn the tools of scientific investigation as part of the curriculum.

Consider the example of a class that is interested in weather patterns, as so many children are. Why is the weather different each day? Many skills are involved in solving this problem (see Table 6.1). First, careful observation is involved. The investigators can begin noting subtle weather indicators by observing any variables that could contribute to the weather changes. These observations can then be classified. Two categories might be atmospheric conditions (e.g., humidity, wind, temperature) and geographic conditions (e.g., latitude, altitude, closeness to water). Each observation could involve measurement, another scientific process. As the class performs their observations, classifications, and measurements, an additional process, communication, simultaneously takes place. At this point, the children are ready to make inferences. In our example, the class might infer that high ground temperature and high humidity are associated with thunderstorms. If so, they might make a prediction that a thunderstorm will occur the next time these conditions are present. Predicting is also a scientific process.

Through performing this complex sequence of procedures, the class gains some knowledge about weather. But unlike the knowledge that is gained from, say, a teacher lecture or textbook description, this is knowledge they have constructed, following scientific procedures. This knowledge is not an abstract generalization concerning weather patterns, but is concrete, based on their own experiences.

As important as knowledge of weather patterns may be, of greater value is growth in using skills related to the scientific process. The ability to observe, classify, measure, communicate, infer, and predict will serve students well in further science investigations, and in other school subjects. These same scientific processes are used in social studies when classifying a culture's characteristics, in music when analyzing the components of a musical piece, in math when making a prediction, in language arts when inferring a character's intentions, and in physical education when observing gymnastic maneuvers.

Process also includes thinking skills, such as inquiry. Students must also learn how to ask scientific questions, construct explanations, test them against current scientific knowledge, and communicate their ideas (National Academy of Sciences, 1996). Without reasoning skills, the science knowledge and process skills will make little sense.

Content and process are both important. Is one more important than the other? To clarify the issue, it would be helpful to consider the goals of science education.

GOALS OF SCIENCE EDUCATION

For many years, the science curriculum was based on essentialist philosophy. Students were taught a body of content based on verified knowledge in biology, chemistry, physical science, and so on. In the late 1950s, the emphasis shifted to the science process, reflecting the progressive philosophy (Cleminson, 1990).

Both Knowledge and Process

Today, science educators, including essentialists, agree that the goals of the curriculum include both process and content goals (Fensham, 1993). Indeed, the two can hardly be separated. To learn science content without using the process is like being told the ending of a mystery without experiencing the joy of figuring it out. On the other hand, to learn the process without focusing on relevant content is an empty exercise that lacks meaning and will not motivate the students. Besides, teaching content and process separately is inefficient.

Using process to teach content satisfies the developmental needs of elementary students. The concrete experiences of scientific problem solving make the content more appropriate to the children's levels of thought. Learned content is more meaningful when it comes from the students' own hypotheses and procedures. Similarly, the process of scientific thinking is better understood when applied to concrete problems that interest the children.

Using real scientific thinking to solve real problems promotes an interest in and appreciation of science. Children may learn to literally "stop and smell the roses." They can focus on the science all around us, from bugs crawling on a leaf, to the components of an automobile engine, to the relationship between the moon and the tides. Having the proper content base and a strong foundation in

Theory to Practice
Science

The first graders in Meg Thompson's Charlotte, North Carolina, class have pets in the back of the room. On a daily basis, the class visits the pet area to feed the animals, observe them, and discuss new developments. There is a gerbil, a hermit crab, a snake, and even a tarantula! For the past few weeks, however, some unusual guests are in the spotlight: a collection of caterpillars are forming their cocoons.

The children have watched the caterpillars munch on leaves and gradually increase in size. Each day the caterpillars are measured, in centimeters, and their growth is recorded on a special calendar created for this purpose. A wide range of predictions are made and questions abound. Ms. Thompson knows the answers to the questions, but her job is to facilitate. "We'll see" is her patient response.

Students then return to their tables where they maintain a log that describes what they have seen. Drawing is encouraged, especially for those who are less skilled at writing. The colors of the cocoon receive a particular amount of attention.

Everything stops a few days later when the first "painted lady" emerges. All eyes are riveted as she snacks on a bowl of sugar water. Additional measurement takes place and the discussion shifts to the ethical problems inherent in maintaining butterflies as pets. The class consensus is to set them free after a brief period of further observation.

As with many activities that go on in a first-grade classroom, the children do not even realize that learning is taking place. Ms. Thompson never announced that the class would be doing a science unit devoted to insects, nor did she mention the need to study metrics. One could say, based on the students' response, that the study of science is occurring naturally.

scientific processes enables students to approach a problem with excitement rather than with a shrug. For instance, a child who has recently studied weather patterns may take an independent interest in observing the sky, studying weather maps, and even creating weather instruments.

Science Careers

One major goal of science education is to prepare students for careers in fields related to science (Harms & Yager, 1981). Science-oriented professionals are needed to solve societal problems, create new technology, and generally fill the demand for doctors, engineers, research scientists, and the like. Elementary school is one place that can kindle an interest in science careers, if the proper combination of content and process experiences is provided. To achieve this goal, Bruner (1960) and other theorists proposed that students study the structure of scientific disciplines.

The idea of using the science curriculum as a tool to attract future scientists has received criticism. After all, a vast majority of students will never seek science-related careers. Although few doubt the need for scientific knowledge, there is debate over whether the curriculum should be geared to the education of an elite group (Fensham, 1993).

Science for Everyone

Others argue that science is not just for those who are gifted in the field. Our society requires that all citizens be scientifically literate, capable of understanding and discussing science issues (Boyer, 1983). Thus, the movement to recast the science curriculum to express this orientation is called "Science for Everyone."

Policy Decisions

Consider some of the policy decisions that communities across the nation are addressing: whether to allow garbage burial, including toxic and nuclear wastes, whether to permit human cloning, how to preserve natural resources ranging from ancient forests to endangered species to mineral deposits, how to prevent pollution, how to prevent AIDS, whether to use chemicals that are linked to cancer. These examples merely scratch the surface.

Because these decisions have profound implications for the quality of life on our planet, including financial, environmental, and health consequences, they must be carefully considered by the citizens in our democracy. The public decision-making process can be influenced through individual and community action. Unfortunately, only 5 percent of the nation may be regarded as scientifically literate (Fort, 1993).

Normally, when one thinks about policy decisions, political science and history are usually considered. However, knowledge of social studies is not sufficient for making the right choices. Often, scientific data must be examined. This requires knowledge of both science content and scientific processes. Those who fail to follow the arguments because of their lack of scientific literacy may be shut out of the debate.

We should not let citizens who are not scientifically literate make decisions for us. For instance, to those who operate on the premise of "out of sight, out of mind," dumping wastes in the sea is not a threat to their lives and livelihood. Yet anyone who has studied the water cycle is aware that today's ocean water is tomorrow's food supply. People must also understand and consider such scientific factors as the frequency of undersea earthquakes, the inclusion of marine animals and fish in the food chain, and the characteristics of toxic chemicals.

It is interesting to note that the factors discussed in our waste example cut across scientific disciplines. Earthquakes are usually studied in earth science, the food chain in biology and zoology, and toxic chemicals in chemistry. This exemplifies the integrated nature of science. Recognizing this interrelationship of scientific disciplines allows us to apply multiple perspectives to a problem; this is another important aspect of the study of science.

Personal Decisions

Knowledge of science is not essential just for making societal policy decisions. Personal decisions are also based on scientific data. The seemingly inconsequential matter of choosing a T-shirt on a warm day involves scientific considerations concerning the cooling properties of cotton versus synthetic materials, the ability of those two fabrics to stay wrinkle-free, and the durability of the garments. Science is involved in many aspects of everyday life, including cooking, selecting cleaning materials, choosing sports equipment, packing fragile objects, and gardening. There is hardly a room in the house or an activity of the day that does not involve scientific content and processes. Students with a good science education will make well-informed decisions that affect their time, energy, and pocketbooks.

HEALTH

The most important personal aspect of scientific awareness is health. All health decisions are based on scientific data. Of course, we rely on experts to help us through the more dangerous and confusing health issues, but those experts cannot advise us on every personal decision. Even for those topics that do require professional assistance, we need to be scientifically literate to understand directions and apply them to our particular situation.

New parents are often acutely aware of the responsibilities of health care. They may never have thought seriously about nutrition, skin care, sanitation, safety, and other aspects of health until they begin making decisions for a small helpless human in a crib. Once they recognize their lack of knowledge, they tend to study everything available on the topic. Indeed, new parents may be considered relative experts on health care because they realize that the doctor cannot be called for every little matter.

Making health decisions can be frustrating because scientific findings often change. At one time, being outdoors on a sunny day was encouraged because the sun was considered an optimum source of vitamin C. Today the dangers of direct sunlight are well recognized. When I was a child, wise mothers tried to include eggs in their family menus to provide protein. Now we are told about the dangers of cholesterol in eggs and the oversupply of protein in the American diet.

Do not rail against the inconclusiveness of scientists; instead applaud the ongoing nature of scientific study. We are fortunate that scientists constantly seek a deeper understanding of health to provide us with the most accurate information available. Students who are acquainted with the tentative nature of scientific findings may experience less frustration and more appreciation when the current wisdom is revised and improved.

Health is probably the most immediately practical topic in the curriculum. Fourth graders studying the human body can use new knowledge about the structure of the muscular system the next time they do stretching exercises before physical activity. A lesson on the nutritional value of various foods can be applied in the cafeteria; a discussion of mental health can be used in students' personal relationships.

Human growth is a fascinating science that incorporates a lot of mathematics.

Integrating Health with Science

A central theme of this book is the integrated nature of knowledge. Nowhere is this more evident than in health. Although the topic has often been taught alone, health education experts have been arguing for a model in which health content is included with other subject matter (Redican, Olsen, & Baffi, 1986).

The possibilities for integration abound. A social studies lesson on the Middle Ages might address the various plagues and epidemics of the period. As the discussion focuses on the way diseases are transmitted, students may not even be aware that they are learning about sanitation and other aspects of preventive health care. A math lesson on decimals might introduce the concept of blood alcohol levels (e.g., .08 or .10), which are used to assess whether drivers are intoxicated. A reading selection might include a character who suffers from mental illness. Physical education, of course, is closely connected to health issues.

Ultimately, any discussion of health becomes a science lesson. The two subjects are inextricably linked. To truly understand any health issue, students must focus on the scientific causes and effects, and the processes used to arrive at a knowledge of those causes and effects. When students are lectured on the dangers of smoking, for instance, the impact of the message tends to be weak. However, examining what happens when tobacco smoke is blown on a slide of live paramecia vividly demonstrates the relationship between smoking and poor health. In performing such an experiment students not only gain a deeper knowledge of science, but they also engage in scientific thought.

Knowledge of scientific processes is particularly useful when new health claims are publicized. Individuals must be cautious in accepting the validity and reliability of medical findings, especially when the findings are popularized in the media. Research conducted on rats, for example, is often used to develop preliminary hypotheses about effects on human health. News reporters often overlook the limitations of such studies and directly link the findings to particular human behaviors. Scientifically literate people can recognize the limitations in such studies and are less apt to jump on the bandwagon. Indeed, skepticism is an important aspect of science and health that should be encouraged by teachers.

SCIENCE STANDARDS

In 1996, the National Academy of Sciences issued a series of standards to assist state and local school systems in the development of a curriculum for science. These standards are designed to highlight and promote outstanding science education, bring coordination, consistency, and coherence to the improvement of science education, and provide criteria for judging progress toward national goals (National Academy of Sciences, 1996).

While the standards address such issues as assessment and the preparation of science teachers, the chapter on content is most useful in understanding changes in the elementary school science curriculum. They are divided into three levels, K–4, 5–8, and 9–12. Within each level, there are eight categories. Table 6.2 lists the standards for the first two levels.

The standards for science content probably differ substantially from the curriculum that you experienced in school. That difference was intended by the National Academy of Sciences when it issued its standards. See Table 6.3 to identify the nature of the proposed changes in emphases for science education.

TABLE 6.2. Science Standards

Unifying Concepts and Processes	Earth and Space Science Standards
Levels K–4 Systems, order, and organization Evidence, models, and explanation Change, constancy, and measurement Evolution and equilibrium Form and function *Levels 5–8* Same as K–4	*Levels K–4* Properties of earth materials Objects in the sky Changes in earth and sky *Levels 5–8* Structure of the earth system Earth's history Earth in the solar system
Science as Inquiry Standards	**Science and Technology Standards**
Levels K–4 Abilities to do scientific inquiry Understanding about scientific inquiry *Levels 5–8* Abilities to do scientific inquiry Understanding about scientific inquiry	*Levels K–4* Abilities to distinguish between natural objects and objects made by humans Abilities of technological design Understanding about science and technology *Levels 5–8* Abilities of technological design Understanding about science and technology
Physical Science Standards	**Science in Personal and Social Perspectives**
Levels K–4 Properties of objects and materials Position and motion of objects Light, heat, electricity, and magnetism *Levels 5–8* Properties and changes of property in matter Motions and forces Transfer of energy	*Levels K–4* Personal health Characteristics and changes in population Types of resources Changes in environments Science and technology in local challenges *Levels 5–8* Personal health Populations, resources, and environments Natural hazards Risks and benefits Science and technology in society
Life Science Standards	**History and Nature of Science Standards**
Levels K–4 Characteristics of organisms Life cycles of organisms Organisms and environments *Levels 5–8* Structure and function in living systems Reproduction and heredity Regulation and behavior Populations and ecosystems Diversity and adaptations of organisms	*Levels K–4* Science as human endeavor *Levels 5–8* Science as human endeavor Nature of science History of science

Source: Adapted from *National Science Education Standards*, 1996, Washington, DC: National Academy Press.

TABLE 6.3. Changing Emphasis

Less emphasis on:	*More emphasis on:*
Knowing scientific facts and information	Understanding scientific concepts and developing abilities of inquiry
Studying subject matter disciplines for their own sake	Learning subject matter disciplines in the context of inquiry, technology, science in personal and social perspectives, and history and nature of science
Separating science knowledge and science process	Integrating all aspects of science content
Covering many science topics	Studying a few fundamental science concepts
Implementing inquiry as a set of processes	Implementing inquiry as instructional strategies, abilities, and ideas to be learned
Demonstrating and verifying science content	Investigating and analyzing science questions
Getting an answer	Using evidence and strategies for developing and revising an explanation

Source: Adapted from *National Science Education Standards*, 1996, Washington, DC: National Academy Press.

You may conclude, after reading about the science standards, that you are not adequately prepared to teach science with such different emphases. You are not alone. Most teachers who have taught and been taught under essentialist principles face the same challenge. The National Academy of Sciences (1996) is well aware of that problem, and have therefore issued standards to govern teacher training and in-service in the same document.

The ripple effect of the proposed science standards illustrates how difficult it is to achieve curriculum reform. It involves more than just changing content and emphasis. Thus, as you will read in Chapters 13, curricular reform requires a careful, systematic effort by educators who seek to improve the quality of education, not just in science, but across the curriculum.

SPECIAL INTEREST GROUPS' INFLUENCE ON THE CURRICULUM

Among the numerous influences on the curriculum are tradition, testing policies, textbooks, and classroom management concerns. But in science and health, additional special interest groups, many outside the field of education, have contributed to the debate on the nature of the curriculum.

Corporations

Industrial organizations support science education as a way to attract bright students to careers in science and technology. Corporations have a great deal of power and they have considerable financial resources to promote their views, both in the public and governmental sectors. They also influence job creation and the general health of the economy. When large corporations call for changes in the curriculum, the public is likely to listen. Their influence, in great part, explains why preparation of future scientists has been regarded as the science curriculum's primary goal (Harms & Yager, 1981).

Many corporations are also interested in promoting the public's general scientific knowledge. Most societal decisions on science issues have a substantial effect on business. The issue of toxic wastes is of prime concern to the chemical and power industries, for example, and governmental investment in AIDS research is of interest to the drug industry. These industries produce educational materials, such as films and brochures, that are distributed to schools. Many teachers rely on these materials, despite their usually one-sided presentation of the issues, because the materials tend to be well written, up-to-date, and free. Teachers who are hesitant to present propaganda can maintain balance by providing alternate viewpoints and encouraging critical thinking. Teachers should not, however, accept the validity of corporate-produced materials simply because of the prestige of the company providing them.

Professional Organizations

Significant influence is also wielded by organizations of science-related professionals such as the American Medical Association. Members of these organizations can afford to support political and public relations campaigns related to education. The high status of their professions brings automatic legitimacy to their views. These organizations are interested in maintaining the importance of their fields. The school curriculum serves as an excellent vehicle to achieve their goals.

Corporations and professional organizations have worked to redesign traditional vocational education courses into technology-oriented ones (Fensham, 1993). Interestingly, some theorists envision technology as a separate subject, independent of science education (American Association for the Advancement of Science, 1989). New York State already requires such a course for middle school students (Fensham, 1993).

Government

It is not surprising that governmental mandates continue to affect the science and health curriculums. The government has long had a strong interest in science and health education. The launching of *Sputnik* in 1957 was seen as a national crisis for the United States, requiring action by national political and military leaders. In recent years, technological advances by various Asian nations, especially Japan, were again viewed as indications of American educational weakness. Unfortunately, educators bore the brunt of the criticism, despite the complex economic, political, and cultural factors that influenced the situation. Politicians were quick to propose governmental solutions to the problem, putting much of their emphasis on the science curriculum. As the American economy becomes increasingly dependent on scientific and technological progress, we can expect continued governmental influence on what is taught in science.

Teacher Organizations

Governmental action on behalf of science education has been supported by teacher organizations, including general teacher groups like the National Education Association and American Federation of Teachers. The most influential organizations, however, are composed of science educators. Science teacher associations, like their counterparts in other subject areas, publish journals that include research reports on the curriculum and essays arguing for particular points of view. They hold conferences and workshops to discuss and disseminate new ideas. Their leaders are usually active in national dialogues concerning the curriculum, and their lobbyists are often represented in local, state, and national deliberations.

Teacher association support for educational reform proposals can be influential in the adoption of new curricula, but the most crucial contribution teachers can make is in implementing the curriculum. As we have seen in Chapter 4, it is in the classroom that curricular reform efforts have broken down. The members of the National Science Teachers Association (NSTA), who have a strong interest in the field, may be active in curricular reform, but their enthusiasm does not necessarily flow to the everyday teacher, especially at the elementary level. Middle and high school teachers dominate subject area organizations such as the NSTA. Few elementary teachers are apt to join an organization focusing on science, and they are probably not familiar with trends in the field. Yet they must be included in any decisions to change the curriculum (Connelly, 1972).

University Professors

The most prominent educators fighting for science education in the 1960s were from the universities. The leadership of such research scientists as Zacharias and Karplus added legitimacy to the work of their less-renowned colleagues in the K–12 and teacher education communities. Ironically, academic scientists have fought against the more recent proposals to reshape the curriculum to emphasize scientific awareness for everyone. The professors object to the requisite dilution of traditional science content. After all, most professors and scientists are experts in one field such as biology or chemistry. They are uncomfortable with a cross-disciplinary approach (Fensham, 1993).

Environmental Groups

Environmental groups hope to use the science curriculum to galvanize public concern for what they view as dangerous environmental practices. Most of the leading environmental organizations conduct workshops, publish educational materials, and take part in political lobbying to influence science education policies. As with the curricular materials produced by corporations, teachers must be cognizant of the potential for bias.

Feminist Organizations

Feminist organizations have been concerned about the weak representation of women in science careers. They have promoted programs that attract girls to the field of science and that attempt to eliminate some of the obstacles that discourage female participation in science courses (Linn & Hyde, 1989). Many of these efforts have been endorsed by educational organizations (National Research Council, 1987).

One of the proposals is to change science from a more "analytic" curriculum to a more "nurturative" one, that would presumably be more appealing to females. This change would include the science-for-everyone orientation plus more interaction, cooperation, consideration of ethical issues, and respect for subjective and irrational forms of knowledge (Manthorpe, 1982). Many educators have cautioned that the lack of science interest is not limited to females (Fensham, 1993). Thus, a recasting of the curriculum may be useful for both sexes.

Other Public Interest Groups

Other public interest groups taking part in the formulation of science and health education policies have delved into more controversial territory. When the topic of sex education is considered, for instance, the school board is likely to hear from local church leaders and the regional chapter of Planned Parenthood. Despite the perception that public outcry prevents the implementation of sex education programs, forty states either require or encourage them (Donovan, 1992). Perhaps the poll results indicating 85 percent support for such programs among the general public (Donovan, 1992) have convinced educational leaders that the loudest objections are likely to come from a small minority.

The Public

Another influential group is the general public. Despite the urgings of political and economic leaders, many people do not consider science an important school subject. Unlike the influence of other groups, however, public disinterest has more subtle effects. When the school budget is being prepared, disinterested citizens do not call for more science equipment. If an elementary teacher omits science from the curriculum, parents do not complain. Their disinterest probably flows from an essentialist orientation and upbringing; for them, science involved only dull memorization and was not emphasized like the so-called basics.

The Media

Many of the science topics that students find most exciting are not part of the official curriculum. When a popular science fiction movie calls attention to the possibilities of alien life forms, robotic police officers, or giant, mutant insects, children's interest in science begins to grow. The same phenomenon occurs throughout society when best-selling books, newspapers, magazines, and television documentaries explore the possibilities of reincarnation, telepathic communication, superhuman powers, or miracle drugs.

All of these topics tend to be part of the null curriculum. They are not discussed in elementary schools because the science curriculum is overwhelmingly focused on proven knowledge, rather than mystical or spiritual topics that may be deemed controversial. It is ironic that schools choose to bypass science topics that lend themselves to animated discussion of scientific principles and processes. Teachers who are committed to scientific learning could contribute to society's understanding of these issues by incorporating them into the science curriculum. Despite the fear that inclusion in the curriculum may serve to promote nonrational topics, teachers may also help students (and their parents) learn how to analyze false and misleading statements and identify poorly designed research studies. In general, they may help to develop better consumers of scientific ideas.

While the media has played a powerful role in the public's fascination with scientific issues, it cannot legitimately be called a special interest group in terms of the elementary school curriculum. Unlike other special interest groups discussed in this chapter, mass media companies do not seem to be attempting to influence what is taught in schools. But they may do so in the future.

Conclusion

Special interest groups seem to place a much higher value on science than those who are less directly involved. In addition, there is generally more emphasis on the formulation of the science curriculum than on its implementation. Elementary teachers are, therefore, not under much pressure to teach science. Those who dislike or feel uncomfortable with the topic—possibly two-thirds of elementary teachers (Fort, 1993)—can probably avoid teaching it. Those instructors who consider science to be valuable will teach it in order to reach the goals identified earlier in this chapter. In other words, the teacher is the ultimate decision maker as to the science curriculum.

Questions

1. What was the emphasis of your science education? How has that emphasis helped or hindered you?

2. Of the various goals of science education, which are most important? Why?
3. What is your opinion on the influence of special interest groups on the science curriculum?
4. Which of the changing emphases for science content will be most difficult to achieve? Why?

References

AMERICAN ASSOCIATION FOR THE ADVANCEMENT OF SCIENCE. (1989). *Science for all Americans.* Washington, DC: Author.

BOYER, E. (1983). *High school: A report for the Carnegie Foundation on Secondary Education in America.* New York: Harper & Row.

BRUNER, J. (1960). *The process of education.* Cambridge, MA: Harvard University Press.

CLEMINSON, A. (1990). Establishing an epistemological base for science teaching in the light of contemporary notions of the nature of science and how children learn science. *Journal of Research in Science Teaching, 27,* 429–447.

CONNELLY, M. (1972). The functions of curriculum development. *Interchange, 3,* 161–177.

DONOVAN, P. (1992). Sex education in American schools: Progress and obstacles. In F. Schultz (Ed.), *Education 93/94* (pp. 188–190). Guilford, CT: Dushkin Publishing Group.

DUSCHL, R. A., & HAMILTON, R. J. (1992). Introduction: Viewing the domain of science education. In R. A. Duschl, & R. J. Hamilton, (Eds.), *Philosophy of science, cognitive psychology, and educational theory in practice* (pp. 1–16). Albany: State University of New York Press.

FENSHAM, P. J. (1993). Science and technology. In P. W. Jackson (Ed.), *Handbook of research on curriculum* (pp. 789–829). New York: Macmillan.

FORT, D. C. (1993). Science shy, science savvy, science smart. *Phi Delta Kappan, 74,* 674–683.

GOODLAD, J. (1984). *A place called school.* New York: McGraw-Hill.

HARMS, N. C., & YAGER, R. E. (1981). *What research says to the science teacher* (Vol. 3). Washington, DC: National Science Teachers Association.

LINN, M., & HYDE, J. (1989). Gender, mathematics, and science. *Educational Researcher, 18,* 17–19, 22–27.

MANTHORPE, C. (1982). Men's science, women's science: Some issues related to the study of girls' science education. *Studies in Science Education, 9,* 65–80.

NATIONAL ACADEMY OF SCIENCES. (1996). *National science education standards.* Washington, DC: National Academy Press.

NATIONAL RESEARCH COUNCIL. (1987). *Women: Their underrepresentation and career differentials in science and engineering.* Washington, DC: National Academy Press.

REDICAN, K. J., OLSEN, L. K., & BAFFI, C. R. (1986). *Organization of school health programs.* New York: Macmillan.

CHAPTER 7

Language Arts

If you ask average citizens about the goals of an elementary school language arts program, the answers are usually simply stated. They will say that children should be able to do the following:

- Read
- Communicate their ideas orally
- Listen and understand what they hear
- Write clearly and legibly

A multitude of language goals are reached when students share their writing with their peers.

These goals have been the foundation of American language arts instruction since the early days of schooling. But, critics ask, are they enough? By reading, do we mean simply pronouncing the words on the page? Shouldn't we be concerned about the ability to comprehend complicated ideas? Then there is a matter of what students read. Should it be limited to fiction? What about reading material such as instruction manuals, poetry, political commentary, and academic discourse?

As for oral expression, how broadly do we want to define the term? Does it include being able to answer questions in class, present an argument to a public group, and perform a dramatic role?

Is listening merely a matter of paying attention? Is listening to a story the same as listening to an argument? What about listening to instructions?

In writing clearly and legibly, are we merely talking about handwriting? Does writing include writing a business letter? Does it include creative expression? Are spelling and handwriting equal in importance to the ideas that are being expressed? Or is one more important?

These questions demonstrate the inherent conflict between the various curricular philosophies. The bottom-line question, as always, is, What are we trying to achieve?

Essentialists are those who seek competency. To them, language arts is a collection of discrete skills that one masters. Teachers must teach those skills to students until they demonstrate competence. Once competence is achieved, students are then presumed to be capable of successfully participating in society.

A second answer comes from a different group of essentialists, those who seek to pass on the American cultural and literacy heritage. They, too, seek competence. But, for them a mastery of skills is not enough. They want students to develop a solid grounding in appreciation for the great works of literature. If all Americans share this understanding, they argue, the nation will be united and citizens will be equally able to succeed.

A third answer is offered by progressives, who are process-oriented. They claim that knowledge of language is constructed, not taught. They want students to grow in their ability to use language. Those who do so, they believe, should be able to demonstrate competence as well as an appreciation for the great works of literature (Farrell, 1991).

Finally, there are reconstructionists, who prefer a critical theorist approach to language arts. Like progressives, critical theorists support the notion of students constructing their knowledge of language, but they go further. Critical theorists want students to be able to analyze a piece of language for any covert assumptions and values (Eisner, 1994). They teach students to consider how the orientation of an author influences the things he or she writes or says.

Each of these schools of thought emphasizes a different orientation toward knowledge and toward the goal of education. We will see that, within each component of the language arts curriculum, these philosophies come to the fore. We will also see how changes in our society may prescribe a different orientation to language arts.

READING

Many Americans see the teaching of reading as the primary purpose of elementary schools. Some even see it as the sole purpose. In one respect, our achievements in literacy are impressive. Fewer Americans are functionally illiterate than ever before. On the other hand, the overall level of reading skill has not risen appreciably (Stedman & Kaestle, 1991). Students also appear to have little interest in reading literature (Speigel, 1981).

Analysis of reading skills has led to a fierce debate over the reading curriculum. One group argues that reading skill is not improving because children are not learning phonics. Phonics is the skill of relating sounds to letters. Proponents of phonics believe that systematic instruction in phonics will give children the foundation for literacy. They believe that a lack of phonics instruction results in a failure to properly read the words on the page, resulting in a society of nonreaders who are frustrated by the reading process (Langer & Allington, 1992).

Critics of phonics claim that the study of letters and their sounds is not interesting to children. They claim that youngsters get so bogged down in deciphering words that reading becomes a tedious chore instead of delightful communication. They cite the evidence that students spend little time actually reading during their so-called reading instruction. Instead, they mostly work on completing worksheets that focus on specific skills (Langer & Allington, 1992).

Much of the debate over phonics has hinged on the definition of reading. If it is defined as merely reading the words on a page, phonics is quite useful. However, comprehension of what one reads is also a major reading goal. One must engage in reading, and not just complete worksheets, to develop such skills as following narration, understanding characters, seeking the main idea, and forming conclusions.

Reading and Whole Language

Reading experts have proposed several alternatives to phonics over the years. The popular alternative today is the whole language approach. Whole language advocates see reading as just one part of the entire spectrum of language skills. This approach will be described throughout the chapter.

To make their point, whole language advocates compare the reading process, which is systematically structured, to the development of oral language, which is relatively ignored by educators. Children experiment with spoken language; they do not master pronunciation of each individual sound in successive fashion. Whole language proponents argue that children should use the knowledge of language that they bring to school to engage in "literary events," which are any activities related to language. Through these events, children will increase their knowledge of letters, words, and other aspects of the reading process, (including phonics!) while they participate in activities that are meaningful to them.

As you have seen in other subjects, the philosophy to which one subscribes is essential in determining curricular goals. Teachers can best develop their reading curriculum when they know what goals they wish to reach. Therefore, further examination of the language arts curriculum is in order.

ORAL LANGUAGE

Children come to school knowing how to speak. Anyone who has conversed with kindergartners, however, knows that they tend to be weak in such skills as describing, organizing ideas, and providing support for an argument. For instance, young children are apt to refer to "that thing over there," instead of using adjectives and landmarks to help the listener locate an object. Similarly, they are likely to answer "Because" instead of explaining their thoughts. Children need instruction and practice in developing oral language.

Unfortunately, the elementary curriculum does not provide sufficient opportunities for developing oral language (Pinnell & Jagger, 1991). Ironically, speaking is increasingly discouraged as students progress through school (Olson, 1977).

Oral Language and Whole Language

Under a whole language format, children are encouraged to speak to each other. Advocates believe that such speaking activities

1. permit experimentation and practice using oral expression,
2. provide the opportunity to practice listening to others,
3. allow children the chance to study other students' oral expression,
4. provide practice in relating written language to oral language,
5. provide exposure to the ideas of others,
6. permit children to use language in a variety of contexts, and
7. encourage experimentation with one's own ideas (Pinnel & Jagger, 1991).

The orientation of whole language toward oral expression demonstrates its alignment with progressivism. Consider the differences between whole language and traditional approaches in Table 7.1. The emphasis on student-centered construction of knowledge reflects a difference in philosophy, not just method.

Critics of whole language sometimes get the impression that teachers merely let children talk in the belief that the unstructured discussion, by itself, will promote competence in oral expression and listening. Although some children are able to intuitively develop their oral expression skills, planned activities are necessary (Rubin, 1985). For instance, studying a videotape of Martin Luther King, Jr.'s, "I Have a Dream" speech allows children to construct their knowledge of effective public speaking. The teacher structures the activity by preparing materials, helping the students analyze what they have seen, and arranging opportunities to practice applying their ideas.

TABLE 7.1. Some Differences Between Whole Language and Traditional Language Arts

Whole Language	Traditional Language Arts
Students construct their knowledge of language.	Students are taught languages rules by others.
Students use language in natural circumstances.	Students give oral reports and speeches that are artificially arranged.
Students constantly interact while the teacher serves as facilitator.	Students listen to the teacher.

One aspect of oral language that is rarely used in schools is improvisational drama (Stewing, 1986). In improvisational drama children develop their own stories and characters rather than merely reading from a script. Although there is strong support for theoretical claims linking drama with growth in other aspects of language, there is not enough empirical support to conclude that one causes the other (Wagner, 1991). Improvisational drama fits the whole language orientation by incorporating many aspects of language (drama, characterization, writing dialogue, oral expression, nonverbal expression) as well as such nonlanguage curriculum components as social psychology and the arts.

LISTENING

Learning activities require listening more than any other means of communication. Therefore, as expected, listening is linked to school achievement (Devine, 1978).

Listening and Whole Language

In a whole language classroom, with its heavy emphasis on children speaking to one another, students will also receive needed experience in listening. Experience, however, is not enough. Substantial data support the use of training in increasing listening comprehension (Pearson & Fielding, 1982).

This idea is often surprising to teachers, who tend to neglect instruction in listening (Strother, 1987). To assume that children only use their ears to listen is to ignore the central cognitive component of the act. Consider some of these listening subskills: attending to cues, identifying the main idea, considering the speaker's intent. They are all significant cognitive factors in the process of comprehending speech. Of course, these skills are also crucial in reading comprehension, thus supporting the concept that whole language cuts across the various language arts. Despite this overlap, specific focus on listening is the best way to promote achievement in that area (Pearson & Fielding, 1982).

In a whole language curriculum, teachers have the opportunity to focus on children's listening. They can assess weaknesses and provide instruction. Both these aspects of the teacher's role are crucial in the lower elementary grades when the amount of listening is highest and understanding others' speech is thus most important.

WRITING

Writing is a complex skill, involving numerous subskills. In the traditional elementary language arts curriculum, each subskill receives separate attention. In accordance with this approach, students may have separate textbooks and report card grades for spelling, handwriting, grammar, and creative writing. In this section, each major subskill will be examined individually.

Spelling

The most important thing to know about skill in spelling is that it is a function of reading ability. Good readers are usually good spellers. Why? Because success in spelling is a function of familiarity with language, or more specifically, with orthography, the graphic representation of the spoken word (Ehri, 1987). One of the methods for spelling correctly, for example, is visualizing the word. Which of these is the correct spelling for a disease of the lungs?

1. emfizema
2. emphysema
3. emphyzema
4. emphosema

If you have never seen the word, you have no way of determining that number 2 is correct. The same problem occurs for children who read below grade level. They cannot identify a correctly spelled word if they have never seen it in written form. Those of us who recognized the correct spelling of emphysema probably relied on past experiences of seeing that word in print.

Usually all children in a class work from the same grade-level speller. It is therefore likely that a number of words on the list will be ones that have yet to appear in some children's reading. Students reading below grade level will fail spelling, and the better readers will have no trouble.

Of course, the relationship between spelling and reading is not a simple one. Research on spelling indicates that individual reading strategies (Frith, 1978), proofreading skills (Personke & Knight, 1967), and word memory (Perin, 1982) also enter into the equation. Most of these factors are related to problems in orthography (Hodges, 1991).

Spelling and Whole Language

The problem with spelling instruction is that it is often isolated from the reading and writing process. Perhaps you know someone who made numerous spelling errors when writing but excelled at the Friday tests. Writing a list of spelling words from memory is not the same as real writing. This issue exemplifies the debate over whole language. Rather than isolate the skill, whole language spelling becomes a component of the writing process, which is related to the reading process, which is related to oral language, and so on.

Another whole language issue addresses the developmental nature of spelling. Research on novice spellers (Hodges, 1991) shows that they go through the stages identified in Table 7.2. Because of educators' growing awareness of spelling development, the idea of "invented spelling" has become popular. With invented spelling students are encouraged to spell the word without worrying about correctness. This method achieves a number of goals:

1. Children whose spelling is not yet in the derivational stage are not penalized for failure to use correct spelling patterns.
2. Children who are below reading level are not penalized for misspelling words they have not seen before.
3. Children practice their phonetic skills by attempting to spell a word the way it sounds, even if the spelling is incorrect.
4. Children are free to focus on the ideas in their writing instead of being distracted or discouraged by technical matters.
5. Rather than pestering a teacher for the correct spelling of a word, children learn to rely on their own judgment.

Invented spelling, like whole language, is a reflection of progressivism. Spelling is learned through experience; students construct their knowledge

TABLE 7.2. Stages in Learning to Spell

1. Prephonemic—using letters arbitrarily to make wordlike configurations
2. Early phonemic—one or two letters are used to represent whole words
3. Letter name—sounds are represented by a letter's most common sound or by the letter's name
4. Transitional—most sounds are written correctly, but many are phonetically logical but incorrect
5. Derivational—patterns and conventions are mastered, but words are not viewed as members of families

as they learn to solve problems. Studying words—their structures, origins, roots, and patterns—encourages the development of generalizations that can be applied during the spelling process.

Some adults fear that with invented spelling children will never learn proper spelling. Keep in mind that invented spelling is an aspect of the *early* elementary curriculum. As children grow in their abilities to read and spell, more emphasis is placed on developing generalizations that will promote correctness. That transition often occurs in second or third grade, when children are mastering decoding skills. In the beginning, spelling is logically viewed as less important than written expression. Accordingly, spelling is now frequently regarded as an upper elementary subject, much like long division. Deemphasizing its role in the early grades allows space in the curriculum for addressing more appropriate knowledge and skills.

Grammar

Grammar is the structure of language. It has long been viewed as a prerequisite to successful written expression. Few among us cannot recall analyzing sentences by underlying subjects, predicates, or objects. Decades of research, however, show that such study has little effect on writing skill (Hillocks, 1986). To add to the problem, teachers persist in teaching the same skills year after year (because their students did not appear to have learned them previously), thus consuming major portions of the language arts curriculum (Smith, Goodman, & Meredith, 1984).

Grammar and Whole Language

The research does not support discontinuing grammar instruction. The problem has been that grammar is usually taught out of context as a discrete set of skills. If it is directly related to the writing process, important lessons can be immediately applied. For example, run-on sentences are typical in elementary students' writing ("I went to the store and I saw my friend and we went over to the park and . . ."). It makes perfect sense to teach the grammatical structure of sentences to students who have this problem. If they learn that a sentence usually has one subject clause, they can recognize when to begin a new sentence.

As with spelling, development is an important factor in teaching grammar. Most grammatical knowledge is abstract. Thus, concrete learners may memorize the various rules but not be able to understand them or apply them when putting pen to paper. Discussions of grammatical terms are more appropriate in later grades when students are more comfortable with the writing process and better able to handle abstract thought.

Spelling and grammar are technical aspects of the writing process. They become important when written work is being polished, not in the early stages of composition. Whole language has encouraged that viewpoint by linking the technical aspects of writing to the overall writing process. Thus students are encouraged to attend to mechanics in the final drafts of a work. The first drafts focus on ideas, so students are free from being distracted by minor matters.

Handwriting

Handwriting is another technical aspect. Like spelling and grammar, it is less important during the drafting process, although it receives a significant share of the time devoted to primary grade language arts. To understand why, let us analyze the nature of the traditional elementary language arts classroom.

Until the 1930s, handwriting was a separate subject (Hodges, 1991). As such, it was given a major block of time and a separate line on the report card, and textbooks were specifically designed for that subject. As we have seen, traditions do not die easily, especially in education. Although most teachers now regard handwriting as part of language arts, the time allotment, textbooks, and report card line may remain. Those three factors influence each other. Given an expensive textbook, many educators assume that it is to be used (Froese, 1981). Similarly, the line on the report card implies that students should receive regular instruction and evaluation in this area.

Another throwback from the earlier years is cursive writing, which many of us know as script. It was only in the 1930s that manuscript writing, or printing, was developed to aid students in their reading. It was believed that learning to write the letters as they appear on the printed page would help bridge the gap between reading and writing (Farris, 1993). Manuscript was also better suited to the slowly developing fine motor skills of young children (Farris, 1993). Note that this approach reflects a whole language orientation long before the approach became popular.

It might be wise to discontinue the teaching of cursive writing. But traditions die hard. Despite the conviction of some that cursive writing can be done more quickly and easily than manuscript and is easier to read, there is not research to support this (Koenke, 1986). Examine your own writing. Do you write in cursive, manuscript, or a combination of the two? The fact that many of us do not write in cursive is an indication that it is not faster or easier to write or read.

A major reason for teaching two handwriting styles is that children consider cursive writing to be something that adults do (Farris, 1993). Therefore, they are eager to learn it. It is gratifying to see students motivated to learn any aspect of language, but you must recognize the drawbacks. First, there is the time element. Every minute that is spent learning a second way to write means less time for the rest of the curriculum. Educators must decide: is cursive writing more important than oral expression or mathematical problem solving or student-directed research (to name three activities that are often neglected because of time)? A second drawback is the developmental factor. The students who are slow in developing their fine motor skills, usually boys, finally will be mastering manuscript when they are told to drop it in favor of cursive writing.

Is it fair to require cursive writing? Is it necessary? Can it be an elective, like playing a musical instrument? Here, too, is a curricular decision that has serious ramifications for students.

Handwriting and Whole Language

As with any skill, the development of good handwriting requires practice. Thus, you will frequently find primary grade students hunched over their desks as they complete a daily handwriting assignment. Many times those assignments involve copying sentences from the chalkboard (e.g., Today is Tuesday, May 11. It is cloudy outside. Tomorrow we go on a field trip.). At other times, students are to copy from a textbook, often in conjunction with grammar instruction (e.g., John went to the circus with [me/I].).

Teachers recognize the benefits of handwriting practice, but they also may value activities that keep students occupied for long periods of time, such as when reading groups require direct instruction for more than an hour. Handwriting (and, later on, much of the rest of the language arts curriculum) may become busywork, which is of little educational value but keeps students engaged.

Although busywork may aid classroom scheduling, it is detrimental to student motivation, interest in language, and school in general. It does not take long for a school-age child to recognize that busywork is boring and does not appear to have any practical use outside of school. Copying from the chalkboard, diagramming sentences, and making sentences out of spelling words are not adult activities. The only reason to participate, therefore, is to receive a good grade or avoid punishment. Intrinsic rewards are absent.

Consider the ultimate goal of the handwriting curriculum, which is to have students write legibly. Traditional handwriting instruction had focused on five key elements: letter formation, spacing, slant, letter alignment, and quality of line (Hodges, 1991). Certainly, these factors are essential if a writer wants readers to understand what has been written. After all, an *a* that looks like an *o* or writing so small that it cannot be deciphered is of little value. However, it is possible to be overzealous in evaluating children's handwriting. Forcing all children to conform to a single style may interfere with individuality and creativity. For instance, penalizing a child for harmlessly making capital letters distinctively wide sends a message that there is only one way to write. Obviously, all of us develop our own individual writing styles. Teachers must be careful not to use handwriting instruction as an exercise in arbitrary power, but instead promote legibility without impeding children's self-expression.

The difference between traditional and whole language handwriting programs is in their purpose. In the whole language approach, children develop good handwriting habits because they care about the legibility of their letters, stories, and reports. They write legibly because they do not want others to have difficulty reading what they have proudly written. Compare that to traditional handwriting activities in which there is no audience for the students' written work.

Writing

Many of the technical aspects of language come together in the writing process. Under optimum circumstances, students apply their constructed knowledge of spelling, grammar, narrative, and other skills to communicate in written form. Writing is a time to play with ideas, develop creativity, and organize thoughts. We learn from writing at the same time that we learn how to write.

The topic of writing is often subject to narrow interpretation. Some teachers define it strictly as creative writing, meaning stories, drama, and poetry. Students, however, should learn to apply poetic expression to all forms of writing, including reports, business letters, and even Post-it notes. Poetic expression is written work that can stand alone and be appreciated for its intrinsic value. Thus, despite its name, it includes prose as well as poetry.

Theory to Practice

Language Arts

In her third-grade class in Charlotte, North Carolina, Donna Weaver centers a portion of her curriculum around the book *My Father's Dragon* (Gannet, 1948). In the book, a classic in children's literature, a young boy travels to a tropical island to rescue a dragon.

The author provides a map in the front of the book to illuminate the boy's situation. Children must develop map skills to track the boy's progress and propose solutions to the problems he faces, such as whether to cross a river filled with crocodiles or walk around a long peninsula. A great deal of discussion is held as the entire class tries to reach a consensus on the best course of action.

Because the setting is a tropical island, a number of geographic concepts are concretely presented. By using the illustrations, the map, and verbal descriptions, the children truly learn the meaning of terms such as island, peninsula, swamp, and river.

A follow-up art assignment has students creating their own islands. Using techniques of design, they plan the features of the island before they build it.

Spelling words appropriate for third graders are pulled from the story. Writing assignments have children exploring the genre of adventure stories. Of course, the narrative features of plot, characterization, and description are explored throughout the unit.

Needless to say, the children love learning in this fashion. *My Father's Dragon* is an excellent choice for the focus of a whole language unit, but so are lots of other books. Teacher planning is the key.

Another narrow view of writing in traditional classrooms sees writing as answers to textbook questions, essays, and filling in blanks on a ditto sheet. In this type of writing, there is little opportunity for self-expression (Applebee, 1984).

Writing and Whole Language

In the whole language classroom, writing is integrated throughout the curriculum. Students do not write for the sake of writing. Instead, they use writing to respond to content in a variety of contexts. A student's daily writing might include a personal journal entry reacting to a piece of sculpture, a research plan for a science experiment, a letter to a city official concerning a community issue, step-by-step directions for solving a mathematical problem, and a story that fits the tall tale genre.

This approach to writing stands in sharp contrast to the traditional language classroom, in which "all writing is really a series of 'dummy runs'—writing being produced mainly as exercises on which the writer is to be judged (and usually convicted)" (Butler, 1991, p. 101). In whole language classrooms, the focus is on the writing process, and evaluation is based on how well the written assignment reflects the author's intentions and satisfies the audience's needs.

HOW TECHNOLOGY IS CHANGING THE LANGUAGE ARTS CURRICULUM

Chapter 2 examined the influence of technology on children's lives and, in turn, on the curriculum. Technology also has a direct effect on the curriculum in general and language arts in particular.

Much technology deals with the communication of information, which is a subcategory of language arts. A visit to the library provides an example. Instead of the cumbersome card catalog of yesteryear, you will find yourself using a computer terminal to find information about library holdings. Having ready access to more details about each item and being able to use multiple methods of searching make using the library much simpler and more efficient.

How does this change affect the curriculum? It is no longer necessary to teach about card catalogs. That aspect of libraries is nearly obsolete. There is also

a greater need to learn keyboard skills and how to interpret information provided on the computer screen. The curriculum must change with the times.

If your next stop in the library requires use of the *Readers' Guide to Periodical Literature,* the large reference book that lists magazine and journal articles by topic, you may be better off using Info-Trac, ERIC, or other CD-ROM software. This technology is remarkably more efficient and informative than the old method of searching through volumes of yearly and monthly indexes. Here, too, the curriculum must adapt.

Examining materials is also easier. Many library systems allow users to view materials on the computer screen. With remote access technology such as the Internet, the user does not even have to be in the library to view certain materials! Researchers have immediate access to photographs, computer graphics, television videos, sound recordings, and reams of statistics that are housed in government offices.

As a result of these technologies, conducting research is no longer a lengthy, tedious affair. For elementary students who may not have access to major libraries or who lack sophisticated reading and research skills, the joy of discovering information on their own can become part of school life. Teachers can no longer claim that they would like to teach research skills, but lack the time and materials to do so. As media collections grow and change, independent study and small-group investigations can become part of the classroom routine instead of a yearly project. The process of inquiry can become a major part of the curriculum.

As we collect our library materials, we may notice that we don't have to rely on reading skills as much. To research a report on a piece of literature, for example, the student can observe a television production of it, listen to a radio review, or view a videotape of an expert discussing the work.

Indeed, more and more information is presented through nonprint means. Language-based materials such as books, articles, analysis, and criticism are no longer beyond the reach of poor readers. For example, some computer programs now "speak," and can assist readers who are confronting unfamiliar words by pronouncing them. Even instructions are available in video form. Complex tasks like putting a bicycle together or wallpapering a room can now be viewed, rerun, and even set in slow motion to provide a perspective that was unavailable through the world of print.

At one time, most people learned about current events by reading the daily newspaper. Today, television is the medium of choice. A large portion of Americans do not even subscribe to newspapers or weekly news magazines (Stedman & Kaestle, 1991). Quite a few people hear about the news only when they watch late-night television comedians do their monologues! Reading skill is not essential to become minimally familiar with current events.

Advances in media permit communication of pictures, animated images, film, and video over a computer screen as well as the television. Major companies often advertise their products using video cassettes sent by mail, thus bypassing the television networks. Fax machines can receive images over the telephone lines.

These developments have a number of implications. For one, like it or not, reading ability is becoming less important. One can still become fairly knowledgeable about the world with less than adequate reading skills. This is not to say that reading need not be taught. It remains a primary method of receiving information, especially when depth is required. The recreational benefits of reading poetry and novels may never be replaced. However, it is fair to say that reading is no longer all-important. It may have to give up some of its share of curricular time.

Another implication is that the language arts must include more instruction in "reading" images. With the growing use of nontext communication, viewers need to develop their skills in interpreting, appreciating, and evaluating different types of visual messages. Political advertisements, commercials, and television film clips must be carefully analyzed if the viewer is to avoid being manipulated. This is a new area requiring the attention of elementary educators.

Finally, schools must recognize that gathering information from the Internet or CD-ROM is so easy that students may not even read the material that is copied! At least, under the old technology, students had to take notes and organize them. Software can now do that for the students. Schools today must help students become ethically responsible in their data collection and reports. Otherwise they may conduct research but learn nothing from the process.

As we wrap up our library trip, it becomes time to present reports on our research. New technology no longer limits reports to the standard term paper. The old options have been expanded considerably. Software programs permit the development of animated cartoons, posters, maps, video excerpts, mock newspaper reports, slick magazine articles, and more. Low-cost video cameras, editing facilities, and recording devices allow for multimedia presentations. Writing a term paper may become an anachronism.

Even for those who choose the traditional methods, however, there are modern options. Obviously, the word processor makes the writing process infinitely easier. It only takes a move of the mouse to rearrange a paragraph. Experiments in organization, style, and mechanics can be conducted without the danger of having to invest time and effort in copying if the result appears unsuccessful. The presence of spelling checks, grammar and usage checks, built-in dictionaries and thesauruses, and other proofreading software allows the writer to focus on the message, knowing that technical matters will, to some extent, take care of themselves.

These developments may transform the language arts curriculum. As access to word processors grows, there is less need for handwriting skill. Children must still learn to write legibly by hand, but the skill will be less important. There will be the occasional shopping list, letter from camp, and birthday card, but most school and office work will surely be performed on keyboards.

Of greater importance will be the ability to work comfortably in a variety of media, often simultaneously. The widening range of options allows creative communicators to go beyond the old parameters. Student creativity must therefore be encouraged. Even students who adhere to the standard writing process can be encouraged to use the technology creatively.

Another change is a reduced need for instruction in spelling, grammar, and other technical skills. These subjects should not be eliminated, because word processors can only make suggestions. They cannot identify misused homophones, nor can they decide which word best communicates the idea in the writer's head. Ultimately, the writer must make the decisions. Thus some attention to technical matters is necessary, even if it is substantially diminished.

As we leave the library, we must ask ourselves if our current language arts curriculum is adequate. Educators must prepare students to live in the future, not the past. As the world changes, the curriculum must adapt.

STANDARDIZED TESTS

In examining ways in which the language arts curriculum has not adapted to children's needs, we must examine the role of standardized tests. Although such tests have been used for many years, their impact became particularly profound in the 1980s, especially in language arts.

During the so-called back-to-basics movement, standardized tests became "high-stakes" measurements. That term is used to signify examinations whose results are used to make major decisions. For example, many state and district policies decreed that students may not graduate or be promoted, regardless of their classroom performance, unless they attained certain test scores. Another aspect of high-stakes testing is the use of test scores to provide merit pay to teachers and principals. Some states punish schools that perform poorly on standardized tests by firing the principal and requiring teachers to take competency tests. Just the publication of district test scores can raise the stakes if an administrator's job is dependent on positive results. Most high-stakes testing has been instituted to provide accountability to the public, to make sure that educators are doing their jobs properly.

Substantial evidence supports the idea that high-stakes testing has had a major effect on the curriculum. Studying its influence (see Figure 7.1) is helpful in analyzing the pace of curricular change in language arts as well as the other subject areas.

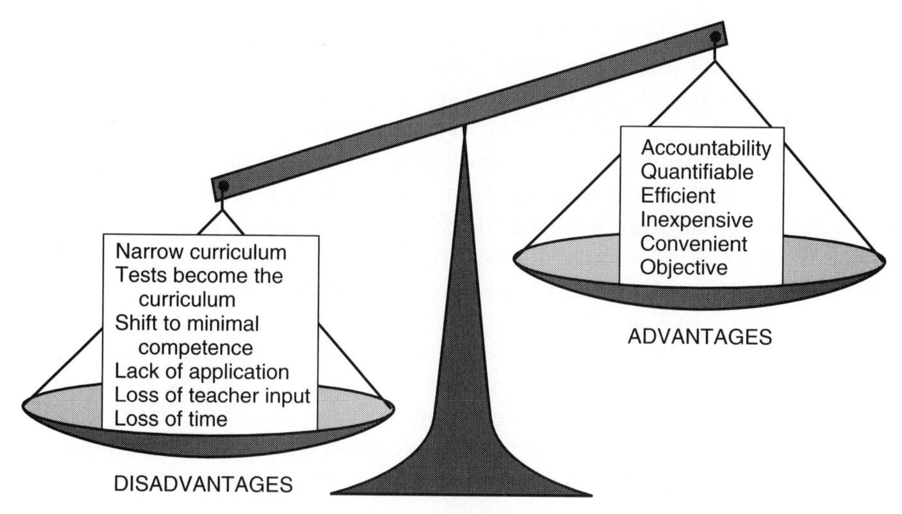

FIGURE 7.1. Advantages and disadvantages of standardized tests.

Negative Developments

The Test Becomes the Curriculum

First, when a standardized test is in place, it is likely to become the curriculum. Teachers may ignore their stated district curriculum if its objectives differ from those being tested. They will also discount their own beliefs about curriculum (Madaus & Kelleghan, 1992).

Applying this finding to language arts, we can see why the teaching of grammar persists. Although many teachers recognize it as ineffective in improving student writing, it receives considerable classroom time because teachers anticipate that students will be tested on grammatical skills such as diagramming sentences. Meanwhile, topics of value, such as oral expression and listening, may get bypassed if students are not tested on those skills.

A Narrowed Curriculum

A second finding, related to the first, is that high-stakes testing narrows the curriculum. When the first high-stakes tests limited their assessment to basic skills in reading and mathematics, the teaching of social studies, science, and the arts was diminished (Stodolsky, 1988). In the same fashion, the tests' emphasis on academic learning shifted some teachers' curriculum away from social, emotional, and physical goals (Madaus & Kelleghan, 1992).

The narrowing of the curriculum has had both positive and negative effects on the language arts. The subject received more teacher preparation, classroom time, and school focus, but the teaching increasingly shifted to cover low-level basic skills.

A Shift to Minimal Competency

This brings us to a third effect of standardized tests: the goals are shifted from maximum performance to minimal competency (Stodolsky, 1988). Many would argue that schools should try to meet each student's needs, but teachers instead feel compelled to bring the greatest number of students above the minimum standard. Thus, in an elementary classroom in which two-thirds of the students read at or above grade level, the emphasis may be on reviewing basic skills in phonics, despite the fact that most students have already mastered them. Writing activities would be likely to focus on avoiding errors in capitalization instead of encouraging already proficient writers to enhance their skills. When the minimum competency test results appear, educators and the public may feel proud of having few students fail, but may be unaware that high-ability students are not reaching their maximum level of capability. High achievers probably consider the basic exercises busywork, and exhibit the boredom and off-task behavior associated with such activities.

Loss of Application

A fourth problem with standardized testing is that classroom activities become geared to testing formats instead of real-life applications (Frederickson, 1984). Evaluating student writing skill, for example, does not lend itself to optical scanning sheets. Handwritten essays require additional testing time, multiple human reviewers, and a lengthy grading and reporting period. There are also problems with validity and reliability. Instead of assessing writing, therefore, test items are often designed to determine whether students can recognize writing errors in a passage. Certainly that skill is related to writing, but it is also quite different from the actual writing process.

Because of the problems in assessing writing using standardized tests, teachers tend to de-emphasize the teaching of writing in favor of activities similar to those on the tests. Classroom time is then spent on activities that may promote high test scores but not help students develop the skills they need to succeed in society. Under a whole language approach, students might engage in small-group discussion to cooperatively write a play. With the threat of high-stakes testing, the teacher may forgo that activity for a lecture on the apostrophe.

The same situation exists for reading, in that reading brief passages for the purpose of answering questions is not the same as reading a book. Thus, the test item may not be a valid indicator of reading achievement. Unfortunately, the influence of these tests may lead to classrooms in which some students never experience the intrinsic joys of reading.

Moving the Locus of Decision Making

Fifth, as we have seen with textbooks, testing allows curricular decision making to be taken out of the hands of the classroom teacher. If teachers teach for the tests, they cannot design the curriculum for students' needs. I know of one teacher who was told by her principal to teach the concept of nouns and verbs to her below–grade-level second graders. When she protested that the children were barely able to decode a sentence, he cut her off: "You have to do it. It will be on the test." As a result, valuable instructional time was devoted to a skill that the students did not need. Their progress in decoding was interrupted to concentrate on a skill they were unlikely to master. In essence, success was replaced by failure for the sake of the test. This can happen when teachers are prevented from using their own discretion. Lowering the stakes would allow teachers to make the curricular decisions they feel are appropriate.

If teachers are not making the curricular decisions, who is responsible for the influence of high-stakes tests? In a sense, all of us are, because we allow this situation to occur. But the specific culprits are those who make the laws and choose the tests, the political and administrative leaders. Those leaders tend to prefer quantifiable, efficient, inexpensive, administratively convenient, and objective ways to solve problems. Standardized testing is perceived by many noneducators as the perfect solution, meeting all those criteria (Madaus & Kelleghan, 1992). The political process of curricular change will be discussed in Chapter 13.

It may be helpful, at this point, to analyze how the topics in standardized tests are chosen. According to court rulings, a test is unfair if it covers topics that were not included in the curriculum that was taught (Madaus & Kelleghan, 1992). Although this is a reasonable principle, it does create problems for curriculum developers.

Teachers occasionally receive surveys from testing companies that ask how much time they devote to various topics. Presumably, those topics will be the ones that the test will measure. Unfortunately, teachers who are already influenced by high-stakes testing will indicate that large portions of time are spent on such topics as grammar and handwriting. Likewise, oral expression and media interpretation will be identified as topics receiving little coverage. The subsequent tests will reflect those time allocations, even if they conflict with teacher beliefs or district and state curriculum guidelines. In other words, we have a vicious cycle, in which the tests influence the teachers, who influence the curriculum, which influences the tests.

Most teachers would agree that an inordinate amount of classroom time is spent preparing for and taking standardized tests (Stodolsky, 1988). Students

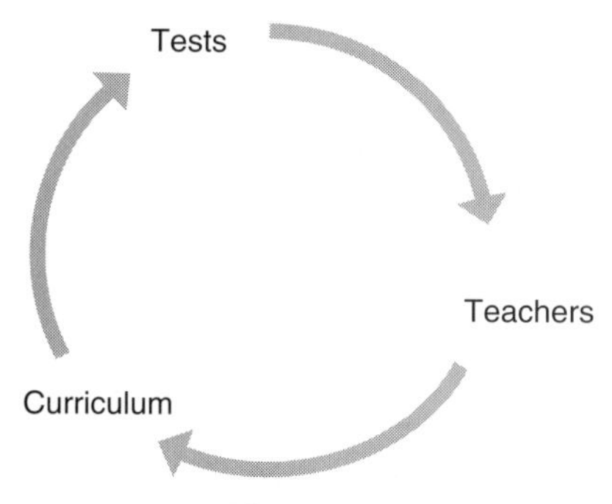

FIGURE 7.2. The vicious testing cycle.

spend hours practicing sample test items and reviewing the basic skills that will be tested. They are also likely to avoid academics during the test-taking period to maximize their alertness. In essence, the curriculum is suspended for this annual ceremony. The dollar cost of this decision has been placed in the hundreds of millions; the educational cost is incalculable (Madaus & Kelleghan, 1992).

Positive Developments

Authentic Assessment

Before becoming discouraged over the negative influence of standardized tests, rest assured that there are a number of positive recent developments. One is that many school districts are aware of the dangers of standardized testing and are moving toward performance-based testing. With performance-based testing, the students actually perform a whole activity, rather than demonstrate mastery of one small aspect of it. For instance, instead of fill-in-the-blank exercises to show how pronouns are used, the students' actual writing is analyzed instead. This can be done under testing situations or from a collection of the student's work kept in a portfolio. Although this assessment method presents administrative difficulties, it is recognized as more valid (Farr & Beck, 1991).

Performance-based testing is sometimes called authentic assessment because it uses authentic tasks instead of highly inferential estimates based on group testing (Meisels, 1993). Although there are several types of authentic assessment, most versions share these goals:

1. using actual student work to evaluate learning,
2. enhancing teacher and student involvement in the evaluation process, and
3. satisfying the accountability demands of the public (Chittenden, 1991).

The Kentucky Education Reform Act of 1990 mandated the use of authentic performance assessment tasks (Melograno, 1994). If other states follow Kentucky's model, many of the drawbacks of high-stakes testing may be minimized.

Redesigned Tests

Another development is that the assessment dilemma has been used to promote positive changes. One of the frustrations of testing and measurement experts is that curriculum development has strayed from the basic model proposed by Ralph Tyler (1949). As we have seen, instead of using the curriculum to design the test, the test is determining the curriculum. In an effort to reform the curriculum, some state education departments have redesigned their tests to emphasize process, higher-level thinking, and performance. By this strategy, they hope that teachers will feel compelled to change their plans to meet those standards.

Some states have changed their curricular standards to emphasize general curricular goals rather than specific facts. Notice the general nature of the state competencies identified in Table 7.3. Test makers can use these broad standards to design test items that are at a higher cognitive level than those on traditional tests.

TABLE 7.3. Sample State Competencies

South Carolina, Mathematics:

Grade 4

Solve problems and make predictions based on collections of data.

Massachusetts, Language Arts

Grades 5–8

Analyze how new words enter languages and how meanings evolve over time.

North Carolina, Science:

Grades 3–5

Observe and investigate the interdependence of plants and animals, including concepts such as food webs, pollination, seed dispersal, and other symbiotic relationships. Through direct and indirect observation discover how common plants and animals are helpful and harmful.

Arkansas, Social Studies

Grades K–4

Illustrate how people, places, events, tools, institutions, attitudes, values, and ideas are the result of what has gone before.

New Mexico, Visual Art

Grades K–4

Understand that works of art come from diverse personal and cultural experiences and inspirations.

Oregon, Reading

Grade 3

Demonstrate literal comprehension of a variety of printed materials. Retell, summarize or identify sequence of events, main ideas, and facts in literary and informative selections.

Educating the Public

Some experts have proposed that the stakes of testing be reduced (Farr & Beck, 1991). Considering that most standardized achievement tests suffer from severe limitations in validity and reliability (Madaus & Kelleghan, 1992), it is probably unfair to make major decisions based on the published scores. At the very least, the media must be educated about the dangers of misinterpreting test scores. Comparison of children, schools, districts, states, or nations can be hazardous without allowing for such major factors as culture, socioeconomic status, and variations in curriculum. The public must be made aware of the limitations of high-stakes standardized testing.

Another fruitful area for change is in the political arena. Because governmental leaders are the ones who ordained the high-stakes tests, they must be the ones to dismantle their creation. Educational leaders continually call for alternatives to the current testing situation. If more teachers raise their voices about the pernicious effects of high-stakes standardized testing, political leaders may choose to listen to them. After all, teachers are the ones who know the situation best. Until those changes occur, the curriculum, especially in language arts, will continue to suffer.

BILINGUAL EDUCATION

The biggest victims of high-stakes standardized testing may be those with limited English proficiency (LEP). Even the brightest of these children will have some difficulty understanding test directions and interpreting reading passages in English. A low test score, which may only reflect unfamiliarity with the language, can lead to inappropriate placement in low-level classes or summer school, or being required to repeat a grade. The self-esteem of a bright student would surely suffer under those conditions.

LEP children may also face an inappropriate curriculum. In a well-meaning attempt to strengthen skills in English, schools are likely to burden the LEP student with phonics and workbook exercises (Wong Fillmore & Meyer, 1992). As discussed throughout this chapter, teaching skills in isolation diminishes student interest and success.

Another harmful effect of standardized testing on LEP students is the reduction of subject-area content. The content areas provide more than specific bodies of knowledge; they also stimulate vocabulary development and discussion. If LEP students are forced to focus on language skills, in what amounts to a back-to-basics program just for them, social studies and science instruction is reduced. They end up studying "how to speak, read, and write English in a learning situation in which there is little of substance worth talking about" (Wong Fillmore & Meyer, 1992, p. 648).

To make matters worse, teachers tend to avoid activities involving higher-level thinking so communication can be kept at a simple level. Thus, mathematical word problems, science experiments, social studies debates, and even great works of literature—the very essence of a high-quality educational program—are not part of the LEP students' curriculum (Wong Fillmore & Meyer, 1992). When some adaptation is made, such as repeating a lesson in the LEP students' first language, instruction in other areas of the curriculum must be reduced; either less content is covered or the coverage is superficial. If the goal of a school is merely knowledge transmission, this is not cause for concern. But the recent emphasis on developing thinking skills means that ignoring this area with LEP students denies them equal opportunity and gives them a second-class education.

The use of these interventions with LEP students has created an unfriendly school environment for recent immigrants. Many already find it difficult to adapt to a new culture. When you add the complications of poverty, as is often the case for first- or second-generation immigrant families, it is a wonder that any students are able to succeed. It is easy to understand the 45 percent dropout rate of Mexican-American students (Gollnick & Chinn, 1990).

A Historical Perspective

As poor as the situation may be for students with limited English proficiency, it has improved. Before 1968, schools used to use the submersion, or sink-or-swim, method, teaching all lessons in English regardless of whether students understood it. Some claim that this was how assimilation took place in earlier periods of American history and regard the method as successful. Unfortunately, as with much of the "good old days" rhetoric, there is little evidence to support this idea. School failure for immigrants was a problem then too (Cohen, 1970).

The situation changed when a lawsuit on behalf of Chinese-speaking children in San Francisco claimed that the schools were not providing equal opportunity for school success. The court ruled that treating everyone the same is insufficient and that special language programs are necessary. After that decision, legislation at the state and federal level mandated bilingual education (Gollnick & Chinn, 1990).

Is Mastery of English a Prerequisite?

As we have seen, the quality of bilingual education today is suspect. Much of the problem stems from the assumption that LEP students must master English before they deal with the rest of the curriculum. This argument has several weaknesses.

Time

Most children need at least four to six years to become competent in English (Allen, 1991). By the time LEP students are ready to move past the basics, they will be in junior high school or else bored and unmotivated.

Cultural Identity

The message that many LEP students receive from school is that their language is inferior and must be replaced. Language is an essential part of one's culture. Replacing it with another language has a negative effect on one's cultural identity (Cummins, 1989). It can also harm relationships between the students and their families and primary communities when different languages create miscommunication (Wong Fillmore & Meyer, 1992).

Language Development

The strongest case against prerequisite mastery of English is the very nature of language learning discussed in this chapter. Success in learning to read is based on one's knowledge of language (Fillmore, 1982). LEP children may not know English, but they know a language. Thus, it makes sense for them to learn to read using the language they know, rather than a new one. For instance, recognizing the written form of *door* is much easier if I know what it means, can use it in context, and am comfortable with the grammatical structure in which it is presented. This position is supported by research showing that what is learned in one language is used in learning other languages

(Engle, 1975). What is more, learning to read in one's native language strengthens skills in both languages (Wong Fillmore & Meyer, 1992).

Dialects

Everybody speaks some dialect of their native language, and the differences between dialects can provide for delightful study of regional influences on language. However, certain dialects are commonly regarded as inferior. For instance, Ebonics, or vernacular black English, is usually corrected by teachers. When one of the 80 percent of African-Americans who speak it (Gollnick & Chinn, 1990) says, "She be here," some form of disapproval will probably follow. Such disapproval, as is the case with LEP students, can be seen as a threat to one's cultural identity. This occurs despite the fact that linguists regard Ebonics as a legitimate form of rule-governed language (Strickland & Ascher, 1992). Other dialects, such as those spoken in the Appalachian region or northern big cities, are also criticized and ridiculed.

The issue of Ebonics, from an instructional perspective, is not whether students should be taught to speak that form of English. Speakers of Ebonics probably do not need further instruction in its use. The issue is whether Ebonics can or should be used to develop students' knowledge of language. Whole language advocates cite research findings that students are less likely to develop their reading and writing skills if forced to do so in an unfamiliar dialect.

Matters of Philosophy

Who is to say what dialects and languages are acceptable? What do we do about LEP students? Can we develop skill in standard English (whatever that is) without harming minority students' precarious sense of cultural identity? The answer to these questions, as always, depends on our philosophical goals. In other words, what are we trying to do in the schools?

A long-standing argument that addresses these issues concerns assimilation versus diversity. Our country's traditional response to minority cultures has been forced assimilation (Gollnick & Chinn, 1990). Hirsch (1987), among others, justifies this approach by arguing that the nation needs a common culture to remain unified. In this spirit, there have been movements to ban all languages but English from public life (Wong Fillmore & Meyer, 1992).

Opponents of assimilation claim that diversity does not rule out unity; it enhances it. Working together toward a common goal unites people. For instance, the patriots of 1776 included those of English, French, Dutch, and Scotch-Irish descent. On the other hand, the Arab world generally has a common culture but still suffers from regional conflicts (Ladson-Billings, 1992).

A good example of unity through diversity is a family. Although the members have different sexes and ages, and various interests and beliefs, they share a number of commonalities that bring them together. Furthermore, they use their different strengths to overcome certain weaknesses. American society, according to proponents of diversity, can operate in a similar fashion. This reflects the vision of our nation's founders: *e pluribus unum,* or "out of many, one." The emphasis on tolerance in our country's basic documents is testimony to this belief.

Educational Application

If the goal of a bilingual program is assimilation, that goal can be reached by transitional programs, but the passage will be a painful one (Wong Fillmore & Meyer, 1992). In a transitional bilingual program, LEP students learn in their native language with reinforcement in English. Eventually, the native language is phased out, which can lead to the type of cultural identity problems discussed above.

If the goal is to maintain diversity while developing skills in English, the curriculum is geared toward maintaining the native language as English is developed. This is called a maintenance bilingual program. This approach contributes to cultural pride and also develops citizens who are fluent in two languages. It is the one most bilingual educators recommend (Gollnick & Chinn, 1990).

Two problems prevent the maintenance bilingual program from being widely implemented. One is the lack of qualified teachers. There may be dozens of languages spoken in a school, and even more in a school district. Not many teachers can offer the kind of instruction demanded by the maintenance bilingual program (Gollnick & Chinn, 1990).

The second problem stems from dialects. A teacher may speak Cantonese, for example, but it may not be the form the student knows. Just as English contains multiple dialects, the same is true for other languages. Providing native language instruction is a challenge, particularly in small school districts. Until these problems are resolved, the transitional bilingual program will remain the norm.

Advantages of Bilingualism

If it can be achieved, bilingualism could provide significant advantages for society. As it is, we spend millions of dollars teaching second languages. International trade and diplomacy are dependent on representatives who can visit another country and speak the language. Bilingualism also contributes to the goals of language arts by developing deeper understanding and appreciation of language in general.

The tenets of bilingualism apply to dialects too. Being able to speak more than one dialect enables people to move comfortably from one social context to another. Ladson-Billings (1992) has described how she is able to assume one dialect in scholarly circles and another when with her African-American cultural group. Former President Jimmy Carter often referred to the differences in his language as president compared to the times he conversed at his brother's filling station in Plains, Georgia. Both examples reflect the importance of language in gaining respect. In the future in our diverse society, having only a single dialect could be a handicap.

To achieve the goal of maintaining a dialect, students must be taught when its use is appropriate. Because prejudice against nonstandard dialects can be harmful in the workplace, schools, and elsewhere, the standard dialect must still be taught, especially in written form. The key is emphasizing that other dialects are legitimate and acceptable in certain situations (Gollnick & Chinn, 1990). This knowledge can motivate students to analyze their own language use and make the proper decisions. However, schools must also make accommodations. Care must be taken to be open to other dialects in word as well as deed. Textbooks, tests, and even offhand comments must reflect acceptance of other dialects.

Multiculturalism

The benefits derived from knowledge and appreciation of other languages and dialects are only one part of multicultural understanding. As indicated in earlier chapters, our society suffers from cultural misperceptions. Maintaining respect for students' native languages as well as their cultures within the classroom can promote the kind of environment that will address this problem.

In a supportive atmosphere, children can learn to appreciate other cultures. This requires using grouping and testing procedures that are sensitive to cultural factors. Learning materials, especially textbooks, must accurately reflect the multicultural nature of society, including problems of discrimination and injustice (Giroux, 1988). Students' backgrounds, interests, and learning styles should be reflected in the choice of topics and activities. In a multicultural classroom, if classroom interaction is student-centered and focused on common goals, intercultural understanding can take place (Ainsworth, 1984).

These improvements demand substantial changes in the way the curriculum is planned and implemented. Many of the requisites of multiculturalism are reflected in other curricular proposals that are discussed in this text. Schools may already be moving in that direction. In the meantime, it is incumbent on individual teachers to develop their own multicultural awareness. Reading about the topic and attending anthropology or world geography classes are two good ways to reach that goal. Studying literature and art from other cultures may also be helpful. The best way, especially in a college environment, may be to develop relationships with classmates and children whose cultures are different from your own. The personal enlightenment and enjoyment you receive from these interactions may even exceed the professional benefits.

Questions

1. In view of technological and educational trends, which language topics should receive more emphasis? Which should receive less emphasis?
2. How did the use of end-of-grade tests affect your education? What role should they play?
3. Where do you stand on the issues of bilingualism and multiculturalism?
4. How would your education be different if your teachers had emphasized authentic assessment.

References

AINSWORTH, N. (1984). The cultural shaping of oral discourse. *Theory into Practice, 23,* 132–137.

ALLEN, V. G. (1991). Teaching bilingual and ESL children. In J. Flood, J. M. Jensen, D. Lapp, & J. R. Squire (Eds.), *Handbook of research on teaching the English language arts* (pp. 356–364). New York: Macmillan.

APPLEBEE, A. N. (1984). Writing and reasoning. *Review of Educational Research, 54* (4), 577–596.

BUTLER, S. (1991). The writing connection. In V. Froese (Ed.), *Whole language: Practice and theory.* Needham Heights, MA: Allyn & Bacon.

CHITTENDEN, E. (1991). Authentic assessment, evaluation, and documentation of student performance. In V. Perrone (Ed.) *Expanding student assessment* (pp. 22–31). Alexandria, VA: ASCD.

COHEN, D. K. (1970). Immigrants and the schools. *Review of Educational Research, 401,* 13–27.

CUMMINS, J. (1989). *Empowering minority students.* Sacramento: California Association for Bilingual Education.

DEVINE, T. (1978). Listening: What do we know after 50 years of research and theorizing? *Journal of Reading, 21,* 296–303.

EHRI, L. C. (1987). Learning to read and spell. *Journal of Reading Behavior, 19,* 5–31.

EISNER, E. (1994). *The educational imagination; On the design and evaluation of school programs.* (3rd ed.). NY: Macmillan.

ENGLE, P. (1975). *The use of vernacular languages in education.* Arlington, VA: Center for Applied Linguistics.

FARR, R., & BECK, M. (1991). Evaluating language development. In J. Flood, J. M. Jensen, D. Lapp, & J. R. Squire (Eds.), *Handbook of research on teaching the English language arts* (pp. 489–501). New York: Macmillan.

FARRIS, P. J. (1993). *Language arts: A process approach.* Madison, WI: Brown & Benchmark.

FARRELL, E. J. (1991). Instructional models for English language arts, K–12. In J. Flood, J. M. Jensen, D. Lapp, & J. R. Squire (Eds.), *Handbook of research on teaching the English language arts* (pp. 63–84). New York: Macmillan.

FILLMORE, C. (1982). Ideal readers and real readers. In D. Tannen (Ed.), *Analyzing discourse: Text and talk.* Washington, DC: Georgetown University Press.

FREDERICKSON, N. (1984). The real test bias: Influence of testing on teaching and learning. *American Psychologist, 39* (3), 193–202.

FRITH, V. (1978). Annotation: Spelling difficulties. *Journal of Child Psychology and Psychiatry, 19,* 279–285.

FROESE, V. (1981). In V. Froese, and S. B. Straw (Eds.), *Research in the language arts: Language and schooling* (pp. 227–243). Baltimore: University Park Press, 1981.

GANNET, R. S. (1948). *My father's dragon.* New York: Random House.

GIROUX, H. (1988). *Teachers as intellectuals.* Granby, MA: Bergin & Garvey.

GOLLNICK, D. M., & CHINN, P. C. (1990). *Multicultural education in a pluralistic society.* Columbus, OH: Macmillan.

HILLOCKS, G. (1986). *Research on written composition: New directions for teaching.* Urbana, IL: ERIC and National Council of Teachers of English.

HIRSCH, E. D., JR. (1987). *Cultural literacy: What every American needs to know.* Boston: Houghton Mifflin.

HODGES, R. E. (1991). The conventions of writing. In J. Flood, J. M. Jensen, D. Lapp, & J. R. Squire (Eds.), *Handbook of research on teaching the English language arts* (pp. 775–786). New York: Macmillan.

KOENKE, K. (1986). Handwriting instruction: What do we know? *The Reading Teacher, 40,* 214–216.

LADSON-BILLINGS, G. (1992). The multicultural mission: Unity and diversity. *Social Education, 56,* 308–311.

LANGER, J. A., & ALLINGTON, R. (1992). Curriculum research in writing and reading. In P. Jackson (Ed.), *Handbook of research on curriculum* (pp. 687–725). New York: Macmillan.

MADAUS, G. F., & KELLEGHAN, T. (1992). Curriculum evaluation and assessment. In P. Jackson (Ed.), *Handbook of research on curriculum* (pp. 119–152). New York: Macmillan.

MEISELS, S. J. (1993). The work sampling system: An authentic performance assessment. *Principal, 72*(5), 5–7.

OLSON, D. (1977). From utterance to text. *Harvard Educational Review, 47,* 257–279.

PEARSON, P. D., & FIELDING, L. O. (1982). Research update: Listening comprehension. *Language Arts, 59,* 617–629.

PERIN, D. (1982). Spelling strategies in good and poor readers. *Applied Psycholinguistics, 3,* 1–14.

PERSONKE, C., & KNIGHT, L. (1967). Proofreading and spelling: A report and a program. *Elementary English, 44,* 767–774.

PINNELL, G. S., & JAGGER, A. M. (1991). Oral language: Speaking and listening in the classroom. In J. Flood, J. M. Jensen, D. Lapp, & J. R. Squire (Eds.), *Handbook of research on teaching the English language arts* (pp. 691–720). New York: Macmillan.

RUBIN, D. L. (1985). Instruction in speaking and listening: Battles and options. *Educational Leadership, 42,* 31–36.

SMITH, E. B., GOODMAN, K. S., AND MERDITH, R. (1984). *Language and thinking in the elementary school* (pp. 155–159, 165–170). New York: Holt, Rinehart & Winston.

SPEIGEL, D. L. (1981). *Reading for pleasure: Guidelines.* Newark, DE: International Reading Association.

STEDMAN, L. C., & KAESTLE, C. F. (1991). Literacy and reading performance in the United States from 1880 to the present. In C. F. Kaestle (Ed.), *Literacy in the United States.* New Haven CT: Yale University Press.

STEWING, J. W. (1986). NCTE centers of excellence: A place for drama. *Youth Theatre Journal, 1* (2), 25–27.

STODOLSKY, S. S. (1988). *The subject matters: Classroom activity in math and social studies.* Chicago: University of Chicago Press.

STRICKLAND, D. S., & ASCHER, C. (1992). Low-income African-American children and public schooling. In P. Jackson (Ed.), *Handbook of research on curriculum* (pp. 609–624). New York: Macmillan.

STROTHER, D. B. (1987). Practical applications of research: On listening. *Phi Delta Kappan, 68,* 625–628.

TYLER, R. W. (1949). *Basic principles of curriculum and instruction.* Chicago: University of Chicago Press.

WAGNER, B. J. (1991). Imaginative expression. In J. Flood, J. M. Jensen, D. Lapp, & J. R. Squire (Eds.), *Handbook of research on teaching the English language arts* (pp. 787–804). New York: Macmillan.

WONG FILLMORE, L., & MEYER, L. M. (1992). The curriculum and linguistic minorities. In P. Jackson (Ed.), *Handbook of research on curriculum* (pp. 626–658). New York: Macmillan.

CHAPTER 8

Mathematics

Why do we need to learn this stuff? That is the plaintive cry of legions of school children when they approach math. The answers they receive are illustrative: "You'll need it when you're older," "You'll need it for the test on Friday," "You'll need it for the next grade level," or (worst of all) "Because I said so!" (Westcott, 1978). These familiar answers demonstrate that teachers often do not know a good reason for teaching mathematics. As a result, they teach it the wrong way, for the wrong purposes, with harmful effects.

Take fractions as an example. Everyone agrees that the learning of fractions is crucial, except perhaps those students who are studying the topic. But what makes it crucial? Let's examine the reasons cited above.

First, there is the matter of needing it when you're older. That's true. Adults do use fractions quite a bit. The applications are endless: in recipes, carpentry, clothing sizes, sports, travel, banking, and so on. But adults are not the only ones who need to learn fractions. Everyone needs it, including children. It's immediately useful.

Second is the argument that the information will be needed for a test. When we make statements like this we are communicating to children that the topic has no practical benefit at all; it is merely something we do in school and then forget. After a while, children absorb this message, which may account, in part, for the lack of motivation and diligence that often emerges during the elementary years.

PEANUTS reprinted by permission of United Feature Syndicate, Inc.

Teachers who motivate by threatening low test scores are doing even further damage. These teachers are promoting the idea that the purpose of education is to get high grades or to avoid failure. There are multiple philosophies concerning the purpose of education, but only cynics would discount the power of knowledge and the joy of acquiring it. Thus, using the test as a threat can obstruct the development of healthy attitudes toward school and learning. This tendency is part of the teacher power game, which will be discussed in Chapter 10.

Knowledge of fractions is valuable. Failing to emphasize the benefits of studying fractions is to miss a powerful teaching opportunity. After all, motivation has been shown to be very effective in promoting achievement. Alerting your students to the usefulness of the topic is a major step in helping them learn it.

The third popular rationalization for teaching fractions is that it will be studied in the next grade level. Some students may conclude that they may as well delay learning about fractions until then since the subject matter will only be useful at that time. Once again, though, we must remind children of the immediate use of whatever we teach. Without application, new knowledge is likely to be forgotten.

As for the argument, "Because I said so," this point is as weak as the learn-it-for-the-test argument. Teachers should not use their power to intimidate when they could be inspiring their students.

WHAT SHOULD BE EMPHASIZED IN MATHEMATICS?

The progressives called attention to the immediate use of knowledge. They stressed that "childhood is for itself and not a preparation for adult life" (Johnson, 1926). Even those opposed to progressivism would agree that mathematics is useful in the daily lives of children. The issue is one of emphasis: which uses are most important? An examination of this issue will clarify the purposes of mathematics education.

The "Transfer" Argument

One often-heard argument is that mathematics teaches us how to think. By learning the process of solving an equation, it is said, we become better able to use logic in solving other problems. We become more intelligent. A good mathematician would, thus, be successful in other subject areas. This concept, whose roots are in perennialism, is known as "transfer."

The idea of transfer was extremely popular at the turn of the century. The concept was also used to justify the teaching of Latin and the diagramming of sentences. Although the argument appears logical, like many other beliefs about education, it has not been supported by research. When educators began to use standardized tests to measure student learning, they discovered that there was no transfer. Children who had studied complex mathematical content did not improve their scores on intelligence tests compared to those who did not learn the math. The same was true for studying Latin and the diagramming of sentences. In addition, student performance in math did not carry over into other subject areas. To plan a curriculum for mathematics, we must find a better rationale.

The "Everyday Use" Argument

The most popular argument for mathematics is that we perform basic mathematical calculations each day. We need to know how much change we should get when we pay with a dollar bill. We must follow the directions on a recipe that calls for a specific measurement, such as half a cup of flour. We need to be able to tell time, divide a pizza into equal portions, and know when halftime occurs. All of these examples, by the way, are as relevant to children as they are to adults.

No one would dispute the need for such mathematical knowledge. But doesn't it seem odd that we spend an hour a day, every school day for twelve years, to learn it? These simple calculations do not require a lot of teaching time. Surely, mathematics has some more valuable use that can justify the inordinate amount of time that is devoted to the subject (Westcott, 1978).

The "Math As a Way of Thinking" Argument

The daily-use argument is primarily an essentialist one. Learning simple addition, subtraction, multiplication, and division gives us the skills to balance our checkbooks and manage our everyday lives. However, critics of essentialism claim that we set our sights too low. They argue that we must go beyond the basics to enable students to become effective members of society. They see math as a way of thinking that helps us understand issues and solve problems. Consider some of the following societal concerns.

Budgets

For many years, Americans have struggled with a massive federal budget deficit. According to some politicians addressing this issue, we merely need to tighten our belts a bit. For instance, some candidates promise to solve the problem by reducing congressional salaries. How much would that save? The entire federal legislative branch cost $2.2 billion in 1997, including about $71 million for congressional salaries. To many citizens, $71 million sounds like a substantial amount of money. It is. Unfortunately, it is less than one-tenth of one percent

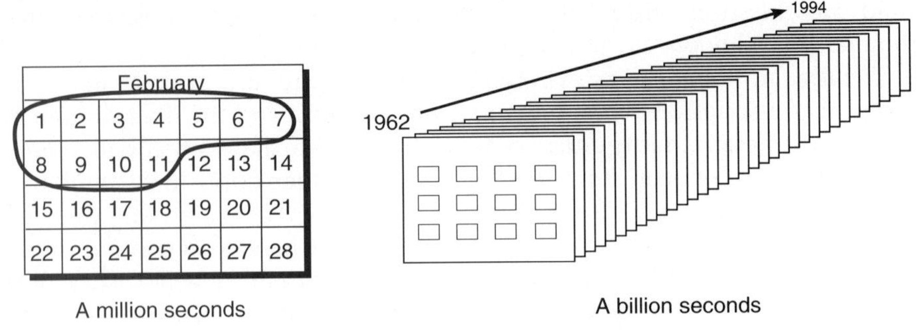

FIGURE 8.1. The difference between a million and a billion.

of the deficit, and an even tinier part of the $1.6 trillion (Office of Management & Budget, 1998) overall budget. All too often, however, the public responds favorably to such inadequate proposals. (Numerous other examples of proposed cuts, to foreign aid, funding for the arts, and public works projects, also receive inordinate attention given their relatively minor impact on the deficit.)

Politicians are able to confuse us on issues like deficit reduction because we do not understand the numbers. We are able to perform simple arithmetic, but too many of us do not know the difference between a million and a billion. We confuse the two, as if they were nearly equivalent. Think of it this way: A million seconds is equal to eleven and a half days, while a billion seconds is the same as thirty-two *years!* (Paulos, 1990) (see Figure 8.1).

Large numbers are abstract. We cannot get a concrete grasp of them as we can with small numbers. Teachers probably taught you how to name millions and billions by abstractly counting zeroes rather than working with concrete examples. This type of instruction, which ignores developmental considerations, accounts for the pervasive curriculum disability that is associated with mathematics.

Safety Threats

To many non-educators, schools seem like terribly unsafe places. To some degree, that perception is caused by the new media. A violent incident on school grounds is likely to be reported in newspapers and on television newscasts in at least a hundred-mile radius. A steady stream of such reports can easily cause one to believe that violence is rampant in the schools and that student safety is at risk.

How serious is school violence? Charlotte, North Carolina, where I live, is on the border between North and South Carolina. The local news media will probably report on violent incidents occurring in a school in either state. That encompasses roughly 4000 schools, including 2000 public schools in North Carolina and 1100 in South Carolina, plus hundreds of private schools across the two states. Thus, every incident only involves 1/4000 of schools in the region, indicating a .00025 chance of the incident occurring in any one school. This miniscule number may reassure parents that the public perception of unsafe schools is greatly exaggerated.

Another common exaggeration concerns missing children. Well-meaning adults constantly emphasize the need to avoid talking to strangers and warn children never to get into unfamiliar cars. Yet in 1992, of the 800,000 children under the age of 18 reported missing, only 300 were taken by total strangers! Almost all missing children are abducted by family members or are runaways (Lee, 1993). Unfortunately, that information has not gotten through to parents and teachers who regard abduction by strangers as a serious threat. Similarly, many people are overly alarmed about the dangers of terrorist attacks, communicable diseases, and major surgery.

Why are people so often fooled by numbers? It may be our unfamiliarity with the problem-solving process. As students, many of us received little or no practice in solving real problems. The exercises at the end of the chapter in a math book usually dealt with simple situations, such as selling one or two apples for ten cents each, not with matters of genuine concern to children. Performing a meaningless problem-solving exercise enables children to practice basic skills, but it doesn't prepare them to address the kinds of issues they care about. Wouldn't it be better to calculate the amount of trash the school produces on a daily basis or how expensive it is to clean up after vandals? This kind of calculation is immediately valuable.

Consumer Awareness

When money is scarce, individuals must be careful in their spending. A foolish decision can cost a fortune. Few adults cannot identify a major financial blunder or two in their lives. For instance, the cost of houses and automobiles is so high that a careless choice can cause financial difficulties that may take years to overcome. Thus, it is in society's interest to help citizens invest their money wisely.

Children do not spend at such high levels, of course, but their need to make wise choices is just as important. When you only have ten dollars, even a toy or movie ticket can be a major purchase. Having empty pockets is devastating, no matter how much you had when you started.

I can recall being fooled by misleading advertisements as a child. The television commercial that stressed the price of a toy as "only $4.95" implied that the product's value was much greater. The plastic piece of junk I bought was not worth it, but my money was already gone.

When merchants advertise "25% Off!" what does it mean? A careful shopper checks whether the reduction is based on the list price (which is almost always higher than the regular price) or the ordinary retail price. Careless shoppers may be so excited about their imagined savings that they never realize they were cheated.

Some advertising is blatantly dishonest in its use of numbers. Perhaps you've seen signs for prices "up to 25% off." That means there may be only a few items marked down 25 percent while most of the items may have smaller reductions or even none at all. A sweepstakes mailing whose envelope proclaims "You may have won," is saying that winning is possible. Only the small print reveals that the chances of winning are, in effect, smaller than the chance of being struck by lightning. However, accepting the negligible chance of success requires understanding the numerical information that appears in the advertisement.

Too many of us avoid analyzing numerical claims because we believe the numerical reasoning behind them is too difficult to understand. While statistical reports can be abstract and dull, in most cases, as in the examples cited above, understanding the reasoning behind them does not require a college degree.

Unfortunately, matters of probability and real-life mathematical application are frequently passed over in elementary schools. The longer problem-solving exercises are commonly offered only as a bonus for extra credit. Students who dislike having to think through such problems will clearly communicate their feelings about the dreaded word problems. Teachers who share their discomfort may also look for ways to avoid teaching mathematical reasoning. Together they conspire to eliminate it from the curriculum! For instance, I have had teachers who offered to skip assigning word problems for homework if the class behaved!

Overall, schools communicate the message that mathematical thinking is extraordinarily difficult and should be reserved for those who are gifted in the subject. Instead of learning the process of solving problems, students receive the dubious favor of being exempted from hard work. Children think they are getting a break, but they will end up paying for their lack of mathematical reasoning skill in the long run. The irony is that math can add clarity and depth to one's thinking when it is applied to real issues. Like the shoppers who thought they were getting a great deal, the students may never realize how they were cheated.

Information Overload

Do you ever feel as if you are overloaded with information? So much so that you have difficulty making decisions? You are not alone! In this new Information Age, we have access to data on every imaginable subject. For example, it is no longer simple to choose the right foods. We have access to nutritional labels that list cholesterol content, calories, fat content, fiber, additives, and other ingredients (see Figure 8.2). If analyzing this information wasn't complicated enough, we are also inundated with conflicting reports about the effects of diet on health. It seems that fat is related to obesity, but some fats are helpful in preventing disease. How does one decide? Some people have given up trying to figure it out.

Moving from the individual to the societal level, citizens are confronted with a myriad of choices when it comes to making public policy. For instance, most scientists believe that improving the environment requires cleaner automobile fuel emissions. Yet some economists tell us that automotive industry jobs will be lost by such a change. Some commentators argue that the environment cannot be sacrificed in the name of jobs. Others claim that air quality is not yet at the crisis stage. Then there are those who believe that improving the environment will create new jobs that will offset the projected industry losses. The average citizen is understandably confused.

To analyze these and the thousands of other issues that must be confronted, we must rely on the objective testimony of those who are more knowledgeable than ourselves. But these experts do not simply tell us what to do. Instead, they present their findings with mathematical reasoning. Thus, we hear that people who have low-fat diets have less chance of suffering from heart disease than those who do not have such diets. Or we hear that the air in a major city can become 50 percent cleaner with higher auto emission standards. Those who have difficulty with math are not likely to benefit from these expert findings.

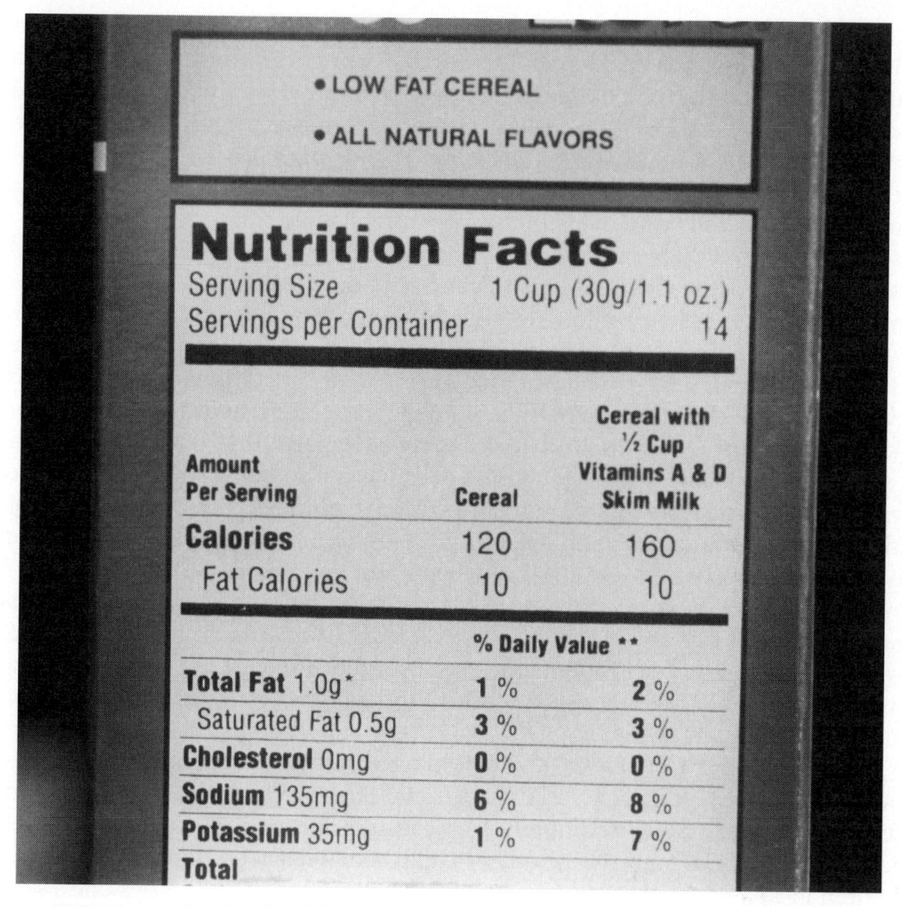

FIGURE 8.2. Staying healthy requires being able to make sense of this label.

Unfortunately for nonmathematical citizens, almost all expert inquiry is conducted and presented using math. Most complex relationships can be reduced to mathematical formulas to provide clarity. Using mathematical reasoning, claims can be tested. Thus, in a sense, mathematics is a tool for testing reality, but it is only for those who can follow the reasoning!

Look around to appreciate the importance of mathematics in everyday life. The light from the lightbulb that is helping you read has been measured in lumens to assess how much brightness is actually provided. A bulb manufacturer cannot claim to have a brighter bulb without proving it mathematically. The furniture on which you sit has been tested by engineers to determine how much weight it can support. These measurements take place mathematically on paper before production begins. The weight and thickness of the paper in this book is mathematically evaluated by the publisher to insure that it can withstand the heavy use that comes from being used as a textbook. A paperback novel or children's book has different paper standards.

Think about other standards. The speed limit on highways is based on calculations that include accident rates, road-grading variables, and pedestrian safety factors—all of which are determined mathematically. When you applied to get into college, all sorts of numbers were examined, including test grades, class rank, grade point average, the rating of your high school, and your qualifications to receive financial aid. If you submitted an essay or appeared for an interview, those too were measured according to some numerical system.

As a teacher, you must constantly consider educational research findings. At one time, much of teacher education was based on a collection of commonsense anecdotes. Only in the past few decades has educational research examined the claims of veteran teachers and professors. It turns out that many long-held assumptions are untrue. For instance, it has been determined that repeating a grade level tends to be ineffective in helping youngsters achieve, ability grouping is unlikely to reduce the gap in student learning rates, and that diagramming sentences does not make for better writers. Despite the seeming logic behind those original ideas, the numbers do not support the claims. Yet teachers who do not understand mathematics are likely to avoid looking at new research data. They continue to implement ideas that have been proven ineffective.

If you choose to ignore the role of mathematics in your life, you will be frustrated. You won't be able to follow the reasoning of scientists, governmental officials, television advertisements, or even weather forecasters. You will be at a disadvantage as a consumer, as a worker, and as a citizen. This is the case for a large portion of our society.

Identifying our collective mathematical weakness helps us understand why so many people make poor individual and societal choices. The inability to understand a problem, analyze data, or comprehend the results of a study leads to helplessness. Helpless individuals must rely on others to tell them what to do, as if they were small children incapable of reason. Giving so much power to others destroys one's sense of autonomy, self-esteem, and ability to make the best choices for oneself. It also leads to corruption among leaders who do not have to undergo the scrutiny of citizens. The dangers of a nonmathematical society are formidable indeed.

So, why do we have to learn this stuff? Not for the test, not for next year, not to learn how to think, and not to perform simple everyday calculations. We need mathematics to solve problems—financial, professional, personal, or societal. We need math to determine what is true. Without it we are a society that cannot use the knowledge it has produced.

WHAT DO THE EXPERTS RECOMMEND?

The National Council of Teachers of Mathematics (NCTM) has issued a set of standards to guide the mathematics curriculum (1989). This group, composed of classroom teachers, college professors, school district administrators, and others interested in mathematics education, hopes that its vision will encourage local school districts to improve their mathematics programs. Although specific grade-level standards are provided, the guidelines have four basic cornerstones:

1. *Mathematics as problem solving*—formulating and solving problems, not just mathematical ones, and developing confidence in the ability to use mathematics meaningfully.
2. *Mathematics as communication*—communicating in various modes, not just numbers, to understand and get meaning from mathematics.
3. *Mathematics as reasoning*—using both inductive and deductive approaches involving investigation, forming and testing conjectures, making and evaluating logical arguments, validating one's own thinking, and appreciating mathematics' contribution to sense-making.

Theory & Practice

Mathematics

When the fourth graders at Idylwild Elementary School in Gainesville, Florida, produced a literary magazine, they wanted to sell copies of it. The profits, they decided, would go toward a pizza party.

How much should they charge? The teacher let the students decide. He had them get into small groups to calculate the cost of the pizza.

"How many do we need?" they immediately asked.

"Figure it out," was his answer.

After much consultation within and between groups, it was decided that each child would have two slices of pizza. Further discussion led to the conclusion that 8 pizzas would be needed for the 32 students in the class (32 people × 2 slices = 64 slices; 64 slices ÷ 8 per pie = 8 pies).

"Doesn't the teacher get any?" they were asked. They decided to order 9 pizzas, with any extra going to the principal, who, after all, would have to approve this exercise in capitalism.

In 1981, when this activity occurred, a pizza cost $5. Thus, students needed to earn $45 (9 pizzas × $5 = $45).

The next decision concerned demand. How many issues of the literary magazine could they sell? Each class member confidently predicted selling five to gullible family members (32 × 5 = 160). Plus, they figured that everyone else in the fourth grade would want one (96 × 1 = 96). Then they determined that half of the other 500 or so students in the school might also buy one (500 × $\frac{1}{2}$ = 250). Careful addition led to the decision to produce 500 copies (160 + 96 + 250 = 506).

The mathematical wizards had already anticipated the next step: with 500 copies, what price would earn them $45? With pencils flashing, they determined that nine cents would do the trick ($45.00 ÷ 500 = $.09).

"Not so fast!" the teacher cautioned. "We have to subtract the cost of the paper. How much paper do we need?" They returned to their groups and figured 16 pages times 500 equals 8,000 sheets. That sounded like a lot. At that point, a few students were ready to settle for a single slice of pizza.

An emissary was sent to the office to find out the price of paper. "Mrs. Holder says we can have it for free!" was the gleeful report.

After a concerted advertising campaign, the magazine sold out in about an hour at ten cents per copy. (The extra penny was the teacher's idea to avoid giving change.) The pizza was delicious. Unfortunately, no one thought about a tip for the delivery boy. He didn't want one of the magazines, so the teacher paid the tip from his own pocket. It was worth it.

4. *Mathematical connections*—appreciating the integrated whole of mathematics as well as the connections with other areas of human thought and activity (NCTM, 1989).

To clarify these standards, it may be helpful to consider some of the changes that would occur if they were implemented.

Changes

Reduced Emphasis on Computation

One major change would be a reduced emphasis on computation. Various studies on the issue show that computation consumes approximately 75 percent of classroom time (Porter et al., 1988). Leaders in the field argue that spending less time on paper-and-pencil calculations would enable students to practice equally valuable skills in mental computation, estimating, and problem solving (Coburn, 1989).

This change is designed to strengthen computation skills by encouraging teachers to develop the underlying concepts through student reasoning about real problems. In the past, teachers have complained about the rush to quickly develop computational skills, often at the expense of deeper understanding. One proposal would make multiplication with a two-digit multiplier a grade 4–5 skill, instead of expecting it to be mastered in fourth grade. This adjustment would allow more time for application and also help reduce the repetition that plagues this subject area (Coburn, 1989).

Frequent Use of Calculators

Another change would involve more frequent use of calculators. Calculators, after all, are designed to make calculations more quickly, easily, and accurately than paper-and-pencil operations. These advantages account for their overwhelming popularity.

Some critics argue that calculator use would result in students' excessive dependence on machines to do mathematics. Yet proponents of increased calculator use make exactly the opposite argument. They claim that freeing the student from mind-numbing, time-consuming exercises in such operations as addition with numerous addends and long division would grant them more opportunity to focus on the nature of the problems, estimating probable answers, and, especially, problem-solving applications. Thus, calculator use would shift the emphasis from performing paper-and-pencil computations to problem solving. Except for unusual circumstances, our society no longer requires skill in doing basic calculations; problem-solving ability is the demand (Coburn, 1989).

Many teachers prefer to teach students addition, subtraction, multiplication, and division before involving them in problem solving (Good, 1979). This approach was criticized by Dewey (1933) many years ago because the emphasis on learning those basic operations promotes mechanical imitation rather than using one's intelligence to figure them out.

Of course, no one is arguing that calculators should replace students' experiences with basic calculations. Experts agree that students must understand the processes involved in basic algorithms before they can ask the calculator to perform them. But students can use the calculator to study how multiplication works or how fractions can be presented as decimals. It can be a tool for learning, not just an answer machine.

THE GAP BETWEEN THE INTENDED CURRICULUM AND THE ACTUAL CURRICULUM

The reasons for curriculum gaps are complex. Multiple forces operate to prevent implementation of the intended curriculum. This problem is more pervasive in mathematics than any other subject area (Romberg, 1992). Many of the issues introduced below are also discussed elsewhere in the text.

Content Perception

One factor is the teacher's perception of content. As we have repeatedly seen, teachers who see mathematics as a collection of mechanical operations are not likely to create the kind of atmosphere that promotes reasoning, communication, and problem solving through connections with other subject areas (Bishop & Nickson, 1983). Contrary to common belief, this situation is not limited to elementary educators. Ball (1990) discovered that even math majors viewed the subject as a set of rules to be memorized!

Perceptions of Student Ability

Teacher perception of student ability is another critical factor. Certain groups of students are often deprived of the opportunity to learn the kind of mathematics that is recommended by the National Council of Teachers of Mathematics. The National Science Foundation (1989) discovered that females, minorities, and working-class students are the least likely groups to continue educational programs in mathematics. They are discouraged by subtle messages in the mathematics classroom that imply that mathematics may be too difficult, by career counseling that steers them away from math-oriented courses and careers, and by limited access to computers compared to those in advanced math classes (Oakes, 1987). Teachers may lower their expectations for these groups, not because of classroom performance, but because of factors such as the vernacular form of English that they speak (Orr, 1987), the level of anxiety they display (Damarin, 1990), or their discomfort with analytic teaching styles that stress order and individuality and discourage all other approaches to problem solving (Stiff, 1990). As a result, members of these groups are not encouraged to understand mathematics, but are merely expected to perform the skills that are taught (Bishop & Nickson, 1983). Members of these groups tend to suffer economically and politically from the inequitable curriculum (National Council of Teachers of Math, 1989).

Emphasis on Behavioral Objectives

A third factor shaping the curriculum is the emphasis on behavioral objectives that appear in textbooks and curriculum guides (Romberg, 1992). Although objectives are necessary to guide instruction and evaluation, they are usually worded so to isolate very specific skills. Working from a behavioral objective (e.g., the students will be able to multiply unlike fractions) shifts the purpose of a math lesson away from reasoning and problem solving. Teachers tend to focus on mastery of the skill instead of using the skill to understand reality. This phenomenon is similar to language arts teachers who emphasize mastery of such specific skills as capitalization or spelling at the expense of developing the overall ability to communicate effectively.

Unrealistic Guidelines

Unrealistic district guidelines also influence how the curriculum is implemented. Many teachers who want to stress conceptual understanding initially design activities that promote the NCTM goals. Unfortunately, they soon become concerned when they perceive that little time is left to "cover" the rest of the mathematics curriculum. Comparisons with other teachers who seek quick mastery of mathematical operations exacerbate their anxiety. In response, the reform-minded teachers feel forced to encourage memorized manipulation of numbers, sacrificing deeper understanding. This approach allows their students to complete the year's work even if they do not quite understand what they have learned (Hyde, 1989).

Standardized Tests

A final factor in the deep-rootedness of the traditional approach is standardized tests. As long as they are computation-based, teachers and schools will tend to ignore problem solving in the curriculum. Fortunately, tests are changing. This trend may move the curriculum closer to the NCTM program in the future. These developments bear watching.

THE ROLE OF TRADITION

Tradition is a major influence on the curriculum, especially in mathematics. Despite the long-standing Piagetian emphasis in elementary teacher training, schools tend to reflect the traditional pattern of students listening to a teacher and then working on pages of drill (Romberg, 1992). For a variety of reasons, beginning teachers are apt to conform to the traditional inactive approach.

Teacher decisions about curriculum and instruction are more likely to be based on the teachers' personal classroom experiences as students than on teacher education courses and in-service training (Lortie, 1975). Most teachers

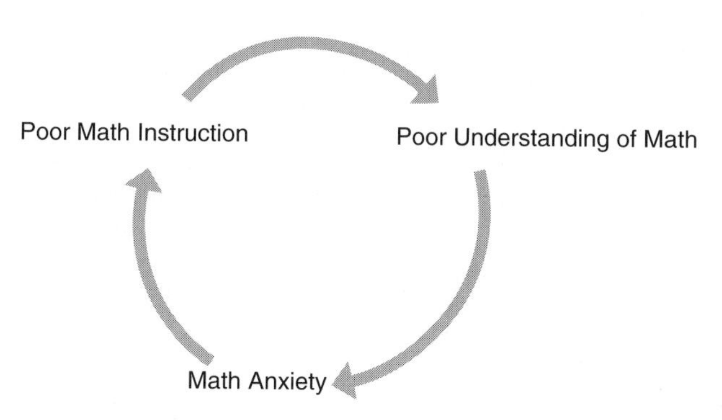

FIGURE 8.3. The cycle of ineffective math instruction.

have only been taught traditional mathematics and have never seen programs that develop concepts, communication, and reasoning. They have no base of experience to provide support for altering the curriculum (Hyde, 1989). A cycle is created in which we learn mathematics in an ineffective manner so that we may use those ineffective methods as teachers.

Because they are not trained to be specialists, elementary school teachers tend to have limited knowledge of mathematics (Hyde, 1989). This fact plus the historical de-emphasis on mathematics for females has produced a high level of math anxiety among predominantly female elementary school teachers (Piel & Green, 1992) (see Figure 8.3). One cannot reasonably expect elementary teachers to pioneer a new curriculum under these conditions.

Implementing the NCTM program (1989) requires skills and powers that new teachers rarely possess. For instance, adapting a curriculum from a textbook orientation to one of active learning requires a strong sense of content and goals, the ability to manage active children, and the strength to deal with criticism from skeptical colleagues, parents, and administrators. Each of these characteristics develops with experience. Thus, a new teacher, seeking to make a good impression, is more likely to use the relatively risk-free traditional approach.

Research studies indicate that teachers who are uncomfortable with subject-matter content will probably rely on traditional methods (Shulman, 1986). Thus, teachers whose mathematics program consists of endless drill may be disguising their lack of mathematical prowess. They could be hesitant to teach for conceptual understanding because they do not possess it themselves. Under such stress, the traditional approach is appealing because it emphasizes correct answers instead of mathematical reasoning and communication. Teachers can relax because they do not have to deal with concepts or explain them.

Using the traditional curriculum may be easier. One does not need extensive knowledge or skill, or have to take responsibility for changing bureaucratic and cultural norms. Unfortunately, children do not learn the mathematics that they need from such an approach. Alternative approaches are essential.

WHAT CAN INDIVIDUAL TEACHERS DO TO REFORM MATHEMATICS EDUCATION?

Individual teachers cannot do a lot, on their own, to change the math curriculum. Of course, for any reform to take place, teachers must believe in the philosophic approach behind the proposals. But changing one's convictions about the curriculum will seldom have effects beyond the individual classroom or school. Most strategies to change a curriculum require a multifaceted approach (Piel & Green, 1992), including group action. These strategies, which will be discussed in Chapter 13, can address some of the institutional and societal constraints to reform.

In the meantime, teachers can remediate their own weaknesses in mathematics. This is not as difficult as it may sound. Remediation does not have to take place in a college classroom. Excellent videotapes, television programs, and even textbooks are infinitely more effective than the educational materials you had in school.

Many teachers experience remediation on their own when they are forced to teach a concept or skill that they never quite understood in the past. By having to analyze the content in order to translate it into meaningful activities for students, teachers discover connections and implications they never quite made during their own schooling.

Many of us have curriculum disabilities from being taught content before we were developmentally ready. Now that we are more capable in a cognitive sense, it is time to relearn mathematics. You may discover, as many do, a beauty in mathematical reasoning, an appreciation for the power of mathematics in understanding reality, and an actual enjoyment of the subject.

Questions

1. Did you learn mathematics as a way of thinking? Or did some other rationale guide your mathematics education?
2. What are your reactions to the proposal by the NCTM?
3. Do you believe there are differing standards in mathematics based on teacher expectations? What are your experiences with this phenomena?
4. How would your life be different if you had the type of mathematics education that was proposed by the NCTM?

References

BALL, D. L. (1990). The mathematical understanding that prospective teachers bring to teaching. *Elementary School Journal, 90*, 449–466.

BISHOP, A. J., & NICKSON, M. (1983). *Research on the social context of mathematics education.* Windsor, U.K.: NFER-Nelson.

COBURN, T. G. (1989). The role of computation in the changing mathematics curriculum. In P. R. Trafton (Ed.), *New directions for elementary school mathematics* (pp. 43–58). Reston, VA: National Council of Teachers of Math.

DAMARIN, S. K. (1990). Teaching mathematics: A feminist perspective. In T. J. Cooney (Ed.), *Teaching and learning mathematics in the 1990s.* Reston, VA: National Council of Teachers of Math.

DEWEY, J. (1933). *How we think.* New York: Heath.

GOOD, T. L. (1979). Teacher effectiveness in the elementary school. *Journal of Teacher Education, 30,* 52–64.

HYDE, A. A. (1989). Staff development: Directions and realities. In P. R. Trafton (Ed.), *New directions for elementary school mathematics.* Reston, VA: National Council of Teachers of Math.

JOHNSON, M. (1926). The educational principles of the school of organic education. In H. Rugg (Ed.), *The foundations and technique for the study of education: Part 1* (p. 349). Bloomington, IN: Public School Publishing.

LEE, F. R. (1993, February 9). Missing children clues often end close to home. *New York Times,* p. A13.

LORTIE, D. (1975). *Schoolteacher: A sociological study.* Chicago: University of Chicago Press.

NATIONAL COUNCIL OF TEACHERS OF MATH. (1989). *Curriculum and evaluation standards for school mathematics.* Reston, VA: Author.

National Science Foundation. (1989). *Everybody counts: A report to the nation on the future of mathematics education.* Washington, DC: National Research Council, National Academy Press.

OAKES, J. (1987). Tracking in secondary schools: A contextual perspective. *Educational Psychologist, 22,* 129–153.

Office of Management and Budget (1998). *A citizen's guide to the federal budget.* Washington, DC: Author.

ORR, E. (1987). *Twice as less: Black English and the performance of black students in mathematics and science.* New York: W. W. Norton.

PAULOS, J. A.(1990). *Innumeracy: Mathematical illiteracy and its consequences.* New York: Vintage.

PIEL, J. A., & GREEN, M. (1992). *Mathematics anxiety in elementary school teachers.* Unpublished paper.

PORTER, A., FLODEN, R., FREEMAN, D., SCHMIDT, W., & SCHWILLE, J. (1988). Content determinants in elementary school mathematics. In D. A. Grouws, and T. J. Cooney (Eds.), *Perspectives on research on effective mathematics teaching.* Reston, VA: National Council of Teachers of Math.

ROMBERG, T. A. (1992). Problematic features of the school mathematics curriculum. In P. W. Jackson (Ed.), *Handbook of research on curriculum.* New York: Macmillan.

SHULMAN, L. S. (1986). Those who understand: Knowledge growth in teaching. *Educational Researcher, 15,* 4–14.

STIFF, L. V. (1990). African-American students and the promise of the curriculum and evaluation standards. In T. J. Cooney (Ed.), *Teaching and learning mathematics in the 1990s.* Reston, VA: National Council of Teachers of Math.

WESTCOTT, A. M. (1978). *Creative teaching of mathematics in the elementary school.* Boston: Allyn & Bacon.

CHAPTER 9

The Arts

I'm no good at art. I can't draw a straight line! To many of us, the word *art* connotes drawing. This is to be expected, because most school experiences in this subject area involve drawing. As a result, a lot of people reject the entire topic of art when it is the physical act of drawing they find unpleasant.

This is a shame. Study of the arts has so many benefits for the individual and society. Learning about art gives us the opportunity to think, grow, communicate, and act; it helps us improve our environment; it provides many of life's greatest joys.

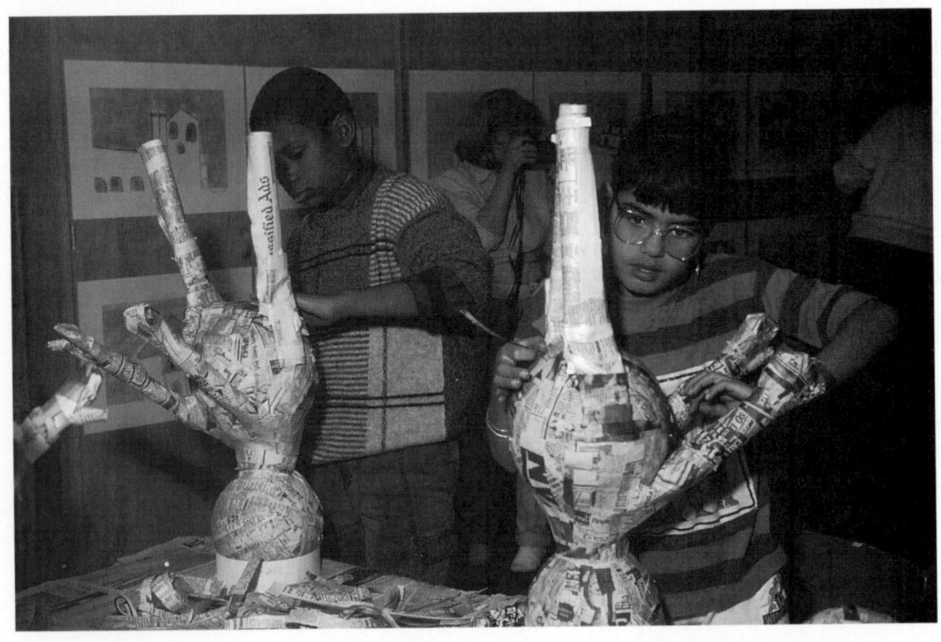

Most elementary school students never get to engage in projects like this.

Does this sound like an overblown endorsement? If it does, you may be overlooking aspects of art that you already enjoy, even if you claim to dislike the subject.

REVISING ONE'S CONCEPTION OF ART

Do you enjoy looking at photographs? Is it fun to examine the latest fashions? Do you listen to music often? Do you get a thrill when you see the skyline of a big city? Is dancing a pleasurable activity for you? How about going to the movies or watching television? Are you ever intrigued by the design of some new product? Do you appreciate a home when it is decorated for the holidays? Can a flower garden stimulate your senses?

Surely you answered yes to some of these questions. Art is clearly more than drawing. It includes music of all kinds, sculpture, photography, architecture, furniture design, media, dance, fashion design, literature, product design, drama, and so much more (see Figure 9.1). All of these arts contribute to our culture.

Culture is a value-laden term often narrowly associated with high-brow activities such as ballet, poetry, classical music, and paintings by the Great Masters. It does not have to be that way. Television programs can be used to teach about drama. Musical composition can be studied through rock music. The elements of dance are evident on music videos. A glance at the television listings will show that even public television recognizes such contemporary aspects of art as country music, film, and modern dance.

As we have seen throughout our study of the curriculum, arts education is not alone in suffering from an outdated curriculum. Like other subject-area educators, leaders in art education have made strides in clearly defining what they teach. A brief historical review will place the changes in context.

For many years, arts education has drifted from one emphasis to another. In nineteenth-century schools, artwork was used as an instrument to promote societal values such as patriotism and hard work, not for developing artistic skill

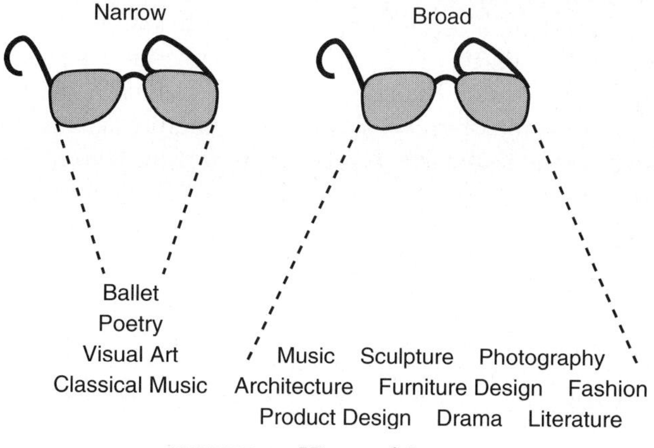

FIGURE 9.1. Views of the arts.

or knowledge. Studio art was viewed as a form of job training in which drawing skills, for example, could be transferred to factory work, such as cloth cutting, which demanded precise lines and curves. In the twentieth century, the emphasis changed when art educators encouraged children's singing, painting, dancing, and pretending as ways of developing creativity and self-expression. Later, the cognitive benefits of art as a way of thinking began to be recognized (Wolf, 1992).

THE NEW ARTS CURRICULUM

Today, the National Art Education Association (NAEA) has incorporated the various emphases into a discipline-based arts education (DBAE), encompassing four major modes: (1) art production, (2) art history, (3) art criticism, and (4) aesthetics. As you will see, these modes provide four different perspectives on art. The overlap between the various modes is not viewed as a detriment. On the contrary, overlaps are opportunities to provide depth:

> We increase our understanding of the meaning of an artwork if we have worked with the materials and processes that artists use to create art. We also broaden our understanding if we know when and where a work was made, something about its creator, the function it served in society, and what art experts have said about it. (Getty Center for Arts Education, 1985, p. 13)

Art Production

Many of the benefits of an arts program come from the creation of art. For instance, painting offers opportunities to experiment, make decisions, develop motor skills, and study such artistic elements as line, texture, and color. It provides for self-expression as well as a greater understanding of what painters do. The development of creativity is a major goal of art production.

Interestingly, elementary students seldom engage in arts production in other areas of artistic expression. Musical instruction usually focuses on singing or playing instruments in a certain way, just as in drama when children follow a script, or in dance when they are to follow a prescribed series of steps. Even drawing is sometimes limited to a coloring activity which provides minimal opportunity for decision making and skill development (Passe, 1984). Depriving students of the benefits that come from creating art may be harmful to the development of their skills and interests in the field. It certainly does nothing for self-expression.

Art History

An old baseball saying is appropriate: you can't tell the players without a scorecard. Indeed, to appreciate a ballgame, it helps to know something of the personalities of the athletes, how their careers have progressed, their strengths and weaknesses, and other items of human interest. The same is true for appreciating works of art. The comedy of Charlie Chaplin or Lucille Ball might not seem particularly clever unless the viewer is aware that those artists' comic performances were among the first to be shown on film and television, respectively. Ancient jars and statues might seem unimpressive without knowing the crudeness of the artists' tools. D. H. Lawrence's daring novels might seem tame without considering the conservative times in which they were published. Thus, not only is the artwork appreciated, but so is the role of the artist in society.

Studying art history also helps us understand other cultures—those of different regions as well as those of different times. Examining ancient Chinese fashion highlights the importance of silk to that culture. Knowing about California gold miners' need for rugged clothing helps us understand why Levi Strauss developed bluejeans in the nineteenth century.

As with other forms of history, studying art history helps us to understand and appreciate the present too. We can see how various historical movements have contributed to contemporary work. For instance, fans of the rock group U2 can identify the influence of Bob Dylan and the Beatles on the band's work. U2's experiments with folk, heavy metal, and the blues can be traced in order to fully appreciate their more recent music.

Art history also gives us conceptual handles that help us categorize artworks in our attempt to understand them. Knowing that a work is from a certain period (e.g., prehistoric, Renaissance), of a certain style (e.g., impressionism), or from a specific culture (e.g., West African, Native American) enables critics to take historical context and circumstances into account when judging the quality of the work.

Art Criticism

Have you ever gone to see a movie because the critics loved it? The phrase seems like a contradiction. If reviewers are critical, how could they love something? The answer is that criticism does not necessarily involve a negative judgment. A critique of one's work may also include description, explanation, analysis, interpretation, and praise.

A critique requires knowledge about a subject. Critics have to know what they are talking about and must use the specialized language of the artistic medium. Some of that knowledge comes from experiences in art production and art history. Art classes must provide such experiences. Students also need to learn about the nature of art criticism. They can study the comments of art critics on a piece of work. They can also develop their own critiques.

The ability to responsibly critique a piece of work is not easily learned. Many of us bear scars from ill-informed and unfair criticism, yet we can profit from thoughtful critiques. They assist us in improving our own work and in appreciating the work of others. Art criticism also promotes objectivity and expressive language (Getty Center for Arts Education, 1985).

One of art criticism's greatest benefits is the depth of understanding it can provide. If you are alerted to the significant elements of a piece of work, you are better able to appreciate it. That is why tour guides are so important on trips to museums, cathedrals, and botanical gardens. This is not to downgrade the value of an intuitive response. But when a friend tells you what to listen for in a great piece of music, for example, you are more likely to respond to it fully.

Perhaps you would be more open to certain forms of art if only someone would guide you through the experience. Think about acquaintances who are arts aficionados, particularly of opera, ballet, and theater. They truly live for those forms of art. Proper exposure to those art forms may possibly have transformed their lives. Such is the power of arts education.

Aesthetics

Any art criticism will ultimately address the nature of art. The philosophical branch of the arts is called aesthetics. It includes topics ranging from the relationship between art and reality to the role of creativity to the issue of censorship.

Can elementary school children engage in philosophical inquiry? Not in an abstract sense, but they do ask a number of aesthetics-related questions for which they usually have answers. For instance, museum trips will often provoke the question of whether a piece of work, say a piece of furniture or an abstract painting, is truly artistic. A related question is whether art must be beautiful. Can a photograph conveying the devastation of war be called artistic, even if the scene it portrays is one of ugliness? Children have no qualms in expressing their opinions on these matters.

One should not expect children to resolve these issues, any more than one should expect adults to do so. Elementary school students can be exposed to various theories concerning aesthetics, and can participate in discussions about them. Doing so may improve their interest in art, their knowledge of it, and their developing skills in cognition, rhetoric, and observation.

CONCERN ABOUT DBAE

Despite the endorsement of DBAE by many educational leaders, the approach has received criticism. The major objection is with the very specific recommendations that have been made for its implementation. Jackson (1987) prefers that the program be implemented at the school level, not at the district level, as proposed by the program founders. He also objects to the rigid, sequential organization of content at each grade level, which limits teacher freedom to interpret the curriculum.

Other concerns focus on the effects of the program. Critics believe that DBAE is too intellectual, too Western- and male-oriented, unsuited for those who are gifted in art, and too limited in its categories, and that it underemphasizes intrinsic rewards (Jackson, 1987). One of the program's founders offers the reminder that an official DBAE curriculum does not yet exist. Thus, the implementation process may remove some of the alleged weaknesses (Eisner, 1987).

THE NATIONAL STANDARDS FOR ARTS EDUCATION

The NAEA joined with other arts organizations to issue a set of standards for education in the arts. Together with the American Alliance for Theatre and Education, the Music Educators National Conference, and the National Dance Association, they produced *The National Standards for Arts Education* (Music Educators National Conference, 1994). That document makes strong claims for the inclusion of art in the curriculum, for its societal benefits (including "making decisions in situations where there is no standard answer" and "learning artistic models of problem solving") but, more important, for the intrinsic value of art for its own sake. It concludes, ". . . there can be no substitute for an education in the arts, which provides bridges to things we can scarcely describe, but respond to deeply." (Music Educators National Conference, 1994, p. 7).

The National Standards for Arts Education identifies the following goals for students upon completion of secondary school:

- "They should be able to communicate at a basic level in the four arts disciplines—dance, music, theatre, and the visual arts.
- They should be able to communicate proficiently in at least one art form, including the ability to define and solve artistic problems, with reason, insight, and technical proficiency.
- They should be able to develop and present basic analyses of works of art from structural, historical, and cultural perspectives, and from combinations of those perspectives.
- They should have an informed acquaintance with exemplary works of art from a variety of cultures and historical periods, and a basic understanding of historical development in the arts disciplines, across the arts as a whole, and within cultures.
- They should be able to relate various types of arts knowledge and skills within and across the arts disciplines.

As a result of developing these capabilities, students can arrive at their own knowledge, beliefs, and values for making personal and artistic decisions. In other terms, they can arrive at a broad-based, well-grounded understanding of the nature, value, and meaning of the arts as a part of their own humanity." (Music Educators National Conference, 1994, pp. 18–19).

THE GAP BETWEEN THE INTENDED CURRICULUM AND THE ACTUAL CURRICULUM

Unless you were unusually talented or interested in the arts, your education probably did not meet the standards identified above. You may wish that your school experiences with the arts were similar to the one proposed by the NAEA and *The National Standards for Arts Education.* Perhaps you would be a more well-rounded person as a result. Consider why your arts education was so different (if it was).

When everyone creates the same product, it is not art.

Teachers' Definitions

Teachers' definitions influence what they teach. Your teachers would not introduce aesthetics or art criticism unless they were aware of and supportive of these aspects of art education. Elementary teachers, who traditionally tend to regard art as a frill, something to do on Friday afternoon after a tough week, tend to have a narrow definition of art.

Ease of Implementation

Many of the activities that elementary teachers provide under the name of art do not promote the goals of thinking, self-expression, experimentation, history, criticism, or aesthetics. Consider, for example, a classroom of students making identical pilgrim hats. In many cases, teachers choose this type of art production activity because it is easy to organize, not disruptive, and likely to result in a product that parents can appreciate. One cannot ignore practical considerations. However, many kinds of truly creative projects can be organized and orderly.

Also, activities that tend to be messy, such as watercolor painting, are worth the extra effort to plan ahead and insure student cooperation. As for parental satisfaction, teachers must ask whether that goal is worth sacrificing the benefits of real arts education.

Differences Between Art and the Rest of the Curriculum

It may be that teachers have removed creativity and self-expression from art education because they (correctly) regard art as different from traditional school practices. At its best, art involves a way of knowing what is different from that in other subjects. It places less emphasis on the one correct answer and more on different versions of the truth. Art includes complex tasks, not the brief, simple chores that comprise much of the elementary curriculum. It requires sustained work and ongoing evaluation, both of which are rarely found elsewhere in schools. Because art is so different, teachers may unconsciously pervert the artistic process so that it better fits the traditional curriculum (Wolf, 1992). Or perhaps the current state of arts education accurately reflects societal preferences for conformity at the expense of individuality. Chapter 10 will address this issue more fully.

Lack of State and District Encouragement

Teachers are certainly not encouraged by state and district policies concerning arts education. As we have seen, when standardized tests are emphasized in a particular subject area, that subject receives more attention. Standardized tests rarely address the arts (National Endowment for the Arts, 1988), so teachers do not feel the pressure to teach them. After all, there have not been any news headlines about dropping test scores in art. It may be no coincidence that the amount of time devoted to the arts has steadily declined (Chira, 1993).

EVALUATION DIFFICULTIES

One reason for the lack of testing in the arts is that it is more difficult to evaluate. Other than art history, much of the arts curriculum does not lend itself to standardized testing. For instance, how can a multiple choice test measure creativity or performance? As a result, many teachers, when they are confronted with the report card space next to art or music, will assign every student the same grade, unless there has been evidence of disinterest or misbehavior. Many school districts do not even refer to the arts on their report cards.

Another daunting challenge is the problem of what, precisely, to test. Each state has an official arts curriculum, but teachers do not always follow it. Besides, many state standards still refer to narrow skills, such as identifying line or rhythm, and ignore broader elements such as theme and style (National Endowment for the Arts, 1988). Because of the problems in evaluating arts achievement, standardized tests do not play a role in shaping the arts curriculum. But the lack of such tests means that the subject is more likely to be overlooked in curricular planning.

Some school districts are experimenting with standardized tests as well as portfolio evaluations. These developments, combined with the publication of national standards may be helpful in strengthening the role of arts education in the elementary school curriculum. But the public has to want it.

Lack of Public Pressure

With little public pressure for improved art education, school districts tend to reduce their support for the program. Art educators are, therefore, forced to teach under conditions that constrain attempts to offer a meaningful curriculum. Consider these limitations: elementary teachers rarely have the benefit of curriculum coordinators in art; textbooks may not be available; and time allocated to art and music is much less than that given to other subject areas. It is hard to imagine providing a quality education under such circumstances (National Endowment for the Arts, 1988).

Lack of Balance

Art instruction tends to focus on the visual arts and music. Other art forms, such as dance, film, and drama are rarely included in most state curriculum guidelines. Classroom time devoted to them is extremely low (National Endowment for the Arts, 1988). While most schools have crayons, paint, and musical instruments, they are less likely to possess video editing equipment or dance studios. Thus, even teachers who follow the curriculum guides are not likely to provide the balanced curriculum proposed by the NAEA.

THE NEED FOR SPECIALISTS

A major concern in arts education is teacher preparation (Boardman, 1990). Teacher education programs demand minimal preparation in the arts. Usually, only one arts course is required, either general arts or music or visual arts. Certification requirements in drama, design, architecture, or other arts are rare (National Endowment for the Arts, 1988). How can one course teach all that is needed to successfully conduct an arts program? It can't. The result is that elementary school teachers are expected to teach unfamiliar knowledge and skills. Is it possible to teach a child about the joys of musical performance when you have never played an instrument?

The problem is compounded by the nature of university arts education courses. Sometimes the instructor of the required course is an expert in methodology. In that case, course content may be inadequate in the areas of art production, history, criticism, and aesthetics (Davis, 1990). In other cases, the instructor is an artist who has never taught in the elementary school and may lack knowledge of effective educational methods. Most artists are expert in a particular aspect of art. So students may gain excellent insights into the nature of, say, music, but not the other arts. It would be wonderful if university arts professors were experts in both art and education, but those individuals are rare (National Endowment for the Arts, 1988).

With an arts preparation that is bound to be incomplete (Boardman, 1990), it is no wonder that elementary teachers have feelings of inadequacy when they address the arts curriculum. Under these conditions, as we have seen with other subject areas, teachers tend to rely on traditional activities that they experienced themselves as students. When these activities fail to meet curricular goals, the entire educational system suffers.

A proposed solution to the weakness in teacher preparation is the use of specialists. An arts specialist would presumably have more training in a variety of arts. With an arts specialist paying closer attention to curricular issues and pedagogical techniques, students may receive a more appropriate education in the arts (Davis, 1990).

Problems with Specialists

Narrow Focus

Unfortunately, like the university professors, arts specialists tend to focus on one area. The music teacher may be a strong piano player but a weak singer. The visual arts teacher may be an expert painter but lack knowledge and experience in sculpture. The multitude of other arts may still only receive minimal attention. In the same vein, many specialists are performers who may not be well versed in history, criticism, or aesthetics.

Weak Qualifications

We assume that specialists are well qualified, but that may not be the case. State certification requirements can be relatively loose. In North Carolina, for example, a teacher who is certified in music may teach band or orchestra, regardless of whether that teacher has any proficiency or experience in those areas! Some schools that have difficulty finding a teacher of the arts must often resort to hiring an uncertified teacher, who agrees to take courses in order to meet the qualifications at a later date. This problem, which plagues middle and secondary schools, is known as *lateral entry.*

Separation

Another problem with specialists is that their presence in the school tends to remove that subject from the teacher's purview. Many teachers justify the lack of art in their daily curriculum by claiming that the music or visual arts specialist will provide that instruction. This attitude creates a series of problems.

Inadequate Time

In most schools, specialists are lucky to have an hour a week with a class. Most educators would acknowledge that little can be accomplished in such a short period of time. That one hour, by the way, includes time spent in transition to the specialist's classroom. Thus, leaving arts education to the specialist would result in an inadequate program.

Inadequate Space

Many specialists do not even have their own classrooms. Space shortages in elementary schools sometimes force specialists to use regular classroom space on a part-time basis, often sharing it with the speech clinician or physical education teacher. When a separate room is unavailable, specialists are obliged to travel from classroom to classroom. Having an itinerant specialist may be economical, but this arrangement creates problems in using specialized equipment and developing ongoing projects. Ironically, these conditions promote activities that are quick and easy, exactly what the use of specialists was designed to prevent.

Inadequate Flexibility

Limiting art to one-hour segments removes flexibility from the arts program. Whereas teachers in self-contained classrooms can manipulate the schedule to allow students to extend a successful arts activity, the specialist must constantly watch the clock in anticipation of the next class's lesson.

Inadequate Integration

The use of specialists mitigates against integration of subject areas. Art is present in every subject, from science's exposure of beautiful forms in nature to social studies' examination of the relationship between the arts and society to the mathematical aspects of musical notation. Specialists have difficulty making these connections when they must deal with two dozen classes per week, each having its own content. Even if they could, the one-hour time period is unlikely to permit much depth.

Curricular Collaboration

Classroom teachers can overcome many of these problems by collaborating on the curriculum with the specialist. Then, connections that are established in specialists' classes can be carried over into the regular classroom. This kind of collaboration

Theory to Practice
Art

Most children grimace at the thought of attending an opera performance. Two hundred students from Charlotte, North Carolina, created their own!

Eight classroom teachers at Irwin Avenue Open Elementary School collaborated with Kevin Eakes, the school's music teacher, to produce a performance of Mozart's classic, *The Magic Flute.* First, Mr. Eakes introduced the students to opera in his music classes. They learned all about the structure of an opera by studying the plot of *Aida.* Then, in their regular classrooms, they examined the history of *The Magic Flute,* including literary aspects of the work. Eventually, the students created their own adaptation of the opera, paring the length down to a manageable 20 minutes. With the help of professionals from Opera Carolina, the students learned about the behind-the-scenes management of an arts company, including such topics as production costs, overhead expenses, and fund raising.

The collaboration between Mr. Eakes and the classroom teachers was extraordinary. Classroom teachers actually came to music class with their students. As the students learned operatic techniques of posture and breath control, the teachers learned along with them, so they could practice and reinforce those skills outside of the music classroom. The teachers also coordinated work on the backdrops, advertising posters, and the program, all of which were student-designed and produced. Students even wrote their own arias by reworking and rewording familiar songs. Poor Mozart would hardly even recognize his masterpiece — the students performed only one of the original arias!

Three principles are evident here. One is that collaboration between the classroom teachers and the specialist permitted the students to engage in an activity that would have been nearly impossible to carry out separately. Classroom teachers lacked the knowledge of music while the specialist lacked the time and energy to work with so many students in so many subject areas. A second point is that incorporating art, literature, and other subject areas provided depth of understanding. Creating an artistic representation allowed the students to understand the process better than any book or lecture. Finally, we see how knowledge logically flows. The study of opera led naturally to study of history, economics, and literature.

Most important is the creative aspects of the project. As one art commentator puts it, "It is only art if the children bring something of themselves and their thoughts and feelings to what they are doing" (Cohen, 1976, p. 153).

requires that the classroom teacher recognize the value of the arts and have a stronger subject knowledge; it also requires additional planning time. Under current conditions, those prerequisites are unlikely to be met.

How do we overcome the constraints that prevent curricular collaboration? Doing so, first of all, requires support from the school administration. Teachers must enlist the cooperation of various political interests to meet that goal. The necessary strategies are discussed in Chapter 13.

In the meantime, you, as a teacher, can develop your interest in the arts. This may be best done with a guide of some sort. University courses, museum programs, public television series, and especially friends who love the arts can be quite helpful in developing your artistic awareness.

Whatever gaps exist in your knowledge can no longer be excused. As an elementary educator, you have a responsibility to teach the arts, even the ones you do not enjoy. (Can you imagine a first-grade teacher ignoring the teaching of reading because he or she personally dislikes novels?)

You may find that the arts that were neglected in your education are actually quite enjoyable. You may develop new insights into the artistic process, aesthetics, and life itself. You may even become a bit of an artist. The arts can change people. That is why arts advocates are so insistent upon their inclusion in the curriculum.

FUNDING AND THE CURRICULUM

Even when a school has a strong arts curriculum plan and dedicated teachers who are committed to its goals, students may still receive an inferior arts education because of inadequate funding. The amount of money schools spend on art determines the limits of students' art experiences.

Funding and Art Production

Art production, in most cases, requires specialized materials and equipment. A curriculum plan may call for student experiences in a variety of media, including tempera paint, oil paint, charcoal, clay, and colored pencils. It may recommend working with different types and sizes of paper, such as construction paper, parchment, and tracing paper. But if the school does not provide a budget to purchase those supplies, alternative art experiences would obviously have to be offered. Inability to buy other art materials may account for some schools' overemphasis on crayon-based art.

Equipment and facilities also make a difference. Some districts equip their elementary schools with kilns for baking clay, darkrooms for photography, and auditoriums with professional quality lighting, sound, and stage areas. Schools with such excellent facilities and equipment can offer a much stronger arts program than schools that do not even have a room set aside for art. A comparison of school districts in Alabama discovered that all of the schools in the state's wealthier districts had art rooms while the poorest districts had none (Ross, et al., 1994).

You may recall being frustrated as an elementary student when your class ran out of paste during an art construction activity or when there were not enough black crayons to create a Halloween picture. An absence of necessary materials forces students to compromise their artistic visions. Having to share basic items such as scissors and paintbrushes can discourage a child from completing a project properly. A student who has only ten minutes at the painting easel, for example, may have to rush through a self-portrait. Contrast that with a student who can leave a painting on the easel and return to it throughout the week. When properly done, art is a slow, careful, thoughtful process, not an assembly line product that must be completed in a set amount of time.

Funding and Art History and Criticism

To develop a knowledge of art history, one must be exposed to historical examples. Funding plays an important role in this issue. One way to study historical art is to examine photos, slides, prints, and reproductions. These materials can be quite expensive, with cost determining their quality. For example, a photograph of a famous painting that is found in the encyclopedia does not create the impact of size, color, and texture compared with a reproduction printed in an expensive coffee-table edition of art masterpieces. Perhaps you have noticed how a well-made movie, such as *Star Wars,* loses a great deal when it is transferred from film to videotape. Sound and screen sizes can make an enormous difference in appreciating artistic quality. Arts education programs that must settle for low-cost reproductions are not likely to promote the same insights and understanding as wealthier programs. When some school districts do not even have libraries to house collections of books or media, the discrepancy is even greater.

The best art history and criticism experiences allow children to view actual artworks as they were created by artists. This is also expensive. Museums offer excellent tours for school groups, but these programs entail admission fees, bus rentals, and other costs. Orchestras, ballet troupes, and theater troupes must also charge for admission, although many do provide free or discount performances for school groups. Transportation remains a problem. Of course, schools with modern auditoriums can invite guest artists to visit, but most schools cannot afford such facilities. Some schools do not have an auditorium and many that do lack lighting, microphones, and a working curtain (Ross, et al., 1994).

When schools are forced to use low-quality materials for lessons in art history and criticism, there may be less appreciation of the artworks and fewer opportunities for informed discussion. A photograph of a Ming vase can never elicit the awe that comes from examining the actual item. Discussions therefore become perfunctory and do not attract students to the arts, thus subverting one of the goals of the curriculum.

Funding and Teacher Training

To implement the DBAE program or any other arts education approach that goes beyond coloring books, teachers need to be properly trained. Because most teachers did not receive an adequate arts education, they tend to be unfamiliar with models that emphasize process or a broad definition of art. Methods of integrating art across the curriculum also need to be taught.

In-service education, unfortunately, can be expensive. School systems with an adequate budget for teacher training can provide assistance for teachers and schools that wish to implement new arts education models. Experts can be hired to present the new models, administrators can be trained to coach teachers in the new methods, and an ongoing teacher training program can be implemented. Poorer school districts, on the other hand, must depend on individual teachers and administrators to try the new approaches without much support. The inability to offer a districtwide approach limits the effectiveness of curricular changes.

Funding and Specialists

Some school systems center their arts education programs around specialists. Specialists may be considered a luxury because, in essence, schools are paying an expert to do a job that many other schools assign to regular classroom teachers. In the Alabama study mentioned earlier, 90 percent of schools in the wealthiest districts had music specialists, compared with 20 percent in the poorer districts (Ross, et al., 1994).

Poorer schools that have specialists sometimes concentrate in-service efforts on them rather than on the entire faculty. Because specialists have already received extensive training in their preservice programs, they are perceived to need less continuing education. (As discussed earlier, specialists may actually need considerably more training if they suffer from poor or narrow training.) There are also a lot fewer specialists to train and coach as compared with all the regular classroom teachers in the system. Thus, having specialists can substantially reduce the in-service budget.

Although less expensive, training that is concentrated on specialists tends to be ineffective unless there is a strong communication link between the specialists and classroom teachers. Otherwise the new ideas do not leave the specialists' rooms. This cost-cutting approach also works against the concept of DBAE, which emphasizes infusing arts education across the curriculum. Schools can handle this problem by encouraging joint planning between regular classroom teachers and specialists. Poorer systems, unfortunately, cannot afford to hire classroom assistants and lunchroom aides to permit this consultation during the school day.

Funding and Teacher Resources

Those of us who attended well-funded schools sometimes take for granted the resources available to teachers and students. We expect all schools to have adequate storage space, media equipment, file cabinets, locks on closet doors, bulletin boards, and smooth desktops. All of these are crucial to the success of an arts education program, yet, poorer schools are less likely to meet these basic requirements. Their arts programs suffer as a result.

THE RELATIONSHIP BETWEEN FUNDING AND LEARNING

Until 1966, most people assumed that funding was tied to student achievement. During that year, James Coleman and his associates (1966) issued a landmark report concluding that there is no relationship between the two variables.

Coleman's findings and those of other researchers provided support for political leaders who argued that educational spending is merely throwing money at our educational problems.

In the late 1980s lawsuits were filed to halt discrepancies in state funding for education. The plaintiffs argued that students in poorer school districts were receiving an inferior education, thereby violating their states' constitutional requirements to provide an equal education to all children. In these cases educational researchers were invited to testify in court. In their preparation, they reexamined the relationship between funding and achievement and discovered a series of errors in the original studies that led to misleading conclusions (Lockwood & McLean, 1994).

Funding Inequities and Education

It seems inconceivable that schools with well-funded arts programs would not have higher achievement in the arts compared with poorer schools. How can anyone reach that conclusion? Actually, no one did. As you may recall, achievement in the arts is rarely measured by standardized achievement tests. The earlier findings looked almost exclusively at scores in reading and mathematics. Thus, the researchers overgeneralized with respect to the arts, as well as physical education, social studies, science, foreign language, and other subject areas.

A second issue dealt with how the schools used their facilities. If schools invest money on expensive science laboratories but only teach a series of definitions, students are unlikely to show significant improvement on a science achievement test related to process skills. Using excess funds to buy workbooks may not be the best way to raise reading scores. The money must be spent according to curricular goals.

A third issue was what the tests measured. A well-stocked library with computerized data searches may promote substantial growth in student research skills, but that achievement may not translate into higher reading scores unless the test is designed to measure research skills. On the other hand, a test that focuses on skill in diagramming sentences is less likely to benefit from schools investing in word processing programs. The test must match the curriculum for scores to improve.

Finally, one must examine how the original conclusions were formed. One mistake that the original researchers made was comparing total school budgets instead of the parts devoted to instruction. By eliminating the variable of teacher pay, which could be accounted for by cost-of-living factors, the discrepancies became more apparent. A teacher in a big city, for example, is usually paid a lot more than rural teachers because it is more expensive to live in the city, not because big-city teachers are inherently better. A second mistake was comparing all schools instead of those that differed. Funding can be so high or so low that any additional expenditure is unlikely to make a difference. To show differences in achievement, wealthy and poor schools must be compared directly. When that was done, the effects on achievement became obvious (Lockwood & McLean, 1994).

THE RELATIONSHIP BETWEEN FUNDING AND OTHER CURRICULUM AREAS

The arts is a subject area that is severely harmed by inadequate funding because so many materials are needed to provide an effective curriculum. Other subjects also suffer, although some of the effects may not appear as obvious.

Physical Education

The differences between wealthy and poor schools can be easily assessed by examining physical education facilities. A quick tour of the playground indicates whether a school has a soccer field with goal posts, a baseball diamond with bases, tennis courts, and an assortment of safe playground equipment such as slides, swings, and climbing bars. Schools that do not have these facilities are less likely to teach these activities properly. They may have playgrounds that become mud bogs after a rainy day or perhaps have no access to grassy fields at all.

Poor schools may not even have gymnasiums. Their students attend physical education outdoors on nice days and indoors in inclement weather. Indoor locations vary between the back of the stage (when there is one), the lunchroom (except during meal times), and an empty classroom if one is available. These schools' opportunities to provide a broad physical education program are limited, to say the least.

A gymnasium does not guarantee appropriate facilities. The size of the playing area, quality of the floor, height of the ceiling, and presence of mats, basketball backboards, and painted lines also contribute to the quality of the curriculum. When schools do not have these basic amenities or students must play outdoors, teachers are limited in the type of activities they can offer.

In wealthy schools, each classroom has its own supply of equipment for baseball, soccer, tennis, and other activities. Poorer schools may not have enough equipment for a single class. One has to wonder how physical their physical education can be.

Language Arts

The language arts program tends to rely extensively on written materials. When a school has an inadequate supply of library books, textbooks, worksheets, and reference materials, the teachers are hampered in their implementation of the curriculum. The development of positive attitudes and skill in reading, for example, is dependent on students having the opportunity to read silently at their own pace with materials of their own choosing. Schools that cannot afford individual materials must make do by having students share reading materials. Thus, they rely on round robin reading or other techniques that make reading seem like a chore. Meaningful homework assignments are limited when there are not enough textbooks for each student to carry one home.

Access to videotape cameras can strengthen an oral language program. Left-handed desks can promote handwriting development for a substantial minority of students. Dictionaries and other reference books can improve student writing, research, and vocabulary. A library with a collection of anthologies can spark an interest in poetry and short stories. Of course, up-to-date encyclopedias are a must for all subjects, not just language arts. In Jonathan Kozol's *Savage Inequalities* (1991), an exposé of school funding inequities, teachers expressed their frustration at trying to teach science when the classroom encyclopedias were twenty years old. Kozol contrasted two schools in New York City. One had reference books in every classroom, 8,000 library books, and a collection of parents who volunteered to run the library. The other had a cubicle with 700 library books, no reference materials, and no adult attendants (Kozol, 1991).

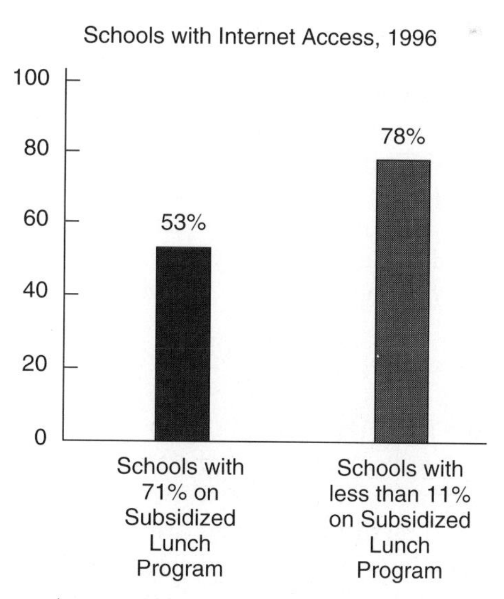

FIGURE 9.2. Internet Access, 1996
Note: All stats are from Statistical Abstract of the United States, 1997.

Even such basic materials as paper and pencils can influence the language arts curriculum. When paper is at a premium, students are less apt to do a second draft of a story. When the only writing instrument is a stubby pencil, the handwriting process becomes a chore and the product is likely to be marred.

Of all the disparities among schools, computer use may be the sharpest. Most computer users are well aware of the advantages computers provide in all aspects of academic work. When students go to schools that do not have computers, they are unable to benefit from those advantages. They receive an inferior education that cuts across subject areas. They will be severely handicapped upon entrance into college or the workplace.

The need for classroom computers is greatest in low-income communities because students are not likely to have computers in their homes (see Table 10.1). A classroom computer for wealthy children is a convenience that allows correlation between home and school. For poor children, it may be their only exposure to the cybernetic world.

Mathematics

For many students, mathematics is simply a matter of textbooks, worksheets, pencil, and paper. They may not be aware of the array of mathematics learning devices that helps translate abstract paper-and-pencil activities into concrete application-oriented mathematics. Learning basic algorithms with the aid of Cuisenaire rods has been shown to be particularly effective. Geometry becomes more understandable when students work with actual cubes, spheres, and cylinders. To learn measurement properly, students need to use measuring devices such as rulers, protractors, scales, and measuring cups. Any real-life problem solving is, of course, made easier and more realistic when calculators are available. Schools that cannot afford these materials must either improvise or rely on textbook drawings.

Audiovisual equipment is frequently used to make mathematics more concrete. An animated film that demonstrates fractions has been a staple of mathematics classrooms for years. Another long-standing tool is the musical recording of songs that help students memorize the multiplication tables. On a more modern level, computer software that allows children to manipulate numbers is extremely popular. All of these cost money for the products and the equipment used to play them. Many schools must do without.

Science

One difference between a content-oriented curriculum that emphasizes definitions and a process-oriented curriculum is the availability of science equipment. When schools have microscopes, slides, telescopes, Bunsen burners, chemicals, and other equipment and facilities, teachers are prepared to implement process goals. Schools that do not have well-stocked science closets are more likely to ignore scientific thinking skills.

Just as the abstraction of mathematics becomes concrete with manipulatives, so does science. A model of the human body with removable organs helps students understand what is hidden underneath the skin. Using an actual pump can teach the process of pressure far more effectively than any textbook diagram or teacher lecture. A computer simulation of seismic shifts is more easily grasped than a written description. Unfortunately, poorer schools cannot afford to provide concrete experiences, and their students become hampered by curriculum disabilities in science. The entire society suffers as a result.

One aspect of funding that is often overlooked is the ability to attract qualified teachers. Most school districts are desperately searching for teachers who are trained in science. College students who are skilled in science tend to opt for higher paying professions instead of teaching. School systems are, therefore, forced to compete for the teachers that are willing to sacrifice earning power for the love and responsibility of teaching science. Most competition revolves around financial issues. A science teacher who lives adjacent to several school districts may choose the one that offers the highest salary. Others may decide based on the quality of the workplace. Thus, a school with a collection of science facilities and materials may be quite attractive. So would a school with smaller classes. It is not unusual for wealthy school districts to steal qualified teachers from surrounding counties by touting their advantages. The poorer districts are then forced to hire teachers who are less qualified.

Social Studies

Social studies is another subject that is primarily associated with textbooks, yet, as we have seen, the abstraction of textbooks can be translated into concrete learning activities when funding is available for that purpose. One popular strategy is to use films. Through the projected image, students can be transported to other places and times. Another approach is to use field trips. Many schools arrange visits to local museums, government buildings, and historical sights. Some even provide travel to the capital cities of the state and country. All of this transportation requires funding that may not be available to poorer school districts.

Such simple learning aids as maps and globes may be in short supply. Teachers in poor districts must refer students to outdated maps that show two Germanys and an intact Soviet Union. Wealthy schools not only have current maps; they also have a variety of wall maps. Their students can examine the population changes of their state, the agricultural products of a particular continent, and the voting districts of their city. The opportunities for understanding social studies content are vastly different.

Conclusions

There is little question that funding influences the curriculum. Despite the protestations of some taxpayer groups, politicians, and conservative commentators, wealthy schools can offer more options with more materials under better conditions than poorer schools. If that were not so, why would residents of wealthy school districts be willing to pay higher taxes to support their schools?

An examination of actual expenditures may be helpful in understanding the disparities. According to Kozol (1991),

> If the New York City schools were funded, for example, at the level of the highest spending suburbs of Long Island, a fourth grade class of 36 children such as those I visited in District 10 would have had *$200,000 more* invested in their education in 1987. Although a portion of this extra money would have gone into administrative costs, the remainder would have been enough to hire two extraordinary teachers at enticing salaries of $50,000 each, divide the class into *two classes* of some 18 children each, provide them with computers, carpets, air conditioning, new texts and reference books and learning games—indeed, with everything available today in the most affluent school districts—and also pay the costs of extra counseling to help those children cope with the dilemmas they face at home. Even the most skeptical detractor of the worth of spending further money in the public schools would hesitate, I think, to face a grade school principal in the South Bronx and try to tell her that this wouldn't make a difference (pp.123–124).

This example comes from an urban school district, but inadequate funding is just as prevalent in rural areas. The Long Island schools Kozol described allotted over $11,000 per pupil in 1987. That same year, schools in some Mississippi counties received about $1,500 per pupil. The schools there could not even afford toilet paper for the bathrooms. The children had to bring it from home (Kozol, 1991).

Analysis of the Funding Situation

When educational reformers address the issue of school funding, two main issues arise. First is the level of spending. The type of curriculum that children need cannot be provided on a shoestring budget. Our societal needs cannot be met without spending more on facilities, supplies, teacher salaries, and inservice training. If taxpayers refuse to pay more, they must be willing to settle for an inferior curriculum.

The second issue is the disparity between wealthy and poor schools. Children will not receive an equal opportunity to learn when some schools spend more than twice as much as others on their curriculum. The principle of equal opportunity has been a hallmark of American life since the founding of the nation. This appears to have been more true in theory than in practice (Kozol, 1991).

> In East Aurora, Illinois, in 1987, a little girl in the fourth grade received an education costing $2,900. Meanwhile, a little boy the same age in the town of Niles could expect some $7,800 to be spent on each year of his elementary education. . . . Over the course of 13 years, from kindergarten to twelfth grade, $38,000 would be spent on the first child's education, and over $100,000 on the second child's education (Kozol, 1991, p. 73).

The reasons for this disparity are complex. Funding formulas differ from state to state. Property tax funds some districts while state money funds others. At times the differences are within school districts based on political and social considerations. A school district concerned about competition from private schools, for example, may put more money into schools in wealthy neighborhoods to keep affluent families in the public school system. Another school system may provide extra funds to certain schools because parents from those schools are more politically powerful than others in the community.

While these matters are being argued in the courts and the political arena, educators have been busy trying to overcome the problems that result from funding inadequacy and inequity. Teachers may need to take a more visible role in the discussion, by publicizing the harm that arises from financial problems and working to ensure that all children receive a curriculum that best meets their needs.

Questions

1. How have your attitudes toward art been affected by your educational experiences?
2. Using the broader definition of the arts, are you an artist in any way? If so, how did you develop your artistic abilities?
3. As a classroom teacher, would you prefer to do your own art, have specialists handle the art curriculum, or have the specialist serve as a consultant? Explain.
4. What should be done about funding inequities?

References

BOARDMAN, E. (1990). Music teacher education. In W. R. Houston (Ed.), *Handbook of research on teacher education* (pp. 730–745). New York: Macmillan.

CHIRA, S. (1993, February 3). As schools cut their budgets, the arts lose a place. *New York Times*, p. A1.

COHEN, E. P. (1976). *Art: Another language for learning*. New York: Citation Press.

DAVIS, D. J. (1990). Teacher education for the visual arts. In W. R. Houston (Ed.), *Handbook of research on teacher education* (pp. 746–757). New York: Macmillan.

EISNER, E. (1987). Discipline-based art education: Its criticisms and its critics. *Art Education, 41*(6), 7–13.

GETTY CENTER FOR ARTS EDUCATION. (1985). *Beyond creating*. Los Angeles: Getty Trust.

JACKSON, P. (1987). Mainstreaming art: An essay on discipline-based arts education. *Educational Researcher, 16*(6), 39–43.

KOZOL, J. (1991). *Savage inequalities*. New York: Crown Publishers, Inc.

LOCKWOOD, R., & MCLEAN, J. (1994). Twenty-five years of data on educational funding and student achievement: What does it mean? Paper presented to the Annual Meeting of the American Educational Research Association, New Orleans.

MUSIC EDUCATORS NATIONAL CONFERENCE. (1994). *The National Standards for Arts Education*. Reston, VA: Author.

NATIONAL ENDOWMENT FOR THE ARTS. (1988). *Toward civilization: A report on arts education*. Washington, DC: Author.

PASSE, J. (1984). Throw away those coloring books! *Mothering, 38*, 53–55.

ROSS, S., SMITH, L., NUNNERY, J., DOUZENIS, C., MCLEAN, J., & TRENTHAM, L. (1994). Do funding inequities produce educational disparity? Research issues in the Alabama case. Paper presented to the Annual Meeting of the American Educational Research Association, New Orleans.

WOLF, D. P. (1992). Becoming knowledge: The evolution of art education curriculum. In P. W. Jackson (Ed.), *Handbook of research on curriculum* (pp. 945–963). New York: Macmillan.

CHAPTER 10

Physical Education

After a week of kindergarten, my son came home with a very important reminder. "I must wear sneakers to school tomorrow, Daddy. I have PE." Curious as to his interpretation, I asked him what PE is. "I don't know, Daddy, but I have to wear my sneakers!"

Ryan's lack of awareness was a function of being told a nickname without an adequate explanation. It also represents a basic problem in the field of physical education. More than any other subject area, physical education suffers from confusion as to its purpose. The failure to clearly define the subject has resulted in a hodgepodge of programs (Steinhardt, 1992). Consider the alternative models.

PHYSICAL EDUCATION CURRICULUM MODELS

Physical Education as Unnecessary

Some people see physical education as an unnecessary component of schooling. They view education as the development of the mind or the transmission of knowledge; therefore, playground activity merely wastes valuable school time that could be devoted to learning. We see this philosophy in critics who propose curtailing athletic programs.

Physical Education as a Break

Another viewpoint is more sympathetic to physical education. Children need a break, it is argued. After being confined to a desk for hours at a time, it does a person good to move the muscles and work up a sweat. Upon returning to class, the child has renewed energy to devote to learning. Physical education, therefore, enables students to learn more in their academic classes because it refreshes the body and rests the brain. This view is popular among classroom teachers

Children love to show off their physical prowess.

who are not physical education specialists. If, in your schooling, you recall a lot of recess, rather than skill instruction, your teachers probably endorsed this viewpoint.

Movement Education

A third approach does not divorce the mind from the body. Advocates of this view see physical education as an opportunity to learn about the body. Learning how to move one's muscles is a valuable skill in itself. The child is learning the science of the human body, the power of physical effort, the influence of space on body movement, and the relationship between those factors. This approach, known as movement education, is particularly popular among elementary school physical education specialists. If you recall activities with parachutes and hula hoops, you were probably taught by a movement education enthusiast.

The Health-Based Model

Another characterization of physical education that connects the mind and the body is the health-based model. In this approach, students are taught skills to promote physical fitness. By learning how to exercise and the benefits of athletic activity, children may develop lifelong habits that will help them maintain healthy lives. If you associate physical education with calisthenics and workouts, you may have had teachers who endorsed this model.

Sports Education

Sports education proponents teach children how to play basketball, tennis, and other sports. Through the learning of games, they expect children to acquire a lifetime love of sports and an appreciation for sportsmanship and competitive effort. A physical education curriculum based on this model will focus on different sports as the seasons evolve.

Developmental Education

The development education model shifts the emphasis of physical education from a product orientation to one that considers process as well. In this approach, activities are chosen that fit developmental needs; they address not just physical development, but social, emotional, and intellectual development too. In this approach, physical education works toward the overall goals of the elementary school program; it is not just an additional subject (Hoffman, Young, & Klesius, 1981). The developmental model, which is widely endorsed by leaders in the field (Steinhardt, 1992), proposes physical education activities that may include aspects of all the previously discussed models, including forays into such matters as self-reliance, expressing feelings, and accepting responsibility.

The Problem of Conflicting Goals

Determining the curriculum model behind a physical education program can be a difficult task because more than one may be present (Steinhardt, 1992). As with other subject areas, teachers may not even be consciously aware of their orientation, and may be teaching based on their own experiences, traditions, or other factors (Ennis & Hooper, 1990).

Various studies support the interpretation that elementary physical education programs have mixed models and conflicting goals. Teachers have identified a broad variety of goals for the subject (Tillman, 1976). Sometimes the orientation is based on grade level. For instance, movement education dominates the curriculum in grades 1 and 2, with a shift to team sports by grades 3 or 4 (U.S. Department of Health and Human Services, 1986). Another difference in orientation is based on who is teaching the subject. In most programs conducted by specialists, the emphasis is on sports and games, with very little time devoted to movement education (Steinhardt, 1992). When physical education is taught by classroom teachers, free play is likely to be the norm (Faucette, McKenzie, & Patterson, 1990). Much of the activity in both program types was not vigorous enough to promote sustained heavy breathing and sweating, as suggested by expert guidelines (U.S. Department of Health and Human Services, 1986). Other program goals, such as allowing for individual differences, are also going unmet (Steinhardt, 1992). Thus, it is safe to conclude that the physical education program, as implemented, is not working as well as it can.

NASPE Goals

To address the hodgepodge problem, the National Association for Sport and Physical Education (NASPE) has developed a framework of goals that incorporate the models presented above (NASPE, 1990). Like the attempts by other professional associations to promote a reconceptualization of their subject areas, this framework is designed to educate the public about physical education. Table 10.1 outlines those goals.

THE BENEFITS OF PHYSICAL EDUCATION FOR ELEMENTARY CHILDREN

If anyone should appreciate the value of movement, it is the educator of young children. The foundation of learning, as Piaget stressed, is interaction between the child and his or her environment. In essence, children learn by doing. Thus, it makes perfect sense for elementary school teachers to include physical activity as part of the curriculum.

Physical activity can be interpreted in many ways. It can be cutting with scissors, measuring with a scale, and practicing sign language. Such activities are often incorporated in the academic course of study.

TABLE 10.1 Curriculum Framework Developed by the National Association for Sport and Physical Education

A physically educated person . . .
has learned skills necessary to perform a variety of physical activities:

1. Moves using concepts of body awareness, effort, and relationships
2. Demonstrates competence in a variety of manipulative, locomotor, and non-locomotor skills
3. Demonstrates competence in combinations of manipulative, locomotor, and nonlocomotor skills performed individually and with others
4. Demonstrates competence in many different forms of physical activity
5. Demonstrates proficiency in a few forms of physical activity
6. Has learned how to learn new skills

Participates regularly in physical activity:

7. Participates in health-enhancing physical activity at least three times a week
8. Selects and regularly participates in lifetime physical activities and is physically fit
9. Assesses, achieves, and maintains physical fitness
10. Designs safe personal fitness programs in accordance with principles of training and conditioning

Knows the implications of and benefits from involvement in physical activities:

11. Identifies the benefits, costs, and obligations associated with regular participation in physical activity
12. Recognizes the risks and safety factors associated with regular participation in physical activity
13. Applies concepts and principles to the development of motor skills
14. Understands that wellness involves more than being physically fit
15. Knows the rules, strategies, and appropriate behaviors for selected physical activities
16. Recognizes that participation in physical activity can lead to multicultural and international understanding
17. Understands that physical activity provides the opportunity for enjoyment, self-expression, and communication

Values physical activity and its contributions to a healthful lifestyle:

18. Appreciates the relationships with others that result from participation in physical activity
19. Respects the role that regular physical activity plays in the pursuit of life-long health and well-being
20. Cherishes the feelings that result from regular participation in physical activity

Source: Definition of the Physically Educated Person: Outcomes of Quality Physical Education Programs by the National Association for Sport and Physical Education, 1990, Reston, VA: Author.

Physical activity can also be interpreted as recess, engaging in stretching exercise between assignments, and walking through the school building en route to the library or cafeteria. These activities are intended to promote physical fitness or a release of energy, and are not directly related to academic goals.

Integrating Physical Education

Both interpretations of physical activity overlook the profound benefits of an academic program that comprehensively integrates movement (or a physical education program that comprehensively integrates academics!). Children learn a great deal from movement activities, far more than how to perform a particular skill or explain the rules of a sport.

Suppose, as part of a first-grade unit on the animal kingdom, children become interested in the climbing skills of monkeys. A teacher with a penchant for integration might seize the opportunity to make a connection with the children's own joy of climbing on the bars in the playground. This might evolve into a study of gymnastics. The resultant series of experiences would probably involve learning about the following:

- Techniques for dismounting from the bars
- The muscles involved in climbing
- The feeling of pride upon reaching the top
- Benefits of working together to perform stunts
- Safety factors associated with climbing
- The idea that climbing promotes coordination.

By engaging in concrete physical activity, the children will learn about technique, muscles, teamwork, safety, and coordination to a degree that can never be achieved by lecture, reading, or other traditional academic means.

In addition, other academic areas are addressed. Students learn

- How climbing bars are constructed to support a great deal of weight
- How gymnastic events are scored
- How our ancestors often had to climb to escape danger or find food (and the relative uselessness of climbing skill in modern society)
- How to measure the height of the bars
- The specialized jargon of gymnastics (e.g., dismount)
- The intrinsic joy of climbing for climbing's sake.

Connections are thus made to the areas of science, aesthetics, social studies, mathematics, and language in a relevant, high-interest fashion. Finally, with so many instrumental learnings taking place, we must not overlook the genuine inner feelings of satisfaction that are associated with physical activity. Physical education is more than just physical. In fact, that is why some educators prefer the term "movement education" (Arnold, 1988).

Theory to Practice
Physical Education

The fourth graders were in their glory! The fourth grade vs. fifth grade kickball tournament finals were being held, and the fourth graders were winning by a landslide.

Their success was not just due to luck. As they developed an interest in kickball (one of the games that grow and recede in popularity during the school year), it had been incorporated into the academic curriculum. Two major themes were integrated: systems and communication.

Their science study of the human body focused on the respiratory, circulatory, and other body systems, so their teacher talked about kickball as a system. He showed them how the outfielders, infielders, pitcher, and catcher all work together to throw out a base runner. In emphasizing teamwork, the students learned the benefits of using relays to move the ball to the right spot and of backing each other up.

Communication, the language arts theme, was easy to relate to kickball. The students discussed how shouting clear directions to your teammates can help make ball movement more efficient. Signals on the base paths were developed to move runners into scoring position.

Both themes were helpful to the team's success. The fourth graders were like a machine as they capitalized on their opponents' mistakes and made the best of their own opportunities. But as they built their lead, the tone of the game changed.

The fifth graders got nasty. In their anger, they became more physical. Fourth graders were "accidentally" knocked over. The ball was thrown excessively hard from a close distance. There were accusations of cheating and ugly taunts.

To the surprise of both teams, the fourth-grade teacher announced that his team would no longer participate. He called his students back to the classroom as the fifth graders cheered at their victory by forfeit.

As they returned to their seats, his students were furious. But rather than launch into a lecture on sportsmanship, he asked them questions so they could analyze the values and feelings of everyone involved:

"Why did the fifth graders act the way they did? How did they feel? Would you have done the same thing if it happened to you?"

"Why do you think I pulled us off the field? What does that say about what is important to me? Which of these values is most important to you—safety? sportsmanship? winning?"

Using this adaptation of value analysis and feeling exploration (Fraenkel, 1977), the students were able to displace some of their anger and frustration. They learned about sports and competition, but mostly about people. They may not have won, in a technical sense, on the ballfield (that issue was discussed for weeks on end), but they grew from the experience. Physical education provides much more than mere physical education.

Cognitive Aspects

Learning a skill or a sport involves a great deal of thinking. The baseball player who makes a diving catch has simultaneously calculated the trajectory of the hit, the speed of the ball, the angle of his or her approach, and the time it will take to slow down enough to make a dive possible. The ballplayer's achievement requires talent, of course, in the form of good hands, agility, and speed, but those talents, by themselves, will not result in catching the ball. We sometimes give too much credit to an athlete's talent (e.g., "the dumb jock") and not enough to the strategies the athlete uses. Those strategies require knowledge of science and math, though not necessarily in abstract terms. The physical education teacher's job is to provide students with opportunities to experiment with their bodies to develop athletic skills.

Another cognitive aspect of physical education is strategy. Successful athletes are able to analyze their performance in order to improve. They must also examine the strengths and weaknesses of the opposition (in competitive activities) and adjust accordingly. Furthermore, in team play there is the matter of studying teammates and team dynamics to efficiently blend individual skills and talents. All of the above require skills in observation, communication, and psychology, as well as science and math skills.

Character Aspects

We must also not ignore the aspects of athletics related to character. Both individual and group activities often demand concentration, leadership, determination, grace, and enthusiasm. Those qualities are not genetic; they must be nurtured. Pep talks and admonitions (e.g., to try hard) are inadequate. Students must be given the opportunity to experience success and defeat and study how their own behavior contributed to the outcome. A strong physical education program allows children to construct their knowledge of movement with a series of active lessons designed to promote cognitive and character-based reflection in addition to physical development.

On a theoretical level, at least, physical education can be a major contributor to the elementary curriculum. Yet, for a variety of reasons, students are not achieving the goals that are identified by the NASPE (1990).

THE GAP BETWEEN THE INTENDED CURRICULUM AND THE ACTUAL CURRICULUM

Lack of a Solid Theoretical Base

One problem is the confusion in curriculum models. Teachers who follow one model and ignore certain others may limit the number of goals that can be reached. For instance, a teacher who stresses the sports model may not develop student awareness about the relationship between fitness and health. This issue comes down to teacher values concerning the curriculum. A solid theoretical base for curricular decision making is needed (Ennis, Mueller, & Hooper, 1990).

In cases when classroom teachers are partially or fully responsible for the physical education curriculum, the curricular planning often suffers because of inadequate training in that subject area. Pre-service preparation for classroom teachers tends to be a single course in which little, if any, hands-on teaching is done (Jones, 1987). As a result, the major influence on the classroom teachers' physical education program is their own experiences as students (Coulon & Reif, 1994). This cycle, which is true for other subject areas in which the training is inadequate, seldom leads to an effective curricular program.

Eclectic Programs

Another aspect of the same problem is that teachers often follow an eclectic program that combines models. Relying on such hodgepodge may result in a program that emphasizes coverage at the expense of depth. Students may not get the prolonged exposure necessary to achieve all of the varied goals (Steinhardt, 1992).

Workplace Constraints

Many physical education teachers cite the constraints of the workplace as an impediment to implementing curriculum goals. They claim that lack of time, oversized classes, inadequate materials and facilities, and student apathy prevent them from doing their jobs effectively (Locke & Griffin, 1986). Because physical education is often a specialized program, classes must be tightly scheduled, allowing little flexibility. If a teacher does indeed have too many students or not enough space, a compromised curriculum model is to be expected.

Low Status

Like the arts, physical education has low status, in part, because it is not usually included in standardized testing programs. The difficulty of measuring student achievement on standardized tests prevents teachers from accurately measuring student performance in physical education. Because much of the physical education curriculum involves skills and attitudes, a paper and pencil test is unlikely to measure students' actual growth in, for example, physical fitness or an overhand throw. New developments in authentic assessment, however, have inspired portfolios for physical education. A physical education portfolio (which could be called a "sportfolio!") may include videotapes, computer grading printouts, and other artifacts of student performance (Melograno, 1994.) With authentic assessment, evaluation in physical education can become more accurate, thus increasing the status of the subject area.

The low status of physical education (Bain, 1990) contributes to constraints on teachers. If citizens and administrators regard physical education as unnecessary or merely a release of energy, insufficient resources will be devoted to the program. On the other hand, if decision makers support one of the curriculum models identified earlier, they will not be likely to assign ninety students to one teacher for a mere thirty minutes a day, once a week. This issue points to the need to educate the public about the benefits of physical education.

Specialization

In addition to schedule constraints, the specialized nature of physical education creates other problems. As discussed in Chapter 9, classroom teachers receive the impression that specialized subject-area teaching should be left to the experts. As a result, when they are expected to supplement the program of the physical education specialist, their curriculum is inadequate. Nonspecialists' activities have been identified as less effective in developing skills and promoting higher levels of activity. Quite often, physical education is dropped from the schedule or replaced with recess (Steinhardt, 1992). In this case, the teachers need further education in teaching PE. Fortunately, studies show that in-service training in physical education can have positive effects on classroom teachers' curriculum in that area (Coulon & Reif, 1994).

The Need for Instruction

The physical education curriculum, whether run by specialists or regular classroom teachers, must be geared to instruction. Merely allowing children to play will not develop a high degree of competency (Hoffman, Young, & Klesius, 1981). Think about an activity that was difficult for you to master, such as riding a bicycle. Most of us, if we had been left on our own, would have eventually given up. Fortunately, we had adults to help us structure the situation—by providing a safe area to learn, a demonstration of the skill, a steady hand on the back of the seat, some feedback when we were unsuccessful, and encouragement when we fell.

This is not to say that some children couldn't teach themselves; all of us do have natural talents in certain areas. However, most people need teachers to maximize their learning potential. The old adage that "practice makes perfect" is mostly untrue. Practice alone may still result in substandard performance; but it will be a *consistent* substandard performance.

Take, for instance, the bowler who constantly throws the ball into the gutter. All the practice in the world will not help if the same poor technique is repeated. Through education, the bowler can learn to release the ball properly to insure a straight shot at the pins. Thus, the adage should be, "Practice *and education* make perfect."

The same is true for the skill of teaching. Though there may be such a thing as a natural teacher, most of us need to be educated concerning matters of development, curriculum, instruction, and evaluation. Otherwise, we will probably copy the standard techniques and appear to be competent at first, but will seldom improve to any degree (Dewey, 1904). If you were to teach physical education without a thoughtful analysis of the issues and a refinement of the proper instructional skills, your program would not yield the benefits that a well-educated teacher might achieve.

IMPLICIT GOALS

Every curriculum has goals that are implicit, that are not identified in planning guides. Teachers may not even be aware of their "hidden curriculum." This existence of a hidden curriculum applies to all subject areas as well as the school system as a whole, but particularly to physical education.

Besides the knowledge, skills, and attitudes that are identified by physical educators, other outcomes are promoted as well: submission to authority, conformity, and stereotyping. It may even be argued that physical education programs encourage a *lack* of sportsmanship! Few teachers would claim these as goals, but their actions may contradict their words.

I became aware of physical education's hidden curriculum as a beginning teacher. I expected my students to return from their twice-a-week sessions with "Coach," the school specialist, demonstrating a love of physical activity, appreciation of their bodies and minds, and a strong sense of self-esteem. What I saw was ugly.

The children arrived in groups. The first to return were some perspiring boys who apparently belonged to the winning team in their sports activity. I knew this because they chanted "We beat! We beat!" all the way down the hallway. Even worse than their poor use of language and lack of consideration for classes in session was their unsportsmanlike conduct. It was not enough to win; they had to rub it in.

Close behind the winners were the sullen losers, mumbling accusations of cheating at the other teams and Coach (who served as referee). I saw no grace in losing, no congratulations for the winners, no pride in their near success, only anger at themselves, their opponents, Coach, and any teammates who happened to make serious errors in the game.

I could only wonder what they were learning on the ballfields. What steps was Coach taking to develop the finer points of athletic competition? And where were the girls during this activity?

I found out a few seconds later when the girls wandered into the classroom in small groups. To my surprise, there was no sign of perspiration. What had they been doing? It seems they had done whatever they wanted. Coach had suggested they play kickball as he went off to get the boys' ballgame started. Some had played on the swings, others played catch with the kickball, and a few just stood around chatting.

Bringing up the rear was a small group of nonathletic boys. They had chosen not to engage in the sports activity and had mixed in with the girls on the playground equipment. Apparently, that was okay with Coach. Upon further investigation, I discovered that Coach never spent any time instructing them in the games. Despite their differing developmental needs, all students received the same instruction: none. It was no wonder, in the unsportsmanlike atmosphere of the physical education program, that some children chose not to participate.

When the boys were not participating in sports, the children frequently took turns being assessed for their physical fitness ability. At those times, the students would stand in a line while one child at a time performed an assigned task, such as the broad jump.

The Hidden Physical Education Curriculum

You may be thinking that this is an unusual situation involving a poor teacher. Research indicates otherwise. An extensive review by Bain (1989) concluded that physical education teachers emphasize attitudes and compliance more than skill and knowledge. This is conveyed in their stated goal preferences, verbal behavior,

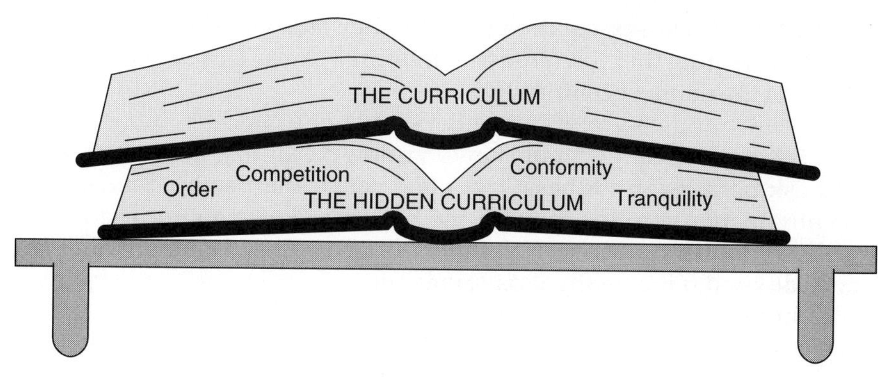

FIGURE 10.1. The hidden curriculum.

and assessment practices. They prefer order and compliance more than achievement (see Figure 10.1). Their attitude preference is for the masculine-athletic-competitive image (Kollen, 1983).

When teachers had lower expectations for certain students, they offered less instruction, less acceptance, and more criticism. The high-expectation students were those who were higher achieving and more compliant. When students chose not to participate in activities they viewed as more appropriate for the opposite sex, teachers tended to accept their decisions (Steinhardt, 1992).

Thus, Coach was in the norm. He provided little instruction, emphasized order instead of skill development, and allowed low-achievers and females to excuse themselves from physical activity. In terms of attitudes, his preference was for the masculine-athletic-competitive image.

Other Hidden Curricula

Before leaping to make snide judgments about physical education, recognize that there is plenty of evidence to indict other subject areas, especially in elementary schools:

- In most science classes, teachers demonstrate experiments instead of having children conduct them. This sacrifices achievement in the name of order.
- Elementary art lessons are more likely to be exercises in following directions. Having each child create the same Thanksgiving turkey made out of a pine cone with construction paper feathers glued to one end avoids having products that may appear unattractive to parents. This sacrifices creativity in the name of public relations.
- Social studies lessons seldom include discussion of controversial topics. This sacrifices self-expression in the name of dispassionate tranquility.
- In language arts class, some teachers are apt to evaluate student stories on the basis of spelling and punctuation rather than on the quality of the students' ideas. This sacrifices originality in the name of precision.
- Math lessons usually focus on only one way of solving a problem. This sacrifices problem solving in the name of efficiency.

- In most music classes, children learn to sing songs like the teacher does, instead of creating their own musical interpretations. This sacrifices individuality in the name of conformity.
- Conformity and control pervade the school day. Students are expected to chant "Good morning" in unison to visitors, to sit in a prescribed fashion, and ask permission for basic tasks like pencil sharpening. Students must silently march in a line through the hallways and may not use the toilet without teacher approval. Rules govern the choice of clothing, the size of notebooks, and the width of paper margins.

Explaining the Hidden Curriculum

Some of the practices and rules that contribute to the hidden curriculum have reasonable explanations. For instance, thirty children walking loudly through the hallways would certainly disrupt other classes. The trouble is that teachers frequently carry rule following to the extreme, constantly admonishing with a "Shhh" and penalizing for the slightest whisper. In too many schools, the mania for rule enforcement has created an atmosphere more like a prison than a place for children to engage in the joy of learning.

Other rules and practices evolve through tradition or thoughtlessness. The singing of teacher-led songs is so ingrained in the school culture that alternative approaches may never have occurred to those who teach music. The science teacher who demonstrates experiments may not realize the inadequacy of this instructional technique.

Most educators would insist that creativity, individuality, originality, and achievement are important, but the overwhelming emphasis of the curriculum works against the achievement of those goals. The reasons for this are numerous, including such previously introduced issues as textbook orientations, teacher knowledge, standardized tests, tradition, and the role of specialists. The role of cultural transmission must also be considered.

Cultural Transmission

Schools are designed to transmit the dominant culture to the young. This is a standard pattern of socialization in all societies. Therefore, it is to be expected that American schools reflect the society of which they are a part.

The values that are emphasized in the physical education program are not promoted accidentally. The masculine-athletic-competitive image could describe American society as well as its schools. Our culture has been geared toward males since the nation's inception. Despite the recent moves toward sexual liberation, few would deny that masculine interests are still quite dominant in areas such as athletics and business. The number of women who are leaders in the arenas of finance, politics, and the sciences is still small. The male-oriented sports receive most of the public's attention.

Athletics is also an emphasis of our society. We see this emphasis in the million-dollar salaries and endorsements of star athletes, the inordinate

The school must counteract the poor role models in the world of sport.

attention given to high school and college sports teams, and the multitudes of people playing every sport from golf and tennis to Little League baseball.

Our capitalist economic system is based on competition. Americans are encouraged to compete in all markets, ranging from international trade to local entrepreneurial opportunities. We see competition in applying for jobs, for scholarships, and even in romance. We have winners and losers in all aspects of life. Our culture is quite competitive.

If one watches professional athletes at work, sportsmanship does not appear to be an important aspect of sporting life. We are likely to see trash talking, hollering at the officials, sulking on the bench, pulling dirty tricks when the referee's head is turned, and fighting with opponents. Because television magnifies star athletes, it is to be expected that youngsters will pattern their behavior on these role models. (It is disappointing that the quiet professionals who go about their business do not get the exposure that their immature teammates receive.)

Thus, physical education emphasizes values that are reflected in the overall society. Perhaps it is unfair to criticize Coach and his subject-area cohorts. That depends on your educational philosophy. If you are a reconstructionist, you would probably prefer to have the physical education curriculum presenting alternate values, such as sex equity, creativity, sportsmanship, and a version of physical activity not limited to athletics. Progressives would encourage having children construct their own value orientations toward these issues, if they arise.

The question for essentialists is not as simple. Some essentialists endorse the transmission of present-day values, no matter how unappealing they may be, since they do, after all, represent our culture. But others may not be as accepting of that viewpoint. Those essentialists do not see the culture in such definitive terms. Yes, competition is part of the capitalist system, but so is cooperation. Corporate executives must work together to provide the best products and services; so must teammates in a football game. However much the culture is dominated by males, there is no question that women are developing greater power and visibility in all facets of life, including athletics. Witness the popularity of the women's tennis tour as well as the increased attention given to women's sports in high schools and colleges. The focus on athletics in our society remains powerful, but its nature is changing. Many Americans appear to be quite interested in health and fitness. Sportsmanship may be in decline, but manners are still basic to most cultures.

One must not overlook the intrinsic rewards of sports and physical activity. Americans have a love of recreation. They enjoy winning, but they mostly love to be active. This is especially true for children. A physical education curriculum that promotes winning at the expense of enjoyment would miss this crucial aspect of our society.

Thus, our culture would not be reliably transmitted by Coach's program. Too many important values would be omitted. A more balanced set of values is needed in the physical education curriculum. Even an essentialist could be comfortable with that view.

What Teachers Can Do

The research on teaching pro-social behavior indicates that it can be effectively taught as part of the physical education program. When teachers have offered instruction in such topics as sportsmanship, conflict resolution, positive leadership, and other social skills, their students have grown in those areas (Sharpe, Brown, & Crider, 1995). These programs, it would seem, could have a profound influence on the students' lives, both in and out of the classroom.

No matter what philosophical beliefs you hold, you will be promoting a hidden curriculum. As we have seen, even a supposedly minor subject area like physical education can make a powerful impression on children. Teachers must explore their belief systems and carefully examine what their students are learning, whether or not those outcomes are identified in a curriculum guide.

Questions

1. Which of the curricular approaches to physical education best fits your beliefs? Why?
2. Which approach to physical education guided most of your schooling? What were the benefits and disadvantages?
3. Identify some aspects of the hidden curriculum in your schooling. How have they affected you?
4. What should schools do to address the masculine-athletic-competitive image of American society?

References

ARNOLD, P. J. (1988). *Education, movement and the curriculum.* London: Falmer Press.

BAIN, L. L. (1989). Implicit values in physical education. In T. J. Templin, & P. G. Schempp (Eds.), *Socialization into physical education: Learning to teach* (pp. 289–314). Indianapolis: Benchmark Press.

BAIN, L. L. (1990). Physical education teacher education. In R. Houston (Ed.), *Handbook for research on teacher education* (pp. 758–781). New York: Macmillan.

COULON, S. C., & REIF, G. (1994) The effect of physical education curriculum development on the instructional behaviors of classroom teachers. *Journal of Teaching in Physical Education, 13,* 179–187.

DEWEY, J. (1904, 1970). The relation of theory to practice in education. In P. Martorella, *Readings in social studies.* New York: Macmillan.

ENNIS, C. D., & HOOPER, L. M. (1990). An analysis of the PPCF as a theoretical framework for an instrument to examine teacher priorities for selecting curriculum content. *Research Quarterly for Exercise and Sport, 56,* 323–333.

ENNIS, C. D., MUELLER, L. K., & HOOPER, L. M. (1990). The influence of teacher value orientations on curriculum planning within the parameters of a theoretical framework. *Research Quarterly for Exercise and Sport, 61,* 360–368.

FAUCETTE, N., MCKENZIE, T. L., & PATTERSON, P. (1990). Descriptive analysis of nonspecialist elementary physical education teachers' curricular choices and class organization. *Journal of Teaching in Physical Education, 9,* 284–293.

FRAENKEL, J. (1977). *How to teach about values: An analytic approach.* Englewood Cliffs, NJ: Prentice-Hall.

HOFFMAN, H. A., YOUNG, J., & KLESIUS, S. E. (1981). *Meaningful movement for children.* Boston: Allyn & Bacon.

JONES, B. J. (1987). Preservice programs for rural environments. *Research in rural education.* 4(1), 3–8.

KOLLEN, P. P. (1983). Fragmentation and integration in movement. In T. Templin and J. Olsen (Eds.), *Teaching in physical education* (pp. 83–89). Champaign, IL: Human Kinetics.

LOCKE, L. F., & GRIFFIN, P. (Eds). (1986). Profiles of struggle. *Journal of Physical Education, Recreation, and Dance, 57,* 32–63.

MELOGRANO, V. J. (1994). Portfolio assessment: Documenting authentic student learning. *Journal of Physical Education, Recreation, and Dance, 65,* 50–61.

NATIONAL ASSOCIATION FOR SPORT AND PHYSICAL EDUCATION. (1990). *Definition of the physically educated person: Outcomes of quality physical education programs.* Reston, VA: Author.

SHARPE, T., BROWN, M., & CRIDER, K. (1995). The effects of a sportsmanship curriculum intervention on generalized positive social behavior of urban elementary school students. *Journal of Applied Behavior Analysis, 28,* 401–416.

STEINHARDT, M. A. (1992). Physical education. In P. W. Jackson (Ed.), *Handbook of research on curriculum.* New York: Macmillan.

TILLMAN, K. (1976). Value shifts by physical educators. *The Reporter, 22,* 12–15.

U.S. DEPARTMENT OF HEALTH AND HUMAN SERVICES. (1986). *Midcourse review: 1990 physical fitness and exercise objectives.* Washington, DC: Government Printing Office.

CHAPTER 11

Organizing Classrooms and Schools

As a university professor, I am sometimes called upon to supervise student teachers. One time, I was observing a student teacher conducting a small-group reading lesson. To promote comfort and informality, she had the eight children stretch out on a small section of carpeted floor behind the teacher's desk. Unfortunately, despite her fine lesson plan and careful monitoring of misbehavior, her children were restless. There were constant complaints: "Johnny is pushing me!" "Susie keeps kicking!"

At the end of the day, when we met to critique her performance, she was distraught over the students' off-task behavior. After I pointed out the many fine decisions she had made, I asked what had caused the misbehavior. She immediately identified the limited space behind the desk as the culprit, but she said, "That's the only place we can meet."

"Is there something you can do about the space problem?" I asked. Smiling, she walked over to the desk and pushed it forward about 18 inches. She had realized what a lot of teachers overlook: we often have more control than we immediately realize.

It is surprising to learn how many options there are for classroom and school organization. It is mistakenly assumed that the predominant graded, self-contained classroom is a given, and that the matter is not within a teacher's purview. In fact, there are numerous models and combinations of models, each with its own strengths and weaknesses. Teachers are often the ones who decide which organizational model will be used in their classrooms, grade levels, or schools. The organizational decisions teachers make can help or hinder the implementation of their curricular philosophies.

GRADED AND NONGRADED SCHOOLS

Graded Schools

In graded schools, children enter kindergarten around age five, move to first grade the following year, and continue through the grades unless a major decision is made to have a child repeat a particular grade.

Small group activities can meet a number of important goals in addition to meeting individual needs and interests.

More than 95 percent of elementary schools are graded (Shepherd & Ragan, 1992), but there has always been criticism of that approach. A major weakness of this model is that children's development varies so greatly. A fourth-grade classroom, for example, includes students entering formal operations and others who are just leaving preoperational thought behind. A typical third-grade class has students who read on the first-grade level as well as those who read on the fifth-grade level. Related to this problem is the fact that development varies within the individual. A child may be ready for a third-grade reading book but struggling with first-grade mathematics.

Teachers in graded schools tend to teach toward the average student, thus boring the academically gifted while the slower students are frustrated. The student who needs more time to learn loses that opportunity when the class moves on to the next topic. Such students may find themselves repeating a grade level because the system failed to allow time for mastery.

A graded school lends itself to a sequence of content set by a governmental body, with textbooks prepared for each grade. Although the simplicity of this system is appealing to administrators, teachers find it difficult to gear the curriculum toward students' needs and interests. For instance, first graders who are interested in earth science must wait until the officially designated grade level (usually fourth) to study it in school. If their teacher bypassed the set curriculum and created a special unit, the required science content for first grade might never be taught. In addition, the possibility of poor performance on the end-of-the-year test would also be a threat.

Nongraded Schools

The nongraded school is designed to avoid these problems. Under this plan, instruction is based on children's needs and maturity level. The term "nongraded" refers to the school's use of performance-based groupings instead of age-based grade levels (see Figure 11.1). It does not refer to grades on report cards or student work.

In a nongraded system an eleven-year-old may learn long division at the same time as a nine-year-old. The key is mastery of the prerequisite steps of subtraction and multiplication. Because no one moves on until mastery is reached, everyone eventually achieves the feeling of success. Instructional groups are formed and reformed as students progress. Individualized instruction is common. Textbooks do not control the curriculum. Instead, the teacher adapts the content to the students' own timetables.

On the surface, nongraded schools seem like the perfect answer to a vexing problem. Indeed, research that compares graded and nongraded schools indicates significant advantages for nongraded programs. In 64 studies published between 1968 and 1991, only 9 percent report lower academic achievement for nongraded students. "In all other studies they performed better (58 percent) or the same (33 percent). As to mental health and school attitudes, 52 percent of the studies indicated nongraded schools as better; 43 percent similar, and only 4 percent worse than graded schools" (Pavan, 1992, p. 7).

Graded Elementary School (K–5)		
Grade 5 10-year-olds Room 4	Grade 4 9-year-olds Room 5	Grade 3 8-year-olds Room 6
Grade K 5-year-olds Room 1	Grade 1 6-year-olds Room 2	Grade 2 7-year-olds Room 3

Nongraded Elementary School (K–5)		
Age 7–10 Room 4	Age 6–9 Room 5	Age 6–10 Room 6
Age 5–10 Room 1	Age 5–7 Room 2	Age 5–10 Room 3

Note: Various age ranges are possible.

FIGURE 11.1. Graded and nongraded elementary schools.

Unfortunately, there are major constraints that have prevented implementation of nongraded programs on a wide scale. First is the demand on teachers. As we have discussed, it is fairly easy for teachers to rely exclusively on textbooks to determine what to teach. A nongraded program requires teachers who understand each individual child's needs, have a good grasp of the curricular sequence, can accurately assess student mastery, and can provide appropriate instruction. Many teachers have not been trained to conduct this type of curricular organization (Miller, 1991). Some may even question whether it is possible to find enough capable teachers to offer this type of organization.

A second problem is disorganization. Keeping track of children at different points of the sequence, with different levels of knowledge requires excellent record keeping. Teachers must also be able to cooperate and communicate with other teachers to avoid redundancy or gaps in the curriculum.

A third problem is public relations. As with any radical change, parents, teachers, students, and citizens are likely to react negatively. Because misconceptions are likely, a major educational effort would be required.

Proponents of nongraded schools are quick to respond to the constraints that are cited by critics of the plan. They point out that teachers are quite capable of conducting a nongraded plan. Such a plan may actually attract and retain talented educators who dislike the rigid system of graded schools.

The response to concerns about disorganization is that those conditions already exist. Students are at different levels of ability and knowledge in every class. The difference is that with graded schools, we treat them as if they were the same, ignoring the differences. As for the need for teacher communication with other teachers, that too is already required. This plan will force teachers to communicate more often.

Finally, proponents of the nongraded approach reject concerns about public reaction because there already are negative feelings about the schools. They believe that if radical change is necessary, it must be carried out. Public education can be conducted properly if steps are taken to avoid the mistakes of previous unsuccessful reform efforts (Fullan, 1991).

HORIZONTAL ORGANIZATION

Because nongraded schools are relatively rare, educators have made attempts to deal with variations in student knowledge and ability within the graded system. These plans are part of a horizontal organization, a way of arranging children within a particular grade level. All eight-year-olds may be randomly assigned to classes, for example, or the most intelligent may be put in one class with the next highest in another class and so on, or alternative arrangements may be made.

Self-Contained Classes

The most popular form of horizontal organization is self-contained classes. As its name implies, all teaching, except for certain special classes like physical education and music, is performed by one teacher in one classroom. There are considerable advantages to this method, but a number of disadvantages too.

Most teachers prefer the autonomy of self-contained classes (Feiman-Nemser & Floden, 1986). This is in part because spending so much time together develops close ties between teachers and children. Indeed, a self-contained class is much like a family. The teacher is able to observe student performance in a wide range of situations, thus seeing "the whole child."

Another major advantage of self-contained classes is the ability to implement a variety of curricular innovations. For the most part, a teacher in a self-contained classroom has control over the schedule and can spend as much or as little time as needed on any subject. This permits additional depth, integration between subjects, and flexible grouping.

The trouble with self-contained classes is that these opportunities are seldom utilized. The curriculum has tended to remain the same, with whole-class instruction geared to the average student, shallow instead of deep coverage, and a separation of subject areas. Many teachers do not have the knowledge and skill to provide depth, integrate subject areas, or manage flexible groups. In a self-contained classroom, a student whose teacher is weak in science or some other subject will suffer. In addition, personality clashes between the teacher and students can lead to a very difficult school year, with the possibility of long-term attitude problems developing.

Departmentalization

To deal with the weaknesses of the self-contained classroom, many elementary schools have tried a departmental approach (see Figure 11.2). With departmentalization, students have different teachers for different subject areas. This approach can be implemented by moving children to different classrooms, as in secondary schools, or having different teachers come to the children.

The basic benefit of departmentalization is that teachers are specialists. This addresses a major weakness of self-contained classrooms. The teacher in charge of social studies, for instance, is likely to be interested in the topic, have considerable

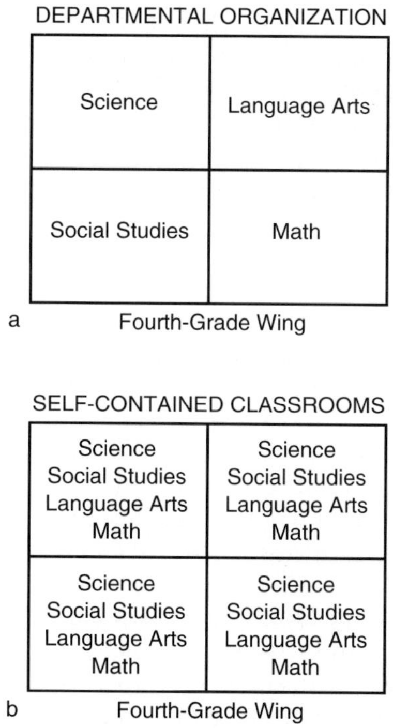

DEPARTMENTAL ORGANIZATION

Science	Language Arts
Social Studies	Math

a Fourth-Grade Wing

SELF-CONTAINED CLASSROOMS

Science Social Studies Language Arts Math	Science Social Studies Language Arts Math
Science Social Studies Language Arts Math	Science Social Studies Language Arts Math

b Fourth-Grade Wing

FIGURE 11.2. Departmental and self-contained configurations.

background knowledge, and be conversant with trends in the field. In addition, if departmental teachers are given their own classrooms, special facilities such as laboratory equipment or maps can be provided.

In departmental horizontal organization, children work with more than one teacher. This avoids the danger of personality conflicts ruining the school year, allows the stronger teachers to be shared by many students, and may promote a sense of responsibility and organization in the children.

The weakness of departmentalization is the strength of self-contained classes. A teacher who sees students for fifty minutes a day only sees the children from one perspective. A child who reads poorly may be an excellent mathematician, but the reading teacher would never know it. A child who misbehaves in science may be an outstanding citizen the rest of the day. In addition, close relationships are more difficult to develop in fifty-minute periods, and integration of subjects is almost impossible. Communication between teachers becomes of critical importance.

With departmentalization, it is easy to become a teacher of the subject instead of a teacher of children. For instance, the mathematics specialist who sees more than a hundred students a day has little opportunity to adjust lessons to individual needs. From the students' perspective, the relationship of mathematics to other subjects is not clear.

Some educators argue that elementary-age children need the security of a single teacher. For that reason, many schools do not begin departmentalization until the upper elementary grades, when it may be valued as preparation for secondary school. Many educators believe that younger students would have difficulty reconciling conflicting teacher demands. They also are concerned about the inefficiency and confusion that results from changing classrooms throughout the day.

Proponents of departmentalization respond that children are already accustomed to dealing with a variety of caregivers. After all, most elementary children are able to adapt to the differing demands of parents, grandparents, Sunday school teachers, coaches, scout leaders, and babysitters. As for inefficiency and confusion, it is argued that this can occur in a self-contained classroom as well; it is a matter of teacher management skills, not the organizational arrangement.

Team Teaching

To create a balance between self-contained and departmental organizations, educators have developed the team-teaching approach (see Figure 11.3). Under this plan, a team of teachers is responsible for coordinating the curriculum for a large group of children.

The actual plan is up to the teachers. They may have four self-contained classes and set up a common planning time. This allows teachers who are stronger in certain areas of the curriculum to help those who are less knowledgeable or inexperienced. Or the team may departmentalize, with each teacher being responsible for a particular subject. The team meets regularly to discuss the curriculum and the individual students, thus avoiding the dangers of

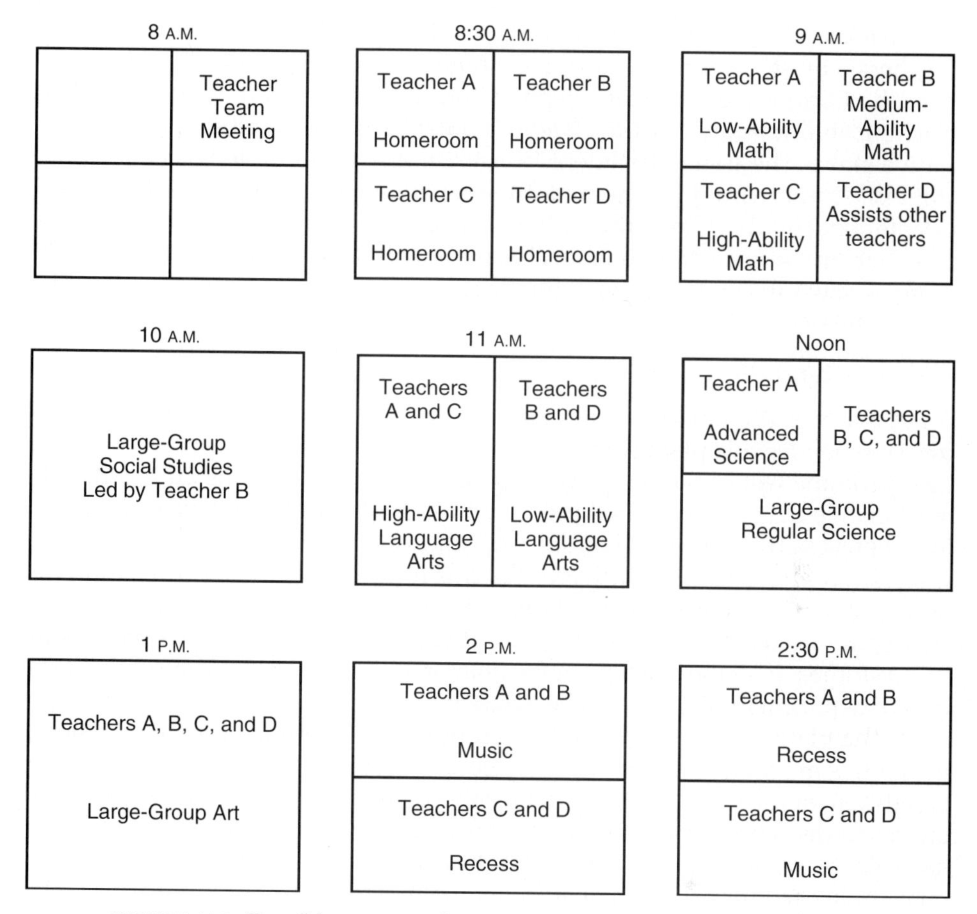

FIGURE 11.3. Possible team configurations, using an open-space facility.

departmentalization. Team teaching also allows for large-group instruction when appropriate, or flexible small groups, or any other arrangement the team may choose. Integration of subjects can also be managed through team planning.

There are a number of administrative benefits to team teaching. A long-standing challenge in education concerns the best way to utilize talented, veteran teachers (Little, 1988). Team teaching allows those teachers to share their knowledge as grade-level chairpersons but still remain in the classroom. Teachers who are weak or inexperienced can benefit from team planning and from observing the stronger teachers, a situation that is difficult to arrange with self-contained classrooms. When the team discusses individual students, the perspectives of a variety of teachers can be considered to gain an accurate reading of a child's strengths and weaknesses.

Unfortunately, team teaching also presents obstacles, the most significant of which is the preference of many teachers to work independently. Another drawback is the considerable amount of time required for team meetings. Teachers working as a team must make numerous compromises. To a large extent, the harmony of the team depends on the chairperson, whose excellent teaching abilities may not translate into outstanding leadership and administrative skills. The issue of student insecurity due to multiple teachers would still exist, but it would be lessened if the team shares a common philosophical orientation. Finally, there is the matter of space. A common area in which pupils can easily move from classroom to classroom will facilitate any team approach. Many school buildings lack such open areas.

Platoon System

A popular variation of team teaching is known as the platoon system (see Figure 11.4). Under this plan, students are taught by specialists for some subjects, but spend the rest of the day with a homeroom teacher. For instance, students may change classes for science and math, but stay with the homeroom teacher for language arts and social studies. This allows the homeroom teachers to develop strong relationships with the students in their classes, but still let the experts provide specialized instruction. Teachers who are weak in math, for instance, are excused from teaching it, but can capitalize on their strengths in social studies. If all the teachers in the platoon work as a team, some of the dangers of departmentalization can be avoided.

Some platoon systems use ability grouping to determine class assignment. Under this method, students are assigned to classes for language arts and math based on their level of proficiency in those subjects, but they stay in heterogenous groups under a homeroom teacher for the rest of the day. Thus, Ms. Smith may have the top readers from 9:00 till 11:00, the average math students from 11:00 till noon, and her randomly assigned homeroom class from noon until 3:00. Ms. Jones, who is particularly adept at teaching low-ability readers, may have the low reading group and the high math group. This type of platoon plan combines many of the benefits of self-contained, departmentalized, and team teaching. Ability grouping, however, is a sensitive topic that deserves special attention.

Ability Grouping

Ability grouping is the assignment of children to academic groups on the basis of achievement or mental maturity. It can take a number of forms (see Figure 11.5). On a district scale, an entire school can be set aside for high achievers, with other schools for average learners and low achievers. Within a single school, self-contained classes can be assigned, with all the high achievers in one class, all the low achievers in another, and average learners in a third. Within a self-contained class, the children can be sorted into instructional groups for various subject areas. As we have seen, a platoon organization can use ability groups for teaching certain subjects. Another variation has children grouped within multiple grade levels, so a low-ability math class may primarily consist of first graders but also include second and third graders.

Time			
8 A.M.	Homeroom (heterogenous)	Homeroom (heterogenous)	Homeroom (heterogenous)
9 A.M.	High-Ability Language Arts	Medium-Ability Language Arts	Low-Ability Language Arts
10 A.M.	PE (heterogenous by homeroom)	Music (heterogenous by homeroom)	Dance (heterogenous by homeroom)

Note: "Specials" rotate on a M-W-F basis.

Time			
11 A.M.	Low-Ability Math	High-Ability Math	Medium-Ability Math
Noon	Art (heterogenous by homeroom)	Social Studies (heterogenous by homeroom)	Science (heterogenous by homeroom)
1 P.M.	Social Studies (heterogenous by homeroom)	Science (heterogenous by homeroom)	Art (heterogenous by homeroom)
2 P.M.	Science (heterogenous by homeroom)	Art (heterogenous by homeroom)	Social Studies (heterogenous by homeroom)

FIGURE 11.4. Possible platoon configurations.

Usually, schools that use ability grouping assess student achievement at the start of the school year. Using mathematics as an example, the teacher of a typical fifth-grade class will discover that some students are weak in addition and subtraction (second-grade level), others are mastering multiplication (third- and fourth-grade level), a few advanced students are ready for algebra (sixth-grade level), while the majority are ready to study decimals and the rest of the fifth-grade curriculum.

If the students are grouped by ability within the classroom, four groups may be created. The teacher would probably work with one group at a time, meeting at a large table, while the other groups work at their desks. Grouping allows the teacher to give additional time and attention to the students below grade level, keep the bright students challenged by algebra instead of being constrained by

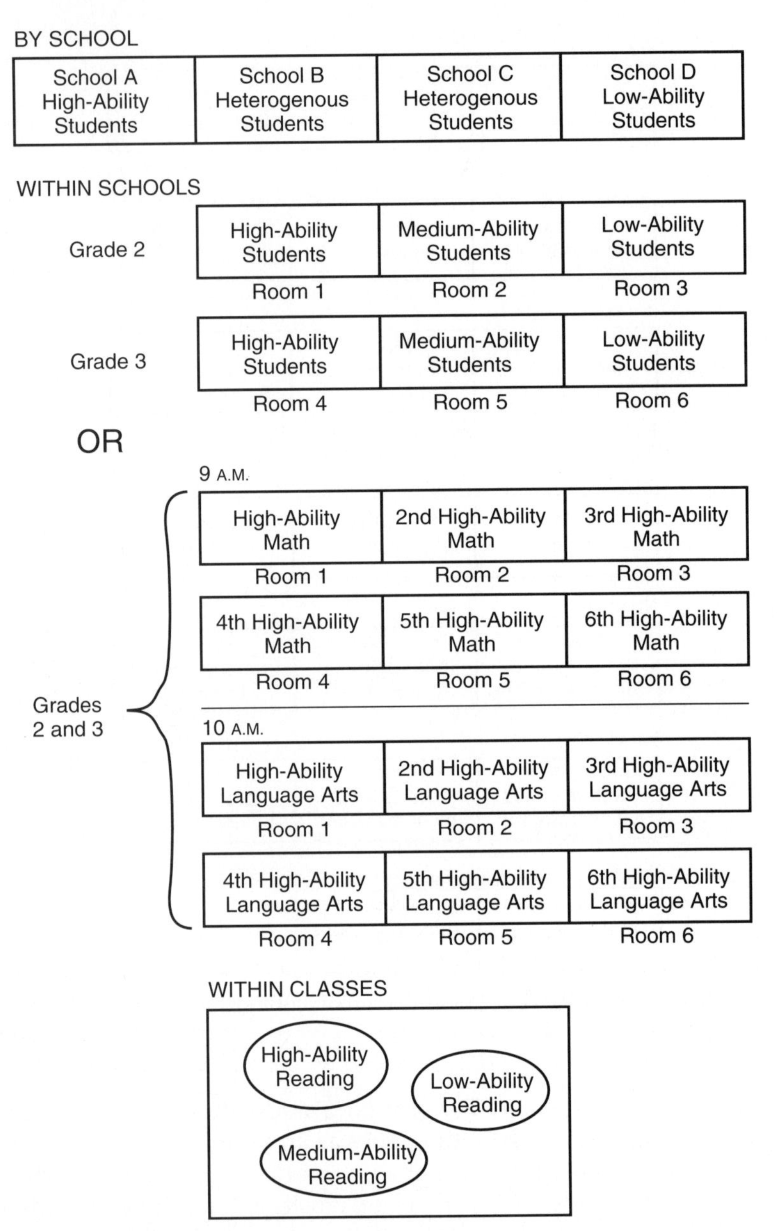

FIGURE 11.5. Types of ability grouping.

their slower classmates, and work at an appropriate pace with the grade-level group, without fear of moving too fast for the weaker students or boring the advanced students.

A drawback for within-class ability grouping is the time it takes to plan and teach four different lessons. Thus, we often see ability grouping across a grade level, or across multiple grade levels, so all the students in one classroom are at the same level. Under this approach, planning time is reduced and instructional time is expanded, thus allowing more opportunities to provide depth, work closely with individual students, and manage the multitude of tasks expected of a teacher.

Ability grouping for mathematics across a grade level or school necessitates abandoning self-contained classrooms. The only exception would be if students are assigned to a single teacher based on ability. This approach, similar to tracking in the secondary school, places students who are viewed as academically similar in the same class with the same teacher throughout the day (except for visiting special teachers in music, physical education, and so on).

The Ability-Grouping Debate

The basic argument for ability grouping is the benefit that comes from teaching students of similar ability. As we have seen, students at the same age can have a wide range of needs, thus necessitating individualized instruction. Ability grouping is designed to reduce the differences within a group, so that the group may be taught as a whole.

Orientation

This approach implies an essentialist orientation. Progressives and reconstructionists tend to prefer students working in groups according to their needs and interests. Such teachers would not be as concerned about students being at different levels as would teachers who build the curriculum around the textbook or lectures.

Student Variations

Even assuming that reduction of differences is intended, does ability grouping achieve that goal? It may reduce differences less than is typically assumed. If students are grouped on the basis of overall reading achievement, there may still be substantial differences in reading subskills. For instance, a child may be strong in decoding but weak in comprehension. If grouping is based on reading ability, there may still be considerable variation in mathematics ability. If intelligence tests are used, the resulting groups may be similar in IQ but not in performance. In matters of physical, social, and emotional development, the correlation would be even smaller (Oakes, Gamoran, & Page, 1993).

Curriculum Differentiation

The curriculum is a major issue in the ability-grouping debate. Students do not simply move at a different pace according to their instructional groups. High-ability classes are taught more of the curriculum than low-ability ones (Gamoran, 1986). They are also far more apt to engage in problem solving, in-depth study, authentic assignments, and higher-order tasks (Oakes, Gamoran, & Page, 1993).

It may be reasonably argued that low-ability students cannot engage in such activities until they are ready, but that too depends on your curricular philosophy. Advocates of whole language do not see reading as a step-by-step process involving a series of prerequisite skills. Nor do proponents of a problem-solving orientation view the learning of mathematics as hierarchical, as is sometimes assumed (Hiebert, 1987). Surely, there are times when it is helpful to learn one thing before another (e.g., place value before subtraction with regrouping), but that is not the only way to learn.

Even if one does endorse a hierarchical sequence of learning, the nature of the assessment system may prevent low-ability students from ever engaging in higher-level activities. Most ability-grouping systems are rigid in that students seldom change groups. For instance, in mathematics, if students in the low group never tackle the higher-level topic of measurement, they will be unable to perform well on the part of the assessment dealing with the topic. Therefore, they will be assigned to the low-ability group again, with its slow pace and low-level assignments, even if they are capable of more challenging work.

This cycle is particularly troubling when one considers that minority and low-SES (low-socioeconomic-status) children tend to score below the average on the types of achievement tests that are often used to assign students to groups (Oakes, Gamoran, & Page, 1993). Grouping often leads to a separation of schooling experiences in which poor and minority students receive an inferior education. Perhaps this pattern could be justified if there was evidence that students from those backgrounds are incapable of achievement at higher levels, but such is not the case (Oakes, 1990). Indeed, the low scores can be better explained by the problems identified in Chapter 2.

Developmental Issues

The nature of cognitive development further complicates ability-group assignments. Children who are not developmentally advanced would probably be placed in a lower group. As these students become concrete-operational, they would presumably be able to learn the same content as those in higher groups. Unfortunately, if they were not exposed to the curriculum of the higher group, they would not do as well on the assessment test, thus remaining in a lower group. To combat this vicious cycle, experts recommend that if grouping is done at all, it should be flexible, so that movement up or down is easily arranged (Good & Brophy, 1991).

Achievement

Proponents of ability grouping predict that it will promote student achievement. Yet an examination of the research shows that only certain kinds of grouping may be considered successful, and then only under certain circumstances (Slavin, 1987). Ability grouping into self-contained classes clearly does not increase academic achievement. However, there is evidence that regrouping for reading and mathematics, as in the platoon approach, may be effective as long as instructional methods are adapted to meet student differences. In other words, using the same techniques to teach all groups is not helpful. Within-class grouping has also been proven effective in the upper elementary grades.

Polarization

Other concerns about ability grouping exist beyond overall academic achievement. One is the indication that high-ability groups benefit more than low-ability groups, thus widening the gap between the two types of students

(Oakes, Gamoran, & Page, 1993). Therefore, the decision to use or not use ability groups may be influenced by whether you value improving the achievement of low-ability students at the expense of higher-ability students, or whether you think society is better served by an arrangement that helps high-ability students more. This societal issue deserves public debate. On one hand, improving the success of those on the bottom may lead to reductions in poverty, crime, drug abuse, and cultural divisiveness. On the other hand, greater success for those at the top may lead to advances in meeting societal goals in science, business, and other important areas.

Nonacademic goals are also a concern. In heterogenous classrooms, students of all abilities are constantly interacting. This may lead to cross-cultural understanding, informal peer tutoring, and cooperative learning. Grouping by ability has the opposite effect, tending to divide students. It may have a number of troublesome effects. For one, the lack of contact between social and racial groups is likely to polarize students, thus counteracting some of the progress made by desegregation and mainstreaming.

A second nonacademic effect of ability grouping is the atmosphere in low-ability classes. The absence of academically successful peers leads to a lack of leadership, numerous behavior problems, and a general attitude of defeatism and alienation (Good & Brophy, 1991). These factors may help explain ability grouping's lack of success. When two students of similar ability are assigned to different groups, the one in the higher group is likely to have higher achievement (Veldman & Sanford, 1984).

The use of platoon systems helps to alleviate some of the polarization caused by grouping because students of differing ability spend the majority of the day together. There are opportunities to interact in art class, physical education, and the lunchroom. The atmosphere in low-ability reading and mathematics classes, however, will still suffer.

A common concern among critics of ability grouping is the effect of labeling on student self-esteem. It is believed that placing students in lower groups calls attention to their lack of ability. Research indicates, however, that elementary students are quite aware of each others' relative ability at an early age (Evert & Barnett, 1982). They learn it from class performance, test results, and differences in learning materials. Besides, one purpose of ability grouping is to inspire low-ability students to work harder so they may join the higher groups (Slavin, 1987). Knowledge of one's relative standing would be necessary to achieve this goal. However, this can only occur when groups are flexible and temporary.

Alternatives to Rigid Ability Grouping

In a self-contained classroom, within-class grouping allows teachers to easily move children in and out of groups as necessary. Based on an analysis of student writing, for example, temporary groups can be created to focus on such topics as expressive language, paragraph formation, and use of apostrophes. Every student has some area in which to improve, and students may be members of more than one group. The teacher can provide appropriate learning experiences for the different groups and disband them when students have mastered the objective.

This flexible approach is not limited to self-contained classes. In a platoon or team-teaching system, teachers can periodically reorganize their groups depending on changes in student performance. This requires considerable administrative and instructional flexibility, but may be worth the effort to avoid the dangers of rigid ability grouping.

Grouping under a progressive philosophy is based more on student interest than ability. In a progressive curriculum, students work together to solve the problems of their groups. For instance, students interested in the clothing of ancient Greece can share the responsibilities of researching the topic, designing costumes, and sewing. Differences in ability level encourage students to help one another learn.

Whole language approaches also involve using mixed-ability groups to read stories, create drama, and critique each other's writing. As indicated in Chapter 7, the emphasis on interaction is a key element in developing language skills.

Cooperative learning groups have proven to be quite effective in improving academic achievement (Slavin, 1983). Research findings indicate particular advantages for minority students whose cultures emphasize interaction and cooperation (Strickland & Ascher, 1993). Related benefits are enhanced self-esteem, cultural awareness, and achievement of other nonacademic goals (Johnson & Johnson, 1989).

These alternatives to rigid ability grouping reflect certain beliefs about the nature of the curriculum. Of course, no method of organization, by itself, will make a difference in student learning. Choosing a system that fits your curriculum goals can help you reach those goals, just as a poor match can hinder you. The decision is one that teachers need to make.

CLASS SIZE

Just as teachers frequently take classroom organization for granted, so too they consider class size to be a given. What is so magical about having twenty-five to thirty students per class? This remnant of nineteenth-century education has harmed the curriculum. The presence of too many students prevents teachers from implementing many of the curricular recommendations discussed in previous chapters. There are numerous examples.

To develop skill in writing, students must be given the opportunity to write and receive feedback. If a teacher in a self-contained classroom with thirty students spends fifteen minutes reviewing each writing assignment, that translates into seven and a half hours of paper grading with a similar amount of time devoted to discussions with the students. That is in addition to grading assignments in five or six other subject areas. For the departmentalized teacher who specializes in language arts and teaches 120 students, the time allotment might be thirty hours of grading papers. This helps to explain why many language arts teachers may choose to assign work that is less useful but easier to grade.

The development of skill in oral expression is also constrained by class size. Listening to thirty students making oral presentations can take up an entire week of class time. Having students give their presentations to another student, in pairs, means that fourteen or fifteen students are speaking at once, which can create enough noise to disturb other classes or invite administrative wrath.

Oral expression is an integral part of the social studies class. Discussion of values and feelings works better when students get to share their ideas aloud. In a large class, however, students have fewer opportunities to speak and even less chance of engaging in thoughtful debate.

The need for hands-on science investigations is quite clear. However, the reality of managing so many students doing experiments presents a major teaching challenge. Helping students plan experiments and then supervising the process (often under somewhat dangerous conditions) requires a great deal of teacher awareness and skill. This constraint could be lessened with fewer students to manage.

The same is true for art. Most teachers would welcome the opportunity to move beyond coloring books and simple cutting and pasting. But the use of such media as paint, sculpture, and papier-mâché can quickly lead to accidents, disorder, and a general mess. How much easier it would be to have fewer paint cans, water jars, and a smaller crowd around the sink!

Mathematics instruction in the elementary school would benefit from the use of manipulatives and computers. However, most schools have limited amounts of materials and an inadequate supply budget. Smaller classes would result in more access to the manipulatives and computers.

Physical education, music, and dance classes often suffer from a lack of individual instruction. To provide proper coaching, time must be spent observing the student, offering feedback, and creating opportunities for students to apply that feedback. Doing so for thirty students takes more time than is usually allowed for special classes. This problem is compounded for specialists who must meet more than one class per period.

Another weakness of larger classes is that they allow inadequate time for lesson planning. A large number of students translates into additional record-keeping and other administrative chores. That leaves less planning time after school to create meaningful activities.

Research on Class Size

It seems apparent that reductions in class size would be a major impetus to curricular reform. There is substantial evidence that smaller classes do actually result in higher achievement. Although the best results were achieved in kindergarten and first grade, teachers of small classes across all grades were able to move quickly beyond the basics. Researchers found significant changes taking place in smaller classrooms, including more enrichment, more in-depth studies, greater use of concrete materials, improved teacher monitoring of misbehavior, more use of feedback, more variety in instructional techniques, and more individualized attention (Word et al., 1990).

Two key findings are crucial in interpreting the research on small classes. First, the number of students must be substantially reduced. Adjusting class size by two or three students does not permit the type of curricular adjustments that are needed. The research cited above is based on a class size of about fifteen students.

Second, the curriculum must be adjusted (Evertson, 1990). To take advantage of reductions in class size, teachers must do things differently. A lecture-oriented approach will yield the same benefits for fifteen students as for thirty. So will cookie-cutter art activities. Reduced class size is an opportunity to implement a more effective curriculum.

The Challenge

Why, then, are schools not immediately cutting class size in half? The answer is simple: money. Smaller classes require twice as many teachers. Since payroll makes up the lion's share of the school budget, it is easy to see how expensive that change would be. School facilities would also have to be altered. One expert indicates that a one-third reduction in class size will result in a one-third increase in costs (Folger, 1990).

Imagine how different American schooling would be if classes were magically cut in half. How many excellent students would be attracted to the teaching profession? How many teachers would remain in the profession and not be discouraged by the amount of work required for so many students? How many weak students would benefit from the extra attention and become successful learners instead of dropping out? How many strong students would be challenged and grow to love learning instead of being bored by the busywork required to manage a large class? Teachers can fight to make this change that could transform the nature of education.

Class size is not normally thought of as a curriculum issue. But, like funding, teacher pay, and, as we shall see, classroom management, decisions in these areas directly affect what is taught and learned.

CLASSROOM MANAGEMENT

Classroom management is related to the size of classes. A decrease in the number of students should result in fewer behavior problems. However, until changes are made, the curriculum will continue to be affected by the threat of disorder. Many of the effects of classroom disorder are obvious, but others may change your way of thinking about schools and discipline.

The Effects of Classroom Disorder

It has been estimated that 40 percent of classroom time is spent on behavior control (Goodlad, 1984). While that percentage must vary considerably among teachers, this finding implies three probable outcomes.

Untaught Content

First, time spent on management leaves insufficient time to teach what is in the curriculum. Therefore, segments of the curriculum go untaught. The math teacher will have to neglect the teaching of measurement, the study of American history must end at the Civil War, and the art teacher must forgo the unit on three-dimensional art. Both the individual and the overall society pay the price for the resulting absence of student knowledge in these and other areas.

Inappropriate Activities

A second outcome of spending so much time on behavior control is that the curriculum must be covered in a hurried manner. Although we do not like to think of teaching as "covering," in this case the word is apt. With so much instructional time devoted to behavior management, there is little opportunity for depth or developmentally appropriate methods. Therefore, teachers may decide to tell the students what happens in a science experiment instead of letting them design and conduct it themselves. In language arts, the students may read a play in class instead of creating their own production. Multiplication might be taught through abstract numerals instead of time-consuming manipulatives. The effect of these decisions is boredom and a loss of student learning, possibly leading to curriculum disabilities (as discussed in Chapter 3).

Further Misbehavior

Ironically, the decisions that are made to accelerate movement through the curriculum are likely to lead to even more student misbehavior. The boring, trivial nature of school tasks is one of the popular explanations for student misbehavior (Doyle, 1986). Thus, eliminating the drama, science experiments, and manipulatives may result in student disinterest, which leads to misbehavior, which leads to even less time for instruction. A vicious circle is created.

Preventing vs. Avoiding Misbehavior

Teachers need to *prevent* misbehavior to allow more time for learning. The recommended approach (Good & Brophy, 1991) is to develop skills in classroom management. Unfortunately, many teachers choose to sidestep (rather than prevent) misbehavior by assigning work that is familiar and easy to complete. Low-level activities and other busywork are often assigned to keep students occupied and out of mischief. These activities are also helpful in minimizing student anxiety. Unfortunately, such learning tasks tend to defeat the purpose of the curriculum (Doyle, 1986). Students may feel more comfortable doing a series of subtraction problems, for example, but that assignment cannot replace the challenge of problem solving.

In their concern for maintaining order, teachers also tend to avoid activity-oriented lessons (McCutcheon, 1988). When concrete and meaningful learning activities are not provided, student understanding of the content suffers. And despite teachers' intentions, misbehavior is likely to increase because of the sameness of the activities that are provided. In a study of effective classroom managers, the use of variety and challenge in seatwork was cited as one of the keys in maintaining student attention (Kounin, 1970). The equation is one we know from our own experiences: lack of challenge and variety leads to off-task behavior.

Reprinted by permission: James Estes

Classrooms as Dictatorships

Teacher interest in maintaining order has another effect on the curriculum, a hidden one. When the class atmosphere emphasizes following directions and avoiding punishment, students are learning how to live in a dictatorship. Alternately, if they engage in a classroom structure that allows them to manage their own behavior, they learn how to live in a democracy.

Most classrooms have a heavy emphasis on teacher control. Children must follow a series of rules or else suffer reprimands and punishment doled out by the teacher, the author of the rules (see Figure 11.6). In a sense, the teacher is the legislator, police officer, judge, and jury. As in any dictatorship, the subjects develop a sense of alienation and an inclination to rebel. Thus, students develop elaborate techniques for working against the system. For instance, to avoid punishments for talking during seatwork, children learn how to pass notes, talk without turning one's head, and meet at the pencil sharpener. Their skill in this area is dependent on learning classroom routines so that the surreptitious talking can be conducted while the teacher's back is turned. (These fairly inconsequential rebellions constitute the majority of elementary school student misbehavior. Despite public perceptions, the misbehavior in the elementary school classroom is fairly benign.) Good classroom managers know how to avoid such situations to prevent the off-task behavior from occurring (Emmer & Evertson, 1981).

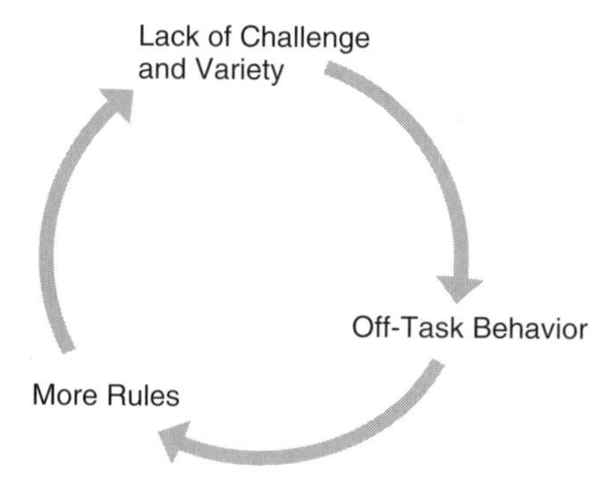

FIGURE 11.6. The vicious classroom management cycle.

When students engage in their minor rebellions, they learn lessons from a hidden curriculum that has harmful aspects. They begin to recognize the absurdity of school life in which they must ask permission to go to the bathroom, get up from their seats, or briefly chat with a neighbor. Children learn that rules tend to be trivial and arbitrary, and that breaking them rarely leads to serious consequences, except when the presiding officer is in a bad mood and may pun-

Theory to Practice
Classroom Management

The gymnasium is not just for physical education classes. It often serves as a site for children to pass the time before and after school and during lunch. Unfortunately, the students of Harmony School in Indiana (as described by Goodman, 1992) were abusing their gym privilege. Their play got so wild that the noise level became extremely high, some equipment was destroyed, and younger children were afraid to enter the area. In response, the gym was placed off limits.

When the children asked when they would be able to use the gym again, they were told that it was not a teacher decision. The faculty wanted the students to come up with a plan. That issue became the focus of a series of school meetings.

The students first suggested having more adult supervision. The teachers objected to that because it would interfere with valuable planning time. To come up with a better plan, a student committee was formed with representatives from each grade level.

Eventually, the committee proposed a set of rules and consequences, a student organization to enforce them, and even an appeals procedure. When the plan was endorsed by both students and staff, the gym was reopened.

Goodman's example demonstrates how students can take responsibility for their own behavior if they are given the chance. Notice that the sharing of power led to a win-win situation. The students benefitted by getting their gym back, and the teachers were able to maintain order without having to sacrifice time and energy. The most important benefit may be the exercise in democratic citizenship that took place.

ish the entire group for the infractions of one or two members. This conception of justice is not one that society would endorse! (See Henry, 1963, for a powerful analysis of this phenomenon.)

Classrooms as Democracies

An alternative approach to classroom management can effectively teach students self-discipline, responsibility for the group, and respect for individual rights and justice. These are central components of democratic life that are already part of the curriculum but disappear in the pervasive atmosphere of teacher control.

The premise, based on Dewey's (1902) concept of classrooms as "embryonic societies," is to pass responsibility for classroom rules to the students (Passe, 1991). Even the youngest students are capable of proposing and implementing rules for distributing playground equipment, cleaning up the art area, and assigning chores.

Of course, as in any democratic system, constitutional limits are placed on legislative acts, so teachers may feel free to veto inappropriate rules (e.g., banning all assignments) or unreasonable consequences (e.g., getting paddled for whispering). However, more important than the ultimate rules and consequences is the student interaction that ensues. Through "moral discourse" (Habermas, 1979), children can discuss what is right and wrong, listen to one another, compromise, and generally experience democratic citizenship. The discourse will probably lead to the approval of fair rules if they are considered along with the more outrageous suggestions.

Students are also more likely to follow their own rules because they understand them better (Good & Brophy, 1991). If the rules or consequences are ineffective, as often happens in society, students can analyze them and revise them accordingly. They learn that maintaining a just, democratic society requires vigilance and flexibility. Many goals from other subject areas will necessarily be integrated through this approach to classroom management: oral expression and listening (during discourse); scientific observation, experimentation, and statistical reports (concerning the success of the rules); sociological and psychological insight (as rules and consequences are analyzed); and the nature of justice, ethics, and responsibility. A democratic classroom exemplifies progressivism, with its emphasis on students constructing their knowledge of society.

An anecdote from my teaching experience may help to illustrate the problems of traditional teacher-centered power and the possible advantages of alternative methods. Like most teachers, I imposed a rule that students must receive permission before leaving to go to the bathroom. To my dismay, I received requests at the most inappropriate times. Typically, during a great class discussion, a weak student would raise his hand and I would eagerly welcome his input only to learn that he merely wanted to leave the room. He would then use the occasion to draw attention to himself as he sauntered out.

One time, I was in an angry mood because my students had been irresponsible. Just then, one of my better students asked permission to go to the bathroom. "No," I replied. Being an obedient sort, she merely nodded and, probably, held her legs a little tighter together than before. At that point, I felt foolish. Why was I so nasty? And what right did I have to decide when someone should use the bathroom?

I decided to present the problem to the class. "I no longer want to be bothered with bathroom decisions. Let's set up a new system." A number of reasonable proposals were proposed, and the class consensus was to have two bathroom passes, one for each sex, to use when they saw fit. I proposed that abusing the bathroom privileges (e.g., by creating mischief) would result in those persons having to ask permission until they demonstrated more responsibility.

For the next few days, you would have thought that free candy was being passed out in the bathrooms. Children raced each other for the pass as soon as it was returned to the room. However, the novelty wore off when the lucky recipients of the bathroom pass found that being in a bathroom is not particularly exciting. The thrill of freedom became rather mundane.

Still, there was a need for revision. I became frustrated when students happened to be in the bathroom while I gave instructions or organized small groups. When I shared my concern, it turned out that the students had a problem too, with the distractions of people leaving the room during whole-class instruction. So, the rule was revised to limit bathroom privileges to independent work time.

This new rule became instantly revised when a student ran up to me during a lesson, gagging, indicating the need to vomit. In an attempt to prevent a humiliating experience and to protect the carpeting, I immediately pointed the student toward the bathroom. I then proposed that the rule be suspended in emergencies. "Tell me about it when you come back," I suggested. My idea passed unanimously.

Eventually the "great bathroom experiment" became common policy in most classrooms in my school. One can only guess how much embarrassment was avoided by students with intestinal problems, how much classroom interruption was curtailed, and, of course, how much citizenship and self-discipline was developed through this program. If we want students to be active citizens, we must give them the opportunity to develop the necessary skills. A teacher-controlled system is not the solution.

Questions

1. Of all the various organizational patterns, which ones appeal to you the most? Why?
2. What experiences have you had with ability grouping? Do the criticisms that have been cited seem accurate? Explain.
3. What are your reactions to the alternatives to teacher-centered power over student behavior?
4. Would reduction in class size be viewed favorably by your community? Why or why not?

References

DEWEY, J. (1902). *The child and the curriculum.* Chicago: University of Chicago Press.

DOYLE, W. (1986). Classroom organization and management. In M. E. Wittrock (Ed.), *Handbook of research on teaching* (3rd ed.) (pp. 392–431). New York: Macmillan.

Emmer, E. T., & Evertson, C. M. (1981). Synthesis of research on classroom management. *Educational Leadership, 38,* 342–347.
Evert, N. N., & Barnett, B. G. (1982). Student perceptions of better readers in elementary classrooms. *Elementary School Journal, 82,* 435–449.
Evertson, C. (1990). Teaching practices and class size: A new look at an old issue. *Contemporary Education, 62,* 85–105.
Feiman-Nemser, S., & Floden, R. E. (1986). The cultures of teaching. In M. E. Wittrock (Ed.), *Handbook of research on teaching* (pp. 505–526). New York: Macmillan.
Folger, J. (1990). Lessons for class size policy and research. *Contemporary Education, 62,* 123–131.
Fullan, M. G. (1991). *The new meaning of educational change* (2nd ed.). New York: Teachers College Press.
Gamoran, A. (1986). Instructional and institutional effects of ability grouping. *Sociology of Education, 59,* 185–198.
Good, T. L., & Brophy, J. E. (1991). *Looking in classrooms* (5th ed.). New York: HarperCollins.
Goodlad, J. I. (1984). *A place called school.* New York: McGraw-Hill.
Goodman, J. (1992). *Elementary schooling for critical democracy.* Albany, New York: State University of New York Press.
Habermas, J. (1979). *Communication and the evolution of society.* Boston: Beacon Press.
Henry, J. (1963). *Culture against man.* New York: Random House.
Hiebert, E. H. (1987). The context of instruction and student learning: An examination of Slavin's assumptions. *Review of Educational Research, 57,* 337–340.
Johnson, D., & Johnson, R. (1989). *Cooperation and competition: Theory and research.* Edina, MN: Interaction Book Co.
Kounin, J. (1970). *Discipline and group management in classrooms.* New York: Holt.
Little, J. (1988). Assessing the prospects for teacher leadership. In A. Lieberman (Ed.), *Building a professional culture in schools* (pp. 147–163). New York: Teachers College Press.
McCutcheon, G. (1988). Curriculum and work of teachers. In L. E. Beyer, and M. W. Apple (Eds.), *The curriculum: Problems, politics, and possibilities* (pp. 191–203). Albany, NY: State University of New York Press.
Miller, B. (1991). Teaching and learning in the multi-grade classroom: Student performance and instructional routines. ERIC Document ED 335178.
Oakes, J. (1990). *Lost talent: The underparticipation of women, minorities, and disabled persons in science.* Santa Monica, CA: Rand.
Oakes, J., Gamoran, A., & Page, R. N. (1993). Curriculum differentiation: Opportunities, outcomes, and meanings. In P. W. Jackson (Ed.), *Handbook of research on curriculum* (pp. 570–608). New York: Macmillan.
Passe, J. (1991). Citizenship knowledge in young learners. *Social Studies and the Young Learner, 31,* 15–17.
Pavan, B. N. (1992) School effectiveness and nongraded schools. Paper presented to the Annual Meeting of the American Educational Research Association, San Francisco. ERIC Document 340008.
Shepherd, G. D., & Ragan, W. B. (1992). *Modern Elementary Curriculum* (7th ed.). Fort Worth, TX: Harcourt Brace Jovanovich.
Slavin, R. E. (1983). *Cooperative learning.* White Plains, NY: Longman.
Slavin, R. E. (1987). Ability grouping: A best-evidence synthesis. *Review of Educational Research, 57,* 293–336.

STRICKLAND, D. S., & ASCHER, C. (1993). Low-income African-American children and public schooling. In P. W. Jackson (Ed.), *Handbook of research on curriculum* (pp. 609–625). New York: Macmillan.

VELDMAN, D. J., & SANFORD, J. P. (1984). The influence of class ability level on student achievement and classroom behavior. *American Educational Research Journal, 21,* 629–644.

WORD, E., ACHILLES, C. M., BAIN, H., FOLGER, J., JOHNSTON, J., & LINTZ, N. (1990). Project Star final executive summary: K through 3rd grade results, 1985–89. *Contemporary Education, 62,* 106–126.

CHAPTER 12

The Integrated Elementary Curriculum

After many years of tinkering with the curriculum, educators are increasingly calling for a restructuring of school subjects. Subject-area leaders have long recognized that no subject is sufficient by itself; each is part of the whole. The National Council of Teachers of Math (1989) identified mathematical connections as a cornerstone of its curriculum standards. Discipline-Based Arts Education is designed to integrate the arts across the curriculum (Getty Center for Arts Education, 1985). The developmental approach to physical education works toward the overall goals of the elementary school program; it is not just an additional subject (Hoffman, Young, & Klesius, 1981). Similar efforts are underway in the fields of science (Hurd, 1991) and social studies (NCSS, 1993). In language arts, the popular whole language movement is based on the premise of integration.

BENEFITS OF THE INTEGRATED CURRICULUM

The traditional curriculum can be substantially improved by integration. Consider just a few of the benefits alluded to in earlier chapters:

- Because "the whole is greater than the sum of its parts," more effective learning can result from an integrated curriculum. Incorporating the arts into the study of history, for instance, may foster a deeper understanding of historical trends as well as a greater appreciation of artistic creations than if the two subjects are taught separately.
- Subjects that have been isolated and de-emphasized because of tradition or the role of specialists can be readily incorporated into the everyday curriculum. For instance, art is no longer "what we do on Friday afternoons" and physical education is not reserved for the specialist.
- The overemphasis on textbooks is diminished. Instead, teachers can create their own curriculum units to meet their students' individual needs. The curriculum can then be better oriented toward children's interests and developmental levels.

- The nature of the integrated curriculum lends itself to joint teacher and student authorship, resulting in a dynamic, interactive process rather than a situation in which teachers simply implement a stale set of objectives created by a set of individuals who are more removed from the classroom. Authorship promotes student interest in the curriculum (Jacobs, 1989). It is likely to do the same for teachers, who are unhappy when teaching topics they find irrelevant.
- An integrated curriculum encourages a whole language orientation. Language skills and knowledge can be developed in the context of other learning, rather than in the isolated fashion of the traditional curriculum.
- With integration, problem solving is not limited to the time set aside for mathematics. Real problems from the worlds of art, physical education, science, and social studies provide a focus.
- Science and social studies are no longer seen as school subjects that bear no relation to everyday life. Students can learn to appreciate these sometimes unpopular subjects by studying the scientific or social aspects of common everyday situations.
- The ever-growing list of mandated school subjects combined with high-stakes testing creates tremendous tension in the curriculum. Every item that is added causes something else to be dropped. Unfortunately, the more meaningful and complex topics are ignored because they are time-consuming. An integrated curriculum, which combines subject areas, may be more efficient in its use of classroom time. Depth usually reached only in long-term projects is achieved because there are fewer artificial time limits (Jacobs, 1989; Passe, 1996).

Drawbacks of the Integrated Curriculum

The vision of the integrated curriculum may be exciting, but it is not the perfect answer. There are no simple solutions to complex problems. Instead, there are alternative visions, and an integrated curriculum is just one.

The integrated curriculum is not for everybody. Some students may be better served by the traditional subject-centered curriculum or some other arrangement. Certainly, some teachers are uncomfortable and ineffective using an integrated approach. Parental and administrative concerns must also be considered.

An integrated curriculum brings with it a variety of problems that must be addressed. Matters of school and classroom organization, testing, resource materials, teacher preparation, the role of specialists, and a host of other serious concerns must be reconsidered in light of a curriculum transformation. As we have seen throughout the history of the schools, every action brings a reaction. Teachers who seek to implement an integrated curriculum will have to prepare for all sorts of consequences, many of which will be unexpected.

The Need to Focus on a Single Approach

The rest of this chapter describes methods of planning an integrated curriculum. At this point you may wonder why, if there are alternative visions, only this particular approach is being presented. Is it a matter of bias? Yes. As indicated in earlier chapters, bias cannot be avoided in education or any decision-making activity. I feel strongly about the need for an integrated curriculum, but I am far from alone in this view. Many authorities in the field of elementary education have endorsed curriculum integration (as have a surprising number of secondary school educators). In fact, this issue has been cited as the number one curricular challenge in a poll of teachers (Jacobs, 1989).

Integration is sometimes regarded as "the approach of the future." By now you know that several major educational approaches were never seriously implemented, but cynical dismissal of this or any other approach can only be harmful. At the very least, this chapter can help you understand the approach to see if it would work for you, or if it can be adapted to fit the needs of you and your students, or if it should be rejected. An informed decision is the best one.

What about techniques for planning the traditional curriculum? This book provides insights into that process too, but in most teacher education programs, traditional methods are demonstrated in the specific methods courses and in visits to schools. This chapter is designed to describe a method that is different. It is rarely experienced by prospective teachers and, thus, a detailed description is necessary. The same is not true for traditional approaches, which are both common and relatively simple in comparison.

Theory to Practice

Integration

Students at Jackson Elementary School in Salt Lake City were studying the important role of trees in maintaining the environment (Lesko, 1992). They wanted to plant trees to prevent erosion, recycle water, and reverse the greenhouse effect. But how can kids raise the necessary funds?

Their studies of the political system came in handy. They decided to contact Utah's Senator Orin Hatch for assistance. But rather than ask for direct assistance, they proposed a matching grant.

Thus, mathematics was introduced with the topic of percentage. The students suggested having kids match 10 to 20 percent of all federal funds for tree planting. To make their case, they pointed out how a single tree saves $62,000 in air pollution costs, thus using large numbers that are not usually used by elementary school children.

The students implemented language arts when they wrote a letter to Senator Hatch. The letter was, apparently, well received because one of the students was invited to Washington to use her skills of persuasion to convince other congressional leaders to support the idea.

Ultimately, a federal law, the America the Beautiful Act of 1990, was created. It included a provision to award matching grants to youth groups for planting and cultivating trees.

This exercise in citizen action combined science, math, social studies, and language arts in a seamless fashion. All the relevant topics were standard parts of the curriculum. By using them in a real-life situation, what the students learned was greater than the sum of its parts.

A verbal description of a model, however, can only provide an overview. You must supplement what you learn from this book with other sources of information such as films, videotapes, lesson plans and, especially, visits to actual schools that use an integrated curriculum. Through this text and your own research, the power of an integrated curriculum will become apparent to you. It is not a new idea. It has excited educators throughout the twentieth century.

TWO APPROACHES TO CURRICULUM INTEGRATION

There are two basic approaches to curriculum integration: adapting an existing curriculum and creating a new curriculum. Deciding which approach to use depends on the situation. Many teachers begin by experimenting with integration. When their adaptations are successful they may then gradually expand its use. This approach is particularly appropriate for inexperienced teachers because they are relatively unfamiliar with the existing curriculum, their students' interests, needs, and capabilities, and their own teaching style.

More experienced teachers who have the freedom to experiment may choose to implement a new curriculum from scratch. This approach is, of course, more challenging, but may also be more effective. Partial integration of the curriculum may create confusion among students, parents, and administrators. Planning two types of curriculum simultaneously can be difficult too.

Creating an Integrated Curriculum from Scratch

Because a totally integrated curriculum is the ultimate goal of either approach, our discussion starts with creating a new curriculum. In that way, you can visualize the destination before choosing a path to follow.

Choosing a Theme

The first step in the process is to decide on a theme. The choice should be based on the following considerations.

Student Interest. To motivate students, the theme should be one that students will find exciting. An integrated unit may last for weeks at a time, so the theme should be one that will get them out of bed in the morning. Some guaranteed winners are dinosaurs, television, pets, and the circus.

The optimum plan is to have the students choose the topic. This insures that the theme will be one they like. It also promotes student responsibility for making decisions (Passe, 1996). The choice of themes can be decided by vote or by consensus.

The drawback to student choice is the lack of preparation time it leaves the teachers. It takes many hours to plan a unit. Letting the children choose their topic during the first days of school will not allow enough leeway to design an appropriate unit.

To avoid the problem of time constraints, many teachers choose the first unit for the students, based on their expectations of what will be appealing. These expectations could come from previous experiences with the topic, conversations with children of the same age, and the recommendations of colleagues and parents.

If the teacher chooses the first unit, the students have the opportunity to see how an integrated unit works, thus preparing them to choose subsequent themes. It also gives the teacher confidence knowing that the students' initial experiences in his or her classroom will be well-planned to promote interest and learning. Once the structure of the classroom has been established, it is easier to manage student-centered activities. Finally, teacher choice of the theme increases the chances that the unit will be educationally valid.

Educational Validity. Combining two or more subject areas may make a unit integrated, but it does not make it educationally valid (Ackerman, 1989). To be valid, the students must learn something valuable. For instance, many teachers attempt to integrate their curriculum by including science terms in the weekly spelling list. That is a legitimate integration combining spelling and science, but it may not meet valid goals. If a fourth-grade class is studying the human body, they will be learning words such as esophagus, larynx, and retina. However, spelling those words is too difficult for most fourth graders, who will only be forced to memorize them temporarily. Studying the unusual spellings will not improve student knowledge of orthography. Thus, the integration has no educational benefits.

Another invalid attempt at integration is the choice of "fun" activities. Some teachers use word-finding activities to integrate social studies and language. For instance, a class studying the thirteen colonies may receive a sheet of paper with each colony's name hidden within a grid of letters.

M	F	G	E	O	R	G	I	A	M	V	B
J	A	T	Y	U	C	V	B	N	A	I	Q
F	D	R	V	B	Y	U	I	O	P	R	M
W	E	T	Y	V	C	D	S	E	W	G	A
L	K	J	H	L	F	D	P	O	I	I	Y
C	X	S	A	Z	A	T	B	H	G	N	M
P	L	M	O	K	J	N	F	W	E	I	P
C	O	C	E	E	C	B	D	S	A	A	U

These activities, like most puzzles, are enjoyable. But what goal does it achieve? It does not develop skill or knowledge in spelling or reading. It really does not help students learn about the colonies either, other than to recognize their names. Integration for the sake of integration (or fun) is educationally invalid. This is not to argue that students should not enjoy learning, but there are numerous pleasurable activities that also meet educational objectives.

Another aspect of educational validity is whether the theme fits with students' needs. A unit on the seasons may be perfectly appropriate for kindergartners but somewhat juvenile for older children. By the same token, a unit on government would be too abstract for those in the early grades.

To ensure that a potential theme is educationally valid, a teacher must take the responsibility of checking to see what goals will be met during the unit. A check of the district's curriculum guide will indicate which topics are appropriate for which age ranges. Teachers can then determine if their choice of units will meet the goals that are identified. Once the objectives are clear, activity planning will be more efficient.

Teacher Interest. Just as students need to be motivated to study a topic for weeks at a time, so must the teacher. Generally, teachers are pleased by any topic that delights children, but there are still limits. If the topic is one that the teacher dislikes (e.g., snakes), it would be wise to steer the students to another choice. Students can quickly assess when teachers are ill at ease or bored.

If the topic children select is one about which the teacher has little knowledge, either the teacher will have to learn about the topic in a hurry or the students must make another choice. In most cases, an unfamiliar topic can provide great dividends. The teacher will be learning along with the students, and increased teacher interest usually translates into enthusiasm. (It's always fun to learn new things; it's one of the joys of teaching.) If the topic is more than the teacher can handle, however, the quality of the unit will suffer. For instance, one student of mine nearly exhausted herself preparing a unit on Australia. There was more information than she ever expected. A brief survey of the topic may help to prevent such an occurrence.

The best themes are usually ones that the teacher likes. A teacher with a strong interest in, say, Native American culture could create a remarkable unit on the subject. The teacher would have a wealth of knowledge to share, access to resources, and an eagerness to learn more. The teacher's enthusiasm could not help but foster student enthusiasm. If you experienced units in your own education when the teacher was knowledgeable and enthusiastic, you probably remember them well.

Time and Focus. A unit must be manageable. If it is too long and complex, boredom results. On the other hand, excessive brevity and simplicity may result in a lack of depth. Keep in mind that the unit is one of many throughout the year. Students are not expected to meet all district goals in a single experience.

To get a sense of the focus, a blueprint must be created. Like any other outline, the blueprint is not a contract but only a device for planning. Anticipating the scope of the unit will increase the chance that it fits the parameters of the classroom situation.

Brainstorming

Once a theme is determined, the curriculum planners (which may include teachers, students, and other interested parties) should think of possible subtopics related to the central theme. Guide the brainstorming by considering, What would the children want to know about this topic?

Before we look at a hypothetical planning session, it may be useful to review the basics of brainstorming (Osborn, 1963). First, any idea is accepted, no matter how illogical or foolish it may seem. What may seem irrelevant at first may later turn out to be an integral idea. Besides, even if the idea is unsuitable, it may provoke a connection in someone else's mind that is more apropos. Second, any criticism is saved for the end of the brainstorming session. This is when the poor ideas are eliminated. Doing so earlier might discourage some participants from contributing because of fear of criticism. By the end of the session, we are unlikely to remember who made which suggestion. Therefore, criticism will be of the idea, not the person, thus promoting honesty and avoiding the problem of anyone taking criticism personally.

Throughout the planning process, but particularly at the beginning, the planners must gather as much information as possible. Consulting encyclopedias, reading children's books on the topic, talking to experts, and writing for information are essential. This research reduces the possibility of overlooking key ideas. It also increases the number of brainstormed topics.

A Sample Unit

Suppose I teach third grade. Based on my knowledge of eight- and nine-year-olds, I choose a unit on bicycles. I know that most children of this age have learned to ride a two-wheeler within the past few years and are interested in a number of related issues.

Brainstorm. Now it is time to brainstorm. What will they want to know about this topic? So many answers come to mind that I jot them all down in haphazard fashion as shown in Table 12.1.

Notice how each idea leads to the next one; there are so many connections that can be made. This list, which could go on and on, merely represents my own thinking. Imagine how many ideas could be suggested by an entire class!

Check Validity. As a spot-check on the educational validity thus far, it is helpful to sort these questions into subject areas (see Table 12.2). This will facilitate checking the district curriculum guide and will also identify any gaps.

Looking at this list, you may be surprised at how wide a scope the unit covers. All subject areas are represented. This will occur with just about any theme, because real life is not subject-centered, it is integrated!

Fill in the Gaps. A few gaps may be noted. For instance, there is only one question that fits under the heading Language Arts. Rather than indicating a weakness in the plan, this fact may more accurately reflect the nature of the subject area. Language arts is primarily concerned with skills. In accordance with whole language philosophy, language experiences will be provided in context. Children will be reading to find the answers to the questions, writing as they learn, speaking to each other throughout the process, and constantly presenting their findings to their classmates. Mathematics and the arts are also primarily skill-based subjects, whereas social studies and science are more concept-based. Physical education may fall somewhere in between, though I am sure you can get a good argument from either viewpoint.

TABLE 12.1. Brainstorming about Bicycles

What makes the bike stay up?
How do the gears work?
Why do we put oil on the chain?
Why are the new styles so popular?
How much does a bicycle cost?
Why does a bike cost so much?
How do designers decide how the bicycle will look?
Have bicycles always looked the way they do?
Why Is It Called a Bicycle?
Are there places where bikes are the main kind of transportation?
Do bike riders have to follow the same rules as drivers?
Is it a law that helmets must be worn?
What do helmets do?
Are there race courses for bicycles?
What is the record for the fastest a bike can go?
How do designers make a bike go fast?
What can I do to be a faster rider?
Why would someone want a stationary bike?

TABLE 12.2 Brainstorming Questions Sorted by Subject Area

Science and Health
What makes the bike stay up? (physics)
How do the gears work? (physics, also math)
Why do we put oil on the chain? (chemistry, physics)
What do helmets do? (safety, physics)
How do designers make a bike go so fast? (physics)
Why would someone want a stationary bike? (health, also physical education)

Social Studies
Why are the new styles so popular? (sociology)
Why does a bike cost so much? (economics, also math)
How do designers decide how the bicycle will look? (sociology, also art)
Have bicycles always looked the way they do? (history)
Are there places where bikes are the main kind of transportation? (geography, anthropology)
Do bike riders have to follow the same rules as drivers? (political science)
Is it a law that helmets must be worn? (political science)

Mathematics
How much does a bicycle cost? (money)
Why does it cost so much? (money, also social studies)
What is the record for the fastest a bike can go? (measurement)

The Arts
How do designers decide how the bicycle will look? (design, also social studies)

Language Arts
Why is it called a bicycle?

Physical Education
Are there race courses for bicycles?
What can I do to be a faster rider?
Why would someone want a stationary bike? (also health)

Establish Follow-Up Activities. We often become so excited about the unit's content, that we overlook skills. Planning must go beyond concept goals. For example, the single question under the Arts can now be expanded. Here is where a logical consideration of follow-up activities takes place. Presumably, if students start examining how bicycles are designed, they will become interested in the design process. The connections might be made as follows:

- How do designers decide how the bicycle will look?
- the function of engineers and design experts who work for bicycle companies (involving interviews with experts, reading bike magazines, writing to the companies for information, consulting a university engineering professor, etc.)
- the actual design process (sketches, blueprints, scale models, etc.)

- comparing designs in terms of efficiency, speed, aesthetic appeal, etc.
- students making their own designs (sketching a rough draft, developing a blueprint, creating a scale model, etc.)

Notice how language, mathematics, and art skills become prominent in this single strand. As students practice these skills and gain knowledge about bicycles, aesthetics, engineering, the structure of the workplace, and the value of planning, they experience a series of interesting, hands-on, educationally meaningful lessons. This can happen with just about any topic provided we look for the connections.

We can now project follow-up activities for the other questions (see Table 12.3). Here again, the connections are the product of one person's thinking. Students will undoubtedly provide numerous other perspectives and directions, as will further research. But the integrated nature of each topic should be apparent from these examples. Students cannot avoid developing skills in mathematics (e.g., using ratios, graphing, tabulating statistics), language arts (e.g., using dictionaries, preparing survey questions, writing explanations) and the arts (e.g., editing videotapes, creating skits, developing brochures). Social studies and science skills also appear (e.g., experimenting, mapping, making cultural comparisons, assessing the influence of social, economic, and historical factors).

Pruning the List

You may be thinking that this list of ideas is rather extensive. Indeed, it would take a long time to carry out all the brainstormed activities. Remember, the plan is an outline. Every activity will not be done by each child. Some may be done by the entire class, such as recording individual performances and interviewing police officers. Others are more appropriate for small groups based on interest. For instance, some students may be fascinated by experiments with aerodynamics while others may be more interested in studying design. There is no rule that every student must do the same activity. However, it is crucial that each small group share what it has learned with the rest of the class. Even if a student did not actually carry out the survey on stationary bikes, she or he could learn what the survey group discovered and try to help them make some sense out of it.

Finally, there will be some topics that should be excluded. Some are just not inspiring. You can try to anticipate what they may be, but ultimately, the students will indicate which topics attract their interest. (A little salesmanship may rescue an idea that seems unappealing at first but is ripe with possibilities.) Do not be concerned about leaving gaps. A topic that is excluded from the bicycle unit is likely to turn up in some other unit. For instance, the study of oil may resurface in units on animals (the use of animal fat), the environment (the Exxon Valdez incident), cooking (fried foods), the Middle East (petroleum), and the 1970s (oil shortages). There are dozens more examples.

Other topics may be excluded because they do not fit the curriculum. For instance, the type of ratios used in bicycle gears involves fractions that go beyond the simple fractions found in the third-grade curriculum guide. Thus, this topic may not be appropriate for your class. However, those students who are more mathematically astute could benefit from a foray into more complex fractions.

TABLE 12.3 Follow-Up Activities for Unit Questions

Science and Health

What makes the bike stay up? → balance → gravity → experiments to determine the relationship between speed and balance → writing clear explanations of the process

How do the gears work? → how simple machines work → creating simple machines → how to measure the power of a gear → ratios → fractions

Why do we put oil on the chain? → machines → lubrication → types of oil

What do helmets do? → experiments with cushioning → the danger of head injuries → statistics on how much helmets have reduced head injuries → creating skits to present findings

How do designers make a bike go so fast? → aerodynamics → experiments on the relationship between weight and speed → graphing results

Why would someone want a stationary bike? → health trends → surveys of stationary bike owners → developing clear survey questions → tabulating results → the benefits of the exercise

Social Studies

Why are the new styles so popular? → marketing → advertising → surveys of bike owners → tabulating results → presenting findings using videotaped reports → using the camcorder → editing

Why does a bike cost so much? → writing to bicycle companies for information → the cost of the materials → design and production costs → marketing costs → middleman costs

Have bicycles always looked the way they do? → library research → the influence of new materials → the influence of new production techniques → the influence of marketing strategies

Are there places where bikes are the main kind of transportation? → encyclopedias → subheadings → cultural comparisons → the influence of economic, social, and historical factors → the use of bicycles by those who cannot afford cars

(*continued*)

Likewise, some students may have already mastered a particular concept or skill. A child who previously studied simple machines in another classroom or in the family garage, for example, can focus on something more challenging or may wish to become a group leader.

This is a benefit of the integrated curriculum: only those who are ready to study a concept or skill will do so. The rest can move in different directions. In an integrated unit, there is always something educationally meaningful to work on. The difficulty is in keeping track of it all. Good record keeping is essential.

Organizing the Curriculum

Because so many curriculum choices are made by the students, it is difficult to predict what they will study and what direction they will follow. All the teacher can do is guess and prepare. Experience can make this planning process more reliable, but even veteran teachers know better than to expect a unit to evolve as planned.

TABLE 12.3 (*continued*)

Do bike riders have to follow the same rules as drivers? → consulting the driver's manual → writing letters to legislators → historical causes → safety benefits

Is it a law that helmets must be worn? → consulting the police → reasons for and against helmet laws → comparisons with motorcycle laws

Mathematics

How much does a bicycle cost? → interview with bike shop owners → comparisons of models and costs → cost opportunity → creating a consumer brochure

Why does a bike cost so much? → writing to bicycle companies for information → the cost of the materials → design and production costs → marketing costs → middleman costs

What is the record for the fastest a bike can go? → using the record book → interpreting miles per hour → comparison of the bicycle record with human, animal, and motor vehicle speeds → recording individual performances → graphing

Language Arts

Why is it called a bicycle? → using a dictionary → word roots → Latin → other uses of *bi-* → other uses of *-cycle* → creating a bulletin board displaying common Latin roots

Physical Education

Are there race courses for bicycles? → using computerized literature searches → bicycle magazines → the table of contents → type of races → rules → location of races → mapping

What can I do to be a faster rider? → consulting with fitness experts → the muscular system → exercising

Why would someone want a stationary bike? → creating a survey → tabulating survey results → analyzing advertisements → testing health claims

As with any prospective journey, a map is useful. The brainstormed topics can be laid out as a curriculum web to help identify the range of possibilities.

1. Begin by writing *bicycles* in a circle in the center of a large piece of paper. Write small because the paper will soon be filled.
2. Using lines and circles, connect brainstormed subthemes, such as balance, gears, cost, design, racing, speed, exercise, safety, and so on, to that central circle (see Figure 12.1).
3. As you notice additional connections between subthemes, draw lines between them. For instance, racing and speed are related, as are cost and design. Connecting lines are important because they indicate potential pathways. Thus, you may anticipate the whole class shifting its attention to racing after they study speed. Or perhaps small groups can be created to work on the two topics simultaneously.
4. Using your brainstormed list, add more topics in circles and connect them to any other related topics. For instance, racing connects with aerodynamics, which relates to weight, which relates to metal. Meanwhile, design also leads to aerodynamics, as does speed. The more possibilities, the better. Just be sure

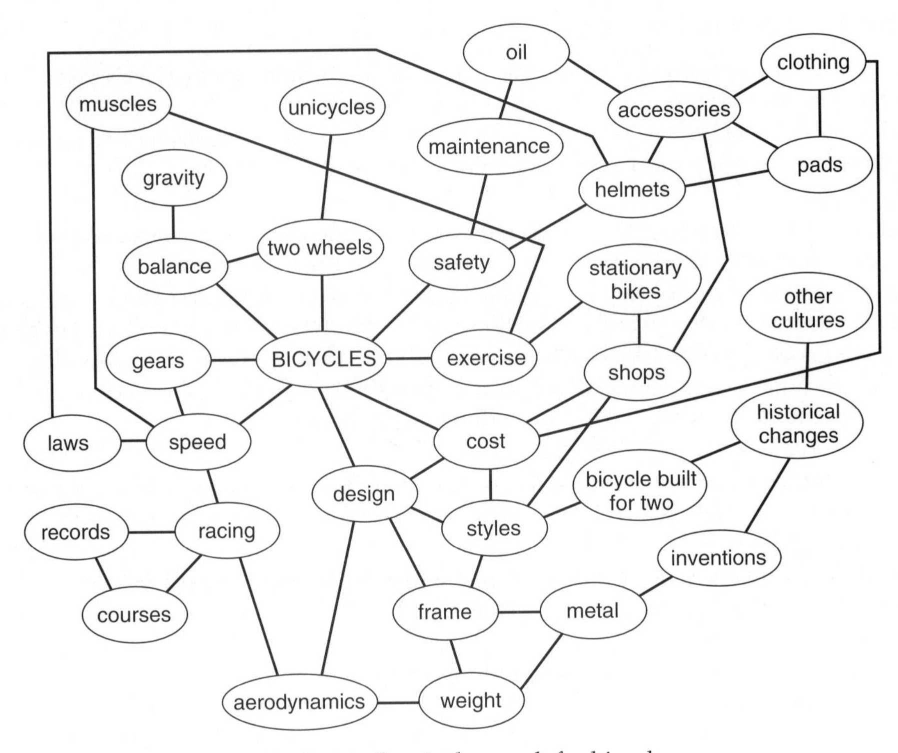

FIGURE 12.1. Curriculum web for bicycles.

to stick to the overall theme. For example, even though aerodynamics relates to airplanes, this subtheme would lead us away from the focus on bicycles. Do not be concerned about unusually long or criss-crossing connecting lines. The web you are creating is only a draft. It can and should be revised later.

5. The connected circles should start forming what looks like a web. Keep adding topics. If you get stuck, come back to the web later, especially after conducting more research (such as going out for a bike ride!). The process actually should never end. Implementation provokes new ideas, as does the post-unit evaluation.
6. Decide where to start. Put yourself in the place of your students. Imagine what topic would most strike their fancy. Where would study of that first topic lead? Then where? Keep track of your pathway on the web with a highlighter. (See Appendix A for examples of sequenced topics in integrated unit plans.)
7. Plan your specific objectives and activities. As indicated earlier, the students are not likely to follow the precise path you have set. A little motivation from the teacher could push them in the desired direction.

Ideas for planning individual objectives and activities are readily available from other sources. A science methods text provides substantial advice on the organizing of experiments, an art professor can offer numerous ideas on getting the design process started, veteran teachers can help you plan a debate on helmet laws, and many activities merely require some quiet reflection. Children's textbooks are very useful in this process. Do not hesitate to pull ideas from them. You may even want to use those textbooks in an activity, such as reading a descriptive passage on bicycle use in China.

Cautions

Whatever your source of ideas, it is essential that you follow a plan. Otherwise, there is no focus to the unit, resulting in what critics refer to as a "potpourri problem." Interdisciplinary units must be held to the same standards as lessons in any curriculum, including a scope and sequence, objectives, and an evaluation plan (Jacobs, 1989).

Another potential problem with integrated units is when one of the subject areas plays a "subservient role" to another. When third graders write letters to the mayor, the activity may meet a language arts goal (i.e., letter writing) but may not meet any social studies goals. If the activity involves study of the mayor's responsibilities, or of local issues, then social studies goals are more likely to be met. The arts frequently serve a subservient role in the curriculum when students sing a song from another culture but do not receive any instruction or analyze the song.

Many integrated activities are not cost-effective, in that they take too much valuable classroom time. Alleman and Brophy (1993) cite examples of students creating scrapbooks or preparing period costumes as activities that place more emphasis on construction than on understanding.

Alleman and Brophy (1993) are also concerned about content distortion. When first graders studying "clothing" created puppets of people dressed in uniforms, it gave too much content emphasis to the relatively minor topic of uniforms. A unit on "clothing" has many more important goals related to the idea of clothing as a basic human need.

Teachers can avoid potential mistakes that arise from an integrated unit by studying the stories of teachers who have implemented them. Books and articles by Levy (1996), Passe (1996), and Stanley (1995) are among the many diverse approaches to curriculum integration that are documented in the literature.

Assessment Issues

The approach toward assessment in an integrated curriculum should be similar to that used in a traditional curricular approach. Teachers must design evaluation devices that will assess whether the objectives of the unit have been met. They may include paper and pencil tests, student projects, presentations, and all the other teacher-developed techniques that have been a staple of elementary classrooms.

One benefit of an integrated curriculum is that it lends itself very well to alternative assessment devices such as portfolios, interviews, and anecdotal records. Because teachers serve as facilitators in an integrated curriculum, they get to observe students as they learn. Formative evaluation is the norm.

"The ongoing assessment process inherent in the integrated approach provides the data that the teacher uses for planning and for evaluating outcomes. It focuses on the individual child, not just in terms of what he or she knows, but also on what the child is in the process of knowing. Without this form of assessment, classroom activity becomes a far less meaningful exercise in which children do things without clear direction as to why" (Charbonneau & Reader, 1995, p. 95).

Adapting an Existing Curriculum

The basic strategy in integrating an existing curriculum is to look for connections. Natural relationships exist between most subjects, but they are often overlooked. Once you find the connections, you can save time and promote cross-disciplinary insight.

For example, many teachers have separate units on nutrition and the metric system. They are unconnected in traditional school life because one deals with science and health, and the other with mathematics. Yet children's basic experience with metric measurement comes from the sides of cereal boxes on which nutritional information is provided in grams. The savvy teacher treats both topics together, using the children's curiosity about the nutritional value of their cereals to get across some points about the sometimes mundane topic of metrics. Students benefit from applying their knowledge of metrics to nutrition, thus promoting depth of understanding.

Connections between subject areas are so plentiful that a series of textbooks would be needed to detail them. For the purpose of this text, we shall merely scratch the surface with an overview of possible connections at the elementary level.

Social Studies and Mathematics

Understanding numbers is essential for understanding historical and present-day social issues. Even rudimentary social studies learning involves the measurement of chronological time, distance, temperature, and other climate indicators; constructing and decoding graphs; and interpreting large numbers (e.g., population, factory output), using place value. More advanced elementary school social studies includes historical changes in prices and salaries, taxation, calculations concerning congressional representation and the electoral college, and other cultures' numerical systems.

Mathematical skills are also applied in many kinds of social decisions. If a class has the opportunity to decide what to do on a major field trip, such as a visit to the state capital, students can determine the best allocation of time and money with regard to potential benefits. Mathematics is also used when, for example, a class is deciding whether a stoplight is needed at a busy intersection. They would probably look at the accident rate and the costs associated with installing a light. A policy decision such as whether to build more prisons would also involve mathematical analysis.

Social Studies and Science

Social behavior is intimately linked with science. Scientific discoveries, from the invention of the wheel to the process of sterilization to the harnessing of nuclear energy, have influenced human lifestyles. In fact, for any science concept to make sense to a concrete learner, it must be applied to children's social lives.

Cultural attitudes toward science often differ. The Native American orientation toward nature could be compared with that of the European settlers. The problems of some developing countries could be traced to their interactions with nature (e.g., sanitation, nutrition, desertification), and the same could be done for economically advanced societies (e.g., destruction of greenspace, pollution, heart disease).

Each science topic has a public policy component (and vice versa). Once we understand the scientific principles behind an issue, what should we do about it? Energy, ecology, nutrition, reproduction, outer space, animal adaptation, weather, and technology are all topics that require significant public discussion and decision making.

Social Studies and Language Arts

As with mathematics, language arts skills are heavily infused into the rest of the curriculum. Almost all social studies topics involve reading, listening, writing, and speaking. But there are some aspects of language arts that are especially suited to social studies.

Because social studies has an affective component involving feelings and values, it frequently involves forms of poetic expression. Emotions ranging from patriotic pride to horror at the destruction of war to love of one's fellow human beings are all expressed in great literature, which can be shared with the class. In addition, students can express their own feelings about social studies content through journals, poetry, stories, and drama.

Two long-standing connections between language arts and social studies are report writing and debate. Both activities require students to apply language arts skills to gain a deeper understanding of social studies.

A fascinating aspect of language that relates to social studies is etymology, the history of words. The fact that every place is named after something is taken for granted in names like Washington, DC, Ecuador, and New Mexico. But we can also trace the origin of street names in the community, the names given to public buildings, and names of bodies of water to gain a sense of the historic and cultural influences around us.

Social Studies and the Arts

The affective component of social studies can also be experienced through the arts. Many of the world's great artistic creations, whether visual art, music, architecture, sculpture, dance, or drama, are linked to the social world. As discussed in Chapter 9, appreciation of other cultures can be achieved by studying their artistic creations. Thus, students can learn about the world and art at the same time.

As with language arts, the performance side of the arts is also geared to social studies. Students can use the arts to express themselves using social studies content as an inspiration.

The social influence of art is an important part of a nation's heritage. Harriet Beecher Stowe's novel *Uncle Tom's Cabin,* Arthur Miller's play *Death of a Salesman,* John Lennon's song "Imagine," and Oliver Stone's film *Platoon* have all had an impact on the American psyche. It is no wonder that art censorship is one of the initial actions of a dictatorial government. The relationship between art and the society is worthy of intense study.

Social Studies and Physical Education

Just as art is a component of a society's culture, so are sports and recreation. We can learn much about such groups as the ancient Greeks, early Native Americans, and present-day Russians by examining their use of leisure time. We can also learn to engage in some of the major activities of those groups, such as track and field, lacrosse, and chess.

Other aspects of the physical education program lend themselves to social studies. The need for teamwork is a social issue that can be learned through games. The need for rules is another game-based lesson. In fact, sports is often viewed as an integral aspect of character building. We often learn to get along with each other by sharing recreational activities (which highlight the *social* in social studies). The two subjects are quite closely linked.

Science and Mathematics

No subjects are more closely connected than these two. Almost all scientific observation is recorded using numbers. Almost all scientific principles are expressed through mathematical formulas. Whether it is the hardness of a rock, the air pressure that influences storms, the nutritional fiber content of a vegetable, or the chemical structure of an element, mathematics is used to describe it. It is fitting that premed and preengineering programs have such stringent mathematical requirements.

The key to the integration of mathematics and science is performing experiments. Traditional science instruction that consists of memorizing definitions allows little opportunity to use mathematical thought, but making hypotheses, setting up a plan, recording data, and looking for patterns all involve mathematics.

Science and Language Arts

Communicating about science is a challenge! One must be precise in describing hypotheses, plans, observations, and conclusions. Directions to "put that green stuff in the little thingamajig and heat it up" could lead to an explosion. Thus, children need to gain experience in scientific communication, including written and oral language.

Students can also benefit from exposure to science-related literature. They can learn to appreciate clear scientific prose by reading about science. Love of the natural and physical world can be broadened by reading and hearing works of literature on those topics. Of course, children's own expressive writing should be included in any science unit.

Science and the Arts

There is a science to art. For instance, the photographic process can best be understood by studying the optics and chemistry involved. Students can also study the physical science of architecture, the biology of floral design, and the principles of sound related to music.

But there is also an art to science. The colors of a sunset, the design of a flower, and even the molecular structure of human skin provide endless visual delights. The sounds of thunder, crickets, and chugging locomotives provide delight for our ears. The feel of cotton cloth, caterpillars, and smooth marble stimulates our sense of touch. Good food appeals to our senses of taste and smell. And one must not overlook the role of the brain in interpreting all this sensory information. Artists have glorified the scientific world from the beginning of human presence on the earth.

Science and Physical Education

Every physical act has a scientific principle to explain it. In exercise, the working of the muscles, the perspiration that results, the increase in heart and lung activity, the burning of calories, and the functioning of exercise machines are integral components of the process. Protection against excessive friction on the feet, the ultraviolet rays of the sun, and poison ivy are also included in a physical education program. It is difficult to separate science and physical education.

Mathematics and Language Arts

The connection between these subject areas is exemplified by the term "word problems." Unlike exercises that involve strictly the manipulation of mathematical symbols, word problems require interpretation of language. When we solve problems in real life, we generally use words to describe situations, analyze them, and generate solutions. Thus, the mathematics that we need to learn is integrated with language arts.

It has been suggested that more experience in communicating about mathematics will improve student skill in this area (NCTM, 1989). Communicating about any subject area is important, but particularly in mathematics because of the often abstract nature of the discipline. Language can make abstract topics more concrete, and thus, promote learning.

Keep in mind that mathematics is a language in itself. It has a series of symbols and a set of rules to govern their use. As children study the language of mathematics, they are learning about language in general. A wise teacher will help students connect the two subjects.

Mathematics and the Arts

Many people who claim to be weak in mathematics may not realize how successfully they use it in the arts. Knitters, weavers, florists, dancers, and musicians all attend to patterns. These patterns, which are mathematical, give structure to the arts.

An artist frequently uses mathematics in a more direct fashion. Art materials such as paper, pencils, film, and wood come in grades that are numerically rated. A photographer selects aperture settings and exposures, a musician works with octaves, and theatre lighting directors make mathematical calculations concerning brightness, angle, and hue.

Just as art is mathematical, math is artistic too. Geometric designs provide a sense of symmetry, the solution to a quadratic equation conveys beauty in its logic, and a simple circle profoundly represents the cycle of our lives. Perhaps in our attention to the instrumentality of mathematics, we tend to overlook its aesthetic qualities.

Mathematics and Physical Education

By now you are aware of how mathematics is used in solving problems; its applicability to physical education should be obvious. However, there is a special connection in childhood.

Many children learn math intuitively during physical activity. Jumping rope, playing jacks, and the hopscotch board all promote mathematical thought. Game rules are very specific about numbers, and keeping score is a time when calculation abilities are truly put to the test. Many of us first learned about statistics when we calculated our own batting averages. Proponents of physical education may accurately cite mathematical competence as a benefit of its inclusion in the curriculum.

Language Arts and the Arts

The title of this section seems a little redundant. By its very name, language arts is a collection of arts. The two subjects share self-expression as a goal.

Looking beyond that major connection, there are other links worth mentioning. Music is a language with symbols and rules to help us communicate. In a more abstract way, so are dance, architecture, and visual art. When we learn to interpret artists' symbolism we gain a better understanding of their work.

The language of art can also provide insights. Knowing that octave comes from the Latin word for "eight" can help us read and play music. Novice ballet dancers can benefit by remembering that *demi-pliet* literally means "half fold." The painting technique called pointillism immediately communicates the use of dots to create an image. To separate the study of language from the study of art is to miss a valuable opportunity for learning.

Language Arts and Physical Education

Just as physical education influences children's conceptions of mathematics, it does the same for language development. Children communicate when they engage in recreational pursuits. Skills in teamwork, conflict resolution, coaching, and clarification are developed through language. The enjoyable nature of recreational activities allows students to improve their communication abilities without realizing it.

In addition, so much of everyday English has evolved from sports, especially slang. One of the biggest difficulties in learning to speak English is understanding idioms from unfamiliar activities. Such terms as "hitting an ace," "going for all the marbles," "getting to first base," and "par for the course" convey the influence sports has had on our language. Physical education is, therefore, an excellent device for promoting language skill with nonnative speakers of English. It also helps native speakers appreciate and enjoy the ever-changing nature of language.

Arts and Physical Education

Both art and physical activity have strong intrinsic rewards. We enjoy a pat on the back or an award for fine work, but the main reason we participate is for the satisfying inner feelings that come from self-improvement.

It may be reasonably argued that athletes are artists. The fluid strokes of a swimmer, the acrobatic grace of a basketball player, and the choreographed movements of a football offense can be likened to the extraordinary body control of dancers and actors. Some fans attend athletic events to enjoy the beauty of the game, not just for the competition.

At the same time, art can be very physical. Many art activities such as cutting, carving, and drawing develop the fine motor control that is so important during the elementary school years. Other activities, such as dance and drama, require more advanced movement education. If the physical education program is to prepare students for wholesome recreation, art must be included. The line between the two subjects is thin indeed.

Combining Subject Areas

When teachers see a possibility for integrating the existing curriculum, adjustments must be made. If long division will be taught in connection with batting averages in fourth-grade physical education, care must be taken to provide preliminary mathematical preparation. To learn division, students must be fairly comfortable with multiplication and subtraction. Thus, the teacher can alter the schedule of topics so students will be ready for division late in the year. Because baseball is traditionally a springtime activity, only minor adjustments are necessary.

If physical education is taught by a specialist, joint planning is needed. Perhaps some form of team teaching can take place to be sure that the two teachers are working together. The frequent consultation that results from this effort may pave the way for other forms of curriculum integration.

One of the great benefits of the entire process is that it forces teachers to critically examine the curriculum. As they look for connections, they may also spot redundancies, unnecessary busywork, and traditional activities that may no longer be appropriate. If teachers are more familiar with the curriculum, they are better able to make it work effectively.

TEACHING IN HIGH POVERTY CLASSROOMS

A series of studies concerning the best ways to meet the needs of classrooms with high rates of poverty, have identified several findings that support the use

TABLE 12.4. Principles Guiding Instruction of Low-SES Students

- Make connections with students' out-of-school experience and culture.
- Embed instruction on basic skills in context of more global tasks.
- Focus on complex, meaningful problems.

(Means & Knapp, 1991, p. 8).

of an integrated curriculum. The researchers have rejected the traditional approach, which they call "conventional wisdom."

> In brief, the conventional wisdom focuses on what children lack (e.g., print awareness, grasp of Standard English syntax, a supportive home environment) and seeks to remedy these deficiencies by teaching discrete skills (e.g., decoding skills, language mechanics, arithmetic computation). Curriculum and instruction follow a fixed sequence from "basic" to "advanced" skills, so that students master simpler tasks as a prerequisite for the more complex activities of comprehension, composition, and reasoning. To inculcate these skills, the conventional wisdom favors a style of teaching in which instruction is fast paced and tightly controlled by the teacher to maximize student time on task (Knapp, 1995, p. 6).

Research on the conventional wisdom approach indicates that it is only effective for certain types of outcomes and only for a short period of time. Low-SES students may show a short-term gain on standardized tests but, after two or three years, they fall behind their classmates. The improvement in standardized test scores is only temporary because the tests present the same type of discrete skill exercises as the conventional wisdom instructional methods (Means & Knapp, 1991). The students' level of understanding is not measured by these tests. While a rise in test scores is often greeted with public enthusiasm, many educators have long recognized that those results do not necessarily translate into present or future success. The true goal is student-motivated learning that is sustained over time (Passe, 1996).

Alternatives to the conventional wisdom approach are called "teaching for meaning." Each of these alternatives

> de-emphasizes the teaching of discrete skills in isolation from the context in which these skills are applied. Each rests on the assumption that knowledge is less discrete, less separable into distinct subject and skill areas. Each fosters connections between academic learning and the world from which children come. And each views the children's cumulative experience of that world as a resource for learning (Knapp, 1995, p. 7).

Means and Knapp (1991) make three main curricular recommendations for teachers who wish to "teach for meaning." (See Table 12.4.) Each is a perfect fit with an integrated curriculum:

1. *Make connections with students' out-of-school experience and culture.* An integrated curriculum, by its very nature, is related to the students' own experiences and culture. Content is related to their lives, unlike

the traditional curriculum, in which content may not be related beyond the subject-area boundaries. Connections are made even stronger when the content is of the students' own choosing (Passe, 1996).

2. *Embed instruction on basic skills in context of more global tasks.* In an integrated curriculum, students learn and practice basic skills as they are learning about some other topic. This is particularly true of skills in reading, language, and mathematics, which students often find tedious.
3. *Focus on complex, meaningful problems.* The traditional curriculum, with its sturdy disciplinary boundaries, prevents students from employing multiple perspectives. To practice skills, therefore, teachers are often forced to develop meaningless problems (e.g., A train leaves San Francisco at 3 P.M. . . .) The integrated curriculum allows students to examine real problems by using skills from several subject areas.

It is ironic that the integrated curriculum is most likely to be found in programs for the academically gifted, while low-ability classes struggle under the conventional approach. When the research by Knapp and his colleagues (1991; 1995) is combined with recent work on multiple intelligences (Gardner, 1993) and the brain (Caine & Caine, 1991), the appeal of an integrated curriculum becomes quite powerful.

Questions

1. How would your knowledge and attitudes be different if your education had been based on an integrated curriculum?
2. If given the choice, would you prefer a totally integrated curriculum, a partially integrated one, or a traditional approach? Why?
3. What objections would you expect from those opposed to the implementation of an integrated elementary school curriculum? How would you respond to those objections?
4. Why would "conventional wisdom" be ineffective with students in high-poverty classrooms?

References

ACKERMAN, D. B. (1989). Intellectual and practical criteria for successful curriculum integration. In H. H. Jacobs (Ed.), *Interdisciplinary curriculum: Design and implementation* (pp. 25–37). Alexandria, VA: Association for Curriculum Supervision and Development.

CAINE, R., & CAINE, G. (1991). *Making connections: Teaching and the human brain.* Alexandria, VA: Association for Supervision and Curriculum Development.

CHARBONNEAU, M. P., & READER, B. E. (1995). *The integrated elementary classroom: A developmental model of education for the 21st century.* Boston: Allyn & Bacon.

GARDNER, H. (1993). *Multiple intelligences: The theory in practice.* New York: Basic Books.

GETTY CENTER FOR ARTS EDUCATION. (1985). *Beyond creating.* Los Angeles: Getty Trust.

HOFFMAN, H. A., YOUNG, J., & KLESIUS, S.E. (1981). *Meaningful movement for children.* Boston: Allyn & Bacon.

HURD, P. D. (1991). Why we must transform science education. *Educational Leadership, 49,* 33–35.

JACOBS, H. H. (1989). The growing need for interdisciplinary curriculum content. In H. H. Jacobs (Ed.), *Interdisciplinary curriculum: Design and implementation* (pp. 1–12). Alexandria, VA: ACSD.

LESKO, W. S. (1993). *No kidding around: America's young activists are changing our world and you can too.* Kensington, MD: Information, USA.

LEVY, S. (1996). *Starting from scratch.* Portsmouth, NH: Heinemann.

NATIONAL COUNCIL OF TEACHERS OF MATH. (1989). *Curriculum and evaluation standards for school mathematics.* Reston, VA: Author.

OSBORN, A. F. (1963). *Applied imagination.* New York: Charles Scribner.

PASSE, J. (1996). *When students choose content.* Thousand Oaks, CA: Corwin Press.

STANLEY, L. R. (1995). A river runs through science learning. *Science and Children, 32*(4), 11–13.

PART FOUR

Politics of the Elementary School Curriculum

CHAPTER 13

How the Curriculum Is Determined

There is an old saying that there are two things people should never watch being made—sausage and legislation. Both can provoke unpleasant reactions when you consider what goes into the process. Unsettling as it may be, educators need to be familiar with the politics of curriculum-making because they are affected by it. If they want to influence the final product, they must engage in the process.

Every political process involves some degree of complexity and variation. As in history, there are rarely simple cause-effect relationships. Most causes have multiple effects and most effects have multiple causes. Connections between factors are seldom direct; they are often dependent on context and other variables.

School boards can have a strong influence on the curriculum.

Therefore, you should take care to develop a solid understanding of the political process as it relates to curriculum as you read this chapter. Those who are uncomfortable with studying government must be especially patient. The long-term benefits of gaining this knowledge, however, will be worth the effort.

THE FEDERAL ROLE IN DETERMINING THE CURRICULUM

The Constitution says nothing at all about education. According to the Tenth Amendment, that right is reserved for the individual states. Although presidential candidates talk about improving education, they can do little to directly affect the quality of teaching and learning.

Federal Financing

Despite this limitation, the federal government has found ways to influence educational policy. Even though Congress and the president cannot dictate what individual states may do about education, they can be very persuasive. The instrument of their persuasion is money. As we saw in Chapter 4, financial support is a powerful weapon. For example, when the politicians in Washington, DC, wanted to improve the quality of education for children with handicaps, they developed a federal grant for school districts that implemented special education programs. The grants had to be optional, but there were so many millions of dollars being offered that almost all school systems signed on.

This type of federal role, called offering inducements, may be viewed as a form of bribery, but inducements have been shown to be quite effective (Knapp et al., 1983). Congressional programs to educate the disadvantaged, provide for bilingual learners, and desegregate school districts have all been successfully carried out through this process. A telling fact is that more than half of all state education department personnel are paid for by federal dollars (Campbell et al., 1990). George Bush's America 2000 and Bill Clinton's Goals 2000 are two recent initiatives that have increased the federal presence in the curriculum development process.

Program Implementation

Because it controls the purse holding federal monies, Congress has some power. But implementation of federal programs falls on the executive branch, which is led by the president. The federal agency in charge of carrying out federal education policies is the Education Department. The head of the ED, as it is known, is the Secretary of Education. The secretary serves as a member of the president's cabinet and is appointed by the president, with the advice and consent of the Senate.

Our secretaries of education, thus far, have only been loosely connected to the profession. A federal judge, a state education officer, a professor, a college president, and two former governors have served in the position since it was created in 1980. When leaders are not specialists in their fields, they must rely heavily on their staff members and the rest of the bureaucracy.

Besides carrying out congressionally authorized programs, the Department of Education has other roles to play in the development of the curriculum. Its leaders have issued reports about the quality of American schooling, made official proposals for change, and generally tried to promote public discussion of educational issues. Another of its curriculum-related powers is deciding what topics are worthy of being awarded research grants. For instance, under the Reagan administration, the ED shifted its research emphasis to issues of school choice and testing (Clark & Astuto, 1987).

THE STATE ROLE IN DETERMINING THE CURRICULUM

Because there is only one federal government and fifty different states, it is more difficult to generalize about how states influence the curriculum. Most observers will agree, however; that state educational policy evolves out of a power struggle between the legislative and executive branches of government.

The State Legislature

The state legislature is a powerful force in educational matters. Its powers, derived from both federal and state constitutions, make it a "big school board" (Campbell et al., 1990). The legislature has the right to set policy, and its power to allocate state revenues enables it to control all aspects of education.

Very few legislators have backgrounds in education, other than having attended school or having relatives who attend school. Their experiences may be twenty or more years old, and may be limited to private schooling, but legislators often rely on those experiences in developing educational policies. The education leaders in the legislature, however, are usually those few senators and representatives who are or have been public school teachers. Their influence is maximized when they serve on the committees that focus exclusively on education policies (Fuhrman, 1981).

The State Board of Education and the CSSO

Legislators do not operate in a vacuum. They rely on a state board of education to propose educational policies and standards concerning such crucial matters as the curriculum, textbook adoption, graduation criteria, and testing. In most states, members of the board of education are appointed by the governor. Noneducators are usually appointed to those positions (Campbell et al., 1990). The board members' lack of knowledge concerning educational issues makes most boards relatively weak. They seldom initiate policies on their own (Campbell & Mazzoni, 1976).

When the state board of education meets, much of its agenda has been created by the state department of education. Like the ED on the federal level, the state department is composed of educational bureaucrats. The head of the state department is the chief state school officer (CSSO), who meets regularly with the board, recommends action, issues reports, and generally serves as the official state spokesperson for education.

In twenty-six states, the CSSO is appointed by the state board of education. Thus, one may say that the CSSO is the state board's hired hand. In seventeen states, the CSSO is elected, meaning that the state board has no power over the CSSO's actions, which sometimes creates tension between them. In seven states, the CSSO is appointed by the governor. If the governor has also appointed the board, little conflict will occur. If not, problems may arise.

CSSOs can have a great deal of power. In addition to their influence on the state board of education, they also appoint members of the state bureaucracy that propose and implement education policies. The quality of those staff appointments becomes more crucial when the CSSO does not have a background in education. This is most likely to occur when the position is elected rather than appointed.

The Policy-making Process

The CSSO and the leaders of the state board of education present their proposals to the state legislative committees on education, which sometimes revise them. After that, the proposals are sent to the entire legislative body, where more revision may take place. If the two houses of the legislature come out with different policies, the differences are resolved in a conference committee. Usually education committee members are active in any resolution of education policies. The legislature votes on the conference committee recommendation, but passage is usually assured. Finally, the compromise bill goes to the governor, who can sign it or veto it.

This complicated process leaves a lot of room for maneuvering by powerful individuals and groups. A study of state decision making (Marshall, Mitchell, & Wirt, 1989) concluded that members of the legislature have the most power in determining state education policy, followed by the legislature as a whole. Somewhat less powerful are the CSSO, the governor, and the variety of educational interest groups that engage in lobbying. Behind them comes the state board of education.

It may seem surprising that the state board has so little influence. Its lack of on-the-job knowledge is the reason. When legislators are working on changing aspects of the educational system, they tend to listen to those who are most closely connected to the classroom—teachers, administrators, school board members, and the parent-teacher associations. Of these interest groups, the teacher organizations appear to have the most power (Marshall, Mitchell, & Wirt, 1989). After all, an organized group of teachers can play a major role in the political process. Their firsthand knowledge of educational issues gives them an authoritative voice. Teachers also make up a significant portion of the voters in every school district, and their organizations often have political action committees that will work for proeducation candidates and contribute to their election campaigns.

School boards also have an association, as do administrators, but they do not have the numbers or the resources to make as large an impact on the political process. Individually, they rank below the state board of education in influencing

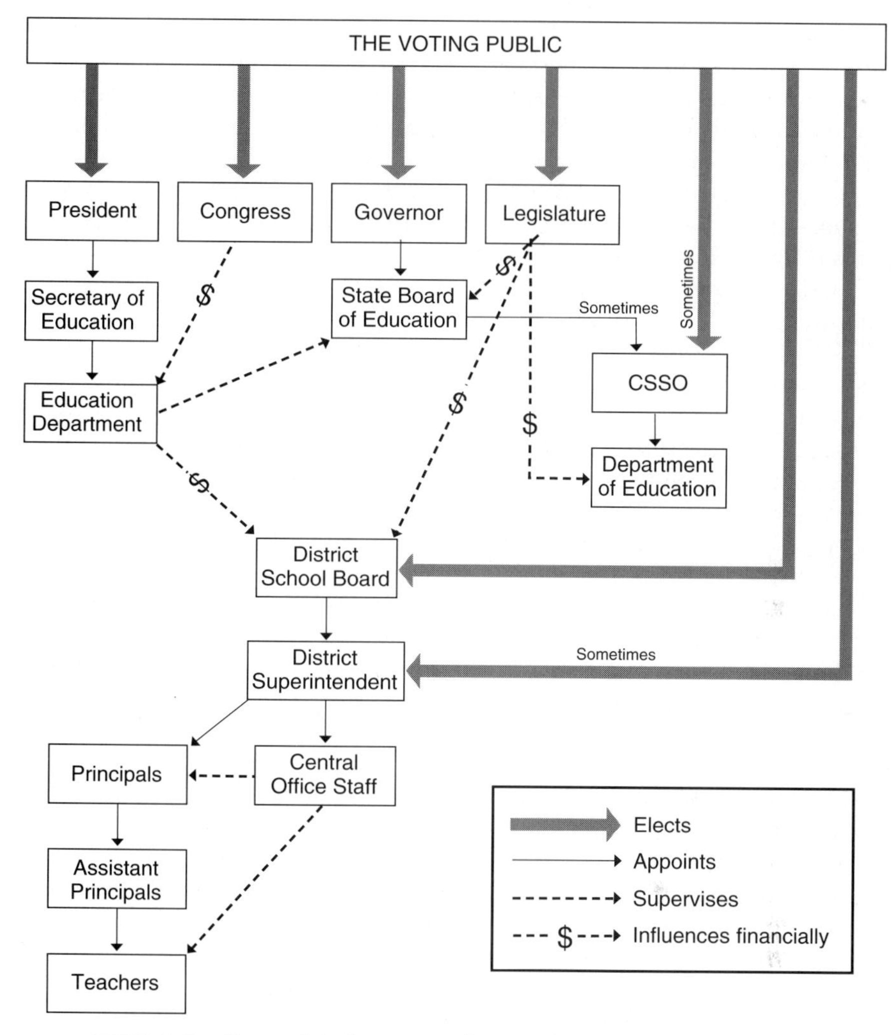

FIGURE 13.1. The political process of curriculum decision making.

the process. A rather insignificant force, mistakenly believed to be powerful, is the publishers of educational materials. As you might expect, there is no mention of students in the discussion of power, despite their obvious high stakes in the matter.

THE ROLE OF SCHOOL DISTRICTS IN DETERMINING THE CURRICULUM

Despite the fact that states have the power to control all aspects of education policy, they do not exercise it. States are too large and diverse to have their schools managed from the state capital. Therefore, all states except Hawaii delegate that power to school districts.

The size and number of school districts vary from state to state. In many states, the counties serve as school districts. In other states, school districts are smaller entities, usually based on town or village lines, but they can also be determined through other means. California and Texas have more than 1,000 school districts while Hawaii has one. California's district size ranges from one with almost 600,000 students to one with less than 10. To further complicate matters, some states have separate school districts for elementary and secondary schools (Campbell et al., 1990).

School Boards

School districts operate under parameters set by the state. Within those parameters, however, they have some flexibility. For example, the state may require that certain science topics be taught but not specify how. Implementation of state guidelines is left to the discretion of local school boards, who are believed to be more knowledgeable about the needs of their particular districts. Basically, the school boards are in charge of all education matters in their districts.

Almost all district school boards are elected, although, as of 1986, 5 percent were appointed, usually in large cities (Campbell et al., 1990). Presumably, anyone of voting age who seeks votes may be elected to the school board. Yet the typical member is a married, middle-class, white male in his early forties who is employed in a professional or managerial position. Women and minorities are underrepresented on school boards compared to their numbers in the overall population (Campbell et al., 1990).

The predominance of the middle class on school boards diminishes board effectiveness. Because members tend to lack access to the influential, wealthy sectors of the community, they must cede power to the professional educators who serve the board, namely the district superintendent and his or her staff (Zeigler, 1973).

Superintendents

Superintendents are hired by the district school board to implement its policies. But, as with the state board, superintendents often control the policy-making apparatus of the board. The reason is the same: the board members are rarely educators; they are usually untrained and do not know enough to make decisions about educational issues. Instead, they tend to defer to the experts. School boards are much more comfortable dealing with the budget, school facilities, pupil assignment, and food service than with curriculum issues. Thus, most decisions that school boards make about the curriculum are based on superintendents' recommendations.

Because members tend to be unfamiliar with matters related to learning, it should not be surprising that school board elections rarely focus on educational issues, or indeed, on any issues at all. The public responds by showing little interest. School board races typically receive far fewer votes than most city, state, and national elections (Zeigler & Tucker, 1981). The only exception is when the community is divided over a particular issue. If a school is to be closed, a principal or coach fired, or pupils reassigned to new schools, public interest is galvanized. But clearly, such issues are barely related to the curriculum.

Superintendents serve at the pleasure of the school board, which means they can be fired at any time. Therefore, it is in their interest to keep the board happy. One way for superintendents to achieve job security is to protect the board from public criticism that may lead to support for challengers in the next election. Another common strategy is to work behind the scenes so the school board members can take credit for all educational policy decisions.

Superintendents have a great deal of responsibility managing all aspects of the district's public schools. They are similar to corporate managers in terms of the scope of their supervision. They handle everything from personnel and payroll to purchasing and maintenance. Curriculum issues actually play a small part in their daily deliberations.

The Central Office Staff

Almost all superintendents hire staff members to assist in running the schools. There is usually one assistant superintendent in charge of curriculum and instruction, although large districts may have dozens of administrators working for the superintendent. These administrators, known as the central office, help to implement the required state curriculum by recommending particular strategies to the superintendent and enforcing them if they are approved by the board. This function is similar to that of the bureaucrats in the state department of education, but the district decisions are, of course, much closer to the classroom. Such matters as class size, the assignment of subject specialists, which topics to emphasize, or which textbooks to use would be carried out by the central office staff in consultation with principals, teachers, and others in the district.

Smaller districts that do not have large central office staffs to help them are sometimes organized into a larger administrative group called an intermediate unit. Typically, all the school districts in a county would make up an intermediate unit. The intermediate unit can provide services more efficiently than each smaller district could. For instance, teacher in-service training or the purchase of cleaning equipment need not be duplicated in each district, but can be coordinated by one office. Some intermediate units even have their own school boards and superintendents (Campbell et al., 1990).

THE SCHOOL'S ROLE IN DETERMINING THE CURRICULUM

When district policies are formulated, school principals have the responsibility to implement them. This task includes interpreting the state and district guidelines, adapting them to the needs and interests of the students, explaining the curriculum goals and methods to the teaching staff, providing the necessary materials, making sure that the guidelines are being observed, and assisting teachers who experience problems.

At one time, principals were only in charge of curriculum and instruction. They were the *principal,* or foremost, teachers in their schools. Today the principal's role has expanded considerably. Principals must tend to the supervision of cafeteria workers, bus drivers, janitorial services, landscaping, the purchase of office supplies, and numerous business matters that support the educational goals of the school. Their attention is divided. A survey discovered that principals plan to spend the major portion of their time on program development, but end up devoting more time to personnel and office matters (Gorton & McIntyre, 1978).

If a principal cannot fully attend to curriculum matters, there are a number of alternatives. In schools with assistant principals, curriculum leadership may be delegated to one of them. In schools without assistant principals, a veteran teacher or a committee of teachers may handle curriculum supervision. Central office staff members sometimes assist. Schools with team-teaching arrangements or strong grade-level organizations may decide the curriculum through those channels. Curriculum issues may even go unattended, with individual teachers making decisions for their own classrooms.

CURRICULUM DECISION MAKING IN ACTION

Now that we have an overview of the process, we can trace an imaginary curriculum change through the system. Suppose that, over the past few years, there has been a movement among educators to expand multicultural education. After attending a conference in which the topic was discussed, State A's social studies director presents a proposal to the CSSO. The CSSO studies the proposal, discusses it at a staff meeting of the state's education department, and consults with legislative leaders, other political leaders, and education interest groups to see if there is support for it. There is, so it is presented to the state board of education as a proposed change in policy.

Legislative Action

At the regular meeting of the state board of education, the policy proposal is discussed and passed, because of the CSSO's recommendation and the broad base of support, including the governor. There are concerns among the more conservative members of the state board of education, but since they were appointed by the governor, they go along with the leader of their political party.

The proposal is included in the annual package that is sent to the state legislature. The education committees of each house consider the proposal first. The chairperson of the Senate committee, who is a former teacher, was briefed by the CSSO before the proposal was ever presented, and her support is assured. However, during public hearings, a lobbyist representing a conservative group claims that the program will discriminate against whites. Immediately, some legislators from the other party threaten to block the bill. To counter their objections, the committee finally passes a bill in which some of the language is softened, making the program optional rather than mandated.

At the same time, the bill is being examined by the other house of the legislature. The problem there is that some members of the education committee are concerned about the cost of new textbooks and in-service training needed to implement the program. Those legislators succeed in cutting state financial support for the program in half.

After being passed by each education committee, the bill goes to the floor of each house. In one house, the proposal is further revised by a coalition of minority legislators who add the requirement that districts must consult a review panel representing various ethnic groups before they can spend state money. The other house passes the bill as presented, because many legislators owe favors to the chair of the education committee.

The two different bills now need to be reconciled before being sent to the governor. A conference committee is formed, and a number of compromises are reached. The governor has threatened to veto the bill unless some of the money is restored. Therefore, the conference committee adds an inducement that promises to match any funding that school districts receive from other sources. The governor signs the bill and the multicultural program is now state policy.

Federal Influence

Meanwhile, at the federal level, Congress develops a grant program to help districts pay for new textbooks with multicultural themes. (This development is not a coincidence; change often occurs at multiple levels of government.) Any school districts that are interested must apply to the ED.

When the new state multicultural policy is announced, the superintendent in School District B has his staff prepare a proposal to the school board about the district's interest in the optional program. When a number of school principals and the head of the teacher's association express enthusiasm, the superintendent decides to request the program. The availability of federal funds is a crucial factor, because of the district's tight budget. He includes the proposal in the agenda for the next monthly school board meeting.

As school board members review the agenda, they discuss the matter with the superintendent and various public leaders. Sensing only minor objections from the community, the school board approves the superintendent's plan, contingent on receiving federal grant money. At this point, the administrator on the central staff in charge of grants develops a proposal to send to the ED in Washington.

Implementation

When the federal grant is received, the district goes through the process of ordering new textbooks and training teachers. However, because of bureaucratic delays, there is inadequate time to properly train the teachers. The plan to hold five one-hour in-service sessions before school starts has to be adjusted. Now, training takes place one afternoon after school during the first week of classes. Only half the district's teachers are able to attend.

In School X, most teachers effectively implement the program. However, the level of effectiveness varies because some classes are not that interested in the topic. In classes where the students react enthusiastically, the content is studied in more depth than in classrooms of uninterested students.

School Y suffers from a teacher morale problem, so the principal decides not to enforce program implementation. Some teachers choose to use the textbooks but skip all multicultural references. A few teachers quietly return to using the old textbooks.

School Z has a strong social studies curriculum committee that immediately hops on the multicultural bandwagon. The committee develops an excellent series of lesson plans to fit the new program. Their ideas are sent to the district social studies coordinator who distributes them throughout the district.

Program Assessment

When the state department of education assesses its new multicultural program, it discovers these variations. At that point, it may recommend withdrawing funds from schools that do not implement the program properly. Or it can propose new state tests that will emphasize knowledge of multicultural issues, thus forcing districts to teach for the test. The state department may even request additional funds from the legislature to expand in-service education for teachers.

How does the story end? It doesn't. The process of changing the curriculum goes on and on. Each district, each school, and each teacher must adapt to the ever-changing circumstances of curriculum reform. How effectively the system is organized will influence the quality of change. The process is not pretty.

ANALYZING THE CURRICULUM DECISION-MAKING SYSTEM

The process of determining the curriculum can be characterized as a "top-down" system. This term is used when those at the top (politicians and superintendents) make decisions to be implemented by those at the bottom (teachers and students). Top-down systems appear in most American institutions, including corporations, the military, and sports teams. One difference between these institutions and education is the consultation that characterizes much of curricular decision making. For instance, teacher associations are involved in the early steps of the curriculum-making process and the state department of education assists in implementation.

Most institutions are "tightly coupled" in that decisions made at the top can be expected to be carried out by those at the bottom. For example, when a general orders troops to move to a particular position by 0800, those troops will be there. The education system does not work that way. Many of the policies that are set by educational leaders are not translated into practice. This is particularly true in the area of curriculum.

Loosely Coupled Systems

The "loosely coupled" nature of curriculum-making (Weick, 1976) reflects the political process. When politicians make curriculum policies, they cannot be very specific in their details, nor should they be. Every local situation requires different adaptations (Sykes & Elmore, 1993). For instance, states may require a certain number of hours of art for each student, but it would be foolish for states to specify the schedule of topics or the amount of integration with other subject areas. Those decisions are best left to the teachers and principals at each local school.

Another reason for the loosely coupled nature of curriculum-making is the process of political decision making. Most governmental policies reflect compromises between different interests. This is why education lobbyists prefer to work behind the scenes to influence the agenda, before the policies are even proposed. For instance, the guideline concerning hours of art education may not be specific because of a conflict between art specialists, who want time to be set aside for art, and regular classroom teachers, who prefer that art be integrated. To settle the conflict, the guideline that is set is deliberately vague on the issue (Sykes & Elmore, 1993).

The loosely coupled system of curriculum decision making is also a result of the uncertainty of the political process. We can never be sure how a particular policy will translate into practice. Unforeseen consequences may occur and unexpected pressures may lead to a different set of actions than was intended (Sykes & Elmore, 1993). When states began to expand standardized testing in the 1980s, for instance, it was not anticipated that social studies and science would become de-emphasized in the curriculum.

A final consideration is the multitude of decision makers (Sykes & Elmore, 1993). As policy is interpreted and reinterpreted as it passes from government to government, to the superintendent to the principal to the teacher, schools may end up with a different policy in practice than was intended. It is much like the children's game of telephone, in which the message changes each time it is passed along. The curriculum message may be further garbled when groups outside the governmental process, such as college professors, textbook publishers, and parents, add their own interpretations. The ultimate interpreter is the classroom teacher, whose decisions behind the classroom door may go unchecked by any authorities.

Advantages and Disadvantages

The loosely coupled nature of curriculum decision making has advantages and disadvantages. Within certain parameters, teachers are free to do as they please. They can avoid curriculum practices that they view as harmful and include some that are not recommended by the curriculum makers. Of course, the educational benefits of this freedom depend on whether the teacher's views are accurate.

A weakness of teachers having individual freedom is that an uncoordinated system may result. When teachers independently develop their own curriculums, they are not working together toward a common goal. The teachers who seek to develop problem-solving skills may have their work cancelled out by those who prefer more traditional approaches.

Of course, teacher independence is a relative term. Teachers may be free to spend more or less time on a particular topic, but they probably cannot choose to ignore mandated textbooks. They certainly have no control over such crucial factors as class size or the choice of standardized tests. Therefore, teachers are fooling themselves if they believe they can effectively implement their own curriculum. The forces that influence the curriculum cannot be stopped by a closed classroom door!

Why Teachers Have So Little Power

A review of the curriculum decision-making process shows that teachers are close to the bottom of the system, with little policy-making power. Their relative position reflects historical and political patterns related to the role of women in society.

In the early days of our nation, teachers were mostly male. Reflecting societal norms at that time, men were given power. Teachers had a great deal of autonomy over the curriculum (Ross, Bondy, & Kyle, 1993).

When the industrial revolution upset the traditional role structure of American families, women moved into the teaching profession. After all, childcare was regarded as a female responsibility that came naturally (Freedman, 1988). Of course, the fact that women were expected to be paid less than men must surely have contributed to the perception of their abilities (Freedman, 1988). Today's problem of low teacher pay can be traced to this early form of sexual discrimination.

In the patriarchal society of the day, women did not yet have the right to vote. Thus, men were expected to handle managerial functions. This division of labor still persists, although there are growing exceptions in both education and other professions. In the meantime, the traditions of educational politics, in which men make the decisions for women to implement, have been institutionalized. (The same is still true for other female-dominated professions such as nursing and secretarial work.)

A second factor in teachers' lack of power is their limited access to the decision-making process. For the most part, political power requires time and money. These are two commodities that have been effectively denied to teachers, especially female teachers. In order to run for office, you must attend meetings, socialize with people of influence, and gather enough financial support to fund a campaign.

Female teachers have typically lacked the ability to attend meetings and social events because, in addition to the ever-growing demands of their jobs, they are usually responsible for running a home. They must run to the day-care center or the supermarket instead of testifying before the school board. Financial support, which for most candidates comes from wealthy contributors, is unlikely because working-class teachers usually cannot afford to attend the events that are frequented by the elite. For instance, teachers have few opportunities to join golf clubs, eat in fancy restaurants, or sit in box seats at sporting events. Yet that is where much of the business of politics takes place.

As societal norms change, and women gain access to the political arena, there may be more opportunity for teachers to gain power in the decision-making process. Another political trend, decentralization, may make that transition easier.

DECENTRALIZED CURRICULUM DECISION MAKING

The weaknesses of curriculum reform through a top-down, loosely coupled approach have been widely noted by blue-ribbon panels (Carnegie Forum on Education and the Economy, 1986; The Holmes Group, 1986; McLaughlin & Marsh, 1978). Various approaches have been recommended by various groups, but most now recommend that the direction of curricular decision making be altered.

Decentralization is the theme of the new curriculum development model (Carlson, 1988). If decisions are made at school and classroom sites rather than a central source, it is argued, the entire educational system will benefit. Students' needs and interests would be better served when teachers are not controlled by an external curriculum. Instead, a more progressive curriculum can evolve based on societal, individual, and developmental considerations (Griffin, 1991).

Decentralization can empower teachers. Giving teachers the opportunity to make important decisions would be a major change from the "deskilled" role of paper-pusher (Apple, 1983). Their new status may promote more feelings of professionalism, efficacy, and dedication to teaching as a career. In addition, the ongoing leadership of veteran teachers could be a major impetus toward improving education (Griffin, 1991).

One benefit of decentralized curriculum decision making that is sometimes overlooked is the opportunity for increased collegiality. Instead of working in stultifying isolation, teachers can learn from each other and develop better professional problem-solving skills (Griffin, 1991).

Rather than suffer from a loss of power, legislators and superintendents can reap the benefits of more effective curriculum reform. Under a top-down system, teachers are not necessarily committed to the changes that are mandated. This is more likely if the reasons for the changes are not clearly articulated and teachers receive poor instruction in implementing the changes. A decentralized system could promote the quality of teacher implementation because the teachers have made the choices themselves based on their own discussion of pros and cons. Responsibility could also be enhanced because teachers have personal stakes in making the right decisions (Carlson, 1988).

Another advantage is an enhanced flow of ideas. Under the current system, teacher ideas tend to be ignored or lost in the din. Under decentralization, teacher ideas can be presented to grade levels or schools, implemented as model programs, and, if successful, eventually adopted by other schools or the entire system (Sykes & Elmore, 1993).

Of course, decentralization has its drawbacks too. Teachers must be prepared to engage in curriculum decision making, an aspect of the profession that is new to many (McLaughlin & Yee, 1988). Knowledge of curriculum history, theory, the political process, issues in different fields, and decision-making skills is needed to successfully achieve reform. Without the necessary prerequisites, teacher curriculum planning may only serve to duplicate already existing curricula. Teacher education courses may have to be adjusted for this new orientation. Time for collegial interaction and extensive planning must also be built into the system. Once all that occurs, the challenge will remain for teachers to alter their long-standing patterns of collegial involvement (Little, 1988). American educators could prepare for these problems by studying curriculum decentralization efforts in other nations (Marsh et al., 1990).

In the meantime, it appears that school-based management is being instituted. There is reason to be optimistic about the prospects of improving the curriculum. The goal will be difficult to achieve, however, without attending to the politics of school systems.

HOW TEACHERS CAN INFLUENCE THE CURRICULUM

Most new teachers set out to implement their philosophical beliefs in a way that will benefit students and society. They want to transform the educational system. Yet, to some degree, all are unsuccessful.

The reason for their limited success is simply that teachers are just one part of a collaborative system of curriculum development. The system can only work when all parties compromise (Goodman, 1992). Compromise occurs when one or more parties sacrifice part of their demands in order to reach an agreement. To be an effective negotiator, it helps to begin in a position of power. Thus, if teachers wish to take part in the decision-making process, they must develop a power base.

Some people are uncomfortable with the process of gaining power. We have seen how difficult politics can be. Teachers, however, cannot avoid making decisions, which is a central element of the political process. Those who choose not to participate in their school or district decision-making process become pawns to be moved around by powerful others. Teachers who allow themselves to become pawns tend to leave the profession in frustration because they are not able to implement their beliefs (McLaughlin & Yee, 1988). Rather than enter the profession armed only with your dreams, it is better to prepare strategies to help you reach them.

THE POWER OF TEACHER ASSOCIATIONS

Federal and state decisions are seldom influenced by individuals. Even presidents and business tycoons, who wield enormous power, are only as strong as their governments, political parties, and companies. Teachers too can be politically effective when they organize.

Groups of teachers working together can overcome many of the constraints that stall curriculum reform.

Subject-Area Organizations

One type of teacher organization is devoted to curriculum issues. In earlier chapters, we have studied recommendations by the National Association for Sport and Physical Education, the National Council of Teachers of Math, and the National Art Education Association. Every subject area has a similar organization.

Teacher subject-area organizations, whose members also include administrators and professors, play a powerful role in determining the curriculum. Their journals, newsletters, and conferences influence educational thought, and in turn curriculum practice. This can occur when a teacher hears about a new curricular approach and attempts to implement it or when publishing company representatives track the latest ideas to incorporate them in a future textbook series.

The public relations office of subject-area organizations promotes the views of its members to the media, to textbook publishers, and especially to political leaders. They have lobbyists who work behind the scenes to influence legislation and policy guidelines. When the organizational voice for, say, the nation's science teachers makes a pronouncement, the message is likely to be heard. After all, there is strength in numbers.

Joining a curriculum-oriented teacher organization only requires payment of an annual membership fee, which usually provides publications and conference discounts. The biggest problem for elementary teachers is not the membership fees (which are relatively low considering the benefits you receive); it is

When teachers get together at the math conference, they learn how to improve the curriculum.

deciding which of the many organizations to join. As an alternative, there are general educational organizations, such as Phi Delta Kappa, an educational honor society, and the Association for Supervision and Curriculum Development, whose focus cuts across subject areas.(See Appendix B for a list of organizations.)

Based on my own professional experiences and those of my colleagues, reading professional journals and attending conferences has had the greatest influence on our careers. Most of the ideas that I have used in my teaching and writing at the elementary, middle, and university levels evolved from exposure to the ideas of others. Once you graduate, you will begin to fall behind. You will no longer have the access to new ideas that is available through higher education. Joining a curriculum-oriented teacher organization can provide this personal benefit while your dues contribute to the overall goals of the organization.

Teacher Associations and Unions

Another type of teacher organization is the teacher association or union. Many people connect teacher unions with the struggle for higher pay, probably due to the media attention that is focused on teacher strikes over that issue. In actuality, the number of teacher strikes is quite low (e.g., 66 out of 15,000 school districts in the 1986–1987 school year). Salary issues may at first seem unrelated to curriculum, but there is a relationship. Higher pay, for example, could reduce the number of teachers who must work a second job—more than 25 percent of all teachers and 75 percent of male teachers (National Education Association,

1987). Only devoting time to teaching would enable teachers to spend more time on curriculum development.

Teacher associations and unions are also concerned with nonfinancial issues, which may affect the curriculum more directly. For example, more than one-third of teacher–school board contracts in some states specify that teachers be involved in curriculum decisions (Johnson, 1988). These provisions alter the traditional top-down approach by including teacher input when choosing textbooks, determining content, and establishing graduation criteria. There probably is much variance in the degree to which this input is valued and used, but it does indicate a promising direction for teachers to influence the curriculum.

Collective bargaining by teacher associations and unions can also have an effect on curricular issues. Many of the constraints on curricular change that have been noted throughout this text are workplace issues. Concerns such as class size, planning time, and the school supply budget are often addressed by the contract that is negotiated between the school board and the teachers. In fact, one of the major events in labor history occurred when teachers in New York City negotiated a reduction in teaching load, a forty-five-minute minimum for elementary teachers to plan, a duty-free lunch, and the hiring of aides to handle noninstructional chores, in addition to substantial salary increases (Campbell et al., 1990). All these changes promoted professionalism.

Perhaps the most profound influence of teacher associations and unions is in the political arena. The two major teacher organizations, the National Education Association (NEA) and the American Federation of Teachers (AFT), spend millions of dollars each year on political campaigns and lobbying. Their power lies in their ability to mobilize more than two million teachers in all fifty states and to contribute time, energy, and money to the election of proeducation candidates. When their candidates win, the NEA and AFT are regularly consulted on educational policy decisions. Of course, when their candidates lose, teachers are left out of the communication loop (Campbell et al., 1990). The latter may not be a big disadvantage because candidates unfriendly to education would probably also be less open to teachers' views.

As this edition is being completed, the NEA and AFT are planning to merge their organizations. If successful, their new organization will be even more powerful in the political arena. At the same time, however, Congress is considering placing limits on the political fund-raising activities of nonprofit groups. While these limitations may reduce some of the financial power of a merged NEA and AFT, the ability of a single teacher association to mobilize its members should become stronger than ever.

Teacher associations wield a great deal of power in the state legislature. They can be influential in local school board deliberations too. Association officers also frequently represent teachers when the media reports on education issues. Sometimes teacher associations join with other groups to form a proeducation coalition. The public relations advantages and joint expertise arising from those alliances can have a major impact on political decisions.

It may seem contradictory to refer to teacher power on the state and federal level within a top-down system. Keep in mind that the top-down system's

Teacher support is valuable to political leaders who could be helpful in curriculum reform.

weaknesses (e.g., decision makers who are not educators) have left room for teachers, and particularly teacher associations, to raise their voice. The nature of the political process also grants power to large, organized groups. The top-down system may exist, but teachers can help decide which decision makers will serve (e.g., as chief state school officer, legislators, school board members) and what decisions they will make (e.g., concerning textbooks, courses, requirements). Teachers have a power that they may not appreciate!

INDIVIDUAL ACTION

As effective as groups are in the political process, individuals can make a difference too. Teachers can participate in politics in the same ways that other citizens do.

Letter Writing

Letters (or calls) to decision makers can be influential when your argument is stated clearly and focuses on one issue. (A poorly written letter can have the opposite effect.) A letter from a teacher to a local representative about educational policy may be the only "expert testimony" that official receives. At higher levels of government, the volume of mail is so great that letters are counted as for and against. In that case, organized letter writing campaigns may have more of an impact.

Another effective strategy is writing letters to the editor of the local newspaper. Decision makers read those letters to get a feel for the mood of the citizenry. When letter writers identify themselves as teachers, the entire community is likely to take notice. Of course, in a public forum, one must be particularly accurate and diplomatic. Therefore, before sending any letters to the editor, it is wise to have them reviewed by someone with a good grasp of both politics and the English language.

Political Activity

Individual political action can also make a difference. Campaign volunteers sometimes find themselves in the inner circle of political advisors. If the politician is unversed in educational matters, who better to consult than a teacher loyal to the cause? Local political activists are often invited to political and social events in which educational policy may be a topic of discussion. Individual teachers stand out in these conversations because of their firsthand knowledge. If ideas are presented in a reasonable way, the decision makers (and future decision makers) will value the teacher's views.

Sometimes individual action evolves from group membership. For instance, political campaign organizations like to have representatives from each constituent group. Therefore, they may contact the local teachers association to suggest a contact person. Letters to the editor may also be coordinated by a larger group, even though the letter is signed by a single person.

Curriculum Committees

Several school districts have curriculum committees composed of representatives from individual schools. These committees, which may be outgrowths of union contracts requiring teacher input, typically focus on specific aspects of the curriculum. For instance, a district committee may be formed to review and recommend mathematics textbooks. Another committee may be charged with proposing a set of objectives for the arts curriculum.

Because so much of what gets taught is based on textbooks and district objectives, committee membership can be influential. Surprisingly, it is not difficult to be appointed to one of these committees. Appointment criteria vary from district to district, but a principal's recommendation may be all that is needed. Sometimes the faculty of a school votes on committee representatives, but competition for the appointment is usually not intense. Committee work is time-consuming and often involves leaving one's classroom to attend meetings. Many dedicated teachers prefer not to make those sacrifices, so the job may be open to volunteers. If a teacher does a particularly good job on one committee, the district's central office staff may request future appointments for that teacher. Committee service can create an excellent opportunity to become a local curriculum leader.

Influencing the Curriculum
Theory to Practice

Barb Grant has been a leader in the effort to integrate her school's curriculum. The factors that led to her success (Hawthorne, 1992) are instructive for anyone attempting educational reform from the inside.

First, she works hard to improve as a teacher. She constantly attends workshops and classes, and reads professional journals voraciously.

Her knowledge is translated into action. What she learns is applied to her own classroom. She designed a new integrated program for her classroom based on her readings. Because she knows what she is doing, her changes are usually successful, resulting in an improved curriculum.

Barb has earned a reputation as a great teacher. Her students have received numerous rewards. Meanwhile, Barb shares her ideas with colleagues. She is recognized as extremely capable.

With a strong reputation as a talented teacher and hard worker, leadership opportunities frequently come her way. She has been asked to coordinate some programs within her school and serves on several district curriculum committees.

All this work brings the reward of power. Her district committee work was influential in revising the district language arts curriculum to stress integration. When it came time to implement the program in her school, she was the logical choice to coordinate the effort.

Thus, Barb Grant enjoys a fulfilling career. No doubt she has extraordinary talent. But what sets her apart from other talented teachers is her constant effort to improve professionally, her collegiality, her classroom success, and her willingness to serve. She is an outstanding model to emulate!

Community Outreach

One responsibility of teachers that is often overlooked is education of the general public. Citizens do not have the knowledge that teachers have acquired from years of practice and study. Confusion about educational goals, child development, and specific aspects of the curriculum is to be expected among nonprofessionals.

In addressing that confusion, teachers can help nonprofessionals deal with educational issues outside the school building. Parents benefit when they can recognize the purposes of their children's assignments, for instance, or relate their children's achievement to a particular developmental stage. A discussion of educational methods can be used by organizations to strengthen their training components. Political leaders can use what they learn to help address educational issues at the governmental level.

When teachers educate the public, they also improve their status in the public's eye and rally support for curriculum reform. The public is eager to hear expert educational testimony, much as they seek medical advice from physicians.

Educating the public may also help in limiting the effectiveness of groups opposed to public education. Unfortunately, a few conservative organizations have

sought to erode confidence in public schools by spreading distortions and misrepresentations about the "hidden goals of the educational establishment" (Brandt, 1993). One example is the accusation that studying the interrelationships of countries around the globe is a subversive attempt to promote a single global government (Simonds, 1993). Discussing these issues in a rational public forum allows for meaningful democratic debate instead of emotional intimidation.

Individual teachers do not have the political power and funding needed to counter opposition groups. Teacher associations, however, and public interest groups such as People for the American Way have paid staff who are experienced in public debate. By joining such organizations, teachers can help insure that the public is receiving an accurate description and explanation of curriculum policies.

POLITICS AT THE SCHOOL LEVEL

Normally politics is regarded as something that occurs among elected officials. By defining politics as the exercise of power, however, we are political actors every time we engage in decision making. Because so many curricular decisions are made at the school level, a savvy teacher can have a major influence on the school's curriculum. In so doing, the teacher can insure that the political situation promotes the kind of atmosphere that leads to professional growth and efficacy.

Choose Your Employer Carefully

One of the first political decisions a teacher can make is where to work. Choosing a district or school that supports your educational philosophy can be a key factor in your professional success (Rosenholtz, 1989). When administrators are supportive of curricular change and shared decision making, and the staff is committed to collegiality, the opportunity for growth is enormous. When the opposite is the case, frustration and burnout result (Ross, Bondy, & Kyle, 1993).

Beginning teachers usually choose the first position that is offered, especially in a tight job market. That decision can backfire if there is a mismatch between the teacher's philosophy and the school or district curriculum. In their disappointment, teachers sometimes choose to leave the profession after sacrificing years of education and a lifetime of dreams.

To prevent such disillusionment, teachers should ask some questions when applying for jobs (Ross, Bondy, & Kyle, 1993). Interviews need not be one-way discussions in which administrators decide whether the candidate is qualified. Candidates should diplomatically make inquiries concerning the degree of input teachers have, the opportunities for collegial interaction, and, most important, the curricular philosophy that is being implemented. (Administrators may be impressed with such insightful questions.) After the interview, questions can also be directed to current and former teachers, university professors, parents, and anyone else who may have knowledge about the district or school. When offered a position, the teacher can make an informed decision.

This approach can make the difference in a teacher's professional satisfaction, but its benefits may be tempered by the fact that administrators and their policies often change. A change-oriented principal may be replaced by one who is less supportive of change. A traditional curriculum can be revised by the school board. Teachers should not expect conditions to remain static.

Research the Political Environment

Once hired, the best advice for a new teacher is to study the school's political system. Rather than immediately engage in the decision-making process and possibly alienate veteran teachers, the wiser course is to analyze how the staff

Influencing the Curriculum
Theory to Practice

The movie *The Dead Poets Society* was well received for its portrayal of a progressive teacher seeking to reform education. In many ways the teacher, John Keating, was unsuccessful. He was able to inspire his students to a love of literature and a spirit of *carpe diem* ("seize the day"). Unfortunately, he was fired long before the end of the school year. An analysis of some of his mistakes may be instructive.

One major error was his failure to seek out allies. He never discussed his ideas with colleagues. The parents of his students did not receive letters describing his curriculum and teaching techniques. When his teaching was criticized, therefore, no one supported him despite his success.

Not only did he not seek allies among his colleagues, he did things that alienated them. His students were frequently on display, engaging in unusual activities that upset the more traditional faculty members. When they tried to intervene, Keating was anything but humble.

Keating's political skills were weak. He never scouted out the social structure of the school. The powerful headmaster who hired him could have been helpful. But Keating's primary allies were students, the politically weakest faction of the school.

Could Keating have been successful if he had been more politically savvy? Perhaps not, but his situation is in the realm of fiction. Most educational reformers would tell you that the methods he used had the least likelihood of being successful. His goals were laudatory, but as a politician he was a negative role model. What good is a great curriculum if you never get to implement it?

and principal operate. When attending faculty meetings, figure out which teachers are most respected and how much discussion the principal allows. Notice which teachers are disinterested in the process and which ones share a philosophy similar to your own. Scope out potential allies, especially ones who are likely to have accurate knowledge of the school's political dynamics (Ball, 1987).

Most staff members will give little credence to the ideas of beginning teachers until those newcomers have proven themselves. First impressions are very important. Actually, the entire first year of teaching creates a first impression. Staff members and administrators will constantly be assessing your dedication and ability. The savvy beginning teacher must work hard to gain respect. Once that respect is earned, entry to the upper levels of school decision making, such as school curriculum committees and representation on district committees, is more readily assured.

Maintain a Professional Image

Professionalism is the key. Teachers respect colleagues who work hard, are interested in professional growth, and are respectful and friendly. Consider the following suggestions:

- Veteran teachers appreciate being asked for advice and think highly of beginning teachers whose comments do not imply that they already know it all. When colleagues feel included in the change process, they are more likely to be committed to the process. If not, they can easily become obstructionists (Fullan, 1991).
- Respect is also crucial during inevitable professional disagreements. Listening carefully and avoiding direct confrontation will create a positive impression and promote the chances for meaningful negotiation to take place (Ball, 1987).
- Beginning teachers are perceived as friendly when they stop to chat in the teacher's lounge or by the school office, but can be perceived as lazy if they spend an inordinate amount of time there. Remember, beginning teachers should be among the busiest people on the planet; they do not have time to become "lounge rats." Besides, any teachers who are usually found in the lounge probably do not spend a lot of time on curriculum development. Potential allies are more likely to be found working in their classrooms. Visit them there.
- When socializing, discretion is the rule. It may have been perfectly acceptable in college student circles to go barhopping or spend the weekend with one's fiancé. Now, however, there may be staff members who object to such behavior. This is not to suggest that beginning teachers should change their lifestyles to please others, but they should limit talk about their private lives.
- Like any social system, schools are hotbeds for gossip. Anything you say may get repeated around the building. This is particularly true for comments made in the classroom, which, more often than not, are repeated inaccurately by the children. Discretion is essential. Any criticism of

administrators or fellow teachers should be addressed in a positive tone and in private. The idea is to develop allies, not enemies!

- First impressions are, unfortunately, frequently based on appearance. Teachers whose appearance differs substantially from the norm may become known for the way they look rather than for their teaching. It is better to be referred to as "that new teacher who does such great art activities" than "the one with the earrings." Your ideas will be taken more seriously when your colleagues recognize you for your hard work and skill.
- Being among the first to arrive and last to leave gives the impression of dedication to those who notice which cars are in the parking lot. Attendance at PTA and other functions is also valued.
- Friendliness and respect must extend beyond the teaching staff. Other school employees deserve equal respect and may also provide crucial support when necessary. For instance, the school secretaries spend more time with administrators than anyone else in the building. Their attitude toward a teacher may sway an administrator's decision one way or another. Secretaries can also protect a teacher from an irate parent or correct a major paperwork error before the principal catches it. Disrespectful teachers do not receive those favors.

  The school custodian may have the final word on how the classroom is arranged. The decision to set up an area for pets may be vetoed because of the mess. Arranging the desks in a circle to promote interaction might be objected to because vacuuming may become too difficult. Consulting the custodian before making classroom changes is a sign of respect and may encourage more flexibility. The cafeteria staff, media specialist, bus drivers, and other personnel are equally valuable allies whose cooperation should be sought.
- The ultimate measure of professionalism is your success as a teacher. When students are happily learning in your classroom, word gets around. It leads to a wonderful cycle: If Johnny Smith is having a good year, his parents will praise you to the principal. Parental support is a key factor in the development of teacher power (Blase, 1988). When you ask the principal for permission to try a more progressive approach, the perception of you as a good teacher may positively influence the decision (Ross, Bondy, & Kyle, 1993). When your new approach leads to classroom success, there will be more praise. And the cycle goes on.

  Colleagues also notice classroom success. They will be more likely to listen to your ideas about social studies when you have earned a reputation for the quality of your social studies program. On the other hand, if your students tend to be unmotivated or unruly colleagues will not have much respect for your views on teaching or classroom management.
- Public relations can be helpful. If the media reports on some of your classroom innovations, your principal and colleagues indirectly share the credit. They would be loath to disregard your ideas while basking in your achievement. Central office administrators might also seek your involvement on curriculum committees. A word of caution, however: if your public relations

efforts are perceived to be excessive, your colleagues may resent you for spending too much time on self-promotion. Moderation is the key.

MANAGING CURRICULUM REFORM

If you mention curriculum reform to some teachers, they may just roll their eyes in response. Teachers are justifiably wary of reform proposals because of their numerous experiences with unsuccessful programs that were supposed to transform education. Still, there have been some success stories over the years in which educational change was properly managed.

- Wheeler Elementary School in Louisville, Kentucky has raised student achievement, eliminated grade-level failure, and promoted teacher and student attitude by "reorganizing the school into five multi-age teams of 88 to 120 students each; instituting shared planning time, . . . thematic curriculum development, and shared decision making; and developing a process for inside-out change that required teachers to decide what they would undertake and how, rather than being told what to do (Darling-Hammond, 1997, p. 100).
- Keels Elementary School in Columbia, South Carolina, despite having more than half its students fail to meet the state's readiness standard in kindergarten, has 90 percent meet state standards in reading and mathematics by the end of first grade. This progress came about through a program that included teacher decision-making, cooperative learning in heterogenous classrooms, whole language instruction, student decision making about school discipline, and a portfolio-based assessment system (Darling-Hammond, 1997).
- The classic success story, Central Park East Elementary School in New York City, has documented extraordinary long-term progress for its mostly low-income, minority students. The school's decision making process includes extensive teacher, student, and parent involvement in hiring, planning, and policy implementation on a collaborative basis (Darling-Hammond, 1997).

The factors that contributed to the success of these programs have been studied extensively, yielding a series of well-supported recommendations. Most of the ideas presented in this section are based on the work of Michael G. Fullan (1991), who has clearly synthesized the research on educational change.

Requirements for Successful Innovations

For educational innovations to be successful, they must meet as many of the following criteria as possible:

- The reform must meet a need that is recognized as a priority. Educators, due to their history, tend to be suspicious of new ideas. They must be committed to the purpose of the change if it is going to succeed. If they are less than fully supportive, they will not put out the energy and resources necessary to achieve the goal. Instead, they will concentrate on other priorities deemed worthier.

- The reform must be formulated very clearly. Educators must know exactly what the reform is and what they must do to implement it. When the precise nature of the reform is misunderstood, implementation becomes haphazard. False clarity—when the change appears simpler than it is—ultimately leads to anxiety, frustration, and distrust.

  Clarity is difficult to achieve because teachers often do not consider written descriptions, theory, and lists of specific student outcomes to be practical. Instead, they tend to understand reforms as they are being implemented. Change cannot simply be mandated through a top-down system. A more collaborative decision-making system is required. (This will be expanded on later.)
- A certain level of complexity is necessary. If the reform is too simple, it may be easy to implement but probably will not make much difference. A complex reform may be more effective in the long run, but is harder to manage. Therefore, Fullan (1991) recommends that complex changes be implemented in small increments.
- The reform must be properly planned and viewed as practical. If the timetable or budget for a change is unrealistic, or if the plan is not viewed as potentially successful, it will not work. The average length of time for an innovation, from initiation until it is institutionalized, is between three and five years. Major restructuring takes twice as long. The process cannot be hurried without harm. As Fullan (1991, p. 49) reminds us, "Change is a process, not an event."

  Teachers will not wholeheartedly implement a program unless they are convinced that the costs (e.g., time, energy, threat to one's sense of adequacy) are outweighed by the benefits (e.g., student success, teacher excitement, sense of accomplishment). A reform proposal must be carefully prepared to convince others of its quality, but must also avoid false clarity.
- The *active* support of higher-ups, from the assistant principal to the school board, is crucial. Support must go beyond words. By providing resources and psychological support as well as personally taking part in the change process, administrators can be substantial contributors to the success of the idea. Therefore, reformers must work hard to recruit active support from supervisors at all levels. Outside assistance from members of corporations, governments, and other sources can also make a difference. They too must be recruited.
- A collaborative work culture must be developed. This is the most difficult of Fullan's (1991) criteria to achieve, but it can yield substantial benefits. Teachers must be included in the process; they will not accept changes just because they are proposed by colleagues. Continuous interaction among teachers will give them a sense of ownership of the reform. As they share successful practices, provide feedback for each other, observe and discuss concrete role models, meet with consultants, and modify procedures throughout the implementation process, the reform will be changed, but the

teachers will be committed to it. As they engage in experimentation with support from each other, they develop a sense of efficacy.

The social process of implementation, with a heavy emphasis on conversation among teachers, results in a shared vision, which is crucial for the successful curriculum reform. This vision cannot evolve from isolated teachers in separate classrooms. That is why teacher associations are seeking changes in the structure of the workplace—not just to gain power, but to share in the responsibility of implementing positive educational change.

How the Reform Process Works

A small group of reformers begins working with an idea that shows potential. When success is achieved on a small scale, momentum is developed by pressuring those holding positions of power to provide support. The plan that evolves, based on a recognized priority, is clearly stated to convince others of its quality and practicality. When support is assured, reformers then work with teachers as they concretely experiment with the changes, offering continuing opportunities for discussion and revision to promote clarity. Together, administrators and teachers engage in the process of transforming the idea, which involves plenty of healthy disagreement, negotiation, and compromise. Even when the reform has become part of the institution, further modification takes place to meet changing situations.

The process may be viewed as a combination of top-down and bottom-up participation (Fullan, 1991) or as a set of concentric circles comprising teachers, students, families, community, school district, and state in which ideas flow in both directions (Darling-Hammond, 1997). The challenge for today's educators is to alter the structure of schools to enable reform to take place. Fortunately, as described earlier in this chapter, that process has already begun. This book will help prepare you for engaging in the reform process.

A FINAL COMMENT

You are probably aware of a common noneducators' judgment of our profession. Many cannot understand why someone would want a job in which the pay and working conditions are below those of more prestigious careers.

These critics overlook the intrinsic benefits of teaching. The joys of working with children, preparing them for meaningful lives, and improving society can offer profound feelings of satisfaction (Lortie, 1975). Few people like having to set an alarm and go to work, but good teachers (after a cup of coffee) are usually eager to see their students and carry out their instructional plans.

Extrinsic rewards such as high pay and a fancy office may improve the quality of life, but the trade-off may not be worth it if you dislike your job. Those who scorn your choice of teaching today may envy your professional happiness in ten years, when they assess the intrinsic benefits of a high-paid but unrewarding job.

This is not to say that teachers should merely settle for intrinsic rewards. If anything, this book takes the opposite viewpoint: teachers are capable of transforming the system. Schools can become wonderful places for teachers to work and students to learn. It will not be an easy transition but, if successful, the rewards are plentiful. You are needed to make it happen. Welcome to the profession.

Questions

1. Of the various strategies for influencing the curriculum, with which are you most comfortable? Why?
2. Should teacher associations have more power, less power, or the same amount of power that they have today? Why?
3. What aspects of the political process of curriculum development would you change? Why?
4. In view of the relative power of various groups in determining the curriculum, what role do you foresee for yourself?

References

APPLE, M. W. (1983). Curricular form and the logic of technical control. In M. W. Apple & L. Weis (Eds.), *Ideology and practice in schooling* (pp. 143–165). New York: Cambridge University Press.

BALL, S. J. (1987). *The micro-politics of the school: Towards a theory of school organization.* New York: Methuen.

BLASE, J. J. (1988). The everyday political perspective of teachers. *International Journal of Qualitative Studies in Education, 1,* 125–142.

BRANDT, R. (1993). Time of trial for public education. *Educational Leadership, 51,* 3.

CAMPBELL, R. F., & MAZZONI, T. L., JR. (1976). *State policy making for the public schools.* Berkeley, CA: McCutchan.

CAMPBELL, R. F., CUNNINGHAM, L. L., NYSTRAND, R. O., & USDAN, M.D. (1990). *The organization and control of American schools.* Columbus, OH: Merrill.

CARLSON, D. L. (1988). Curriculum planning and the state: The dynamics of control in education. In L. E. Beyer & M. W. Apple (Eds.), *The curriculum: Problems, politics, and possibilities* (pp. 98–118). Albany, NY: State University of New York Press.

CARNEGIE FORUM ON EDUCATION AND THE ECONOMY. (1986). *A nation prepared: Teachers for the 21st century.* New York: Carnegie Forum on Education and the Economy.

CLARK, D. L., & ASTUTO, T. A. (1987). The implications for educational research of a changing federal education policy. ERIC Document ED 297426.

DARLING-HAMMOND, L. (1997) *The right to learn.* San Francisco: Jossey-Bass.

FREEDMAN, S. E. (1988). Teaching, gender, and curriculum. In M. F. Klein (Ed.), *The politics of curriculum decision-making* (pp. 204–218). Albany, NY: State University of New York Press.

FUHRMAN, S. (1981). Introduction. In S. Fuhrman & A. Rosenthal (Eds.), *Shaping education policy in the states.* Washington, DC: Institute for Educational Leadership.

FULLAN, M. G. (1991). *The new meaning of educational change* (2nd ed.). New York: Teachers College Press.

GOODMAN, J. (1992). *Elementary schooling for critical democracy.* Albany, NY: State University of New York Press.

GORTON, R. A., & MCINTYRE, K. E. (1978). *The effective principal.* Reston, VA: National Association of Secondary School Principals.

GRIFFIN, G. (1991). Teacher education and curriculum decision making: The issue of teacher proliferation. In M. F. Klein (Ed.), *The politics of curriculum decision-making* (pp. 121–150). Albany, NY: State University of New York Press.

HAWTHORNE, R. K. (1992). *Curriculum in the making: Teacher choice and the classroom experience.* New York: Teachers College Press.

HOLMES GROUP. (1986). *Tomorrow's teachers.* East Lansing, MI: Author.

JOHNSON, S. (1988). Unionism and collective bargaining in the public schools. In N. Boyan (Ed.), *Handbook of research in educational administration.* New York: Longman.

KNAPP, M., STEARNS, M., TRUNBULL, B., DAVID, J., & PETERSON, S. (1983). *Cumulative effects of federal education policies on schools and districts.* Menlo Park, CA: SRI International.

LITTLE, J. (1988). Assessing the prospects for teacher leadership. In A. Lieberman (Ed.), *Building a professional culture in schools* (pp. 147–163). New York: Teachers College Press.

LORTIE, D. (1975). *Schoolteacher.* Chicago: University of Chicago Press.

MCLAUGHLIN, M. W., & MARSH, D. D. (1978). Staff development and school change. *Teachers College Record, 80,* 69–94.

MCLAUGHLIN, M. W., & YEE, S. M. (1988). School as a place to have a career. In A. Lieberman (Ed.), *Building a professional culture in schools.* New York: Teachers College Press.

MARSH, C., DAY, C., HANNAY, L., & MCCUTCHEON, G. (1990). *Reconceptualizing school-based curriculum development.* London: Falmer Press.

MARSHALL, C., MITCHELL, D., & WIRT, F. (1989). *Culture and education policy in the American states.* New York: Falmer Press.

NATIONAL EDUCATION ASSOCIATION. (1987). *Status of the American public school teacher, 1985–86.* Washington, DC: Author.

ROSENHOLTZ, S. J. (1989). *Teachers' workplace.* New York: Longman.

ROSS, D. D., BONDY, E., & KYLE, D. W. (1993). *Reflective teaching for student empowerment.* New York: Macmillan.

SIMONDS, R. L. (1993). A plea for the children. *Educational Leadership, 51,* 12–15.

SYKES, G., & ELMORE, R. (1993). Curriculum policy. In P. W. Jackson (Ed.), *Handbook of research on curriculum* (pp. 185–214). New York: Macmillan.

WEICK, K. (1976). Educational organizations as loosely coupled systems. *Administrative Science Quarterly, 21,* 1–19.

ZEIGLER, L. H. (1973). Creating responsive schools. *Urban Review, 6,* 40.

ZEIGLER, L. H., & TUCKER, H. J. (1981). Who governs American education: One more time? In D. Davies (Ed.), *Communities and their schools,* pp. 23–37. New York: McGraw-Hill.

Appendix
Integrated Unit Plans—Samples

INTRODUCTION

The unit plans included in the following section represent the type of unit that is recommended in Chapter 12. They are based on curriculum webs developed around a topic that would be appealing to children at particular grade levels. These units were primarily developed by preservice teachers as part of their course requirements and revised in places by the author.

COMPONENTS

Each sample unit begins with a projected sequence of topics. Under each topic, relevant generalizations are listed. Each generalization includes a rationale and understandings. Each component of the process is explained below.

Projected Topic Sequence

The topics in the sequence are selected to represent the probable flow of student interests, as described in Chapter 12. The first topic should be one that has particular motivational and introductory impact. The second topic on the list is that which the students would probably choose as their next focus, as predicted by the teacher. Of course, the flow of topics is always dictated by the interests of the students, the salesmanship of the teacher, the nature of the topic, and several other factors, so the plan must always be considered tentative. The set of topics from which these choices are made comes from the curriculum web that the teacher designed. Each topic is related to the previous and subsequent topics in some fashion. Sometimes the connection is apparent from the topic heading; at other times the connection may be through the understandings.

Generalizations

Generalizations are statements that are true for many times and places. By definition, they are general, with no specific references. That makes them useful in other units, as described in Chapter 5. The generalizations in these units are important ideas that students can use throughout their lives. They tend to be abstract. In a strong unit plan, the generalizations come from a variety of subject areas, as described in Chapter 12. Most topics lend themselves to several generalizations, although for some units, only one generalization may fit.

Generalizations are used mainly as a teacher planning device. They help the teacher identify what is important to teach, but they can seldom be used with students because of their abstract nature. Generalizations help us design understandings, which are discussed below.

Rationales

Rationales are statements that justify the teaching of a particular generalization. They indicate a benefit, for the individual or the society, if the generalization is learned. Rationales should be written to show what people will do with the knowledge. Thus, they do not include verbs like know, see, or understand. Rationales differ from behavioral objectives because they may not be measurable. Rationales usually indicate long-term benefits rather than immediate ones.

If teachers use rationales in their planning, they can insure that the generalizations they are teaching are of value. A generalization that cannot be justified is probably not worthy of inclusion in the curriculum. It would be difficult, for instance, to write a rationale for teaching about the capital cities of distant nations.

Understandings

Understandings are specific examples of the generalization. Because generalizations tend to be abstract, and therefore inaccessible to the primarily concrete-operational learners of the elementary school, teachers must teach concrete examples of the generalizations instead. Understandings are specific to the topic and the unit. They are written in children's language to promote maximum comprehension.

THE INSTRUCTIONAL PLAN

Once the teacher has planned the sequence of topics, the generalizations, rationales, and understandings, the curricular portion of the unit plan is complete. The teacher is equipped with a plan for the content that the children are expected to learn. The following step, which is not included in these sample unit plans, is the instructional methods that are to be used to teach the content. Although certain understandings lend themselves to specific types of lessons, that is not the focus of this book. Obviously, there are a variety of methods that can be used to teach these ideas. Most methods courses in the teacher education program address this issue in great detail.

It may be helpful to use the format described in Chapter 12 to critique the units that follow. By identifying how the units address the needs of elementary school learners, your own planning may be enhanced.

INTEGRATED UNIT: PETS

Grade: 1
—BY ASHLEY L. BASS

SEQUENCE OF TOPICS

1. Responsibility
2. Laws
3. Public Health
4. Animal Control
5. Taxes
6. Expense
7. Care of Pets
8. Friendship
9. Companionship
10. Symbolism

TOPIC: RESPONSIBILITY

Generalization: Responsible individuals are rewarded by society.

Rationale: People will act responsibly.

Understandings:

- If you show your parents that you can be trusted to take care of your own pet, they might allow you other privileges.
- If you prove that you are responsible by taking good care of your own pet, other people might pay you to take care of their pets when they are away.
- If you show your parents that you are responsible by doing your household chores, they may give you a pet for your birthday.
- Dog owners that groom their poodles very well may win a prize in a dog show.

Generalization: Irresponsible behavior can harm others.

Rationale: People will act responsibly.

Understandings:

- If you don't keep the gate closed, your dog may get out and bite someone.
- Forgetting to clean the fish tank may kill your fish.
- If you don't clean the cats' litter box they might leave their droppings on the carpet.
- If dogs are not given enough room to exercise they get sick.

TOPIC: LAWS

Generalization: Laws help to protect living things.

Rationale: People will obey the laws.

Understandings:

- Leash laws protect people from being bit by dogs.
- Laws that require pet vaccinations can keep people from getting diseases like rabies.
- The law allows the police to take pets away from people who don't take care of them properly.

TOPIC: PUBLIC HEALTH

Generalization: When the public is threatened, preventive action is necessary.

Rationale: People will exercise prevention when appropriate.

Understandings:

- To make sure that rabies does not spread, pets are required to get a shot to prevent it.
- When the disease of feline leukemia was spreading, veterinarians encouraged pet owners to get their cats vaccinated.
- To make sure that germs are not spread, some communities do not allow stores to sell box turtles.
- Communities that have a problem with packs of stray dogs may require that all pets have leashes so that animal wardens can remove the strays.

TOPIC: ANIMAL CONTROL

Generalization: Communities develop programs to do jobs more effectively.

Rationale: People will support community services.

Understandings:

- Instead of each person trying to catch stray animals, most communities hire animal wardens who have been trained to catch them safely.
- To make it easier to choose new pets, many communities keep stray animals in animal shelters.
- Because most people do not want to clean up the bodies of animals that were killed on the highways, communities have special workers to do the job.

TOPIC: TAXES

Generalization: Citizens pay taxes to support community services.

Rationale: People will support tax increases for programs they endorse.

Understandings:

- Part of the property tax that people pay to their community may be spent on animal shelters.
- The tax fee that people pay when they register their pets usually pays for animal wardens.
- Part of the tax that people pay on gasoline may help pay for programs that clean animal bodies from the highways.
- Part of the sales tax money that everyone pays may help pay for police officers that arrest people who abuse their pets.

TOPIC: EXPENSE

Generalization: Hidden consequences may change the effects of a decision.

Rationale: People will consider consequences before they act.

Understandings:

- The cost of getting a hamster for a pet includes not only the hamster, but also the cage, bedding, food, food containers, and an exercise wheel.
- Someone who buys a dog also spends hundreds of dollars a year to pay the veterinarian.
- People who buy horses often have to pay for space in a stable.
- A baby kitten may be free but the cost of cat litter, food, and vaccinations can be a few dollars a week.

TOPIC: CARE OF PETS

Generalization: Unless essential needs are met, living things will suffer.

Rationale: People will strive to meet the essential needs of living things.

Understandings:

- Dogs must drink water every day to remain healthy.
- Cats must have shots to prevent worms from making them sick.

- Horses need lots of space so they can run and exercise to remain healthy.
- A pet hamster needs an exercise wheel in the cage or it will become bored and unhealthy.

Generalization: Choices affect our lives.

Rationale: People will consider consequences before they act.

Understandings:

- If you choose to buy a large dog rather than a small dog, you will pay a lot more to feed it.
- If you choose a long haired kitten instead of a short hair, you will have to spend more time brushing its coat and cleaning the furniture.
- If you choose to own a pet you must set time aside each day to take care of it.
- If you choose to spend a lot of time taking care of your pet, you will receive many years of friendship.

TOPIC: FRIENDSHIP

Generalization: Interactions between living creatures promote healthy lives.

Rationale: People will work harder to develop relationships.

Understandings:

- Without love and affection from its owner, a baby kitten may die.
- When a new kitten or puppy stays with its brother or sister, it is usually happier.
- When people who are sick have a pet to take care of they sometimes get better sooner.

Generalization: People with common interests often become friends.

Rationale: People with things in common will seek out each other.

Understandings:

- Dog owners often become friends when they stop to talk while walking their dogs.
- People whose horses are in the same stable may become friends as they talk to each other while grooming their horses.
- Cat owners become friendly if they join a club for people who love cats.

TOPIC: COMPANIONSHIP

Generalization: Other living things can meet human needs.

Rationale: People will take care of other living things.

Understandings:

- A cat can provide friendship to an elderly person living alone.
- A child who comes home to an empty house after school may enjoy having a pet to keep from feeling all alone.
- Joggers can feel safer having a dog running alongside them.
- A Seeing Eye dog helps blind people get where they need to go.

Generalization: People derive pleasure from other living things.

Rationale: People will take advantage of the pleasure other living things have to offer.

Understandings:

- A person who owns a horse can enjoy riding it through the woods.
- Parrot owners often laugh at the things their birds will repeat.
- Watching kittens play is a favorite activity of many families.
- Having a dog waiting for them at the front step makes people smile.

TOPIC: SYMBOLISM

Generalization: Living things are associated with their unique characteristics.

Rationale: People will gain better appreciation of language and the arts.

Understandings:

- A dog is thought of as "Man's Best Friend."
- Cats represent cleverness.
- When people are sloppy, we may call them pigs.
- Because horses eat so much we may say that we are "as hungry as a horse."

INTEGRATED UNIT: SOAP

Grade: 2

—BY JACKIE SCHACHT AND INGRID WARD

SEQUENCE OF TOPICS

1. Hygiene
2. History
3. Ingredients
4. Manufacturing
5. Pollution
6. Package Design
7. Advertising
8. Consumers
9. Safety
10. Bubbles

TOPIC: HYGIENE

Generalization: Habits affect health.

Rationale: People will have better health.

Understandings:

- Washing hands with anitbactieral soap before eating or handling food kills germs that could make you sick.
- Keeping bodies washed with soap keeps skin healthier by washing away dirt and oils which carry germs.
- Dental mirrors and scrapers are regularly washed with special medical soap that kills germs before use so they do not spread disease to patients.
- In the 1800s, because surgeons did not wash their hands before performing surgery, patients would die from staph infections even when the surgery went well.

TOPIC: HISTORY

Generalization: Inventions are often the unintended side effect of another practice.

Rationale: People will look at practices from a different point of view to discover another useful purpose besides what was originally intended.

Understanding:

- Soap was developed on Sapo Hill near Rome 3000 years ago when animal fat drippings combined with the ashes of the fire and someone discovered the soapy clay substance helped clean clothes.

Generalization: Available resources affect product development.

Rationale: People will use everyday resources to make something new.

Understandings:

- In the spring, pioneers made lye by pouring water in a barrel containing a year's worth of ashes. The brown liquid that trickled out a hole in the bottom of the barrel was the lye used in soap-making.
- Pioneers used animal fats, saved from butchering, and grease, saved from cooking, to mix with lye to make soap.

TOPIC: INGREDIENTS

Generalization: New discoveries affect effectiveness.

Rationale: When people hear of new discoveries, they will consider how they might improve products and whether the improvement is worth having.

Understandings:

- When the chemicals called surfactants were discovered and added to detergents, they helped remove more dirt.
- Phosphates added to detergents were found to work better than detergents without phosphates for cleaning very dirty laundry.

Generalization: New discoveries affect availability.

Rationale: People will make new discoveries to improve previous products that may have had a limited availability.

Understandings:

- In the 1700s, Nicholas Leblanc, a French scientist, found that lye could be made from table salt, which made soap easier to make and more people could buy it.
- Scientists found that plant oils (coconut and olive) could be substituted for animal fat and mixed with an alkali (lye, salt, caustic soda, or potash) to produce more soap and make it more available.

TOPIC: MANUFACTURING

Generalization: Ideas can have a long-lasting effect.

Rationale: People will consider long-lasting effects of new ideas.

Understanding:

- When making soap today, alkali salt is still added, just as Nicholas Leblanc discovered in the 1700s.

Generalization: Modernization affects production.

Rationale: People may explore ways to modernize processes in order to improve production.

Understandings:

- Today some soap is made using large, steel kettles that are three stories high. This method makes more soap in less time.
- A method called continuous processing is now used even more than the kettle method. This process makes soap in the form of bars, flakes, and granules.

TOPIC: POLLUTION

Generalization: Behavior of living things affects the environment.

Rationale: People will make wise decisions regarding the environment.

Understandings:

- Phosphates that make detergents clean better are not added anymore because they cause more algae to grow in rivers and it suffocates the fish.
- People who reuse or recycle the cardboard boxes that laundry detergent comes in, help save trees from being cut down to make more cardboard.
- When people recycle plastic detergent bottles, the plastic can be used by manufacturers to make new items like car parts and new containers which reduces air and water pollution that come from the manufacturing of plastics.
- When people recycle plastic laundry bottles, in places where trash is incinerated (burned), harmful, acid gases that form from burning plastic are kept out of the air.
- Recycling laundry detergent bottles and boxes keeps less waste from going to landfills.
- Scientists developed biodegradable plastic that breaks down with time by microorganisms in landfills to reduce waste in the landfill.

TOPIC: PACKAGE DESIGN

Generalization: Aesthetics affect desirability.

Rationale: People will make wise decisions when buying products, knowing that the product is packaged to influence their buying decision.

Understandings:

- Children's liquid soap is available in bright colors and sometimes with objects floating in it, like little Matchbox cars, to attract children, who then ask their parents to buy it.
- Children's shampoo bottles are available with cartoon characters' heads on them to attract children to buy that shampoo.
- Bright colors are used on detergent boxes and bottles to make people notice them and want to buy them more often.
- A soap company makes more than one brand of detergent, but uses different color boxes for each brand to attract people who might like a certain color.

Generalization: Convenience affects desirability.

Rationale: People will make wise decisions when buying products, knowing that the product is packaged to influence their buying decision.

Understandings:

- Customers like the smaller containers that concentrated detergent comes in because it is easier to carry than larger containers.
- Large packages of detergent are often bought by families who wash a lot of laundry so they do not have to make as many trips to the store.

TOPIC: ADVERTISING

Generalization: Advertising affects desirability.

Rationale: People will make wise decisions when buying products, knowing that the product is advertised to influence their buying decision.

Understandings:

- If Kirstie Alley is seen in a commercial using a certain shampoo, it can influence people to buy it because they think their hair will look like Kirstie Alley's hair.
- Soap companies spend a lot of their budget on advertisements in women's magazines so more women will want to buy their products.

- Some soap products are advertised as "natural" to appeal to people who don't want to use extra chemicals and additives.
- One dish soap advertises that it will soften hands so more women will buy that brand.
- A baby shampoo may advertise "No More Tears" so parents will buy their product to keep their children happy during bath time.

TOPIC: CONSUMERS

Generalization: Cost influences consumers.

Rationale: People will be smart consumers by realizing cost does not always reflect quality.

Understandings:

- A soap company may distribute coupons to decrease the cost of their products so more people will buy them.
- A lower unit price on a generic detergent will attract people to buy that product.
- Sometimes a higher price on a soap product means better quality, which is attractive to people who believe that more expensive soap will be better for their skin.

TOPIC: SAFETY

Generalization: Every problem has a solution.

Rationale: People will be less likely to be overwhelmed by any problem.

Understandings:

- If a child swallows detergent, he or she can follow the instructions of the box's caution label that says to drink water or milk so the child does not get sick.
- When children get dish soap in their eyes, they can rinse the eyes with water or they will sting and be irritated.
- If bubbles got in a child's eyes, with no adult present, and the rinsing of the eyes did not help, 911 could be called and medical help would come and make them feel better.

TOPIC: BUBBLES

Generalization: Products often have uses beyond their original use.

Rationale: People will explore alternative uses of products for different means, such as recreation.

Understandings:

- Dish soap, which is made to wash dishes, is also used as bubble soap by children for fun.
- Everyday items, including paper towel tubes, straws or string, which are made for other purposes, can be used to blow bubbles for fun.

Generalization: Experiments influence knowledge.

Rationale: New knowledge will come from experiments.

Understandings:

- If children take wire bubble wands and bend them into any shape, such as a circle, triangle or square, they will learn that because of the even distribution of air pressure inside the bubble, it will always be a sphere.
- Children can observe the effect of adding glycerine to dish soap and see that it makes bigger, longer-lasting bubbles than dish soap alone.
- Using various food colorings in a bubble mixture and allowing the bubbles of different colors to pop on top of each other, lets children observe what colors result from mixing the different colors.
- Blowing bubbles on a sunny day allows children to learn that reflected light separates into the rainbow's colors.

INTEGRATED UNIT: THE OCEAN

Grade: 5

BY GINA M. CENTOFANNI AND TINA SMALL

SEQUENCE OF TOPICS

1. Pollution
2. The Environment
3. The Greenhouse Effect
4. The Ozone Layer
5. Ocean Levels
6. Laws and Treaties
7. Whaling
8. Supply and Demand
9. Technology
10. Ecology

TOPIC: POLLUTION

Generalization: Actions can cause disastrous results.

Rationale: Individuals will become responsible for their actions.

Understandings:

- When just one person litters on the beach, hundreds of sea animals can be killed.
- When people carelessly threw garbage in the ocean at Wrightsville Beach, a young whale ate the garbage and it killed him.
- Backyard mechanics who change their automobile oil and pour it down the sewer cause more yearly pollution than the tanker Exxon Valdez did with its giant 1989 oil spill.

Generalization: New ideas are developed to solve problems.

Rationale: People will look for solutions to problems.

Understandings:

- New energy sources like solar power may help prevent the need for oil and thus reduce ocean oil spills.

- Bacteria that eat oil may help to clean up oil spills.
- Placing limits on what can be dumped into the ocean may reduce pollution.

Generalization: Things are not always as they seem.

Rationale: People will challenge their assumptions and make wiser decisions.

Understandings:

- Many people think we will always have plenty of fish to eat, but pollution has reduced the amount of fish available to us.
- Ocean water may appear to be clean but may actually contain millions of tiny, dangerous bacteria.
- The water that is closest to the surface may seem clean, but many pollutants sit on the bottom of the ocean.
- A fish living in polluted water may appear healthy but actually be dangerous to eat.

TOPIC: THE ENVIRONMENT

Generalization: Organisms need a healthy environment to thrive.

Rationale: People will make wiser decisions to insure a healthy, balanced environment.

Understandings:

- If sea turtles do not have clean beaches on which to lay their eggs, they will not reproduce and may become extinct.
- If seagulls eat polluted shellfish, they will die.
- If fish swallow dangerous bacteria, they may lay deformed eggs that never hatch.

TOPIC: THE GREENHOUSE EFFECT

Generalization: Progress often leads to negative consequences.

Rationale: People will be more cautious when considering new ideas.

Understandings:

- Spray cans are very convenient, but their ingredients may harm the ozone layer, creating the greenhouse effect, which causes the ice caps to melt.
- Cars have made transportation very easy, but their exhaust contributes to smog that creates the greenhouse effect.
- Car air conditioners make us cooler, but when some of their chemicals leak out it damages the ozone layer.

TOPIC: THE OZONE LAYER

Generalization: Things are not always as they seem.

Rationale: People will challenge their assumptions and make wiser decisions.

Understandings:

- We cannot see the ozone layer wearing away, but it is.
- The polar ice caps seem like they will always be there, but they are beginning to melt.
- The ocean appears to stay the same size, but when the ice cap melts it gets bigger.
- We cannot see the sun's rays causing skin cancer when we tan ourselves on the beach, but it happens anyway.

Generalization: For every action, there is a reaction.

Rationale: People will consider consequences before they act.

Understandings:

- If people cut down on the use of spray propellants, the ozone layer will become stronger.
- Spending too much time in the direct sun may cause skin cancer.
- By changing the type of chemical used in car air conditioners, the ozone layer may be restored.

TOPIC: OCEAN LEVELS

Generalization: There are some forces that people are not able to control.

Rationale: People will be cautious when confronted with powerful forces.

Understandings:

- Scientists do not know how to prevent rising ocean levels from rising over the land.
- We are not able to limit the power of the sun to melt the polar ice caps.

TOPIC: LAWS AND TREATIES

Generalization: Laws are made to protect people.

Rationale: People will obey the law.

Understandings:

- The law that requires car makers to use less harmful chemicals was made to protect people from the sun's rays.

- The law that limits what can be dumped into the ocean was made to protect people from getting sick by eating diseased fish.
- The law that makes oil companies get permission before drilling was made to keep ocean habitats clean for people and animals.

Generalization: Cooperation is helpful in solving problems.

Rationale: People will cooperate when they face problems.

Understandings:

- By agreeing to reduce the amount of air pollution, all of the countries in the world are trying to restore the ozone layer.
- To protect the supply of fish, the world's countries have agreed not to fish in certain areas.
- Because there are so few whales left, countries that hunt them have agreed to hunt only a small number of whales each year.

TOPIC: WHALING

Generalization: Cultures use what is available to meet their needs.

Rationale: People will treat other cultures with respect.

Understandings:

- The Inuit people of northern Canada and Alaska used the whale to provide the food, clothing, fuel oil, and tools that they needed to survive.
- Because whales were so plentiful in colonial Massachusetts, sailors hunted and sold them in return for money to buy food and clothing.
- Because Norway, Iceland, Japan, and Russia are located where whales live, many people in those countries use whaling as a way to make a living.

TOPIC: SUPPLY AND DEMAND

Generalization: Demand influences supply.

Rationale: People will consider supply and demand when making economic decisions.

Understandings:

- When petroleum was discovered in 1859, there was less need for whale oil and whaling decreased.

- When scientists discovered that whale oil could be used to make soap and margarine, whaling became popular again.

TOPIC: TECHNOLOGY

Generalization: Technology increases economic development.

Rationale: Society will encourage technological innovation.

Understandings:

- When the invention of a harpoon gun made it easier to catch whales, whaling became popular again.
- The invention of hydrogenation that converts whale fat to soap and margarine made whaling profitable so more whaling was done.
- The invention of sonar made it so easy to catch whales that entire schools of whales were caught in one whaling trip.

Generalization: Technological progress often leads to undesirable effects.

Rationale: People will be cautious about implementing technological innovations.

Understandings:

- Sonar made it easy to catch whales but it almost made them extinct.
- Modern fishing nets are much more efficient but they also endanger our supply of fish.
- Oil drillers have found a less expensive way of searching for oil under the sea, but the search may destroy ocean habitats.

TOPIC: ECOLOGY

Generalization: When values are in competition, a balance between them is usually successful.

Rationale: People will seek to restore balance in their lives.

Understandings:

- When oil companies and environmentalists argued between economic development and environmental safety, the United States government made a compromise plan that allowed some ocean oil drilling, but only in certain areas.
- When environmentalists tried to ban whaling, groups like the Inuits whose culture depends on the whale were allowed to continue doing so.

Generalization: Maintaining balance requires constant monitoring.

Rationale: People will be vigilant in seeking balance.

Understandings:

- Scientists must study the effects of the ban on spray propellants to make sure that it is helping to restore the ozone layer.
- Conservation groups must keep count of the number of whales to be sure that the ban on commercial whaling is successful.
- Geologists must study the amount of pollution on the ocean floor to maintain a safe environment for the fish, plants, and mammals that live there.

INTEGRATED UNIT: HORSES

Grade: 6

BY VICKI M. WALKUP AND ANDREA DEANA ELMS

SEQUENCE OF TOPICS

1. Anatomy
2. Care
3. Habitat
4. Domestication
5. Recreation
6. Training
7. Rodeos
8. Cowboys
9. History
10. Preventing Mistakes

TOPIC: ANATOMY

Generalization: Animals are used to overcome the inadequacies of humans.

Rationale: People will take care of animals.

Understandings:

- Because horses are faster than humans, they have been used in transportation and war.
- Because horses are stronger than humans, they have been used to pull heavy loads.
- Because ponies are small but strong, they have been used to do work in mines.

Generalization: Organisms use their attributes to adapt to their environment.

Rationale: People will be tolerant of change.

Understandings:

- Horses use their long necks and wide set eyes to easily recognize danger.
- Horses use the speed from their long legs to escape danger.
- Horses' large lungs give them great endurance.

TOPIC: CARE

Generalization: All living things have certain requirements to sustain their lives.

Rationale: Individuals will care for other living things.

Understandings:

- Horses need small meals a few times a day because if you let them keep eating they would become sick.
- Horses need their hooves filed or they could grow too long and lead to leg problems.
- Horses need their teeth filed or their teeth would grow until they were unable to chew.

Generalization: Poor health can sometimes be traced to insufficient care.

Rationale: Individuals will take better care of other living things.

Understandings:

- Thrush, a disease that causes lameness in horses, can be caused by wet and dirty bedding and failure to pick out the feet regularly.
- Colic can be caused by horses eating wet hay.
- Horses that develop heart disease may not get enough exercise.

TOPIC: HABITAT

Generalization: Organisms can adjust to variations in their environment.

Rationale: Individuals will be open minded and try to adjust to the changing world.

Understandings:

- A horse that has been stabled can adjust to life in a grass pasture.
- A horse that has lived in a grass pasture can adjust to life in a stable.
- A wild horse that lives on its own can be tamed to respond to human commands.

TOPIC: DOMESTICATION

Generalization: People use available resources to solve problems.

Rationale: Individuals will protect their resources.

Understandings:

- When early Europeans needed to travel quickly, they tamed wild horses and taught them to pull chariots.
- Texas cowboys used horses to help them drive cattle herds to market.
- Plains Indians used horses to help them catch buffalo.

Generalization: Changing habitats requires adaptation.

Rationale: Society will be cautious about altering existing habitats.

Understandings:

- When a horse becomes a barn animal, it no longer runs free and must be taken out for exercise.
- When a horse becomes a barn animal, it no longer feeds itself and must be fed regularly.
- When a horse becomes a barn animal, it no longer has much chance to play with other animals, so its owner must give it attention.

TOPIC: RECREATION

Generalization: All activities can provide economic benefits.

Rationale: People will consider all economic possibilities when making decisions.

Understandings:

- The hobby of horseback riding can lead to a career as a stable owner, riding instructor, trainer, breeder, or groomer.
- People who are good with horses can make money by winning horse shows.
- Horse racing attracts tourists who spend a lot of money at tracks.

Generalization: Recreation provides health benefits.

Rationale: People will be healthier.

Understandings:

- Horseback riding is a relaxing way to reduce stress.

- Horseback riding can develop muscles and improve overall strength.
- Working around a barn provides enough exercise to strengthen your heart.

TOPIC: TRAINING

Generalization: Individuals improve their skills through practice.

Rationale: Individuals will spend more time practicing.

Understandings:

- When horses practice running for many hours between races, they improve their speed.
- Horse show winners are successful because they spend a lot of time practicing their tricks.
- Rodeo stars who spend time each day on riding and lassoing are more prepared for competition.

Generalization: Athletic success requires more than physical skill.

Rationale: People will seek to develop their minds.

Understandings:

- A champion rider must develop different strategies for dry and muddy tracks.
- Champion trainers must understand the personality of their horses.
- A rodeo star must figure out how to be as efficient as possible in roping a calf.

TOPIC: RODEOS

Generalization: Cultures have different ways of expressing values.

Rationale: Society will treat other cultures with respect.

Understandings:

- Rodeos were started as a way of celebrating the work that cowboys did during a roundup.
- Americans attend rodeos today to express the value of tradition and their appreciation of the cowboy heritage.

Generalization: Societal traditions often become controversial.

Rationale: People will consider positive and negative consequences.

Understandings:

- Even though many people enjoy watching rodeos, some people object to them because the animals are suffering.
- Horse racing is very popular but some people criticize how horses are treated during training.

TOPIC: COWBOYS

Generalization: People use available resources to reach goals.

Rationale: Individuals will protect available resources.

Understandings:

- Cowboys used horses to round up cattle.
- Cowboys used horses to maintain the fences around the ranch.
- Cowboys used horses to drive the cattle to the railroad.

Generalization: Things are not always as they appear.

Rationale: People will look beyond initial impressions.

Understandings:

- Although their lives appear to be exciting, most cowboys spent a lot of their time alone.
- Although it appears to be simple, the job of a cowboy was very challenging.
- Although cowboys appear to be in good health, many of them suffered from injuries, poor nutrition, and poor sleeping habits.

TOPIC: HISTORY

Generalization: People's needs create economic opportunities.

Rationale: Individuals will treat others with respect.

Understandings:

- When Americans demanded beef, cowboys were needed to move the cattle from the ranch to the railroad.
- When people wanted cheap meat for pet food, some companies used horse meat.
- When people in the western United States needed a quicker way to receive mail, the Pony Express was started.

Generalization: Technology influences change.

Rationale: People will prepare for change.

Understandings:

- The spread of the railroads put an end to the Pony Express.
- The development of tractors resulted in less need for horses to work on the farm.
- The popularity of cars and jeeps reduced the need for horses on a ranch.
- The development of a highway system reduced the amount of room for wild horses to run.

TOPIC: PREVENTING MISTAKES

Generalization: Governing bodies attempt to solve problems through regulation.

Rationale: People will support governmental regulation when appropriate.

Understandings:

- To prevent wild horses from becoming extinct, the U.S. government set aside land for them to live on that is off limits to hunters.
- Because people did not want to eat horse meat, the U.S. government requires the source of all meat to be labeled on the package.
- To stop animal cruelty, the rodeo association set up rules concerning how animals are treated in rodeos.

Generalization: Change usually occurs gradually.

Rationale: People will be patient when working toward change.

Understandings:

- It will take several years before wild horses are no longer endangered.
- Rodeo performers are slowly changing the way they treat animals.
- Even though farm equipment is now stronger than horses, some farmers still use horses for work.

Photo Research by Michelle Oberhoffer

Part Openers
1: © Mary Kate Denny/PhotoEdit; 2&3: © James Shaffer; 4: © Mike Penny/David Frazier Photolibrary;
Chapter 1
p.3: © Mary Kate Denny/PhotoEdit;
Chapter 2
p.15: © David Frazier Photo CD; p.27: © Mike Penny/David Frazier Photo CD;
Chapter 3
p.44: PhotoDisc/Health and Medicine;
Chapter 4
p.81: © James Shaffer;
Chapter 5
p.81: © Elizabeth Crews/Stock Boston; p.89: © Jean-Claude Lejeune;
Chapter 6
p.102: PhotoDisc/Education; p.109: © James Shaffer; p.115: David Frazier Photo CD;
Chapter 7
p.118: © Jean-Claude Lejeune; p.129, 132: David Frazier Photo CD;
Chapter 8
p.145: © Bob Daemmrich Photo, Inc.; figure 9.2 © James Shaffer
Chapter 9
p.160, p.166: © Mary Kate Denny/PhotoEdit; p.176: © Bob Daemmrich Photo, Inc.; p.183: © Mary Kate Denny/PhotoEdit; p.195(both): © Wide World Photos;
Chapter 11
p.199: © Jean-Claude Lejeune;
Chapter 12
p.228: © James Shaffer;
Chapter 13
p.247: © Mike Penny/David Frazier Photolibrary; p.261: © James Shaffer; p.262: © Mike Penny/David Frazier Photolibrary; p.264: © Wide World Photos; p.267: © Bob Daemmrich Photo, Inc.

Addresses and Web Sites of Teacher Organizations

American Alliance for Health, Physical Education, Recreation, and Dance
1900 Association Drive
Reston, VA 22091
www.aahperd.org

American Educational Research Association (AERA)
1230 17th St., NW
Washington, DC 20036-3078
www.aera.net

American Federation of Teachers (AFT)
555 New Jersey Avenue, NW
Washington, DC 20001
www.aft.org

Association for Supervision and Curriculum Development (ASCD)
1250 North Pitt St.
Alexandria, VA 22314-1453
www.ascd.org

International Reading Association (IRA)
800 Barksdale Road
PO Box 1839
Newark, DE 19714
www.ira.org

Music Teachers National Association (MTNA)
441 Vine St., Ste. 505
Cincinnati, OH 45202-2814
www.mtna.org

National Art Education Association (NAEA)
1916 Association Drive
Reston, VA 22091-1590
www.naea-reston.org

National Council of Teachers of English (NCTE)
1111 Kenyon Road
Urbana, IL 61801
www.ncte.org

National Council of Teachers of Mathematics (NCTM)
1906 Association Drive
Reston, Virginia 20191-1593
www.nctm.org

National Council for the Social Studies
3501 Newark St., NW
Washington, DC 20016
www.ncss.org

National Education Association (NEA)
1201 16th Street, NW6
Washington, DC 20036
www.nea.org

National Parent-Teacher Association (PTA)
330 N. Wabash Avenue, Suite 2100
Chicago, Illinois 60611
www.pta.org

National Science Teachers Association (NSTA)
1840 Wilson Boulevard
Arlington VA 22201-3000
www.nsta.org

Teachers of English to Speakers of Other Languages (TESOL)
1600 Cameron Street, Suite 300
Alexandria, Virginia 22314-2751
www.tesol.edu

Index

Note: Page numbers in *italics* indicate illustrations; those followed by t indicate tables.